£2.

RINKAGATE

RINKAGATE

The Rise and Fall of Jeremy Thorpe

SIMON FREEMAN

WITH

BARRIE PENROSE

BLOOMSBURY

First published 1996

This paperback edition published 1997

Copyright © Barrie Penrose and Simon Freeman 1996

The right of Barrie Penrose and Simon Freeman to be identified as authors of this
work has been asserted by them in accordance with the Copyright, Designs and
Patents Act 1988

Bloomsbury Publishing Plc, 38 Soho Square, London W1V 5DF

A CIP catalogue record for this book
is available from the British Library

ISBN 0 7475 3339 3

Typeset in Great Britain by Hewer Text Composition Services, Edinburgh

Printed and bound by CPI Group (UK) Ltd, Croydon, CR0 4YY

ACKNOWLEDGEMENTS

I am grateful to the many people who spoke to me about the events that led to Jeremy Thorpe's trial at the Old Bailey in 1979. I have acknowledged their contribution in the source notes.

I must thank Bill Hamilton and Sam Boyce at A.M. Heath, my literary agent, for their efficiency. Thanks also, at Bloomsbury Publishing, to Liz Calder and James Gill, and to Mary Tomlinson, for editing the manuscript so quickly. Richard Murray offered perceptive legal advice as well as useful suggestions on improving the text. I am indebted to Barrie Penrose for his anecdotes, patience and his good humour, despite my criticisms of his original investigation into the Thorpe story twenty years earlier.

My mother, Doris Freeman, was an inspiration, as she has been throughout my career. I would also like to record my gratitude to my brother, Michael, and to Allan and Elsie Corkindale for their support. Finally, I must pay tribute to Gillian Cribbs, a talented writer who had her own pressing projects, but who was always ready to encourage and advise me. Without her this book would not exist.

Simon Freeman

ILLUSTRATIONS

10 John Le Mesurier, the carpet dealer who was accused of conspiracy to murder with Thorpe, David Holmes and George Deakin. © *Syndication International Ltd*

11. David Holmes, Thorpe's loyal friend, who organised the plot to silence Norman Scott. © *Syndication International Ltd*

12. George Deakin celebrates his acquittal at the Old Bailey in June 1979. His wife, Wendy, is more restrained. © *Hulton Getty Picture Collection Ltd*

13. Andrew Newton, the bungling hitman. © *Syndication International Ltd*

14. After his acquittal in June 1979 Thorpe and his wife Marion wave triumphantly from the balcony of their home near Hyde Park. His mother Ursula (left) always believed he was innocent. © *Syndication International Ltd*

INTRODUCTION

At 2.34 p.m. on Friday, 22 June 1979 the jurors in what had been billed as 'The Trial of the Century' filed into Number One Court at the Old Bailey to deliver their verdict on the Rt. Hon. Jeremy Thorpe, Privy Counsellor, the former MP for North Devon and ex-leader of the Liberal Party, who had once threatened to smash the two-party mould of British politics.

For nearly seven weeks these nine men and three women had listened, open-mouthed, as Crown prosecutors alleged that Thorpe and three other men had recruited an airline pilot called Andrew Newton to kill Norman Scott, a strange character who claimed that he had once been Thorpe's lover.

It was a gripping story, which dominated front pages in Britain and around the world. It was about homosexual love and revenge, ambition, greed and fear and was set against the backcloth of Westminster, the West Country, California and the Caribbean. This was rich enough for most people but, for those who wanted more than human drama from their breakfast reading, there were allegations of cover-ups and dirty tricks by politicians, civil servants, police and the intelligence services of Britain, the United States and South Africa.

The prosecution had three star witnesses. First, there was Scott. He had briefly been a model as a young man and was still a striking figure, with his shock of dark hair, defiant eyes and sensual pout, though he was now in his late thirties. He lived a solitary life high on the moors in Devon, surrounded by his beloved animals, and was obsessed with Jeremy Thorpe, who he claimed had infected him with the 'disease' of homosexuality when he was 21 years old. He was not an attractive character; he was an hysteric who had a history of attention-seeking failed suicides and had lurched from one disastrous affair to another, with women as well as men.

Then there was Peter Bessell, who was also unappealing. He was a former Liberal MP and failed businessman, who lived in impecunious exile in California. He had dyed hair, which glowed orange under the Old Bailey lights, and a face that had been beaten into parchment by the West Coast sun. He had once been Thorpe's confidant but had turned against him, which added the delicious dimension of betrayal to the proceedings.

Finally, there was Andrew Newton. The prosecution argued that he set out to fulfil his first contract as a highly paid professional assassin in October 1975 when he planned to shoot Scott on Exmoor using an ancient German pistol which he had borrowed from a friend.

Unfortunately, he had a lifelong phobia of dogs and was horrified when Scott arrived for the expedition on a windy autumn night with a huge beast, a 5-year-old Great Dane bitch called Rinka. Newton said that he did want not the monster in his car but Scott refused to move without her.

Newton scowled and Rinka bounded on to the back seat, where she sat patiently, hoping for a run on the moor. After a short drive he pulled up at a suitably deserted spot and got out, ready to kill Scott. Then Rinka leapt from the car. Great Danes are exuberant and playful but Newton thought that he was being attacked by a man-eating donkey. Quivering with fear he shot her with a single bullet to the head. He was so shaken by the experience, and by the sight of a sobbing Scott administering the kiss of life to a dead dog, that he was unable to proceed with his mission and drove off. Newton had been offered immunity from prosecution in return for his testimony at the Old Bailey. He admitted that he had murdered Rinka but he was such an inveterate liar that no one believed anything else he said, except when he cheerfully confessed that he hoped to make a great deal of money from the case.

Mr Justice Cantley, the judge, gave a virtuoso performance. He had spent most of his judicial career in the North of England, far from the glamour of the showcase courts in London, and was an unexpected choice for such a high-profile trial. But he rose to the challenge magnificently and became a celebrity. One minute he was cantankerous and the next was cackling at one of his own lame jokes. He was spectacularly rude to Scott, Bessell and Newton, whom he obviously thought deserved a good flogging, and indicated that, in his opinion, Thorpe was a great man who should have been dealing with important matters of State rather than wasting his time at the Old Bailey. In his summing-up, which was so biased that it assured him a place in legal history, he virtually instructed the jury to acquit Thorpe. He was also sympathetic to the other gentleman in the dock, David Holmes, Thorpe's friend from Oxford University, who described himself as a merchant banker. But Cantley was a snob and was not interested in the other defendants: John Le Mesurier, a fat jolly businessman who sold cut-price carpets in Wales, and George Deakin, a diminutive figure who wore lurid suits and dealt in fruit machines in the Cardiff area.

The jury listened respectfully to Cantley and did as they were told; they returned a unanimous verdict of not guilty on all the defendants. Thorpe strode out of court, arms aloft, as if he had just won a general election. He faced an uncertain future but made one immediate decision: to abandon David Holmes. Even by Thorpe's selfish standards this was brutal; Holmes was a godfather of his son, had been his companion when he travelled to the Mediterranean in search of lithe young men and had only become involved in the plot to silence Scott because he was ferociously loyal to Thorpe.

Journalists who had followed the case were astonished by the verdict and grumbled that the Establishment had saved Thorpe from the prison sentence which he deserved.

The BBC and London Weekend Televison scrapped documentaries which portrayed him as a homosexual who had tried to kill his former lover to prevent him telling the world about their affair. Newspapers tore up their damning background articles about him. A book by three *Sunday Times* reporters, Lewis Chester, Magnus Linklater and David May, which described how the passionate affair between Scott and Thorpe became a bitter feud, had to be rewritten hastily under the eyes of libel lawyers.

But ordinary people, who did not have confidential files bulging with explicit details of Thorpe's sex life, did not care that he had been acquitted. The trial had been an entertaining soap opera but had been spoilt by the sub-plots, which involved Harold Wilson, the former Prime Minister, a millionaire philanthropist from Wolverhampton who lived in the Bahamas, South African spies and much else besides. It had all been fun but the country had had enough of Messrs Scott, Thorpe, Bessell and Newton, and Rinka, the late Great Dane.

I was a young trainee reporter in Plymouth, working for a regional Sunday newspaper, when Norman Scott exploded on to the front pages in spring 1976 with his allegations about Thorpe. This was the biggest West Country story in living memory so my newspaper, which was famously mean, grudgingly dispatched me north to Barnstaple, in the heart of Thorpe's constituency, to gauge the reaction of locals. The evidence suggested that Thorpe and Scott had been lovers, but everyone whom I interviewed, Conservative and Labour voters as well as Liberals, thought that Scott was a wicked liar who should be locked up in an asylum. But a few days later Thorpe was forced to resign the leadership and, just over two years later, was charged with incitement and conspiracy to murder Scott.

When he appeared at the Old Bailey I was a reporter on the London *Evening Standard*. I was not covering the trial so I only knew what I read in the newspapers; like everyone else, I thoroughly enjoyed the tales of homosexual passion and revenge but was bored by the minutiae of the alleged conspiracy to murder Scott and by the background hubbub of cover-ups. But colleagues who had followed the case were furious when he was acquitted, which I thought was melodramatic; even if he had slept with Scott it had happened a long time ago and did not matter.

In the early 1980s I worked with Barrie Penrose at the *Sunday Times*. We drifted together by accident and only had official status as a team when we were briefly co-editors of Insight, the legendary investigative unit, which had a hierarchy of editor, reporters, researchers and secretaries, a budget and an office packed with neatly labelled files. I knew that Penrose was an authority on Thorpe and had written a book called *The Pencourt File*, with Roger Courtiour, a colleague from his days at the BBC, which had, somehow, led to Thorpe being charged in late summer 1978. *The Pencourt File* had been serialised by the *Daily Mirror* and had made Pencourt a great deal of money, though the literary critics dismissed it as a shambles.

Penrose was a fine reporter, who had a rare talent for finding original stories but was not a member of the aristocracy of wordsmiths at the *Sunday Times*, who spent their days chatting and eating sandwiches, waiting to be given a story. Thus, executives were grateful to Penrose, who had a habit of popping up on a Saturday morning with the material for a ripping front-page exclusive. Most journalists on the newspaper thought that they were such brilliant writers that they threw tantrums if anyone tried to change a comma in their copy but Penrose was not like that; he relished the chase, of a guilty man, a defective part or a conspiracy, and seemed to regard the actual writing of the story as a chore. He was generous with his information and did not mind if people rewrote his copy, providing, of course, that his name was on the story when it was published. On a newspaper riven by the bickering of talented men and women with enormous egos this was a refreshing approach.

He rarely mentioned Thorpe to me though sometimes he would pull a scoop from what he called his Pencourt files. For example, when newspapers in Moscow reported that the KGB had tried to trap two American diplomats there with young women, I asked him if he had any ideas on how to develop the story for the weekend. He said that he vaguely recalled that Marcia Falkender, private secretary and influential adviser to Labour's Harold Wilson when he was Prime Minister, had told Pencourt that Sir Geoffrey Harrison, the British Ambassador in Moscow in the mid-1960s, had been 'compromised' by a chambermaid who worked for the KGB; Harrison had to be recalled, which left Britain without an ambassador when the Soviets invaded Czechoslovakia in 1968. But Penrose said that they had not included the story in *The Pencourt File* because it had nothing to do with Thorpe and Wilson. I telephoned Harrison, who said that, unfortunately, it was all true; that weekend, thanks to the Pencourt files, readers of the *Sunday Times* enjoyed the uplifting story of the Ambassador and the KGB temptress.

This was the era when spies were big news. Retired, previously tight-lipped British Intelligence officers seemed to have contracted a tongue-loosening virus. Most talked because they were bored with retirement or wanted public acknowledgement for saving Western democracy from the communist menace but a few hoped that newspapers would reopen debates which they had lost many years earlier with their superiors. This little band required tactful handling because they could not understand why we did not rush into print with their 'revelations', such as the fact that a KGB officer who defected in Sweden thirty years earlier had really been a double (or triple) agent.

Occasionally these ex-spies did leak genuinely sensational stories. They identified Sir Anthony Blunt, the distinguished art historian who was a former Surveyor of the Queen's Pictures, as a former Soviet spy, which was cracking stuff. They also revealed that Sir Roger Hollis, who from 1956 until 1965 had been Director-General of MI5, Britain's counter-espionage agency responsible for catching Soviet spies, was, himself, suspected of being a KGB agent. This was also fun.

Then there was Peter Wright, a former MI5 officer who was struggling to make a living breeding horses in Tasmania, Australia. In the mid-1980s he defied the British government and wrote a book called *Spycatcher: The Candid Autobiography of a Senior Intelligence Officer*. The British government was not pleased by his excursion into literature and tried to persuade the courts in Australia to ban the book. But the judge in Sydney was unmoved by the arguments of Whitehall mandarins that MI5 officers owed a lifelong duty of confidentiality and that publication would cause irreparable damage to the West.

If the British had ignored *Spycatcher*, then it would probably have sunk without trace. But, by trying to ban it in such a hamfisted manner, the government ensured that it became an international bestseller. Wright argued that the West had been deceived totally by Soviet Intelligence since the war. In his view, nothing was as it seemed; even the Sino-Soviet split was a KGB disinformation exercise, which was like saying that the Falklands War had been staged by right-wing intelligence chiefs in London and Buenos Aires to mislead Moscow. He thought that *Spycatcher* would force the West's intelligence services to re-examine all their files, a massive exercise which would, he hinted, require the expertise of a veteran like himself. But it had the opposite effect because, unwittingly, he condemned himself and MI5. His ideas on global politics were curious but harmless but his views on Britain were mad and dangerous. He thought that anyone who was on the far left, or just left, of politics was a potential traitor. The centrepiece of his theory about Soviet 'penetration' of Britain was that Harold Wilson had been a KGB agent but, instead of being sacked for peddling rubbish like this, he had been congratulated by his colleagues for his lateral thinking, which said as much about MI5 as him.

The press competed frantically for new angles on *Spycatcher* but Penrose had ready-made scoops in his Pencourt files. He had many hours of tape recordings with Wilson and Falkender from the mid-1970s, where they complained that MI5 thought that socialism was a different way of spelling communism. They had told Pencourt that some right-wing extremists in MI5 had tried to discredit senior Labour Party figures, by, for example, breaking into their offices and homes in the hope of finding embarrassing documents. Thus, while other journalists scrabbled to find anyone who had suffered at the hands of Wright and his chums, Penrose was able to extract a string of exclusives from his files.

Over the following months the *Sunday Times* and its rivals published hundreds of thousands of words about MI5, the KGB, the CIA, moles, double agents and the Fifth (or Sixth or Seventh) Man of the Cambridge spyring of the 1930s but spymania could not last for ever and one day there was nothing left to say. Penrose and I knew that the spy game was over and parted company.

In spring 1995 I visited Penrose at his home in the Kent countryside. Outside his study I noticed two cupboards that were overflowing with papers and cassettes. I asked him why he did not clear out this rubbish; he said that these were his Pencourt files and, though he knew that no one was interested in Thorpe and Scott, he could not bear to toss them in a dustbin.

For the first time we talked at length about Thorpe. Penrose told me that in spring 1976 he had been a young reporter with *BBC Television News* when, inexplicably, he was summoned to meet Harold Wilson, who had just retired as Prime Minister. For internal political reasons, Penrose asked his friend, Roger Courtiour, who was a researcher in the rival current affairs department, to join him. At best, they thought Wilson might explain exclusively why he had resigned but, instead, the meeting launched them on a long and painful odyssey. They were driven out of the BBC and ridiculed by Fleet Street as purveyors of daft conspiracy theories but they kept going, convinced that they were uncovering the British Watergate.

Penrose told me about the plot to kill Scott, which he insisted had been masterminded by Thorpe. He moved on to BOSS, the Bureau of State Security, South Africa's feared intelligence service, who had interfered, and MI5, who had known everything. Then he talked about Wilson's resignation and Princess Margaret's divorce from Lord Snowdon, both of which had been orchestrated by a sinister lawyer called Lord Goodman, who serviced the rich and powerful, to distract attention from Scott. Finally, there was Thorpe's acquittal, which marked the culmination of the Establishment cover-up. This was head-spinning stuff but, if a fraction of what Penrose said was true, then this was the untold scandal of post-war Britain.

I said that it would be interesting to re-examine the story. Enough time had passed for wounds to heal but, in another few years, it would be too late because there would be no one

left to interview. Many of the protagonists, including Bessell and
Holmes, were already dead and, then, as we discussed the idea, as
if to emphasise the point, Wilson passed away. But Penrose was
not sure: he had devoted several years of his life to Thorpe and did
not want to start grappling again with the same old questions. On
the other hand, he said that it was a hell of a good story which had
never been told properly, so he agreed. I said that we would have
to divide the work; he should sort through his Pencourt material,
piled up in his cupboard, while I read the books on Thorpe.

The first was Barrie Penrose and Roger Courtiour's *The Pencourt
File* which was published early in 1978. It was a testament to the
determination of the authors but, as a book, it was definitely not
a triumph. There were a number of stories jostling for attention
inside its red covers: the plot to kill Scott and the cover-up to protect
Thorpe; Wilson's allegations that MI5 tried to destabilise him and
his conviction that Thorpe had been framed by BOSS and, finally,
the authors' account of their investigation. It defied the conventions
of style and structure and was the literary equivalent of a pile of
bricks at an exhibition of 'modern' art, which everyone circles,
puzzled, but certain that it must mean something. Eventually I
gave up trying to make sense of the jumble of names and dates,
just like the visitor to the art gallery who cannot understand the
bricks and wanders off in search of a proper painting.

The next book on my reading list was *Jeremy Thorpe: A Secret
Life*, written by the journalists from the *Sunday Times* and
published after the trial. In contrast to *The Pencourt File* this was
sharply written and orderly but it was ultimately unsatisfactory.
The evidence that the authors had amassed suggested that Thorpe
was not a nice or honest man. But the narrative was punctuated by
awkward affirmations, obviously inserted by libel lawyers, that he
was a splendid fellow who might have had 'homosexual tendencies'
as a young man but had certainly never plotted to kill Scott.

Finally, there was *The Last Word: An Eye-witness Account
of the Thorpe Trial*, by Auberon Waugh, the funniest satirist
in the country. This was published in 1980 and was ostensibly
a straightforward report of the trial but it captured the essence
of the story, which was love and revenge, greed and hypocrisy.

The next stage was to discover whether we could persuade people
who had either refused to say anything or had lied in the 1970s
to tell the truth now. It was possible, I told Penrose, that I would

conclude that Thorpe was a decent man who had been unfairly vilified by Scott, which would make it rather hard for us to collaborate on a book about him. Penrose sorted through his transcripts, police statements and documents from his days as half of Pencourt. To encourage him, I decided that we should invest his cupboards with some dignity, so I called them 'the Pencourt archive', which we both thought was amusing. Meanwhile, I traced Thorpe's friends. They still talked about him fondly, as they had twenty years ago, but admitted now that he was arrogant, vain and homosexual. One opened the interview with me by saying, 'I suppose you want to know about Jeremy and sex.' For two hours he talked about Thorpe's taste for 'rough trade'. He talked, too, about the toll inflicted on homosexuals of Thorpe's generation, who had to disguise their sexuality and, in the process, often became addicted to lying for lying's sake.

Other people also spoke for the first time, such as the television executive who had lived with Holmes for many years and gay Liberals who revealed that they had warned senior members of the Party that Thorpe was risking everything by cruising the streets in search of young men. Other sources thought in broader terms and said that this was a story about that amorphous institution, known as the Establishment, which always protected its own. They argued that it had tried to save Thorpe and then, having failed to silence Scott, rigged the trial.

Pencourt had worked tirelessly to prove that Thorpe masterminded the plot to murder Scott but Penrose agreed with me that it did not matter whether Thorpe had known about the recruitment of Andrew Newton; the jury had acquitted him and we could not, and should not, retry the case. We had to explain, for the first time, how this Privy Counsellor, Liberal leader and Member of Parliament for North Devon was destroyed by a neurotic for whom sex was an addiction.

Penrose gave me hundreds of pages of notes, based on his 'archive'. But there were nuggets buried here, mostly about Scott. I extracted them, drew on the new information I had gathered from Thorpe's friends and enemies and wrote the first half of the book. I traced the lives of the young Thorpe and Scott until their collision in 1960, when Thorpe visited a stables in Oxfordshire where Scott was working. The attraction was instant and fatal; a year later he seduced Scott. There were frequent rows and separations but there was real affection on both sides, although the impression given at the trial, and in subsequent books, was that the relationship was nothing more than a one-night stand.

In 1965 they drifted apart. Over the next decade Scott's life disintegrated; he lurched from one affair to another in a drunken, drugged daze while Thorpe prospered as the happily married leader of the Liberal Party. But neither could forget the other; love and hate became one overpowering emotion which had to end with the destruction of one of them.

It was less than twenty years since the trial but the society that produced Thorpe belonged to another world. His Britain was a country where homosexuals lived in constant fear of exposure and had to lie to survive, where men were judged by the school they attended and where national security was invoked whenever the press probed too hard.

I decided to open the second half of the book with the arrival of Penrose and Courtiour on Harold Wilson's doorstep in May 1976. I described their laudable, but not very efficient, pursuit of Thorpe over the next two years and his desperate attempts to shake them off. But this was much more than a detective story. It was also about the police, who were not allowed to investigate the case properly, politicians of all parties, who did not want to see one of their own disgraced, and the gay community, who despised Thorpe because he was a relic from the bad old days, when homosexuals were pariahs. Finally, I moved to the trial at the Old Bailey of Thorpe and his cronies. Like most journalists, Pencourt had been astonished by the verdict but, almost twenty years later, it was obvious now that the prosecution had been doomed from the moment that Thorpe was charged.

My best source for the period leading to the trial was Penrose himself. During the first eight months of research I lived in a cottage on his land in Kent, where he talked to me, perceptively and self-deprecatingly, about Pencourt's triumphs and disasters, Bessell's guilt-ridden outpourings, Thorpe's empty threats that he would sue anyone who suggested that he was not one hundred per cent heterosexual, the West Country detectives who were investigating Rinka's death and Falkender's intimate, but asexual, relationship with Wilson. He was especially strong on Scott; he said that I had to appreciate that beneath the exterior of the anguished homosexual was a tough and dangerous character.

There were further gems in his cupboard, which Courtiour and he had largely ignored when they were writing their book because they had nothing to do with Thorpe and 'the South African dimension'. Most important was *The Red File*, a secret diary they had kept when they were working at the BBC. This was a fascinating document because it showed how two young journalists, who believed that they had discovered a shocking conspiracy, were bullied and threatened by BBC executives who did not care for the tone of their investigation. There were other folders that had been gathering dust, unnoticed, for twenty years, such as the statement by a detective who revealed, in unintentionally hilarious detail, how the police had privately relied on Pencourt while protesting publicly that they never spoke to journalists.

Pencourt made many mistakes as they moved unsteadily towards their public denunciation of Thorpe; like astronomers searching for the explanation for life itself, they tried to erect one, grand theory to explain *everything*, from Harold Wilson's resignation as Prime Minister to the fact that a news agency in Washington was once offered a story about Scott. But it had been a fine effort; they had beaten Britain's political, media and legal establishments, which was not a bad achievment for a television reporter and researcher who had been advised by their elders and betters that they were committing professional suicide by suggesting that Thorpe was not a gentleman.

In America, Bob Woodward and Carl Bernstein, two hitherto unknown reporters on the *Washington Post*, had teamed up to investigate a routine burglary at the Watergate apartment building and, two years later, forced Richard Nixon out of the White House in 1974 and created the legend of the investigative journalist as fearless nemesis of the corrupt.

It would be silly to pretend that Rinkagate was in the same league as Watergate; Woodstein uncovered a conspiracy at the heart of the government in the richest country in history while Pencourt proved that the former leader of a political party in a little island off the coast of Europe was a secret homosexual who wanted his ex-lover killed. But that does not detract from Pencourt's achievement, which was to show that dedicated journalists could discover unwelcome truths, even in a chronically secretive country like Britain.

Editors remembered the lesson of Thorpe; never again did they trust a politician just because he had gone to Eton, Oxford and enjoyed opera at Covent Garden. The British press became less reverential and more sceptical, which was good for democracy and bad for politicians. During the 1980s and 1990s there were a stream of stories, in left and right-wing newspapers, tabloid, middle market and broadsheet, about womanising MPs, with their mistresses and illegitimate children, and corrupt MPs, who regarded their membership of the House of Commons as a licence to print money.

Of course, there were many, complex reasons for this new, aggressive reporting, such as the competition for scoops between newspapers and television and the erosion of deference, which had begun after the Second World War and accelerated under Margaret Thatcher. But, when the history of late 20th century journalism is written, Pencourt will surely deserve an honourable mention for demonstrating how reporters with guts and perseverance can change society.

When the hardback edition of this book was published in the autumn of 1996, after it had been serialised over four weeks by the *Sunday Times*, Thorpe's friends protested that he was a good and decent man. They talked about his wit, idealism and kindness but they did not dispute the key facts: that he was a promiscuous homosexual who had an affair with Scott, that he had lied about it and had then helped organise a plot to murder him. They also complained that it was wrong to criticise someone who was ill (Thorpe had been suffering from Parkinson's Disease for many years), which was like saying that American journalists should not attack Ronald Reagan's presidency because he was now very sick. They also said that I had gloated that Thorpe was a broken man. This was not only offensive but also naive because it would have been better for the book if he had been in robust health and had been able to defend himself.

There are important issues here, such as human weakness, the amorality of politics, official secrecy and cynicism and idealism in journalism. But it is difficult not to smile when you are writing about Norman Scott, who once carved the word 'incurable' on his arm with a razor blade and then summoned his doctor to repair the damage, Jeremy Thorpe, an old Etonian snob who had a weakness for young men with firm bodies, and Peter Bessell, who spent his life chasing the Big Deal which would make him a millionaire.

Only Andrew Newton, a greedy and violent liar, was truly bad; otherwise, there were no real villains or victims and certainly no heroes here. The only living creature who deserves our wholehearted sympathy was a large, friendly dog called Rinka, who was in the wrong place at the wrong time.

Simon Freeman
London, April, 1997

CHAPTER ONE

John Jeremy Thorpe was born on 29 April 1929. His father was John Thorpe, a King's Counsel and Conservative MP for Rusholme in Manchester from 1919 to 1924. He was a warm and romantic Irishman from Cork who had been brought up in England and had married Ursula Norton-Griffiths in 1922, when she was still a teenager. John and Ursula had two daughters when Jeremy was born: Lavinia, and Camilla, who committed suicide in 1974.[1]

Ursula was the elder daughter of Sir John Norton-Griffiths, 1st Bt., KCB, DSO, and a Conservative MP from 1910 until 1924. Although her father owed his baronetcy to David Lloyd George, the Welsh Liberal who led the coalition government during the First World War, he was known, to his delight, as 'Empire Jack' because of his Tory devotion to the Empire.

Thorpe's pedigree suggested that he should have become a staunch Conservative yet he turned leftwards, perhaps from the natural rebelliousness of the child against parental values, or perhaps because his father died when he was in the vulnerable years of puberty. He was proud of his family and particularly his father, who lavished affection on his only son, to the irritation of Lavinia and Camilla. Many years later he reflected: 'My father had been terrified of his own father, who was a bigoted, bullying man – a really monstrous man. My father was so influenced by the total lack of warmth shown him that he wanted to compensate for it with me.'[2]

His mother, Ursula, was a monocled authoritarian, who dominated her children by 'the sheer force of her personality'. As an adult Jeremy struggled to reconcile the conflicting emotions of love and anger which she provoked in him; she was his most loyal supporter and adviser, on everything from the content of his speeches to the style of his hats, despite the fact that she was an active Conservative in her local constituency in Surrey, but was also unable to accept that his life was his own. When he was 6 years old tubercular glands were discovered in his stomach. This led to seven months of discomfort in a device known as a spinal carriage. His mother recalled: 'He was very philosophical. He had his own little cottage in Littlehampton with his little *ménage* – his cook-housekeeper and his nanny. I was constantly on the move between him and the rest of the family.'

Thorpe said later that the illness had not scarred him emotionally although it had left him with a permanently weakened spine, which meant that his back would often 'seize up'. When that happened he would seek assistance from the nearest able-bodied men: 'I say to them, I am going to hang from that beam and when I say pull, each of you wrench down hard on my legs. Then I jump down as good as new.'

It meant that he could not enjoy the camaraderie of sport, which was essential if a boy was to be accepted in an English public school. He developed interests which were not exactly designed to win friends, such as playing the violin, and compensated for his physical handicap by becoming a show-off; he was a natural mimic, but always wanted to be centre stage, which did not endear him to his schoolfriends. His mother recalled this instance of her son's precocious self-confidence:

> It never occurred to him that anybody might not be glad to see him. One day we were at a concert and he said, 'I want to go and talk to Sir Thomas Beecham.' 'You can't, Jeremy. We don't know him.' He was quite determined and went backstage, stood in the queue and eventually was ushered in to see the old man. 'What do you want?' asked Sir Thomas. 'I just wanted to talk to you,' said this little boy. After that – we always sat in the front stalls – when Sir Thomas made his bow he would always turn and give this little boy an enormous wink.

Then the war came. The Thorpes had always taken for granted that they would have the necessities of life: the large houses in West London and Surrey, servants, bespoke clothes, dinner parties and the best seats at the opera. It did not occur to them that this all depended on money, which, like other respectable people, they did not talk about. Thorpe senior's practice at the Bar fell apart and he became a badly paid civil servant. Christopher Bourke, who was one of Thorpe's closest friends at Oxford after the war, said, 'Jeremy had always been at home with privilege. Ursula had always moved in illustrious circles politically and socially and was connected to highly acclaimed figures. They used to have a great income and that was cut off. The London house went and they had to move to Surrey.'[3]

Ursula had to adapt to their reduced circumstances, without the servants whom she could summon, and sack, with a flick of the hand. But she was determined not to show her pain. Thorpe recalled:

> She ran the house, did the cooking and washing-up. I remember hearing someone say, 'Mrs Thorpe has come down in the world better than anyone I know.' She had three wartime functions: she was a billeting officer, she delivered groceries and she cut up those green horses, which were horse carcasses intended for dog food and painted green so humans couldn't eat them. Nobody in Surrey wanted the unpalatable job of cutting them up so this enormous table was set in our household and there my mother would stand, wearing great rubber gloves, chopping up these green horses.

In 1940 the Thorpes decided to arrange the escape of their children from German bombs and possible invasion. Jeremy, aged 11, and his younger sister, Camilla, were packed off to the United States to stay with their aunt, Lady Norton-Griffiths, in Connecticut. He was one of forty pupils, including other English exiles, at the Rectory School, which the headmaster, John Bigelow, described as 'more like an overgrown family than a school'.

Thorpe thrived there; the fact that he could not play bone-crunching, character-forming games, like rugby, did not matter here. Later he claimed that he was so impressed by America's dynamic meritocracy that he began to veer leftwards, away from his parents' Conservatism. In 1943, however, he was summoned home by his mother. She said that his father was missing him and that it was time for Jeremy to commence his real education: at Eton College.

He had just arrived at Eton when his father had a stroke. Jeremy sought out faith healers who, he hoped, might be able to restore him. But he died in 1944. Thorpe senior's death exacerbated the family's financial problems and Ursula feared that she would have to withdraw Jeremy from Eton, but her brother-in-law stepped in with a seven-year covenant. Yet it might have been better for him

if he had gone elsewhere since, like many boys, he did not care for
the school. Even rugged characters like Alan Clark, sportsman,
womaniser, millionaire, maverick Conservative minister and bestselling diarist, could not stand the place. Clark, a year older than
Thorpe, said, 'It was an early introduction to human cruelty,
treachery and extreme physical hardship.' Another non-wimpish
survivor was the explorer, Sir Ranulph Fiennes, who was Thorpe's
junior by fifteen years. He said, 'No leper can have suffered so
long or so sharply as I did as I struggled to live with the taunts
and subtle cruelties of my fellow Etonians.'[4]

Eton College was founded in 1440 and is the second oldest British
public school, after Winchester, which edges it by fifty-eight years.
By the 1990s, like its equally expensive rivals, it had become sleek
and modern, though it remained resolutely politically incorrect. But
in the 1940s it was different: the hierachy of boys, symbolised by
fagging, the feudal system of junior boys waiting on older boys,
was still unquestioned. Sometimes, if not as often as popularly
rumoured, the relationship moved beyond toasting crumpets and
cleaning rugger boots and involved sex. (*The Oxford English Dictionary* defines 'fag' as slang for a homosexual.) This might be initiated by older boys, who had emerged from the spotty confusion of
puberty with raging sexual appetites, or by younger boys infatuated
by their strapping seniors. Either way, the sex usually amounted to
no more than fumbling masturbation sessions, memories of which
were erased once boys had entered a world inhabited by girls.

Quentin Crewe, a confirmed heterosexual, who later became
a professional journalist, left Eton shortly after Thorpe arrived
in 1943; the two did not meet until the late forties. Crewe
said:

> Homosexuality was rife at Eton. Often it would be an older
> boy seducing a younger one. It was very much frowned upon
> by the school and if you were caught you could be sacked
> [expelled]. The thing is, we never saw any girls and everyone
> was pretty randy. It didn't mean you were gay, quite often
> the reverse. Boys were just in a high state of sexuality and
> didn't have any outlets. They might make a pass at you
> but if you weren't interested they would leave you alone.
> I don't think there was much buggery. Usually it was just
> mutual masturbation. I suppose it might have given some
> people a taste for homosexuality but most people I know

who carried on like that there turned out to be perfectly normal later.[5]

But Thorpe's friends insisted that he was not involved even in immature groping like this: 'People have said that he must been queer at Eton. Absolute rubbish. I know that is simply not true,' said Stanley Brodie, a lawyer who was one of Thorpe's closest friends at Oxford.[6] Another friend of Thorpe, a member of his entourage when he was Liberal leader, said, 'Boys at Eton were fascinated by sex. They used to get rulers and measure each other's penises. But I know for a fact that Jeremy didn't even get up to that kind of thing.'[7]

Thorpe enjoyed his school holidays at home in Surrey, where his mother epitomised the sensibly shoed, church-going lady who was the backbone of the Tory Party, only distinguished from thousands like her in the shires by her monocle, cigars and cosmopolitan friends. These included Megan Lloyd George, youngest daughter of David Lloyd George, the Welsh Liberal who had been Prime Minister from 1916 to 1922. Megan was a year younger than Ursula and was Jeremy's godmother. She had been elected Liberal MP for Anglesey in the late 1920s and survived there until 1945, although, by then, the Liberals had long since been broken as a major force after the long, acrimonious feud between her father and Herbert Asquith which had begun in 1916.[8] Jeremy loved listening to his godmother talk about her father. She said that, of course, he had had his faults but added that he had changed society for the better by, for example, introducing old-age pensions before the First World War.[9] Jeremy decided that this was his vocation: he would revive the corpse of Liberalism, the only party that was not shackled to interest groups, such as Conservatism's greedy capitalists and Labour's dogmatic trade unionists, and make it a great political force again.

He knew the route that he had to take: Oxford University, 'the place where the emerging Establishment, not all of it especially brilliant, frolics for three years in unique and glorious surroundings and where those with ambition and an eye for the main chance invest heavily in the networking that will set them up for the rest of their lives'.[10]

In 1949, however, he faced the unwelcome interruption of two years of compulsory National Service in the Armed Forces. His career in the Army's Rifle Brigade lasted for just six weeks. He told friends that he had been judged 'psychologically unsuitable' for military life, which they interpreted as meaning that good old

Jeremy had cunningly managed 'to convince the Army that they wouldn't survive if he stayed'. At the time it seemed plausible that he had joked his way out of uniform but later there were doubts about this story, like many of his self-serving anecdotes. Lord Rees-Mogg, who later edited *The Times* for fourteen years, said, 'He told us that he had had a breakdown. That is possible. But after the Scott business came to light I suspected that he had left the Army because of his homosexuality. If he had told them about that they would certainly have pushed him out.'[11]

Every generation that pours into Oxford each autumn believes that it is unique but some generations are certainly special. When Jeremy Thorpe arrived in Oxford in October 1948, aged 19, to take up his place at Trinity College to read law, the same subject as his late father, he was more fortunate than he knew.[12] Instead of the usual influx of pimply, virginal youths there were also young men in their mid-20s, who had fought in the war and who had the far-away look of those who have witnessed terrible things. Superficially, the war veterans were just as competitive and eager to win the glittering prizes as the Thorpes but most held back a fraction because they were men and not boys.

Sir Robin Day, for many years the television interviewer whom politicians most feared, was a National Service veteran on the eve of his 24th birthday when he arrived at St Edmund Hall in autumn 1947 to study law. In his bestselling autobiography Day said that this was 'the golden age' of Oxford, where he was 'privileged to enjoy the most memorable and exciting time of my life'. He wrote:

> There have doubtless been other golden ages but, in contrast to the normal peacetime intake of schoolboys, 75 per cent of the post-war undergraduates were ex-servicemen on government grants. Oxford was a broader, less exclusive place. No one cared, no one asked, which school you had been to, or what your father was, or what rank you had held in the service. Such irrelevant details emerged by accident, if at all, and only in conversation with close friends. There was a marked absence of snobbery. Decadence was not in vogue. But the atmosphere was not earnest or humourless. Post-war Oxford sparkled and bubbled with talent and originality. A brilliant array of characters went up during those years 1945–1950.[13]

This was not how the 19-year-old Jeremy Thorpe saw Oxford; he was determined to become a star, using whatever methods were necessary. (Day, himself, could not have been exactly self-effacing because, like Thorpe, he also managed to conquer Oxford's most treacherous peak when he became President of the Union in 1950.)

Thorpe was not concerned about his law degree – he thought that, with last-minute cramming, he would scrape through and, in any case, the class of your degree did not matter, providing you had made an impact – and law books and weekly essays did not occupy much space in his diary. He vowed to be exceptional: he would be a stylish wit; he would be a *personality* and would collect a string of trophies – by bagging the presidencies of the most prestigious university clubs and societies – which would lay the foundation for his career in politics after Oxford. So despite his lack of army experience, he planned his time at university as if it was a military campaign. First, he had to be noticed. He achieved this by wearing outfits that seemed to have come from his great-grandfather's wardrobe: frock coats, stove-pipe trousers, brocade waistcoats and buckled shoes, set off by a gold-knobbed walking stick, suggesting that this was man of substance who was also a wag. Friends thought that Jeremy had style but many dismissed him as a vulgar show-off.

He also developed eccentric pastimes, such as collecting Chinese ceramics and giving impromptu violin recitals, when he would protest that he had once been an accomplished player but had sacrificed music to more pressing concerns, such as making his way in the world. He could afford weekly lunches with friends at a restaurant called the Shamrock which overlooked the Union. One of that circle was Stanley Brodie: 'We used to have a jolly lunch once a week at a bay window overlooking the street. We weren't rich but we didn't have the money problems that students have today. We still had ration books in 1949 and you couldn't, by law, sell a meal for more than five shillings. So, we managed quite well.'[14]

Thorpe's first goal was to establish his credentials as a Liberal, a party that seemed to be heading for oblivion after decades of self-destructive squabbling. He joined the Liberal Club and soon rose to become Secretary. Ann Chesney, later Mrs Ann Dummett, a respected commentator on race relations, was President. She said:

Jeremy was intensely ambitious but he believed in the Party and thought that Liberalism was good and right. His Liberalism was not cynical. It was the core of him. He thought that one day he would be Prime Minister. We were walking past Downing Street after some meeting or other in London and he pointed to Number 10 and said, 'Ann, I am going to get there.' He was 20 years old. But there was nothing bad about that. That is what political people are like.

Thorpe completed his conquest of the Liberal Club, the first trophy of his Oxford career, when he became President in the first, or Hilary, term, of 1950. He was not an original thinker but he was an instinctive speaker, who could win over a hostile audience with non-stop jokes and mimicry. Ann Dummett said, 'He was an enormously effective President. Membership was higher than ever before under his presidency, thanks to his charisma.'

Thus, the Thorpe of the 1960s was already taking shape: a man of style and wit but who lacked the intellectual equipment to master complicated issues. His Liberalism was a gut reaction against the two dominant philosophies, *laissez-faire* capitalism and socialism, rather than a positive statement of belief. He was passionate on the big questions in foreign affairs, such as the legacy of colonialism, but when he moved closer to home and to dull but important issues, such as education, housing and transport, he could only mouth platitudes about wanting a fairer society. He also cultivated senior Liberals outside Oxford, notably Dingle Foot, Liberal MP for Dundee from 1931 until 1945, whose father Isaac had been a Liberal MP in the West Country during the 1920s and 1930s.[15]

In 1949 Thorpe shot off to Bodmin in Cornwall, where John Foot, Dingle's brother, was standing for the Liberals, and dazzled the voters with his verbal pyrotechnics. John Foot said, 'It was bally-hoo but perfectly legitimate. Even in those days Jeremy had this astonishing instinct for politicking. You knew that this was a very remarkable chap.' However, despite Thorpe's efforts, Foot still lost in 1950.

In the two general elections of 1950 and 1951, which left the Liberals with nine and then six MPs, Thorpe threw himself into campaigning with manic energy. With other young Liberals, such as Ann Dummett, he hurled himself at the voters around Oxford. She said:

We had to visit 130 villages in three weeks. We had to warm up an audience, sometimes just three men and a dog, before the

Liberal candidate arrived. Once we were going to one village which was supposed to be rather inbred. Jeremy asked me to help him beef up on the economy and said tell me, Ann, what is capital investment? I did my best to explain in words of one syllable. Then, at the meeting, when Jeremy was speaking, a man in the audience rose and said yes, but how do you reconcile that with the leader in last week's *Economist*? He was a natural speaker though he was not a great thinker, but then not many politicians are.

Some of Thorpe's contemporaries were not so keen; they thought that he was an unscrupulous showman who shamelessly cultivated useful contacts, such as the Foots. But he was not concerned about this jealous sniping.

Having collected the Liberal Club presidency he moved to his next target, the Law Society. By now his campaigning style had begun to disturb his peers. Dick Taverne, a brilliant Balliol student who later became a Labour MP, said that Thorpe broke every rule:

He got people over from Cambridge so that they could vote for him. Several people, including barristers in London, were surprised to get letters from Thorpe, saying I hope you will vote for me, your Liberal candidate for the presidency. He just wanted to use the society as another of his jumping-off points to fight for the Union presidency. He carried it off with great *élan* and good cheer. He didn't make any bones about it. It was as if he gloried in his misdeeds.

As Taverne rightly judged, the Law Society was just a staging post; the goal was the presidency of the Oxford Union. Thorpe took a year off from his law studies so that he could concentrate on this, which he calculated would be a lot more useful in adult life than a good degree.

The Union building, dating from 1857 and set just off Cornmarket, in the heart of the city, has always been the scene for Machiavellian intrigues by students eager to be elected to one of the senior positions there. By the 1990s, when even the Conservatives preached egalitarianism, the fact that a student had become President guaranteed him or her (women were given full membership rights in 1963) nothing. The Union is, and always has been, just a good library, dining room and debating chamber, where students in dinner jackets show-off amongst adult guests, ranging from American presidents to stars of television soap operas.

But it was different in Thorpe's day; the presidency was a passport bearing the Establishment's seal of approval. He swept aside the obstacles which were placed in his path. He had already had a rehearsal – in 1950, when he had lost to Robin Day – and now, at the beginning of the last, otherwise Michaelmas, term of 1950 he began to eliminate his rivals. First, he had to ensure that Keith Kyle, a popular war veteran, could not stand for the presidency. This was tricky since Thorpe had been on the Union committee that had agreed that the rules governing the eligibility of presidential candidates should be amended so that men like Kyle, whose university careers had been interrupted by war, should not be barred from standing. Kyle, who had a long and varied career in journalism after Oxford, said that friends had persuaded him to be a candidate:

> I told them that I would withdraw if there was any contro-
> versy. Then there was a move to reverse the rule change. This
> was masterminded by Thorpe. So I stood down. Thorpe was a
> good speaker and a brilliant mimic but he wasn't particularly
> bright. He gave the impression of being ruthlessly ambitious.
> He seemed to want to be President of anything. He hated not
> being a president.

Thorpe then outmanoeuvred the incumbent president, Godfrey Smith, later a columnist on the *Sunday Times*, over the choice of speakers in a debate. The details of the argument between the two are irrelevant now but the tactics that Thorpe used, saying one thing in public and doing the opposite in private, were the same as he employed many years later when he was the Liberal leader.

He also displayed an ability as an undergraduate politician to escape the consequences of his actions, just as he managed to convince Liberal colleagues in the early 1970s that he barely knew Norman Scott. The Union held an inquiry into his row with Smith and let him off with a censure. Thorpe told friends that the affair had been a plot by students from Balliol to discredit him and that he did not care if they called him 'a fiddler'. He crowed, 'I will fiddle till Balliol burns.'

He could not be stopped now and he was elected President for the eight-week term which began in January 1951. One of his defeated opponents, William Rees-Mogg for the Conservatives, definitely did not think that the best man had won. Rees-Mogg, who succeeded Thorpe as President, said, 'Thorpe was a superb debater but there was not much content in what he said. My style was based on picking on the arguments of the other side and showing them to be false. But Jeremy gave me nothing to argue against.'

As President Thorpe thoroughly enjoyed himself. He had a small group of trusted friends, some of whom played significant roles in his later secret life as a homosexual. Most important was a homosexual history student from Yorkshire called David Holmes, who became a lifelong confidant. There was also Philip Watkins, a quiet young man who was rumoured to be homosexual and who became the Liberals' treasurer in the 1970s when Thorpe controlled the Party's funds as if they existed solely for the promotion of J. Thorpe. He also knew George Carman, a brilliant law student from Balliol who collected a First and went on to win a succession of celebrated cases, including the defence of Thorpe at the Old Bailey in 1979.

Ursula Thorpe had become a regular visitor to the Union and now, with natural maternal pride, revelled in her son's glory. She was yet another element, like the clothes and the mimicry, in the creation of Thorpe's image. Yet astute observers had picked up clues from her about the contradictions of her son: a Liberal whose roots were buried beneath the debris of shattered privilege and a man who both needed his mother and craved to escape from her.

By summer 1951 the widespread belief that Thorpe was a light-weight performer who could not be trusted meant that, for once, he failed to get what he wanted. He had hoped to be a member of the two-man debating team that Oxford traditionally sent on a tour of American universities but Rees-Mogg and Taverne were chosen because the selection committee thought that Thorpe's ego would be disruptive in the States. But he did not care. He had been President of the Union and had already made many useful contacts in the Liberal Party. 'If you were *determined* to achieve office some of the Union Set thought this was muck politics. I didn't. I am not English. I am three-quarters Celt. And I'm bilingual: I speak American as well as English,' he said.

He took solace from the fact that he had emerged from the mêlée and become a name. The student magazine *Isis* profiled him in 1951; the author Ivan Yates, who later worked for the *Observer*, detected the flaws which later destroyed him: 'His likes and dislikes are are often too violently expressed, and some feel that as a future politician he would be wise to be more discreet. An interesting and stimulating career lies ahead of him, provided he does not let his enthusiasm over-reach his wisdom.'

Thorpe's contemporaries might have congratulated themselves in the summer of 1951 that, finally, they had got the measure of him. But they had missed one, important element: he found men sexually attractive. Although homosexuality was still a criminal offence then, some brave souls, such as Kenneth Tynan, the playwright, made no attempt to hide their sexuality. Others were more cautious but, nonetheless, were the subject of well-informed rumours. But no one suspected that Thorpe was gay, which suggests that his discovery of sex came later. He was a master of deceit, who gave the impression to confidants that he was entrusting them, and them alone, with the secrets of his true self. However, even a man like this would have found it hard to fool all the people, all of the time in the small, gossipy village of Oxford.

'There was not a single hint that he had gay leanings,' said Stanley Brodie. 'He was not the sort of chap to leap into bed with every woman he met but that was because he was determined to further his political career. He was a busy fellow and didn't have time to play about.' Ann Dummett said, ' It was very smart to be homosexual but we had no idea about Jeremy. He didn't seem interested in women but then sex was not the main subject of people's vocabulary, unlike today.' That critical observer, Lord Rees-Mogg, also did not suspect: 'I had no idea that he was gay. None at all.' Another Oxford contemporary said, 'It never entered my head that he might be gay. No one knew and at Oxford everyone knew everything about everyone. But perhaps he did not know either; perhaps his ambition contributed to the repression of his sexual feelings.'

When Thorpe left Oxford in the summer of 1952, having scraped a Third, his mother said that he had 'carried all before him, except his degree'. Despite an unremarkable mind, he had stood out; many at Oxford were cleverer and nicer but few excited such interest. It was impossible to be neutral about him. Stanley Brodie said, 'He was remarkable and charismatic. He did not have the greatest intellect in the world but was superb at picking up other people's ideas. He would always help someone with a sob story. Perhaps that was his undoing.' Michael Ogle (whose friendship with Thorpe was platonic) said that he was proud to have shared rooms with him. Ann Dummett was also faithful. 'There was nothing bad about him. He was a fundamentally decent man who had his faults, like all of us. He had a burning push to do good things.'

Christopher Bourke, a gentle courteous man who later became a lawyer in the office of the Director of Public Prosecutions, said, 'He was the most warm-hearted and amusing man I have ever met. I am proud to have counted him as a friend.'

But equally distinguished alumnae had a different view. Lord Rees-Mogg said:

> He was exceptionally ambitious in a way that was outside the conventions of the time. He was ambitious in an obsessive rather than a balanced way. Yes, we were all ambitious but not so that we would do silly things. I remember having a conversation with some people when we decided that Jeremy had behaved in a way at Oxford which left the impression that he couldn't be trusted.

Dick Taverne said, 'Jeremy Thorpe was a brilliant and entertaining mimic. He was also a totally unscrupulous student politician. But he did it with such *bonhomie* and so blatantly that I have to admit that it was curiously inoffensive. He was likeable but totally dishonest and amoral.' Keith Kyle thought that Thorpe had never been able to tell right from wrong: 'Most of us thought that he was a bounder but, by jove, a bounder with style.'

Another Oxford contemporary said, 'It all went beyond normal ambition with Jeremy. He had the reputation amongst his friends as being a crook, a twister, who would do the dirty on you. It was a widely held view at Oxford that it would all end in some frightful financial fraud. It didn't occur to us that it would be a sexual scandal. But everyone agreed that his career would end in a smash-up.'[16]

CHAPTER TWO

Jeremy Thorpe left Oxford with his presidential trophies, the suitcases packed with his neatly pressed antique outfits, and an address book stuffed with important names. His abysmal class of degree was traditionally acquired only by the stupid or lazy or, as Thorpe explained, by those who had been too busy to study. But he was confident that, with so many influential contacts, he would still be able to earn a comfortable living as a barrister while he worked towards his next goal: to become a Liberal Member of Parliament. He knew that it would be easy to become a Liberal candidate but that it would be immeasurably harder to win a seat. The Party's representation in the House of Commons was shrinking inexorably: in 1945 it had twelve MPs, in 1950 nine and, after the general election in 1951, six. It had polled 743,512 votes, a mere 2.6 per cent of the total of almost 29 million, which reduced it 'to the status of a music-hall joke'.[1] Liberal grandees deluded themselves that the Party was still a major political force but Thorpe could see that it was ideologically and financially bankrupt and depended for survival on well-meaning, unpaid and elderly volunteers. Young, ambitious would-be MPs did not want to waste their time on the Liberals and joined the Conservatives or Labour, which meant that almost anyone who was sane, keen and did not have a criminal record could become a Liberal candidate. No one knew whether the Party was radical right or radical left or just a sanctuary for oddballs. Only in the rural fringes of political and religious non-conformity, the South West, North East Scotland and North Wales, was Liberalism still vigorous, though loyalists there had little in common with each other or the sophisticates in London.

These grim statistics show that, for all his faults, Thorpe cannot be accused of opportunism; many equally promising student Liberals joined the Big Two after university because they calculated that there was little hope of a parliamentary seat as Liberals, let alone glory. Later, when the Liberal revival was under way, first under Jo Grimond and then Thorpe, critics said that he had only stuck with the Party because he knew that he was sure to rise to the top in a party of nonentities; but this theory ignores the fact that in 1952 it seemed likely that there would soon be no party for Thorpe to rise in.

But first he had to find a constituency to fight. His contacts with the Lloyd Georges meant that Wales was a possibility but he was also attracted to the West Country, which had once been a bastion of Liberalism, in the pre-war days when Liberalism and non-conformity were synonymous. North Devon, centred on Barnstaple, was vacant and Thorpe made his move, deploying his considerable persuasive skills when he met the selection committee of the local Liberal Association in November 1952. It is part of the game of politics that, in these circumstances, the applicant has to claim a long, deep love of the constituency he (or she) hopes to represent, and Thorpe did this superbly. He was knocking at a door which was jammed open; he was articulate, elegantly, if curiously, dressed and was well-connected. The North Devon Liberals could not believe that this bright young man wanted to fight for them and snapped him up. Lillian Prowse, then a volunteer worker for the Party, who later became Thorpe's full-time agent, recalled, 'We had come bottom in the 1951 election and we were delighted when Jeremy said he wanted to fight for us. He was a very charming young man. He was charismatic. He inspired great affection. He was extraordinary. He said that he intended to win and we believed him. He said he would come second in the next election. He did. He said he would win the second time. He did.'[2]

At first, however, Thorpe and North Devon seemed ill-matched. The constituency was sprawling and rural: villages and hamlets haphazardly linked to each other by winding lanes and isolated from the rest of Britain, who saw Devon as that pretty place you went to in the summer to eat cream teas.

The moors were rugged and so were the people, who were conservative with a small 'c', and suspicious of outsiders, especially posh-sounding ones from that ungodly place called London. North Devon had been staunchly Liberal before the war but was now Conservative. Its MPs tended to be local and well-to-do. Thorpe was not a member of the landowning class from whom the locals habitually took their lead; he was public school and Oxbridge and

knew more about tribalism in Africa than pig farming in the West
Country. Everything suggested that he had made a disastrous
decision; friends said that he should have been a left-of-centre
Tory candidate, fighting a prosperous seat near London, where the
voters would appreciate his progressive theories on international
affairs.

This was certainly the view of his mother, who was appalled
that her son was throwing away his life; she had no objections to
him becoming a politician but she could not understand why he
had chosen the scruffy Liberals when he could have had a brilliant
career as a Tory. But it was her duty to support Jeremy:

> When I first realised that Jeremy was going to fight North
> Devon as a Liberal, I didn't know what I was going to do. I
> was very active in the Tory Party in Surrey. I was chairman of
> the Women's Advisory Committee. I said to a friend, 'I *can't*
> let Jeremy drive down there by himself.' She said, 'You must
> drive and cherish.' So I went down in our only car and drove
> and cherished. From then I went to every single meeting with
> him. I made it clear to my friends that blood is thicker than
> water.[3]

At first, the North Devon Liberals did not know what to make of
this severe woman who smoked cigars and seemed to think that
she was in charge of Jeremy and them (they later warmed to her).
But they were sure from the start that, in Thorpe, they had netted
a star of the future. At the Party's annual conference in 1953,
held in Ilfracombe, Thorpe confirmed the impression that he was
destined to do more than just win a seat in Parliament, which would
have been a remarkable enough achievement in itself; he told the
assembled Liberal leadership, made up of earnest ageing bankers,
industrialists, wealthy titled philanthropists and intellectuals, that
he would not endorse the Party's policies on Free Trade, which,
he said, were absurdly outdated. And he warned that at least a
dozen other Liberal candidates shared his view. He walked out
and formed the Radical Reform Group, but remained a Liberal.

For the next two and a half years he set about transforming the
moribund Party organisation in North Devon. During the week
he was a barrister in London, though he was still living with
his mother in Surrey to save money, and at weekends would
drive to Devon, where he stayed at the Broomhill Hotel, near

Barnstaple, which was run by an elderly lady who treated him like a son.

The Liberals had no money and only a handful of activists, who sprang into not very professional action during an election. But Thorpe's apprenticeship at Oxford served him well; he could convince people to vote for him and to pay for the privilege of doing so. He dashed around North Devon in his fogeyish suits and the brown bowler which became his trademark. (This was an unhappy choice of headwear since 'brown bowler' was slang then for homosexual, though at the time no one made the connection, at least publicly.) Lillian Prowse watched his progress with awe:

> He would spend a whole day in a village, meeting people and listening to their problems. He had an incredible memory. He would talk to someone who would tell him that their dog was ill. A year later he would meet the same person again and ask, 'How is your dog?' And he did it all without taking notes. He genuinely cared about people. That was his secret. I have seen him almost in tears when a constituent lost a relative. He was very human and people loved him for that.[4]

Michael Barnes, a solicitor in Barnstaple who occasionally used Thorpe when he was a barrister on the Western Circuit said, 'He was a scintillating wit and a charmer. He also really cared about people and became the finest MP this constituency ever had.'[5]

In his set-piece speeches, which were designed to establish his credentials as a national politician with the press, he concentrated on the big issues, such as the injustice of apartheid and the madness of the Cold War. No one could accuse him of taking easy options: he opposed the invasion of Suez in 1956 by British and French troops, when the country was swept by nationalist fervour, next seen during the Falklands War in 1982; he supported closer ties with Europe, which was not what Devon farmers wanted to hear; and he opposed capital punishment and advocated legalised abortion, which were also not vote-winning ideas. He deserved praise for standing up for his Liberal principles; on the other hand, attitudes such as these were less important to the folk of Devon than his appreciation of the small problems which worried them.

When he was out in the villages, he was a Man of the People; he talked about the bend in the road that was too narrow for the new tractor Mr Jones had just bought, or the disgraceful behaviour of the local squire, who seemed to think he could sack old John with the bad back after thirty years' loyal service as a farmhand. He summed up his campaign philosophy thus: 'Show me a village with no electricity and I will show you a village which is going to vote Liberal next time.' He also made people laugh, which helped.

In May 1955 Thorpe's hard work was tested in a general election. Nationally, the Party did appallingly: it polled 722,402 votes, fewer than in 1951, and just managed to hang on to its six seats in the Commons. During the campaign the Party had been tugged left and right by its senior figures, some of whom wanted Liberals to back the Tories if they did not have their own candidate in a seat, while other Liberals, such as Megan Lloyd George, urged Liberals to back Labour where necessary. But Thorpe had performed brilliantly. On an 82 per cent turn-out, he had halved the Tory majority of 1951. He had persuaded 11,588 people to vote Liberal and had pushed Labour into third place. Next time, he told Lillian Prowse, North Devon will be ours.

Now, he set about turning the Liberals into a lean, mean fighting machine which would have 5,000 paid-up members. He launched this ambitious scheme when he was re-adopted two months after the May election. Flanked by Jo Grimond, who became the Liberal leader the next year, and Peter Bessell, a Liberal candidate who had just fought and lost in Torquay, he told a crowd in Barnstaple that the Party need money if it wanted to make sure that they won the next election. He bet the crowd his wing collar and tie that they could not raise £300; thirty minutes later, having collected £475, Thorpe handed over his collar and tie, having demonstrated again that he was a populist of genius who could persuade people to open their wallets for him.

By 1958 Lillian Prowse was his full-time agent on a small salary and was working tirelessly to put into effect Thorpe's dream. She said, 'We ended up with the best organisation in the country. Jeremy would come down at the weekends and I would arrange his diary. There were fifty polling districts and each had its own committee. We had 1,000 people who would work for us on a polling day. That was a huge number in those days. Jeremy always said that I was the boss and he was very good at doing what we wanted.'[6]

While Prowse was knocking the local Liberals into shape Thorpe was making his mark with the leadership in London. He pushed his way on to the national committee that had been set up to plan the next general-election campaign and he sat on a dull little committee which examined agricultural policy; he was not interested in the minutiae of wheat production or dairy subsidies but was determined to be at the nerve centre of the Party, being seen and picking up gossip, while he nudged Liberals towards the policies espoused by his Radical Reform Group. The new Liberalism that he envisaged would, of course, require a young and vigorous leader; and the obvious candidate would be Jeremy Thorpe.

At the Party assembly at Folkestone in September 1956 the Old Guard retreated further when Clement Davies, then aged 72, a Welsh lawyer who had led the Party since 1945, resigned. He was replaced by Grimond, a fast-thinking 43-year-old Scot, an Old Etonian and Oxford-educated lawyer who understood that television had created a new politics. Thorpe watched approvingly and calculated rightly, as it happened, that he was just the sort of chap whom Grimond would need as the Party searched for a vote-winning identity.

Thorpe worked ceaselessly during the mid-1950s to ensure that he became an MP. But he also tried, in case it all went wrong, to expand his practice as a barrister. He was a polished performer but was more actor than advocate, which might have been effective at a meeting in a village hall in Devon or a dinner party in Chelsea but was not what was required in a court.

Then Dominic Le Foe transformed his life. Le Foe was a Liberal activist and actor-manager who was, according to him, a genius in the fledgling industry of political public relations. He had first met Thorpe in the late 1940s, when he had begun to make his way in the theatre. He recalled, 'I was a young Liberal then and we met on a speaking tour. I had already made my name as a very clever speaker. I didn't know it then but Thorpe was a two-sided character and one side was very dark. His sense of loyalty could be extremely weak. He was very ambitious and thought that he could do as he liked.'[7]

Late in 1955 Le Foe was asked to help a Liberal candidate, Frank Owen, a former editor of the London *Evening Standard* and the *Daily Mail*, fight a by-election in Hereford. To general astonishment Owen came second when the votes were counted the following February. Le Foe said, 'I ran Owen's campaign with showbiz professionalism. The result was a sensation because Liberals usually got a few hundred votes. Thorpe saw what I had done for Frank and wanted me to do it for him.'

By now Le Foe was running his own theatrical agency in London, called, for reasons known only to him, Max Allington. He said: 'Thorpe was desperately keen to get into television. He needed the money to keep body and soul together while he was nursing North Devon. But he was also an actor *manqué*.'[8] He found Thorpe a job in television, as a presenter on *This Week*, the new flagship, go-anywhere programme of Independent Television. This was well-paid and glamorous work. He interviewed foreign leaders, such as King Hussein of Jordan, which reinforced the impression in London's media-political circles that he was a heavyweight operator. But he was not a hit, either with his bosses or with the audience. One former colleague said:

Jeremy was amusing and great company. He was the best mimic I had ever heard. It wasn't just that he could imitate someone's voice; he could get inside their head and think like them. I remember once I heard Michael Foot talking in a *This Week* office. I knew Michael and so I went in to say hello. And there was Jeremy, being Michael Foot. But the closer you got to Thorpe the less you liked him. He also wasn't much good on television. He always wanted an audience. He couldn't just talk to you. You felt you were part of a crowd and that Jeremy was putting on a show. He was always performing. But that didn't work in television. You have to talk to the camera as if you are having a conversation with one person. So he was not kept on by *This Week*.[9]

Thorpe did not mind because he needed to concentrate on North Devon, which was his passport into the House of Commons. In autumn 1959 the Conservative Prime Minister, Harold Macmillan, called a general election for October. This was Thorpe's moment of truth; he was 30 years old, had been a candidate for seven years and knew that failure now would probably mean the end of his political ambitions. The North Devon Liberals went to battle stations, marshalled by Lillian Prowse. Dominic Le Foe directed the public-relations offensive, with posters: 'Make it a Liberal North Devon,' plastered everywhere. Today this does not sound very sophisticated but in the 1950s, when politics had not been taken over by Armani-suited advertising gurus with multi-million-pound budgets, Le Foe's marketing of Thorpe was innovative and effective. Thorpe rose to the occasion superbly, hurdling fences, cracking jokes and promising that, unlike the current Tory incumbent, he would fight for North Devon in the House of Commons.

But, as always, there was a problem with money. Thorpe felt that, as a *big* politician, he deserved the razzmatazz of an American-style election campaign; so he splashed out on cars and posters to create an image that proclaimed that Jeremy Thorpe was a man who was going places. This was another theme of his career: spending money that his party did not have because he thought that he was the only man who could carry the Liberals to glory.

One and a half million people voted for the Liberals, more than twice as many as in 1955, but the Party still only had six MPs, including a new Member for North Devon, Jeremy Thorpe. He had squeezed home by 362 votes. He marched in triumph from the Town Hall to the Party headquarters in Barnstaple. Flanked by his mother, he declared, 'This is not my victory, but our victory. I think you know how much I love North Devon and the people who live within its borders.' Ursula thought that his brown bowler had, on balance, been a mistake but she glowed with pride: 'I pooh-poohed some of his clothes but I don't think he would have had this success without his personal magnetism and exhibitionism.'[10]

That autumn Thorpe took his place in the Commons alongside his five Liberal colleagues, swamped by the 258 Labour members and the 365 Conservatives who cheered and waved their order papers in homage to their leader, Harold Macmillan, the patrician who, at 65, was beginning his second term as Prime Minister.

Thorpe felt as if he had come home. He knew that MPs would flock to hear his jokes and acidic observations. In the corridors, restaurants and bars he would lobby and plot, just as he had done at Oxford, but this time no one would criticise him because winners were appreciated here.[11] The press soon marked him down as a name of the future. He was a master heckler, able to bring guffaws from all sides of the House and reduce speakers to red-faced silence; hence, he was often given an honourable mention in the dispatches of the parliamentary sketch writers, whose columns were eagerly scanned by MPs who wanted to discover who amongst them was tipped for stardom. When Harold Macmillan sacked seven members of his Cabinet in 1962 Thorpe came up with this comment, which the press agreed was the wittiest verdict ever delivered on a face-saving prime-ministerial reshuffle: 'Greater love hath no man than this, that he lay down his friends for his life.'

He confirmed his reputation as a radical thinker who was passionate about human rights abroad, especially in South Africa. Russell Johnston, the Liberal MP for Inverness from 1964, who was knighted in 1985, said:

> He was well-informed about Africa. He was also strong on domestic human rights, divorce, and capital punishment. I remember hearing him once tell an audience of rural Liberals that we had to stand up for persecuted minorities like homosexuals. It was brave of him to say that to people like that. But he wasn't interested in a wide range of policies, on things like housing, transport and the environment.[12]

In Pretoria the South African intelligence service, whose idea of a good laugh was to drop a black man from a ten-storey building, watched the emergence of Mr Thorpe with interest. The Liberals were irritating but unimportant; BOSS knew, however, that this could change. Although BOSS officers loathed Britain as the lowest form of political life, a multi-cultural democracy, they did not allow hatred to influence their analysis of British politics. They calculated that one day the Liberals might be more than just an irrelevant parliamentary rump and so they opened a file on the emerging Liberal star, Jeremy Thorpe, Kaffir-lover and enemy of South Africa. But BOSS's representatives in Britain were already stretched by the effort of monitoring the myriad of organisations dedicated to the overthrow of apartheid and there is no evidence that they managed to find out anything about Thorpe that was not already common knowledge.

Liberals, however, were thrilled with the new Member for North Devon and thought that he was the perfect foil to the leader, Jo Grimond. While Grimond was a solid intellectual who did not have much flair for the drudgery of actually running a party, young Thorpe was waspish and a natural organiser. Thorpe convinced influential Liberals that he was shrewd and caring.

Grimond's wife Laura was so impressed that she said that he was her husband's 'heir apparent'.[13]

It might have seemed, therefore, that Thorpe had made the perfect start to his parliamentary career. But the timebombs that destroyed him sixteen years later were laid and primed in 1960. First, on Friday, 28 February, Buckingham Palace announced the engagement of Princess Margaret, the Queen's 29-year-old younger sister, to a dashing society photographer, Antony Armstrong-Jones. These were respectful times, before the Royal Family became a tabloid soap opera, so newspapers did not spoil the Princess's happiness by reminding her that Armstrong-Jones, a debonair Old Etonian who had coxed Cambridge in the Boat Race in 1950, was not her first choice. In 1955 she had wanted to marry Group Captain Peter Townsend, who was an equerry to the royal household. But Buckingham Palace told her that this was impossible because he was divorced.

Thorpe, however, was not pleased by the news. He had often told friends that it would be jolly helpful to his career if he could marry Margaret, which was not the kind of thing an aspiring Prime Minister, even one who was famous as an irreverent wit, should have said. Now he decided to crack the same joke again. He scribbled a note on a blank postcard carrying the House of Commons crest: 'What a pity about HRH. I rather hoped to marry the one and seduce the other!' He did, at least, have the sense to enclose this tasteless observation in an envelope before posting it to a friend.

He chose the wrong friend: Brecht Van de Vater, an accomplished horseman who ran the Kingham Stables at Chipping Norton, Oxfordshire, and who later rode for Ireland in the Olympics in Montreal in 1976. Like many of Thorpe's friends, he was not quite what he seemed; he had been born Norman Vivian Vater and was the son of a Welsh coal miner but, *en route* to ownership of a stables in the fashionable shires, had acquired a more interesting pedigree. His name had evolved over the years, which caused considerable confusion: the 'Van' and the 'de' often went missing and sometimes swapped position and 'Brecht' occasionally transmuted into 'Breck', while plain Norman became 'Normand'. Finally, at some point, he added the prefix 'the Honourable'. But he did not care what people thought about him or his name: 'So much has been written about me that is absolutely appalling. You people never get my name right. It's all rot. I am not interested in what people write about me. I couldn't care a damn. Everything is wrong about me. Let them get on with it. They can write whatever they bloody well like.'[14]

Unfortunately for Thorpe, Vater did not destroy the postcard, which would have saved them both a great deal of trouble. It found its way into Norman Josiffe's, alias Norman Scott's, suitcase before ending up at Scotland Yard in December 1962. There it lay, gathering layers of spurious importance until it became The Postcard, a top-secret document, the release of which, so it was feared in Whitehall, could bring down the Monarchy because it suggested, wrongly, that Armstrong-Jones was sexually involved with Scott and Thorpe.

Timebomb number two was also planted as a result of the royal engagement in February 1960. There were rumours that Armstrong-Jones might invite Thorpe, whom he knew from Eton, to be his best man. So MI5, the Security Service, asked the Chief Constable of Devon, Lieutenant-Colonel Ranulph Bacon, a 53-year-old former Inspector-General of the Ceylon Police, who was known, with the leaden humour of the police, as either Streaky or Rasher, to investigate Thorpe's suitability for such a high-profile honour.

Bacon was an experienced policeman who had once worked in some of the toughest areas of London and went about his task efficiently but discreetly. There were no leaks at the time but many years later it emerged that he had interviewed what the police called 'known associates' of Thorpe as well as keeping the man himself under surveillance. As a result, he concluded that Thorpe had 'homosexual tendencies'. Bacon was thanked and his report was included in MI5's dossier on Thorpe, the first of many such documents which indicated that the MP for North Devon had a colourful sex life.

But timebomb number three proved fatal. Late in 1960 or early in 1961 – no one has ever established the exact date – Thorpe visited Vater's stables in Oxfordshire, and met a young stable lad called Norman Josiffe: 'He was leaning over a stable door. He was simply heaven,' he told a friend many years later.[15] Josiffe also never forgot that moment.[16] Grooms were oiling saddles, brushing the huge show-jumpers with metal curry combs, tossing fresh straw into the loose boxes and stuffing hay, scented with clover and timothy, into string-nets for the first feed of the day. Then the dark-haired figure strode into the yard, wearing a curious old-fashioned suit and tight waistcoat, set off with a gold pocket watch and silk tie.

Jossiffe recalled: 'He began by talking to me about horses and various things that he really wasn't interested in. He said he was worried about Vater. He said if anything should happen I should get in touch with him.'

Jeremy Thorpe was sure that destiny had marked out him out to achieve greatness. He was also a homosexual. He knew that, one day, in the interests of his career, he would need a wife; but at 31 he was still young enough for people to assume that he was avoiding the commitment of marriage because he was having such a good time playing the field.

At the age of 20 Norman Josiffe was neither confident nor certain about his sexuality. He was a mixed-up young man, who lurched from amusing self-deprecation to suicidal self-pity. He was tall, slim and had the healthy sheen which comes with a life in the open air. His years of working with horses had turned a delicate boy who was hopeless at sport into a strong-limbed young adult. The overall effect was striking; he was good-looking enough to be a model and yet there was something that was not quite right. He did not mince, in the way that homosexuals were caricatured in those politically incorrect times, but there was sexual ambiguity in his expression; his mouth was a little too full, suggesting a pout, while his eyes revealed gnawing inner doubts.[17]

He was born, the fifth child of Ena Josiffe, on 12 February 1940 in Sidcup, a suburban sprawl sandwiched between the greyness of South London and Kent, the Garden of England. Ena's life was a struggle against misfortune. Her first husband, and father of her first four children, had been Albert Merritt, a shipping clerk. But he had died of leukaemia, leaving Ena a widow with a large family and no prospects. In 1942, however, she found a new husband, Albert Josiffe, an accountant of French extraction and friend of the late Mr Merritt.

The Josiffes moved to Bexleyheath with Norman and his three brothers and sister so that they could be close to Ena's mother, known by the family as Grandma Lynch, an Irish woman who impressed her strong Catholicism on her grandchildren. There was another son but the marriage crumbled and Albert decamped to Orpington. But there was another problem, which Norman did not discover until he was a teenager: he was illegitimate. He had always assumed that Josiffe was his natural father until he was rummaging idly amongst some papers at home. He recalled: 'When Albert

Merritt died my mother had been given a trip by his shipping line to Australia and New Zealand. She didn't come back for quite a while. I've still got telegrams from her on the boat and she didn't come back until 1939 so I was obviously conceived when she was abroad.' Ena's reticence was understandable: she was a Catholic in the 1940s, when single mothers were called sluts, or worse, and their children were bastards. Nonetheless, the traumatic discovery that he did not know the identity of his father further weakened Norman's already tenuous grasp on reality.

Ena had already despaired of her infuriatingly sensitive son. She had to support her family and worked long hours at Pan American Airways in Piccadilly. She also had an active social life, which disturbed Norman, who felt that she did not really care for him because she preferred the company of these men. But it hardly ranked as a deprived childhood. He enjoyed his primary school in Bexleyheath, where he was a dunce in arithmetic, good at English and excellent at religious instruction. Like his grandmother he took religion seriously and adored the rich ritual of Mass on Sundays.

He failed his eleven-plus and was sent to St Stephen's, a rugged Roman Catholic school. He did not enjoy it: 'I always wanted something different, better. I became isolated. But I couldn't hide my feelings or my thoughts which is not always a way to make others like you.' He was rescued when the family moved and he was transferred to another, more relaxed school. But he was still not happy, either with himself or his mother. He said, 'I just didn't use my brain at school because I was so confused over my mother and all her boyfriends. I now realise that she wanted me out of the way. I hated her. I thought that she just wanted to enjoy herself.'

The onset of puberty brought further turmoil. He knew nothing about homosexuality but, as a church-going Catholic, he was aware that it was a sin for men to love each other, though he had no conception of how such emotions were expressed. But he could not help himself; he liked other boys. People were a problem but animals were different. He adored them for their unconditional loyalty and they, in turn, understood him. He was especially fond of dogs and horses and, by the age of fourteen, was a rider of promise. After his mother refused to buy him a pony he wrote to the Blue Cross, an animal-welfare charity, and, a few weeks later, became the proud owner of a pony called Listowel. But he managed to twist this against his mother and decided that his mother only allowed him to keep his pony because she wanted him out of the house while she entertained her boyfriends. He retreated into himself and spent his free time riding Listowel around the countryside.

He left school when he was 15, without any qualifications, and within a few months showed that he had not grasped a fundamental principle of adult life: actions have consequences. His pony was hungry and his mother would not give him the money for feed so Norman stole what he needed; as a result on 23 April 1956 he appeared, now aged 16, at Bromley Juvenile Court in Kent. He was convicted of stealing feed and a saddle for his pony and put on probation. But in his own mind he was the wronged party because his mother had forced him to steal. The pattern of his life was set: he always tried to do what was right but his good intentions were misunderstood.

His probation officer, however, was sympathetic to this naive young criminal and encouraged him to pursue his passion for horses by becoming a pupil at the Westerham Riding School near Oxted, Surrey, in the heart of the stockbroker belt. Josiffe thrived here. For the first time in his life he felt that he was worth something; locals told him that he was a fine rider who had an instinctive understanding of horses. He decided that his future was in the country, far from cities, where people did not love animals. When he was 17 he found a job as a riding instructor at a stables in Altrincham, Cheshire. He spent two years there improving his dressage skills, interrupted briefly by National Service. But the Army decided, wisely, that it could manage without this emotional young man who was only interested in horses. He said; 'I don't think they thought that I was front-line regiment material.'[18]

Late in 1959 he was offered a job by the Honourable Norman Van de Brecht de Vater (this was how he arranged his name at that time) at his Kingham Stables. Norman seemed set for a fulfilling career; he had a home, Squirrel Cottage, which was in the grounds of the stables, and a patron who thought that he had talent. But he showed that he had an ability to snatch disaster from the jaws of certain victory.

At first he was over-awed by Vater, a loud and aggressive man who was used to underlings such as Josiffe showing the respect which his position warranted. (Josiffe later complained that his duties included shaving Vater's back in the bath, which had not been mentioned in the original job description.) Then he came heartily to dislike his employer; he made no attempt to disguise his feelings and relations beween the two deteriorated. Josiffe's refusal to participate in life's little compromises was also evident by the regularity with which he argued with other riders.

It was after one such row that Josiffe returned to Squirrel Cottage. He said that he could hardly push the door open because of the bills that were piled inside. He was horrified, he claimed, when he opened the envelopes; thousands of pounds had been spent in his name on items, including a Land Rover, which he knew nothing about. He blamed Vater for this unwelcome spending spree and fled to friends, who took pity on him and offered him a room. Again a pattern was being established that was to be repeated many times in his life; faced with a problem Norman would run and, pleading a nervous breakdown, would throw himself on the mercy of people who felt sorry for him and who would put up with him for months until they were forced to ask him to leave to preserve their own sanity.

But, chronic emotional instability apart, there was a new problem, which was to prove a constant factor in his feud with Jeremy Thorpe: he had no National Insurance card. Today, when virtually every task of daily life involves computers, it is difficult to imagine a world where Insurance cards mattered. But these little green books were important and their loss could be both inconvenient and expensive. Employers were legally obliged to buy stamps weekly for their employees; Insurance cards also showed whether an individual was eligible for state unemployment and pension benefits. Josiffe, however, had been too scared to ask Vater for the return of his card. This should not have been a catastrophe; he was young, had no dependents and no immediate need of state help. He could have applied for a replacement and carried on with his life. But that was too rational: his lost card represented the theft of his identity and an excuse for failing to find happiness.

However, he did not leave the Kingham Stables empty-handed. He scouped up letters and The Postcard which Thorpe had written to Vater. Like his National Insurance card, these became vital pieces of evidence in the Scott–Thorpe affair, analysed over the years as if they were classified government documents.

The card was not the most pressing problem facing him that spring. He felt that his sanity was slipping away and turned to his local GP, for help. The doctor prescribed the tranquilliser

Largactil and referred him to the Ashurst Clinic, which was attached to the Littlemore Hospital in Oxford. Patients like Josiffe were treated with a combination of drugs, psychotherapy and contact with others suffering similar symptoms. On 12 May 1961 he attended the Ashurst's out-patient unit but failed to keep his next appointment. On 24 May he was admitted to the emergency department at Oxford's Radcliffe Infirmary after taking an overdose of Largactil. Doctors who treated him did not believe that he had seriously been trying to kill himself and concluded that this had been a cry for attention and help. In June he became a voluntary in-patient at the Ashurst.

There he poured out his troubles to a psychiatrist, Dr Anthony Willems. The story was long and disjointed. He rambled about a monster called Vater. With tears streaming down his face, he recounted the tragedy of his father. Josiffe senior, he explained, had been an architect who had died in a plane crash in Brazil. This was an ingenious lie which had grown out of the fact that Vater's wife had once been married to an architect. He also talked about Jeremy Thorpe, an important man who loved him. He said that he had letters and a postcard which showed how much Jeremy cared. In his own mind that brief conversation with Thorpe over a stable door many months ago, and a subsequent written invitation to him to visit London for dinner, had become a loving relationship.

In July he discharged himself from the Ashurst at the same time as two other patients, Ann Gray, a middle-aged married woman, and Brian Wade, an older man who was bisexual. Both had crushes on Josiffe, which did not make for a happy atmosphere when they set up home together in Oxford. Within a month this unlikely household had disintegrated and Gray and Wade returned to the relative sanity of the Ashurst. Josiffe also went back but left after two days, to continue his erratic progress around Oxfordshire.

He set up home with a young man in a farmhouse in the village of Church Enstone. But inevitably there were problems, which led to two police officers and a doctor, John Poole, knocking on the door. Poole recalled that Josiffe was 'six feet tall, thinly built, dark-haired and effeminate in appearance and speech' and kept shouting that he was not homosexual, even if we thought he was. Poole never forgot the encounter:

> It was obvious from his mental state that he needed medical help and it was arranged that he would be admitted to the

Littlemore. These arrangements took a long time and, whilst waiting, I entered into a conversation with this man to try and calm him down. He told me that his father had been an architect and had designed buildings in a new city in Brazil. But he had been killed when the plane carrying the VIPs to the opening of the new city had crashed. He went on to say that his mother had either married or was living with a younger man in either Surrey or Sussex. Mention was made of his love for horses and either working at a stables or being involved in show-jumping. He was very concerned as to where he would live when he left hospital and hinted that he was very friendly with an important person called J.T. He then said that this person's name was Jeremy and he lived at Westminster. He then inferred that he would go to see this person when he felt better. After a while he told me that this person was Jeremy Thorpe, MP. He made no allegation of any homosexual activity with Mr Thorpe.[19]

Poole recommended that he should be sectioned, under section 29 of the Mental Health Act, 1959, which allowed compulsory detention in a mental institution for three days. On 28 October 1961 Norman was taken back to the Ashurst for renewed treatment. Three days later he left the clinic. In theory doctors could have detained him under the Mental Health Act but they did not believe that it would serve any useful purpose; he was unstable but not dangerous.

Josiffe set off to London to see Jeremy Thorpe, who had been so interested and kind when they had met a year ago. He was accompanied, as always, by a pet, a Jack Russell terrier called Mrs Tish; but, amid the tangle of complexes and neuroses, there was one certainty, that nice Mr Thorpe would make it all come right.

In the early afternoon of 8 November 1961 Josiffe, his well-travelled suitcase and Mrs Tish arrived at the House of Commons. A policeman at the St Stephen's entrance told him dogs were not allowed in Parliament so he left her at the Whitehall office of the Anti-Vivisection League. He returned and made his way into the domed visitors' lobby where an official in a Victorian black swallow-tail coat and starched wing collar asked him to fill in the regulation green card for visitors. He signed it 'Norman

Lianche-Josiffe'. Like his ertswhile patron Vater, Norman had experimented with his name and now called himself Lianche-Josiffe, created by Frenchifying his Irish grandmother's surname of Lynch. Occasionally, though not that day, he affixed an 'Honourable' to add gravitas.

A messenger was sent to Thorpe while Norman tried to look as if he belonged amid the important people who hurried past him carrying sheaves of documents. Then Thorpe appeared, waving and smiling, and guided him to a room where they could chat privately. He tutted indulgently when young Norman complained that poor Mrs Tish had been banned by the horrid policemen; Thorpe said that it was a tradition that only cavalier spaniels, named after Charles I, were allowed within Parliament. The balance of power of their relationship was being defined here; Thorpe was the guide, who would help Norman survive in a glamorous new world which he did not understand.

Then Josiffe began to pour out his troubles. He talked about Vater, hospitals and his attempts to end it all. He complained that he had nowhere to live and no money and no prospect of either because he had 'lost' his National Insurance card. He opened his suitcase and handed Thorpe a bundle of letters which Thorpe had sent Vater. Like a small child hoping to win approval from a parent, Josiffe said that he had been worried that Vater could use them to embarrass Thorpe. But he also kept The Postcard which Thorpe had written, regretting that Princess Margaret was no longer single and that he would not have the opportunity to seduce Mr Armstrong-Jones.

Like many people who met Josiffe, Thorpe underestimated him. His failure to hand over The Postcard showed that he was not as naive as Thorpe imagined. Superficially he was a highly-strung, vulnerable young man, but he also possessed cunning, a steely inner core and a potential for vindictiveness. It would be absurd to suggest that, as he flirted with Thorpe that day in the Commons, he knew how important The Postcard would be. But he knew instinctively that this was a valuable document which he should keep.[20]

If Thorpe had been sensible he would have sighed, regretted that an affair was not possible and sent him packing. But he wanted Josiffe and was addicted to the danger that accompanied homosexuality. He was also so arrogant that he felt that, whatever he did, no one could touch him. He told Josiffe that everything would be fine and said that they would meet later that day, an invitation that signalled the beginning of the end for him.

Even Peter Bessell, who had a prodigious sexual appetite, was baffled by Thorpe's decision:

> As an MP Jeremy should have adopted one of two proper courses of action open to him. Since he had known Vater for years and Josiffe was no more than an acquaintance, his most sensible reaction would have been to phone Vater and hear his side of the story. Alternatively, since Josiffe was not Jeremy's constituent, he should have arranged for him to see the MP who represented the part of Oxfordshire where Vater lived. Jeremy did neither. He took the neurotic boy to his mother's home in Surrey for the night.

That evening Thorpe, Josiffe and Mrs Tish roared away from the Commons in Thorpe's sporty dark-blue Sunbeam Rapier towards Ursula Thorpe's house at Limpsfield in Surrey, then a seventy-five-minute drive away. On the way they stopped in Dulwich, South London, where Thorpe proudly introduced Josiffe to two homosexual friends as his latest conquest. He told Josiffe that he would be away for two weeks in Malta, filming with a television crew, and that he should contact the two men if he needed help. This meeting, which seemed inconsequential at the time, was another nail in the coffin of Thorpe's career because one of the men was called Tony. This helped fuel the mad theory of The Postcard in the 1970s: that Josiffe had become entangled in a homosexual ring which involved Armstrong-Jones.

Josiffe was delighted that Mr Thorpe was taking so much trouble; now, as they headed towards Surrey, he claimed that he did not understand what was expected of him, which was sex. He said that he had fumbled inadequately with men and women but added, 'I didn't really know very much about homosexuality although I suppose I had homosexual tendencies. We all have this [sic], channelled the wrong way.' They drove into Limpsfield, the epitome of respectable, prosperous Middle England. There were half-timbered houses in the High Street, through which horse boxes regularly trundled as the well-off locals set off to hunt foxes. They pulled up outside Ursula Thorpe's home, Stonewalls, a period house perched on a hill a few hundred yards from the village centre.

Josiffe said:

Just before we got out of the car Jeremy told me I must tell his mother I was part of the television camera crew who was going abroad with him the following day. I thought it very strange at the time. We drove into the garage and went up some steps into the main house and Mrs Thorpe was there. I was a bit worried whether Mrs Thorpe would mind the dog being with me. I was also worried how the lie would work because what was I going to do with the dog on the way to Malta? She seemed very nice but a little reserved. Then he introduced me to her as 'Peter,' saying I lived in Colchester. She asked me to sign the visitors' book. I think I signed the name 'Peter Johnson', the name he had told me to use that evening. I didn't know where Colchester was and I turned to him and asked him in a whisper: Where is Colchester? He told me it was in Essex. By now I was very tired. I felt rather strange in this grand house and said I would like to go to bed. Ursula Thorpe showed me where I was to sleep. This was almost opposite his bedroom. He asked me whether I'd like to have a book to read. I said, 'Very well.' I thought: I mustn't refuse anything, I must be polite. So he gave me a book called *Giovanni's Room* by James Baldwin. It's the story of a homosexual couple and a rather beautiful book. It was a bit staggering for me to read at the time.[21]

Baldwin's book, first published in Britain in 1957, had been hailed as 'a landmark in gay writing'. Baldwin, a New Yorker who died in 1987, set the book in Paris in the 1950s. He wanted to explore 'a young man's awakening to the insistent possibilities of his true homosexual nature'. The hero, David, an American writer, meets Giovanni, a barman, and agrees to spend the night with him; one night becomes three months of 'covert passion'.[22]

As Josiffe was struggling with this complex novel, Thorpe knocked on the bedroom door. What happened next was bitterly disputed by the two men when they faced each other at the Old Bailey in 1979. Thorpe maintained that he had not 'made love' to Josiffe. He said:

I wish, with all the emphasis which I can command, to

deny that I was at any time engaged in any homosexual relationship with Josiffe-Scott whatsoever, or that I was, at any time, a party to any homosexual familiarity with him. I believed that he was a person who was desperately in need of help and support in that he was in a suicidal and unbalanced state. The action which, in the circumstances, I followed was attributable solely to what I saw as my duty having regard to the conditions under which he approached me, and in the event my compassion and kindness towards him was in due course repaid with malevolence and resentment.[23]

Josiffe, however, insisted that Thorpe had gone further than offer help:

> He was wearing a dressing gown and pyjamas. He just began talking to me about how I looked so ill, that things would be all right. He said, 'You look like a frightened rabbit, which isn't very complimentary. Never mind. You look like a frightened rabbit.' He then leant forward and put his arm round me. He hugged me and called me 'poor bunny'. Then he kissed me. I was very frightened and nervous. He had a towel with him and some Vaseline. He put the Vaseline on his penis and put the towel on the bed. I was just biting the pillow. He was cutting me open with his penis. I did not scream because I was frightened of waking Mrs Thorpe. I just couldn't believe it. I thought I was being killed. It was horrible. I couldn't be sure whether he ejaculated but he seemed satisfied.

Thorpe got up, patted Josiffe on the thigh and left. He cuddled up to his terrier, Mrs Tish, and cried. Next morning Thorpe appeared at the bedroom door and asked Josiffe how he liked his eggs cooked. Then Thorpe drove to Heathrow to catch his flight to Malta. *En route* he picked up his Commons secretary, Jennifer King, and told her that she should help Norman if necessary while he was abroad. He handed Josiffe £5 and said that he would be able to find a selection of 'flats' advertised in a shop window in the King's Road, Chelsea. A few hours later Josiffe was installed in Draycott Place in what he liked to call a 'service room', though it was only a bed-sit, costing £8 a week. As Thorpe flew off to Malta, glowing with the pleasure that finally he had seduced the dreamboat stable boy, Josiffe was experiencing very different emotions: confusion, disgust and self-loathing.

He was also a Catholic, which made what had happened unbearable. He loved Thorpe but also blamed him: 'What happened to me that night was very sinful as far as the Church was concerned. I knew that. Homosexuality was an illness, a disease, and I had been infected by Jeremy Thorpe. If he had not seduced me I may have had a different life, a heterosexual life with a conventional family, a wife and children. I would not have been put through hell.'[24]

CHAPTER THREE

Norman Josiffe felt that finally he had found someone who cared for him. The sex was a problem because it was painful and a sin but he was sure that there would be no more mental hospitals, drugs and long dark days when despair choked him. His room at 21 Draycott Place was tiny but he knew that Jeremy would soon find him somewhere nicer. Chelsea and the King's Road, however, more than compensated. There were famous actors, such as Laurence Olivier, and philosphers, like Bertrand Russell, Nobel Prize-winner and doyen of the peace movement, who held court in his house in Hasker Street when he was not in jail for squatting outside Parliament. Norman also enjoyed the café near his bed-sit, where young artists sipped *cappuccinos* (a recent import) and plotted the overthrow of philistines at the Royal Academy who dismissed Picasso as a worthless dauber. Norman loved it all and knew that life with Jeremy would be wonderful.

Then Thorpe returned from Malta. He determined to re-style Norman so that he could show him off at his London clubs. Josiffe said, 'He noticed my shoes were not in very good condition so he told me to go to Gieves in Old Bond Street and get whatever I wanted in the way of clothes, underwear, vests and pants and a pair of shoes. I had also had two pale-blue shirts from Thresher and Glenny.'[1]

But there was a price. Josiffe wanted Thorpe to be father, friend and lover, though this last function was the not wholly desirable consequence of the first two. Anger that he had been 'infected' with homosexuality was compounded by resentment that Thorpe was a perfunctory and selfish lover:

Jeremy would arrive at Draycott Place, ring the bell, look up and wave. I'd drop the keys down to him outside. Sometimes he was so short of time he would tell me to join him in his car and we would drive to a quiet spot near Battersea Bridge. Then he got me to jerk him off into a handkerchief before he disappeared into the night. I had to walk back to Draycott Place. I used to think: Poor Norman. What will become of me?

He also knew that Thorpe wanted other men, whom he would find in pubs or on the street: 'I was walking in St James's Park one day and realised a man was following me. I turned round and saw it was Jeremy. He hadn't realised it was me and looked really surprised. He was out trying to pick up another man and he had been caught out.' On another occasion he arrived at Thorpe's flat at Marsham Court, Victoria, and found him with a Swedish sailor.

By now Josiffe had renounced any semblance of independence. On Thorpe's instructions he embarked on an exhausting and disorientating odyssey, shuttling between his bed-sit and Marsham Court and various addresses in the West Country, where Thorpe's friends put him up. Thorpe thought that it was splendid; he did not want Josiffe in London all the time, which would have been tedious, but he wanted to see him when and where he wanted. People in the West Country were either naive or discreet, which meant that they would not gossip about his regular visits to this odd young man. For example, Thorpe arranged for Josiffe and Mrs Tish to spend Christmas 1961 with Jimmy Collier, the prospective Liberal candidate for Tiverton, Devon, and his wife Mary at their farm just outside the town. The Colliers were decent people and were anxious to help Josiffe, whom Thorpe said was trying to recover from the death of his father in a plane crash.

The Colliers and Josiffe were invited to lunch over Christmas with Thorpe and his mother at the Broomhill Hotel in Barnstaple. After lunch Mary and Ursula suggested a walk but Thorpe said that he wanted Norman to try on some shirts. Jimmy Collier, who was becoming suspicious about the friendship between Thorpe and Josiffe, thought that this was peculiar but shrugged it off and decided to get some air. Meanwhile, Thorpe hauled Josiffe to his room for another bout of hasty sex. More cynical, metropolitan characters guessed what was going on. Dominic Le Foe, Thorpe's public-relations guru, said, 'Of course I knew about Norman. Jimmy Collier and his poor wife were lumbered with him over Christmas. Thorpe just foisted him on them and made no attempt to hide it.'[2]

Josiffe was back in London in the New Year but disaster tracked

him down again when Ann Gray, his admirer from his time in the
Ashurst Clinic, turned up at Draycott Place and rented a room.
Having been initiated in the dubious pleasures of full sex Josiffe
now proved, and did so many times in the future, that he could
not resist an invitation, from a man or a woman, to go to bed.
He slept with Gray and then, because he thought it was the right
thing to do, told her, with breathtaking insensitivity, that he was
having an affair with Thorpe. She was not pleased: 'She was terribly
shocked and I suppose felt like a woman scorned,' he said.

He decided to slip away from Draycott Place and found another
room in West London. Gray, however, was determined to find
him and complained to the police that he had stolen her suede
coat. But, when the police told Josiffe that they would like to
question him about the missing coat, Thorpe stepped in and told
them that, as Josiffe's guardian, he had a right to be present. The
interview was scheduled for 4.15 p.m. on 8 February 1962 at his
office in Westminster. Josiffe was nervous, though he knew nothing
about Gray's coat, but Thorpe was excited by the prospect of a
confrontation with the police. Josiffe said, 'I told him I wanted to
stop this sex thing, and I said I thought it better if we didn't see
each other again. He said he wanted to carry on, and he tried to
kiss me in the room, and tried to get hold of my penis, but I moved
towards the door when someone came to the door. He told me to
keep quiet. Then a detective from Chelsea police station came to
ask me about Ann Gray.'

Detective Constable Raymond Whitmore-Smith did not like the
way that Thorpe dominated Josiffe:

It is abundantly clear that Josiffe himself is still suffering
from a nervous breakdown and states he is still under drugs.
He did, however, agree to write a statement under caution,
copy attached, and it will be seen that he gives as a possible
reason for this allegation the fact that Mrs Gray has been
trying for some time to ascertain his whereabouts. This
claim is substantiated by Mr Jeremy Thorpe and is a matter
already in the hands of his solicitors. During the interview
with Josiffe in the presence of Mr Jeremy Thorpe, it was
patently obvious that Josiffe was a rather weak personality,
apparently labouring under considerable mental strain, and
completely domineered by Mr Thorpe who was acting in an
advisory capacity to Josiffe. During the period when Josiffe

was writing a statement, Mr Thorpe left his office to attend a Division in the House of Commons, and during his absence, Josiffe was noticeably relaxed and more talkative.

The police closed the investigation after establishing that both Gray and Josiffe had a history of mental illness. They also decided that it would be wise if Gray was not given Josiffe's new address.

Thorpe packed Josiffe off to stay with the Colliers again. On 13 February 1962 he sent this letter:

My Dear Norman,

Since my letters normally go to the House, yours arrived all by itself at my breakfast table at the Reform, and gave me tremendous pleasure. I cannot tell you just how happy I am to feel that you are really settling down, and feeling that life has something to offer.

This is really wonderful and you can always feel that whatever happens Jimmy and Mary and I are right behind you. The next thing is to solve your financial problems and this James Walters and I are on to. The really important point is that you are now a member of a 'family' doing a useful job of work – with Tish – which you enjoy. Hooray! Faced with all that, no more bloody clinics.

I think you can now take the Ann Gray incident as over and done with. Enclosed another letter!! I suggest you keep them all – just in case – but will you send back the photo? Thank the guy but say you are fixed up.

In haste.

Bunnies can (and will) go to France.

Yours affectionately,

Jeremy.

I miss you.

If Thorpe had chucked this letter in the rubbish bin he might well have survived Josiffe's campaign to ruin him. When it was published in 1976 in a newspaper it fatally undermined his protestations that he barely knew Josiffe; it might not have been erotic but it was not the sort of letter that platonic friends sent each other. The letter itself was bad enough but Thorpe compounded the mistake by misdating it February 1961, instead of February 1962. Josiffe assumed in the mid-1970s that the date on it was correct, so he calculated, quite reasonably, that their affair had begun when he was only 20 years old. (He was in fact 21 years old, and this was a genuine mistake by him.) Buggery was a serious offence but it was unforgivable when it involved a minor; hence, everyone who was caught up in the scandal, politicians, civil servants, policemen and intelligence officers, thought that they were dealing with allegations of under-age homosexuality.

Like most letters between lovers it was written in code. James Walters was a London lawyer who had been asked by Thorpe to establish whether Josiffe would inherit anything from the estate of his father. Jimmy and Mary were the Colliers, with whom Josiffe was staying. 'Bunny' was Thorpe's nickname for him, first used when he had consoled Josiffe in bed at his mother's house. The trip to France was a reference to Norman's ambition to study dressage there.

The letter that Thorpe had enclosed was a reply to an advertisement in *Country Life* magazine, which he had placed in an effort to find Norman a job. The advertisement had said, 'Ex-public-school boy, 21, wishes to live with family and work on farm. Skilled horses. Former Badminton competitor. Willing to undertake any work. Pocket money only expected.' There were some replies but, alas, most came from men who were not interested in Norman's ability with horses.

It is conceivable that when he wrote the letter he believed that Norman was settling down; it is more likely, however, that he was trying to assure Josiffe, and himself, that the worst was over. It was not, as he realised during one of his trips to Devon. Josiffe needed Thorpe but did not want to be treated like a sex object and his resentment exploded when they were enjoying the Devon air in Thorpe's sports car. He said:

We had a dreadful row. I'm not trying to excuse myself. I just didn't want the sexual part of it – the friendship was nice. It always came down to the wretched sexual thing and I just hated it. He kissed me. I said I just wanted the whole thing to end. I began to cry: it was stupid of me. I said, 'I must end it, I don't know how.' He laughed at me. I said I thought he was absolutely rotten. It sounds ridiculous now but I said, 'I'll show you up in public if you don't leave me alone.' He laughed and said I sounded like a suburban person. Anyway, he said, 'One of my greatest friends is the Director of Public Prosecutions, Sir Norman Skelhorn.' [Skelhorn did not become DPP until 1964.]

By now the Colliers had had enough of their guest. Josiffe saw their point: 'I think it must have been very difficult for them because I was in a very nervous state. They had two girls who must have been frightened when I used to cry in my room. I think the Colliers asked Thorpe to find somewhere else for me to live.'

If Thorpe had dumped him now Josiffe would have found it impossible to take revenge. He could have offered the love letters to a newspaper but would have been told to clear off; no editor would have taken the word of an unbalanced loser like him against that of a respected MP. But Thorpe was still besotted, so he told Norman that he was moving him to North Devon, where he would be able to stay for nothing with Liberal activists. He would also be offered a job canvassing for the Party. This idea underlined the scale of Thorpe's obsession; it was extraordinary that the constituency MP should suggest that someone like Josiffe, for whom liberalism, socialism and capitalism were long words with the same ending, should be allowed to roam the streets under the Party flag trying to convert voters to an ideology of which he was entirely ignorant. Josiffe was delighted at the prospect of employment. But this meant that, once again, he was anxious about his missing National Insurance card and asked Thorpe if he had any news of it. Thorpe told him that his solicitor, James Walters, was working on it, as well as investigating his late father's estate.

While Josiffe looked forward to a bright future as a Liberal canvasser Thorpe was given more bad news, which confirmed that Josiffe had a vivid and dangerous imagination. In February Walters reported that he had doubts about the Brazilian plane-crash story. He urged Thorpe to forget the investigation, 'since if we press too far and destroy the story with which we have been presented we may well find that this has disastrous consequences so far as Josiffe himself is concerned'. Thorpe agreed and Walters ceased work but answers to his enquiries continued to trickle in; in April he was informed that Josiffe's father, a successful architect who had perished in the Amazon rain forest, was, in fact, an accountant in Orpington. Norman's mother was also alive, but not happy; in May she told Walters that Thorpe was destroying her son. Josiffe, meanwhile, was also mounting his own probe into his late father's estate. He took advantage of the government's Legal Aid scheme and asked a firm of solicitors in Exeter, Sparkes and Company, to find out whether he stood to inherit anything from his late father. As a result, Mr D. Lyon-Smith, a senior partner at the firm, wrote to Thorpe, asking if he had any information about the late Mr Josiffe senior. Thorpe passed the letter to Walters, who told Mr Lyon-Smith that he feared that Josiffe was not entirely reliable. This was surreal: two lawyers, one of whom had been instructed by Josiffe, were chasing the non-existent inheritance of a fictitious father.

But Thorpe was not worried and, instead of dumping Josiffe, worked hard to obtain a new National Insurance card. In March he telephoned the Ministry of Pensions and asked if Josiffe could be given one. The following month a new card, which gave Josiffe's National Insurance number as ZT.7115160, was sent to Thorpe. He was so pleased that he wrote to Thomas Howell, the official who had dealt with the case, thanking him for the trouble he had taken. This meant that, as far as Josiffe and the Ministry of Pensions were concerned, Thorpe was now Josiffe's employer and was, therefore, legally obliged to pay for Norman's Insurance stamps. This was a heavy responsibility and one which Thorpe, who was notoriously mean, had no intention of fulfilling.

Josiffe was now a Liberal Party canvasser in Lynton and Lynmouth in North Devon. He did his best, knocking on doors of voters whom the Party felt might support Thorpe but neither his mind nor his heart was in it. When people asked him about the Liberals' policy on law and order, Europe, agricultural subsidies or South Africa Norman could only smile good-humouredly since he had absolutely no idea what they were talking about. He told Jeremy that he was keen to get back to horses.

Then fate intervened. Thorpe read a report in a Devon newspaper that a female groom to a local farmer, Major Nigel Hambro, from Hawkridge, near Dulverton, had been killed in an accident. He telephoned Hambro, offered his condolences and suggested that the Major might care to consider a friend called Norman Josiffe as a replacement. Hambro said, 'He was trying to help a young man who was familiar with horses and, as I had no groom, he wondered whether he could help me out for a time. I thought this was just the kind thought of a Member of Parliament towards a constituent. I welcomed the thought of some help and shortly afterwards Norman Josiffe came to my farm.'

But Hambro refused formally to employ Josiffe. He told him that he could live in his house and would receive a few pounds a week as 'pocket money'. As a former military man he was, however, less sympathetic than the Colliers to Josiffe's moods. Norman, for his part, talked incessantly about his Insurance card for which, he claimed, Thorpe was responsible. After ten weeks Hambro told him to leave. So Josiffe moved on, though another fantasy was taking shape in his mind. He now decided that he was the illegitimate son of John Scott, 4th Earl of Eldon, who owned the neighbouring Rackenford Manor.

Having been fired by Hambro he found a job at the Metropole Riding School in Minehead, run by a lady called Mrs Webber. He said, 'Mrs Webber asked me for my Insurance card and so I telephoned Thorpe and asked him if I could have it. But he felt he was going to lose me. Once I had my Insurance card I would have had my own identity. So he wouldn't give it to me and Mrs Webber said that she was sorry but that was it.' Thus, in May 1962 Josiffe was in the familiar position of having no job, nowhere to live and no National Insurance card. Faced with these difficulties he reacted as he always did in moments of crisis: 'I just got very nervous again and had another breakdown.'

At some point during his perambulations around Devon the Ministry of Pensions had posted a new card to him, but he never received it; even if he had he would certainly have 'lost' it immediately since it had become a symbol of the independence which he claimed he wanted but could not face. However much he might protest that he wanted a new life he was bonded to Thorpe, as Thorpe was to him.

He could have applied for a new card but that did not appeal to him:

> My lifestyle was so disjointed that I really couldn't have done that. How could I? Technically, Jeremy Thorpe was my employer. Officials would ask where I had been working. Well, you could hardly say, 'I was sleeping with Mr Thorpe.' Regardless of what people say I am an honest person and I couldn't have lied. I mean, I'd lied enough already for him, beginning with the bogus name I was asked to put in the visitors' book at his mother's home.

His next move was predictable: he went to see a doctor and asked for his favourite drug, Largactil. Once again, he showed that, while he could not earn a living or obtain a National Insurance card, he was a master at making people feel sorry for him. The doctor, Keith

Lister, a happily married man, invited Josiffe to stay at his home, at Worthey Manor, Porlock Weir in Somerset. While Josiffe recovered his poise with the help of a stable family, country air, animals and tranquillisers, Dr Lister decided to contact his guardian, Jeremy Thorpe. But Thorpe was not pleased that a country doctor knew about his relationship with Norman; he replied curtly, giving the address of Norman's mother. In September Mrs Tish, Josiffe's loyal terrier, inadvertently set the stage for a reconciliation of the two men when she ran amok amongst Dr Lister's ducks and had to be put down. Josiffe was distraught and wrote to Thorpe, requesting the return of a photograph of his late Jack Russell. On 30 September 1962 Thorpe replied:

> My dear Norman,
>   This is indeed terribly sad news about poor little Mrs Tish, and I know what a blow this must have been to you. You have all my sympathy.
>   I am afraid that I shall not be home for a little while and cannot therefore send you the photo (at the moment I'm in N. Devon). I have a horrible feeling I may have pasted it into an album which will make it difficult for me to dislodge. However . . .
>   I hope otherwise things go well.
>   Yours,
>   Jeremy.

Josiffe realised now that he would have to leave the Listers'. 'They already had four children, they didn't need me as a fifth. They were sweet children. Because I was so unhappy I was incarcerated in my bedroom and they used to push flowers under the door with a little note saying, "Oh Norman, do get better,"' he said.

Inevitably, there was another half-hearted attempt at suicide: 'I was terribly troubled about Thorpe and tried to kill myself because I felt there was no way out. I was very frightened and tried to slash my wrists after taking an overdose, which all sounds rather ridiculous. I was in such a terrible state. Totally broken.'

Even the saintly Listers had had enough; their ducks had been slaughtered and their house guest was overdosing on drugs prescribed by the host and making a mess by slashing his wrists. Esther Lister, the doctor's wife, drove Josiffe to London, with his suitcase containing his love letters from Thorpe and The Postcard which mentioned Armstrong-Jones, the latest recruit to the Royal Family.

He spent a few tense days with his mother in Bexleyheath. As a good Catholic Mrs Josiffe did not, of course, approve of Norman's relationship with Thorpe, which he had told her about as soon as it had started. But she did not have the power to stop Norman returning to Thorpe. Josiffe moved back to Marsham Court. But the one-bedroom flat, with a tiny kitchen off the living room, was too small for two men. Norman was still tormented by what he called 'the inevitable sex thing'; this took place in Thorpe's single bed, after which he was forced to move to a camp bed, where he would lie awake and sob that life was 'grotesque'. But there were small consolations. He loved watching Thorpe perform in the Commons: 'It was a marvellous feeling to be in the Mother of Parliaments. I very rarely heard him speak there but I was very proud. It was just enough that I was with him. I was proud of the man, not the relationship.'

He now decided that he had to confess 'the sex thing' and ask forgiveness. He told a priest at Westminster Cathedral that he was having sexual relations with a man, though he did not identify Thorpe. These were unenlightened times and the priest was not sympathetic. Josiffe recalled: 'The priest said he would not absolve me unless I promised I would never do it again. He suggested I went to a Salvation Army hostel but I told him that I couldn't do that.' Having failed to find solace from his church he returned to Marsham Court.

He turned for advice to a new friend, Caroline Barrington-Ward, the daughter of a former editor of *The Times*, who also lived in Draycott Place. She knew Thorpe, which had encouraged Josiffe to regale her with stories of their affair, though he would probably have done this whether or not she had ever met Thorpe. On 19 December there was another row and Josiffe stormed out of the flat. He fled to Barrington-Ward and told her that he intended to commit suicide after killing Thorpe. Then he decided that he would stay in a hotel for the night, although he had no money. He walked the streets until he spotted the Easton Hotel, by Victoria Station.

By his own, admittedly shabby, standards Thorpe had treated Norman well. He had given him money, bought him clothes and found him work. But Norman did not see things like that. When he trudged into the reception at the Easton Hotel he met his friend and protector from the West Country, Mary Collier. Another receptionist would have turned him away but Collier, who was helping her sister-in-law who owned the hotel, took pity on him: 'I let him have a room although I wasn't happy about it. He had no money but he was in an emotional state.'[3]

That was an understatement. He telephoned Caroline Barrington-Ward and told her again that he would kill himself because he could no longer tolerate his 'sordid relationship', but first he said that he would shoot Thorpe. With Josiffian bathos he complained that he had a bullet but no gun, which was obviously a problem. She asked where he was and told him that she would come immediately. But she also had to avert a bloodbath: 'I did what any public-spirited citizen would do in the circumstances. I called the police.' This was not what Norman had in mind; he had hoped that she would contact Thorpe, who would rush to assure him that he still loved him.

Detective Sergeant Edward Smith and a colleague were on the scene within a few minutes of Barrington-Ward's call. They asked Josiffe if he knew Mr Thorpe. Josiffe said that he did and that they had had a 'horrible' affair. Smith asked if he could prove this, which was the signal for Josiffe to open his suitcase and produce his treasured bundle of love letters and The Postcard, which he had taken when he had fled in tears over eighteen months earlier from the beastly Van de Vater's employment. Smith had that sinking feeling, familiar to experienced police officers who know that they are about to be dragged into a case which is not going to do them any good. The priority was to make sure that Josiffe was not going to murder Thorpe or anybody else and then let someone else sort the whole thing out. Josiffe was calmer now and, since he had no gun, could not shoot anyone. Smith told him to report the next day to the station at Cale Street, off the King's Road, which had handled the inquiry in February into Ann Gray's missing suede coat.

Next day, Josiffe was being questioned by one of the Metropolitan Police's rising stars, Detective Inspector Robert Huntley, who later commanded Scotland Yard's bomb squad at the height of the IRA's bombing campaign on mainland Britain in the mid-1970s. Like every office in the country the station in Cale Street was festooned with Christmas cards. Norman, however, was not in festive mood but he was talkative. Huntley was a subtle interrogator but only had to listen as Josiffe gushed out his statement. Norman had been both dreading, and dreaming about, this moment, when he would confess his sins and destroy Thorpe, the man whom he loved. He began: 'I have come to tell you about my homosexual relations with Jeremy Thorpe, MP, because these relations have caused me so much purgatory and I am afraid it might happen to someone else.' He gave his address as Worthey Manor, Porlock Weir, Somerset, which was the Listers' home, and described himself as a horse trainer. Technically this was untrue – he no longer lived at the Listers' and had never been employed there – but the description showed his genius for spreading confusion. If Huntley had called the Listers, which he did not, they would have spoken fondly of him, said that he was always welcome there and confirmed that he had, in fact, looked after horses on the manor, thus turning what should have been a routine police inquiry about an address into a mind-bending debate.

Josiffe described how Thorpe had ruined his life. He had a fine memory for gory details, which meant that he talked about pots of Vaseline and his flies being unzipped in the House of Commons. The statement ran to six pages and Josiffe signed and dated it 20 December 1962. Then he offered Huntley the corroboration, a selection from his treasure-trove of love letters. He gave him the misdated 'Bunny' letter, which suggested that Thorpe had buggered a minor, The Postcard, which hinted at royal involvement in a homosexual ring, and Thorpe's expression of sympathy that Mrs Tish had been put down after killing Dr Lister's ducks. He also handed over another letter, which never emerged again from police files; Thorpe had opened this by saying, 'My angel, all I want is to share a Devon farm with you,' and had then gone on to describe how he adored 'making love' to Norman.

Before he left the station, with his suitcase containing his reserve stock of love letters, Norman was examined by a police surgeon, which was standard procedure when allegations of homosexuality were made. The doctor concluded that Josiffe was a practising homosexual. Norman then returned home, to Marsham Court and Thorpe. He did not tell him that he had made a statement that could have resulted in both of them being charged with buggery; Norman waited, hoping, but also dreading, that the police would take action.

Huntley was not impressed by the evidence. He said, 'The letters showed that there had been a relationship but not a homosexual relationship. With allegations like this we had to have corroboration. We did not have any.'[4]

This was not the entire story. As Huntley knew very well, there were issues here that deserved to be investigated; whether it was in anyone's interests to do so was another matter. Josiffe was a neurotic wreck and Thorpe was an MP and any police officer who took Josiffe's word against that of Thorpe would be signing his career death warrant. Huntley was an honest man but he was also realistic and wanted to offload the Thorpe file on to his superiors as quickly as possible. He asked the police in Barnstaple if they would check to see if they had any evidence to indicate that Scott was telling the truth. But the police there were also not enthusiastic about pursuing an investigation into their local MP based on the complaints of a creature like Josiffe. After a few cursory checks Barnstaple reported to Huntley that they had found nothing to substantiate the allegations. So he wrote his report and sent it to Scotland Yard.

Since Thorpe was an MP, Huntley's report, Josiffe's statement, Thorpe's letters and The Postcard were passed to Special Branch, who gave a summary to MI5. This was included in the folder that had been opened on Thorpe when he had become an MP in 1959. There was nothing sinister about this – MI5 opened files on all new members, which were top-secret and were normally only read by the Director-General or his deputy – but Thorpe's file was already fatter than that of other recent recruits to the Commons. There was the 1960 report by Lt.-Colonel Streaky Bacon, Devon's Chief Constable, which stated that Thorpe was probably a homosexual. There was also the report from the interview with Scott and Thorpe at the Commons in February 1962 after Ann Gray complained that her coat had been stolen.

Huntley's report, the letters and The Postcard were deposited in the safe of Assistant Commissioner (Crime) Richard Jackson and Huntley returned to his normal duties. He said, 'Thorpe wasn't interviewed because we knew he would deny it all and without evidence it would have been a waste of time to see him. So the papers were submitted to my superiors and then dealt with by the Yard. I didn't hear any more.'[5]

No one actually said that Thorpe should be protected but there was a tacit understanding amongst everyone, civil servants, police and intelligence officers, that it would not be right for an MP, who had been educated at Eton and Oxford, and Antony

Armstrong-Jones, the new husband of a princess, to be dragged into the gutter by a loathsome thing called Norman Josiffe.

The Liberal revival of the early 1960s was inspired by Jo Grimond but Thorpe's waspish and stylish presence in the Commons boosted the Party's self-esteem, both within Parliament and amongst the foot soldiers in the constituencies who spent their evenings banging on voters' doors. He was a brilliant money-raiser, which was much appreciated in a party that lacked the guaranteed financial support which the Conservatives and Labour enjoyed. Now he persuaded Grimond to let him control a new secret fund, which would be spent on constituencies which Thorpe thought were winnable. He did not become Liberal treasurer until 1965 but he already knew that whoever had access to Party funds also had power. He also believed that, since he had raised the money, it was up to him how he spent it.

Russell Johnston was adopted as the Liberal candidate for Inverness in 1961 and recalled that Thorpe designated it as a 'special' seat, which merited an injection of money from the secret fund. He said, 'The Liberals had no money and if Thorpe could raise it himself then we thought it only fair that he spent it. We didn't care if he spent a bit on hotels and a decent dinner. It's not as if he was buying villas in Spain.'[6]

In 1961 Liberals performed well in a series of by-elections, though they did not win any; in March 1962 a Liberal came within 973 votes of capturing the rock-solid Conservative seat of Blackpool North. Then came one of those extraordinary victories which seems to presage a new political order: a Conservative majority of over 14,000 in the middle-class commuter suburb of Orpington in Kent was overturned by the Liberal's Eric Lubbock, whose winning margin was 7,855. Later that month an opinion poll in the *Daily Mail* showed that the Liberals were the most popular party in the country.[7]

Thorpe's future, therefore, looked bright. He had been marked down as Grimond's heir; a sensible man would have lived blamelessly while he waited for the day when he was anointed leader. But Thorpe was not like that. He would not, and could not, give up the lifestyle that threatened to destroy him. It has to be emphasised that his behaviour was extraordinarily dangerous. Homosexuality was not decriminalised until 1967, indeed until then it carried a maximum sentence of life imprisonment.

Ian Harvey was a Conservative MP and a junior minister at
the Foreign Office in November 1958 when he was charged
with committing an act of gross indecency in St James's Park
with Anthony Plant, aged 19, of the Coldstream Guards. He
escaped with a fine but, as he left the court in Bow Street on a
chilly December day, he said, 'When you fall below the standards
you expect of others in public life, you must quit. That is why I
shall never try to go back into public life.'

He spent the next twenty years as a campaigner for homosexual rights:

> Society has continued to ostracise homosexuals, to victimise
> them at work and to make it impossible for them to hold
> positions of authority and responsibility. Because of society's
> own attitude to homosexuality, and only because of that,
> they are regarded as a security risk. They are, in effect,
> denied both their civil rights and prevented from placing
> their abilities at the service of the community. Thus we
> have in our midst an oppressed and depressed minority, a
> minority far larger than that of the Jews or Roman Catholics.
> The medical profession bears a high degree of responsibility
> for present attitudes. Many doctors and psychiatrists still
> treat homosexuality as either a disease or a sickness and
> consider that all homosexuals ought to be 'cured'. Lawyers
> and judges, in particular, make derogatory remarks about
> homosexuals which tend to encourage the police to act
> against them. Churchmen of all denominations continue
> to denounce homosexuality as a sin although they have
> no divine right to do so. Finally, politicians are reluctant
> to carry further reforms, although they are needed, lest they
> themselves should be regarded as homosexually inclined and
> lose votes as a result.[8]

Thus, Thorpe knew what he was risking by continuing his affair
with Josiffe. At best, publicity would wreck his career; at worst
he would be sent to jail, facing anything from a life sentence for
buggery to two years for gross indecency, the euphemism for sex
which did not involve anal penetration.[9]

The generally unflattering contemporary view of gays was
reinforced in 1956 when the report of the Conference of Privy
Counsellors published its report on the defections five years
earlier of two suspected KGB agents, Guy Burgess and Donald

Maclean, to the Soviet Union. It said that the cases of Burgess, an open and flamboyant homosexual, and Maclean, an icy Foreign Office careerist who was bisexual, proved that it was not enough to vet people to check that they were politically reliable; 'character defects', including homosexuality, had to be investigated. These defects included 'drunkenness, addiction to drugs, homosexuality or any loose living'. The report concluded: 'It is right to continue the practice of tilting the balance in favour of offering greater protection to the security of the State rather than in the direction of safeguarding the rights of the individual.'

In 1957 Sir John Wolfenden produced a report on female prostitution and homosexuality, in which he recommended that homosexual acts in private between consenting men who were aged 21 or over should be legalised. He also argued for greater understanding of homosexuals, who were not, he said, diseased, inherently unstable or necessarily promiscuous. (It took a decade for his recommendations to become law.) As Wolfenden suggested, there were many homosexuals who led balanced lives. For example, the novelist Francis King was never troubled by his homosexuality. He was born in 1923 in Switzerland and spent his childhood in India, where his father was a civil servant, before being sent to Shrewsbury, one of Britain's leading public schools. Sex education was not part of the curriculum then but King had an intimation that he might not be developing conventionally when masters there told him repeatedly that he was 'girlish'.[10]

When he went to Balliol College, Oxford, in 1942 he was still not sure why he was different, though he enjoyed visiting the George Street Milk Bar, which, he later wrote, 'was a favourite haunt for homosexuals'.[11] He was in his mid-20s before he discovered himself. Like many latent homosexuals he had ignored the emotions which disturbed him at home but Europe was different. He was on holiday in Venice when he met a gondolier called Gino; after a brief courtship they had sex, as King later recalled: 'I was pitifully maladroit, greedy, precipitate. "All these years I've lived for this," I told him. It was only the truth. But of course he did not understand my English, merely shaking his head and laughing.'[12]

From that moment King was at peace with himself. He worked abroad for the British Council for many years before settling in England in the mid-1960s. But he realised that he had been lucky to come to terms so painlessly with his homosexuality: 'Some of my friends felt that there was something wrong with them. One friend in the 1940s went through a terrible time having aversion therapy because he thought it would cure him of his homosexuality.'[13]

It was not easy, he said, to be a homosexual in Britain:

> We all lived, to some extent, in fear of the police. Fortunately, I was not interested in 'rough trade' but people were always worried about blackmail. It was very dangerous. The builder, truck driver or whatever might say, 'I want five hundred quid or I will go to the police.' Why did people want 'rough trade'? I think that it was because they thought homosexuality was dirty and they didn't think it was right to use their peers. So, they went to men outside their social circle. It was like a married man who goes to a prostitute.

Many politicians were unmoved, however, by the argument that homosexuals deserved to be treated as ordinary human beings. In her famous diaries, compiled during her long career as a Cabinet minister, Barbara Castle recalled an incident in February 1966, when she was the controversial Minister of Transport, responsible for a number of reforms, such as a 70-m.p.h. speed limit and the breathalyser. She noted the reaction of her Cabinet colleague, George Brown, the economic-affairs supremo whose drinking and womanising were legendary, to the Sexual Offences Bill then making its way through Parliament. Castle wrote that he was not pleased by the Bill, which incorporated the essential points of the 1957 Wolfenden Report and aimed to decriminalise homosexuality between consenting adults. He described it as 'the Buggers' Charter' and then revealed that prejudice against homosexuals was just as strong amongst socialists as Conservatives. Castle wrote, 'George [set] off on a remarkable diatribe against homosexuality. As an Anglo-Catholic and Socialist, he thought society ought to have higher standards . . . He got very passionate: "This is how Rome came down. And I care deeply about it . . . don't think teenagers are able to evaluate your liberal ideas. You will have a totally disorganised, indecent and unpleasant society. You must have rules! We've gone too damned far on sex already. I don't regard sex as pleasant. It's pretty undignified and I've always thought so." '[14]

Brown would probably have become even angrier if he had known that Jeremy Thorpe, MP, who was sitting on the Liberal benches, had spent his adult life breaking those rules that were 'essential for a civilized society'.

CHAPTER FOUR

Norman was exhausted by his exertions at the Easton Hotel, Victoria and Chelsea police station in December 1962 and slumped back into his role as Thorpe's moody lover in the cramped flat at Marsham Court. After a quiet Christmas, the two men agreed that they needed time and space. So they turned to *Horse and Hound*, the magazine which was the employment exchange for people who worked with horses. Josiffe wanted to move up the riding ladder, from being a groom to an instructor, and spotted an advertisement for a job at the Castle Riding School at Comber, Northern Ireland. He applied for and was offered the position. He packed his battered suitcase with his riding gear and his precious love letters, and left the bustle and grime of London for his new life in the rolling green countryside of Ulster.

After Josiffe had departed a bill plopped on to the doormat at Marsham Court. It came from Gieves Ltd, the gentlemen's outfitters in Bond Street, and requested payment for a pair of silk pyjamas which Mr Josiffe had billed to Thorpe's account. He was irritated that Norman had splashed out on fripperies like pyjamas without his permission, so he wrote to the shop and denied responsibility: 'Unfortunately, I have no idea of Mr Josiffe's present whereabouts, although I believe he has gone abroad.'

Norman's foray into the world of Irish equestrianism marked the start of two years of misery for him, which made his first fourteen months with Thorpe seem blissfully happy. He was sacked or stormed out from a succession of jobs in Ulster and mainland Britain. He hurt himself in bad falls. He became addicted to tranquillisers and when he was especially distressed tried to commit suicide, in his usual unenthusiastic way. He rowed with Thorpe but continued to sleep with him, though he despised himself for doing so. He had no money, no home and no National Insurance card. Finally, he ended up in the winter of 1964 shivering in a loft in Switzerland, having taken a job he did not want.

He felt that he had been deserted in Ireland although a neutral observer would have said that Thorpe did his best to stay in touch. Sometimes they spoke on the phone but they could not have a private conversation if Josiffe was in the riding school, and making long-distance calls from rural public phone boxes required patience, acute hearing and a bagful of coins to feed into the slot marked with a large 'A'. Letters were more efficient and intimate. Josiffe was still settling in at Comber when he received a note from Thorpe, who had just moved into a new office in Bridge Street. There was a suggestion of wariness – there was no 'Dear Norman' – but this was a pointless precaution because the letter itself was so explicit:

> House of Commons. 1.50 (p.m.). I've claimed my desk and got my own special key to No. 1 Bridge St . . . the subway entrance. The (telephone) extension is 755 and you have to go through the attendant; who are on duty now very helpful – nice desk – I didn't talk to the girls – hundreds of them. How shall I get typewriter moved and from where?
>
> Cable and Wireless says has Sir Walter got Gorillas again?!
>
> I'm going shopping with 01 now, slight cooling again! i.e. since your telephone call. I wasn't going to write anything compromising but can't stop myself saying I love you and can't wait to see you.[1]

To outsiders this letter would have been gibberish ('01' referred to a woman who was keen on Thorpe and 'Gorillas' was a little joke about the poor quality of the telephone lines from Northern Ireland) but there would have been no difficulty interpreting the final sentence: writer and recipient were lovers. Josiffe folded it and deposited it in his suitcase, where there were over fifty affectionate letters, a documentary bomb waiting to destroy Thorpe's career.

It was not enough that Jeremy still cared for him; in his befuddled mind there was still the problem of his National Insurance card. He had two contradictory views on this; first, Thorpe was his employer and should have been stamping the card for the past year, which was obviously untrue; second, Thorpe would not return it because he did not want him to be independent, which was also nonsense. But Josiffe was sure that the card held the key to future happiness:

Thorpe was very pleased that I had a job. But I told him, 'I will have to have my Insurance card and fill in some forms about tax.' At once he replied, 'Oh yes, I'll send it over.' But he didn't. That situation went on for weeks. My employers had just started in business and wanted to do the right thing. I lied to protect him and fob them off about the delay. Of course I couldn't tell them that Thorpe should have been stamping my card. So they said, 'I'm sorry, but you'll have to go.'[2]

Once again someone took pity on him. This time his saviour was Billy Lowry, who sold animal feed in County Antrim and inhabited a rambling house called Rokeby Hall, along with his mother, brother and seven sisters. Mrs Lowry agreed that Billy's new friend could move into the house until he found a cottage to rent. The Lowrys did not actually employ him but horses were part of life in the Irish countryside, which meant that he was soon basking in the status of an accomplished rider. He also had a gift for story-telling, which did not bring the same approval. He revived the idea, which he had picked up in Devon in 1962 when he was briefly semi-employed by Major Hambro, that he was the illegitimate son of Lord Eldon. He further confused people when he told them his full name was the Honourable Norman Lianche-Josiffe. He had other stories, too, about a horrible man called Thorpe, who had ruined his life, which he backed up with his bundle of letters on House of Commons notepaper.

Occasionally he travelled to London to Marsham Court, but the sex was as brief and joyless as ever and, once Thorpe was satisfied, Norman was ejected on to the stiff little camp bed: 'Every time I came over it was only for one reason. It was not to pick up the Insurance cards. It was for him, so he could screw me,' he said. Yet, while he claimed to hate homosexual sex, he now began an affair with a man in Belfast; if sex was an exciting recreation for Thorpe then for Norman it was consolation and comfort. He told everyone that he was desperately unhappy but he had a foolproof routine to lift his spirits after a night with Thorpe: a haircut in Chelsea, followed by lunch at an Italian restaurant.

In Northern Ireland the initial sympathy he always provoked in people was superceded by the inevitable doubts about his sanity. Lord Dunleath and his wife, Lady Dorinda Dunleath, who lived near the Lowrys, came to dread their encounters with him. Lady Dunleath said that he claimed to be the illegitimate son of a peer and said that he would shortly be undergoing a lobotomy. (He did not confide that he hoped the operation would 'cure' him of his homosexuality.)[3]

The Dunleaths also had to endure his tears as he explained that his life had been destroyed by Thorpe. She said:

> People befriended him and were kind to him. But one never knew what were lies and what was fantasy. He roared around the countryside, involving everybody. His net was wide and a lot of people got caught in it. If I saw him in the distance I used to get out of sight very quickly and make definite attempts not to meet him. People used mistakenly to think they'd seen him around the place. Everybody was sighting him everywhere, like Lord Lucan.[4]

Thorpe, on the other hand, thrived, as if he took sustenance from Josiffe's struggles. He was in marvellous form at the Liberal Assembly in 1963, when he delivered a classic Thorpian attack, full of jokes and impersonations, on the Conservatives. He told the Party faithful that a Conservative MP only needed to be loyal to the Party whip to be honoured: 'How justly we refer to the Tories as the party of dreadful knights.' The next year he craftily grabbed national headlines with a campaign against bureaucratic incompetence in the Egg Marketing Board.

But he ignored the danger signals. He had given Norman money, bought him clothes, showed him off at his London clubs and forgiven his regular black moods. He did not know about Norman's treacherous statement to the police in Chelsea, where he had accused Thorpe of buggery, but he was certainly aware that he regaled total strangers with details of their domestic difficulties. Yet he would not drop him; indeed, he continued to write letters declaring his love, which Norman hoarded in his suitcase for some future, unspecified purpose. In view of Josiffe's volatile nature, Thorpe should have realised that this was unlikely to be benign. Thorpe also ignored the lessons of espionage scandals which dominated the press in 1962 and 1963. The first centred on John Vassall, a 38-year-old homosexual clerk at the Admiralty who had been blackmailed into spying for the Soviets by the KGB; he was sentenced to eighteen years in prison at the Old Bailey late in 1962.

If Francis King showed how homosexuals could lead fulfilling lives despite the law then the Vassall affair demonstrated what could go wrong if it was not changed. Vassall came from a solidly respectable family – his father was an RAF chaplain, his mother a nurse – and they did their best for their son by scraping together enough money to send him to a minor public school, where he realised that he was sexually attracted to other boys.[5]

In the 1950s he was posted to the British Embassy in Moscow where, predictably, he was targeted by the KGB. They drugged him and photographed him naked in bed with men, engaged in a variety of sexual acts, and then blackmailed him into handing them information, which he did, until he was arrested in 1962 in London. That same year, after Vassall had been packed off to prison, there was a limp inquiry by an eminent judge, which was the normal government response to a spy scandal. The judge, Lord Radcliffe, seemed to be more irritated by Fleet Street's investigations into the affair (he jailed two reporters for refusing to name their sources) than by the fact that a lonely and vulnerable homosexual such as Vassall had been sent to Moscow.[6]

Then there was the Profumo affair, which generated millions of words in newspapers and spawned bestselling books and a successful film. In June 1963 John Profumo, the Minister for War in Harold Macmillan's government, was forced to resign after lying in the Commons about his relationship with a young woman called Christine Keeler, who had also been having an affair with a KGB officer called Eugène Ivanov, ostensibly a naval attaché at the Soviet Embassy in London. Both Harold Wilson, who had become the leader of the Labour Party in February, and Thorpe tried to take advantage as Macmillan squirmed with embarrassment over the behaviour of Profumo and the inexplicable failure of MI5 to discover that a minister and a KGB spy were sleeping with the same woman. Wilson thundered in the Commons, 'What we are seeing is the diseased excrescence, a corrupted and poisoned appendix, of a small and unrepresentative section of society that makes no contribution to what Britain is, still less what Britain can be.' Thorpe was also determined to make his mark and announced to the House that two other ministers would be forced to resign 'for personal reasons'.

In September 1963 Lord Denning's inquiry was published. But there were no new names and Thorpe was forced to apologise to the Commons: 'I accept Lord Denning's findings and I would wish to apologise for any pain which this publicity might have caused. This in itself indicates that standards of our public life stand higher than many at times thought possible.'

MPs who admit their errors are always forgiven by their colleagues and no more was said about his allegation, though privately his rivals in the Liberal Party were thrilled that he had blundered so spectacularly. There were more pressing matters to gossip about; in October 1963 Macmillan resigned and was replaced, to the delight of Labour and the Liberals, by a charming Scottish aristocrat called Lord Home, who looked like a frightened stag when he appeared on television and who, Labour and Liberals hoped, would be crushed by Wilson and Grimond in the election that was scheduled for October 1964.

No one remembered Thorpe's confident claims about the two ministers. Yet he had been right, which proved that, for a young MP, he had unusually good contacts in the intelligence services. In a report on the private lives of ministers and senior civil servants, commissioned secretly by Macmillan and written as a private letter, Denning said that most of the rumours swirling around Westminster about ministers were 'mischievous and without foundation'. But he added that, regretfully, two had been guilty of conduct that exposed them to possible blackmail: Ernest Marples, the Minister of Transport, and Denzil Freeth, the 39-year-old MP for Basingstoke who was Parliamentary Secretary at the Ministry of Science.[7] Denning wrote:

I am satisfied that for a considerable number of years and up to a few years ago Mr Marples had an association with a prostitute and that, in the course of this association, conduct took place of such a character as would expose Mr Marples to a risk of undue pressure.

It is right that I should add that I am satisfied that he has not been subjected to such pressure and that national security has not in fact been endangered, but I am also satisfied that the conduct was of such a nature as to constitute a security risk.

Mr Denzil Freeth, a junior Member of your government, invited me to inquire into certain rumours about him. I have done so and regret to inform you that Mr Freeth did three years ago go to a party of a homosexual character and that he there participated in homosexual conduct.

His report remained secret for thirty years. Then an historian called Richard Lamb found a copy while he was researching in Denning's personal archive. Denning, a former Master of the Rolls and one of the most respected judges this century, was not pleased; he later said that he had forgotten that the letter was there and that he regretted that it had become public.[8]

Freeth's political career was ended by Denning's letter. He resigned as a minister and in 1964 stood down as an MP. He moved into the City but never discussed the reasons for his abrupt and mysterious departure from politics. In 1995, living in retirement, he said that he had never been told officially about the letter but admitted that he had been questioned and that he had feared the worst after seeing Denning: 'I wasn't aware that he had written to the Prime Minister. But this sort of allegation hardly helps your political career, does it?'[9]

Freeth's fate contrasted sharply with Thorpe's, who prospered for years, despite a private life that made most MPs seem positively saintly. While Freeth was consigned to political oblivion for what Denning described as a single lapse, Thorpe became the leader of the Liberal Party and a Privy Counsellor, though the police and MI5 knew that he was a practising homosexual.

Yet Freeth had as much right as Thorpe to expect generosity from the Establishment. After wartime service as a pilot in the RAF he went to Cambridge as a scholar at Trinity Hall. In 1949 he became President of the Union and Chairman of the university's Conservative Association, which marked him out as a Tory high-flier. He was elected to the Commons in 1955 and seemed set for a glittering career; a year later he became Parliamentary Private Secretary to the Trade Minister, the first step on the ladder to full ministerial rank. He moved steadily upwards; he had excellent connections in the City (he was a partner in a stockbroking firm) and was tipped for major office. There was a blip in May 1962 when he was fined £1 for being drunk and disorderly. He offered to resign from his job at the Ministry of Science but Macmillan told him that he had already been punished and that the offence was too trivial to warrant resignation.

In 1963, however, Freeth heard that Denning had been told that he had visited homosexual parties. Freeth said that he told Denning that he was totally innocent: 'I know who made the allegation about me to Denning but that person is dead and I believe that he got the wrong end of the stick. I had to invite Denning to speak to me because it was reported to me that this allegation had been made. I was interrogated but I was obviously unable to persuade him that the allegation was untrue. I never saw Denning's letter but my political life was finished.'

The Vassall case reinforced the prejudice that homosexuals could not be trusted and were susceptible to blackmail. But, more disturbing from Thorpe's point of view, was the Profumo affair; it did not require a Master's degree in the new discipline of media science to see how the media, which had crucified Profumo for sleeping with a beautiful young woman, would treat a Liberal MP who was having a homosexual affair with a riding instructor. Thorpe remained certain, however, that he would escape exposure.

There was one final example of the realities of power in London in the 1960s, where compromises were struck which would have appalled ordinary people, who believed they were governed by men and women of principle.

Alex Kellar was a popular officer who headed F Branch at MI5, which monitored political parties, from 1956 until he retired in 1965. He was also a homosexual, as everyone in MI5 knew. One retired officer said of him, 'He was an amusing and sweet man. I knew him very well indeed. He fostered the romance between myself and my husband. He was extremely camp and was known as Liberace. Did he marry? Gosh, no, of course not.'[10]

The service could not afford to be too choosy during the war about the sexual predilections of its recruits but it was a different matter after 1945. NATO and the Warsaw Pact employed every dirty trick in the espionage handbook in an effort to demoralise and discredit the other, including blackmailing homosexuals. Paranoia was a fact of life in the intelligence services on both sides of the Iron Curtain during these years; MI5, the CIA, the KGB and the rest spent as much time hunting traitors in their own ranks as chasing spies in the real world.

Yet Kellar prospered. This was a credit to the humanity of his colleagues but these same, commendably tolerant officers were also convinced that homosexuals in general, though not Kellar, had to be weeded out of government and the Civil Service because they were 'security risks'.

Kellar was born in 1905, read law at Edinburgh University and was President of the National Union of Students. He studied law at Yale, became a barrister in London in the mid-1930s and joined MI5 in 1941. His promotion as head of F Branch was widely welcomed: 'He modernised it . . . it was under his direction that F completed a vast survey of Communist Party of Great Britain affiliations and sympathisers at Oxford and Cambridge Universities.'[11] It is likely that he would have seen or heard about the growing files on Jeremy Thorpe, the Liberal MP for North Devon, who was reported to be a homosexual and, therefore, a possible target for blackmail.

Kellar had a busy retirement until his death in the late 1980s. He had spells with the English Tourist Board and the Ministry for Overseas Development and, in his spare time, was a popular member of the literary gay scene in Brighton and London. Francis King, the novelist, recalled his first meeting with Kellar: 'A distinguished-looking man in a beautifully cut grey suit, purple socks and purple watered-silk tie appeared . . . we became neighbours and close friends.'[12]

In his autobiography, published after Kellar's death, King said that everyone had known that Kellar had been a senior officer in MI5.

> He was essentially a serious figure, and yet at the same time a preposterous one. A tremendous snob, he pursued anyone with a title . . . All too obviously a homosexual, he blissfully thought that no one was aware of this. After we had known each other for two or three years, he suddenly said to me, when the two of us were alone together, 'Forgive me for asking this question, Francis, but would I be right in thinking you were homosexual?' It amazed me that someone who had risen so high in MI5 should not long before have intuited the answer to this question. In fact, I was so amazed by it that I failed to say, 'And would I be right in thinking you are also homosexual?'[13]

King also recalled with amusement Kellar's black-tie dinner parties: 'They were extraordinary. One would be waited on by these very handsome hunks in white monkey jackets from the Brigade of Guards and the Household Cavalry. Alex used to hire them for the night.[14]

He thought that it was splendid that MI5 had valued Kellar: 'His colleagues knew that he was homosexual but they knew that didn't mean he would become a traitor. He used to wear the most

extraordinarily garish ties and socks. Maybe that was his way of
declaring himself. He was always asking my friend, David, round
to his flat to repair his toaster or whatever. He obviously took
great pleasure in having David there but he never made a pass at
him. Poor chap, you know I don't know whether he ever had any
sexual relations when he was in Intelligence.'

Norman Josiffe's riding career in Ulster, which had seemed so
promising, was brought to an abrupt end in the summer of
1963 at the Royal Dublin Show when his horse took a fence
badly and fell on him, crushing six vertebrae. As he was
recuperating he decided to see if he would have better luck in
England.

Once again, he turned to the magazine *Horse and Hound*.
There was a vacancy at a stables in Wolverhampton, run by
Fred Hartill, who trained show-jumpers. But, as usual, there
were complications. He became friendly with Heather Simpson,
who was a groom at the stables, and, though he was still sleeping
with Thorpe, proposed to her.

A further difficulty was his friendship with one of his riding
students, a woman called Sheila Weight, whose husband Charles
ran a company making tractor parts. She thought a great deal of
her instructor, the Honourable Norman Lianche-Josiffe:

> He was gentlemanly and sympathetic. He had a very good
> sense of humour and, in fact, it would be true to say he
> became a friend of the family. But there was no sexual
> attraction between us. He never made any sort of pass at
> me and his rather effeminate personality made him more like
> a sister towards me. He was very funny and a truly excellent
> rider and instructor. But he did go on about Thorpe.[15]

But Fred Hartill was not a fan. Norman was incapable of taking
advice from employers who did not know as much about horses
as he did, which meant everyone for whom he worked. On 23
December 1963 there was another row and Josiffe stomped
off. He turned up at the Weights' house in Muchall Road,
Wolverhampton's equivalent of Hampstead, where Charles, then
in his early 50s, was anticipating a quiet family Christmas. 'Sheila,
I have been kicked out,' Josiffe announced, adding that he had
nowhere to stay. He said that Hartill had ordered him off the

premises and out of the accommodation that went with the job. But he hoped that money would arrive soon from a benefactor in London, though he did not mention Thorpe by name. Reluctantly Charles Weight agreed, under pressure from his wife, to let Norman stay with them for a few days.

Predictably, the money did not arrive from London and the few days became weeks and then months. The Weights, especially Sheila, were remarkably patient. She took him on shopping expeditions to Fortnum and Mason and Harrods and introduced him to her doctor in Harley Street, Dr Campbell Connolly, a neuro-surgeon who had treated her for problems with the blood supply to her brain. Josiffe had a private consultation with him but his difficulties were psychological rather than neurological and Connolly was unable to help.

Back in Muchall Road, the atmosphere became tense. Charles Weight accused Josiffe of spending his money on champagne and riding boots; Norman claimed that they were presents. He was convinced Sheila wanted to go into business with him, breeding Russian horses, which were then fashionable. After an angry discussion he stormed out. Hours later he was admitted to hospital after swallowing an overdose of drugs. The police telephoned at 3 a.m. and told the Weights that Josiffe had tried to kill himself. Mrs Weight had had enough and said that, while she was sorry that he was not well, she did not want to see him again. Next day she spoke to one of Norman's ex-hosts, Esther Lister, wife of the West Country doctor, whose ducks Josiffe's dog had killed. Mrs Lister assured her that Josiffe was not really trying to kill himself: 'Esther told me, "Don't worry, we had five attempts and this is Norman's method of obtaining his own way." '

Next day, having recovered, Josiffe turned up at the Weights', pleading to be given a second chance. But Charles Weight had seen enough of young Norman; he escorted him to the Park Hall Hotel and paid for his room. He also gave him the money for the train fare to London.[16]

Naturally, he returned to Marsham Court. Thorpe was in fine form. The election of October 1964 had once again shown the iniquities of the voting system; the Party polled over 3 million votes, compared to just over 12 million each for Labour and the Conservatives, but had won only nine out of 630 seats in the Commons. The Party had almost doubled its share of the vote since 1959 but was no better off, although Labour's tiny majority meant that the Liberals could expect to wield an influence far beyond their actual seats. But for Thorpe the election was a triumph; he now had a majority in North Devon of 5,136.

Norman was not interested in Thorpe's success. Christmas was approaching again and as he surveyed his life he did not like what he saw. So, yet again, he tried to commit suicide. Many years later he said that he had tried to kill himself so often during the 1960s that he could not remember each attempt clearly. But he thought that, on this occasion, he had ended up in St George's Hospital, Hyde Park, a huge building overlooking the gardens of Buckingham Palace. He said, 'I suppose I tried to kill myself because I was depressed. But it happened so often I can't remember exactly. I know that I did not tell the doctors about Thorpe. I just discharged myself and went back to Marsham Court.'[17]

As always, suicide proved cathartic and, after he had had his stomach pumped by doctors, he decided it was time to pull himself together. He turned once more to *Horse and Hound*.

As he was browsing the predictable dead-end jobs in the West Country, the Midlands and Ireland he spotted one that offered him the kind of fresh start which he craved: Dr François Choquard, a vet in Porrentruy, a small town near Basle in north-west Switzerland, wanted a groom. He read out the advertisement to Thorpe who, said Josiffe, seemed 'thrilled' at the possibility that he might leave the country. But then Norman began to fret and said that, perhaps, it was not such a good idea after all; he had never been abroad before and did not have a passport. But Thorpe was determined and, over supper, told him that the job would be fun and challenging and that bracing Alpine air was exactly what he needed after his recent difficulties in the Midlands. Norman was still not sure but Switzerland sounded exciting – and there was the advantage that he would not need a National Insurance card. So, as they cleared the dishes away, he agreed to go.

Over the next few days there was a flurry of telegrams between Thorpe and Dr Choquard, which ended with Josiffe's appointment as groom-in-residence in Porrentruy. The doctor concluded the arrangements by sending Thorpe a money order for the train fare from London. Thorpe moved quickly before Norman could change his mind. 'Jeremy got a passport for me. We had photographs taken and went to Petty France in London where he counter-signed the picture on the back, saying he had known me for two years.' Then he dispatched his secretary to the bank to draw pocket money for Norman's first overseas excursion.

Norman went to say goodbye to his mother in Bexleyheath, who was worried that he would not be able to cope abroad but was also relieved that he was escaping the dreadful Thorpe. Then her son set off manfully to Victoria Station to catch the boat train, clutching his new passport, and his trusty suitcase, containing the love letters.

But disaster was inexorably tracking Norman. He said:

In my suitcase were all the letters he'd ever written to me apart from those taken by Scotland Yard two years earlier. As ill-luck would have it my suitcase was thrown off the train at a place called Versoul in France, which was miles from Porrentruy. I was wearing this very thin suit and there was thick snow about. I suppose there would be in Switzerland at that time of the year. There was nobody to meet me and it was just the most horrible anti-climax and I felt it wasn't going to work.

Shivering in his thin suit, he trudged through the snow to Choquard's house over two miles away, where he was met by the vet, who showed him to his accommodation. This did not meet with Norman's approval: 'It was a loft full of rats. There was an all-pervading stench of horse manure, no light and no warmth.' He was not prepared to ruin his suit and refused to begin work. But he was happy to talk and explained to the Choquards that he was missing his good friend and protector, Mr Thorpe, a British Member of Parliament.

In between regaling his employer with stories about Thorpe, Norman found time to send a postcard to his mother: 'Impossible to be here! The conditions are impossible . . . I wish things were different but no. Can't say anything on paper. You know I would stay if I could. Pleace [sic] do not worry.'

Two days after he had first breathed the fresh Alpine air which Thorpe had hoped would prove so invigorating Norman was on the train back to London, courtesy of a loan of 300 Swiss francs from Choquard. With the commendable financial prudence for which his fellow countrymen are renowned, he had decided that, when Norman's missing suitcase did turn up, he would hold it as collateral against the loan.

Josiffe arrived in London with half a franc and no clothes. He
called Thorpe at Marsham Court: 'He said, "Well, you'd better
come back here for the night," and so I did and stayed for a week
or so. I told him I had nowhere to go and nothing to wear as I'd
lost my suitcase.'

No one was glad to see him. Mrs Josiffe thought that it was
'absolutely ghastly' that Norman had been sucked back into the
homosexual relationship which had ruined his life. Thorpe was
also not pleased. Much as he enjoyed taking Norman to bed the
relationship brought only problems, which, as he clawed his way
up politics' treacherous pole, he could well do without. And he
was incandescent when he heard that his letters were in an old
suitcase, trundling somewhere between Vesoul and Porrentruy.
Supremely confident though he was that he could not be touched
by the media, he sensed that it would hardly boost his career if
the letters were examined by nosy customs officers as the suitcase
made its way across the Franco-Swiss border. He told Norman
that it had to be recovered, unopened. But Norman insisted that
there was nothing he could do since he had no money and, after
a tense Christmas, he set off on his travels again. His friend, Billy
Lowry, the animal-feed dealer in County Antrim, had told him
that he would find a job easily in the Irish Republic. And, since
this was another country, Norman would not need a National
Insurance card.

In January 1965 he found a live-in job as chief riding instructor
at the Grand Hotel in Malahide, twenty minutes from Dublin's
city centre. But then he invited Lowry to stay the night, which
was against hotel rules, and he was sacked. A week later he
found a new job, at the Ballyrogan Stud in Redcross, County
Wicklow, thirty-eight miles outside Dublin, which was owned
by Mr and Mrs Quirke; like other kindly couples who had felt
sorry for Norman, such as the Listers of Devon and the Weights
of Wolverhampton, they were soon bit-players in his ongoing
drama with Thorpe.

Superficially things were going well; he was building a reputation
as a fine show-jumper, and emotionally he felt at home in a
country where Catholicism was part of the fabric of daily life.
But Norman could always find darkness inside a cloud's silver
exterior and he began to brood again: 'I kept writing and
telephoning Jeremy, asking him to send the Insurance card
because I was getting quite a name and people wanted me to

ride their horses in England. Without the card I couldn't go over and ride.'

He also had a new obsession: his suitcase. He badgered Thorpe about this, though for once Thorpe was just as worried as he. On 2 February 1965 Thorpe telephoned the British Consulate in Berne and said that it was time that they sorted out the mess of a British subject's missing suitcase. Then he stepped up the pressure. On 28 February 1965 he wrote to the Foreign Office in London and demanded action.

The negotiations had drained Norman and in early March he returned the Quirkes' hospitality in his own inimitable way; he stormed off. Mrs Marie Quirke was so concerned about his mental health that, reluctantly, she decided to contact Norman's great friend Mr Thorpe, the MP. She wrote on 6 March 1965:

Dear Mr Thorpe,

Three weeks ago Norman Josiffe came here to learn Stud work. I met him in Dublin and drove him down. The first morning, within half an hour, he came in and told me he was going and would I take him to Dublin. A friend staying with us drove him into Wicklow where he could catch a bus. Even though he insisted he could take a taxi – Dublin is thirty-eight miles from us! That afternoon he telephoned from Dublin to apologise and said he would like to come back. A friend drove him down the next day but wouldn't come in.

My husband offered him pocket money whilst he was learning the job £3 a week and he would live with us as one of the family. Norman said he would not dream of accepting anything and it was very good of us to have him. We just put it down to foolish pride.

We did everything we could to make him feel at home, especially as he then told us he was an orphan. He then went on to say his mother was French and his father a well-known English Peer. He travelled on a French passport and his name Josiffe was his mother's name also, his mother was dead.

Three times in as many weeks he said he was going and the last time, two evenings ago when he was talking about a certain horse with my husband and they disagreed as to ownership I told him to look it up in *Horses in Training*. He did so and was proved wrong. He turned on my husband

and said 'I'm not spending all night arguing with you. I will be leaving here tomorrow morning.'

Frankly we were shocked. The next morning (yesterday) we drove him into Dublin parting on good terms . . .

I am writing to you as he told us you were his Guardian and we feel there is something wrong with the boy. We have made all the efforts, especially as he was widowed [sic] at such an early age and his past history seems to play on his mind.

A stud farm is very exacting work and we run it seriously. It is not a holiday camp. It is quite impossible to teach Norman anything as he will not be told but at the same time asks plenty of questions. Then walks away whilst one is trying to tell him.

He will certainly have to pull up his socks if he intends to settle down to anything, and as his Guardian I feel you have a right to know what has happened here. My husband gave Norman £10 yesterday and had given him a couple of pounds before. We wouldn't like to see him stranded. It's such a pity as he can be such a charming boy and just as quickly he can be very nasty.

Please let us know if he turns up alright. If you are ever over in Ireland we would be delighted if you would give us a call.

Yours sincerely,
Mrs M. Quirke.

On 11 March, Thorpe replied on House of Commons note-paper:

Dear Mrs Quirke,

Thank you so much for your letter of 6 March. I am very sorry you have had so many unfortunate experiences with Norman Josiffe.

In fact I am not his Guardian, but merely tried to help him on occasions which have proved at times rather hair-raising. I think honestly that he has a split personality and does seem incapable of standing on his own feet for long.

I fear I have no responsibility for his actions. I believe that his mother is alive and lives in Kent.

Yours sincerely . . .

This was not a sensible letter. It outraged Josiffe, who thought that Thorpe had abandoned him. He drifted from one job to another until he ended up at a stables in Dunboyne, County Meath, near Dublin, which was run by a well-known breeder called Nat Galway-Greer, who owned some of the finest hunters in Ireland. Galway-Greer's daughter Betty was a sensitive girl and saw that poor Catholic Norman was tormented; she advised him to speak to a priest and suggested Father Michael Sweetman, whose order was based at Milldown Park in Dublin.

But Josiffe clung to Thorpe. He telephoned him in London and was incensed when he complained about how much money it was costing to sort out his various problems. 'I had become very depressed again and burned the new passport Thorpe had arranged for me. After a great deal of soul-searching I thought: Well, if he won't sort out the Insurance card for me, I must ask his mother. I know people will say that I was being spiteful but I had to do what was necessary.'

He travelled to Dublin and checked into a hotel, which, he assumed, Thorpe would pay for. Unfortunately for Norman, Thorpe refused point-blank to do so when the hotel telephoned him. Things were now looking even bleaker than normal but, once again, Norman found a saviour; Father Sweetman came to the hotel and promised to help with the bill and find cheaper accommodation. He poured out his story to the priest, who talked about sin, forgiveness and finding God through suffering. This was thought-provoking stuff but Norman was not strong on abstract concepts and he now focused, as if he was lining up a horse to jump the biggest fence at a show, on Ursula Thorpe. In mid-March he wrote her a seventeen-page letter. He opened with this bleak but effective statement:

For the last five years, as you probably know, Jeremy and I have had a 'homosexual' relationship. To go into it too deeply will not help either of us. When I came down to Stonewalls that was when I first met him. Though he told you something about the TV programme and Malta. That was all not so true. What remains is the fact that through my meeting with Jeremy that day I gave birth to this vice that lies latent in every man.

He went on to summarise his life after that night at Stonewalls. He wrote about the room at Draycott Place in Chelsea, his stay with the Collier family and her son's callousness at the flat in Marsham Court: 'When he had satisfied himself he put me to sleep on a little camp bed. This was when I realised that he didn't care for me as a friend but only as . . . Oh! How I hate to write that! It upset me terribly and I was rather sick because, you see, I was looking for a friend in the real sense of the word.'

He wrote about his desperation in Ireland and how he had returned to Jeremy, seeking comfort:

> I was to go to England – to Jeremy – corruption. Your son offered me two pounds after he had satisfied himself . . . I came to England with the determination that I would never see Jeremy again. Got very depressed, took all my sleeeping tablets and woke up in St George's Hospital. I was able to discharge myself pretty simply, but they asked me why I had done the whole thing. Could I tell them? No, I am too loyal – a quality your son fails at so miserably.

He was bitter that Thorpe had complained about the cost of securing the return of the suitcase: 'This was the last straw. Was our "love" to be measured in monetary values? £30 is so little. I was so hurt.'

He talked, too, about finding 'a cure' for the homosexuality that he had caught from Thorpe. 'I have heard of a splendid doctor who I shall go to when I have paid off all my other commitments who can cure this "thing".' He ended the letter:

> You are probably shattered by all this. I am so sorry, but what can I do? Will you ask Jeremy to please lend me at least the money for the luggage. I hate asking because I know it may cause friction, and I know how close you both are. This is really why I am writing to you. Jeremy owes me nothing. Possibly I owe him a lot, though I feel we balance out. Now instead of helping a cast-off 'friend' I appeal to his finer feelings as a 'man' to help me who is in real need. I promise I shall repay every penny as soon as I am on my feet. Believe me, I mean this.

He added this sad little postscript: 'Can you understand any of this, Mrs Thorpe? I'm so sorry. Please believe me, I'm desperate for help.'

This was not blackmail, though Thorpe's lawyers at the Old Bailey in 1979 suggested to the jury that this had been Josiffe's main purpose in writing the letter. Many normally well-balanced people behave strangely when a love affair disintegrates and Norman was neither normal nor well-balanced. This was the revenge of the lover who had been discarded. On Friday, 26 March 1965 the letter arrived at Stonewalls. Ursula Thorpe read it and gave it to her son, thus opening the next act in the drama.

CHAPTER FIVE

Thorpe assured his mother that the letter from Dublin was one long lie. He admitted that he had once tried to help Josiffe but said that he had severed contact when he realised that he was a fantasist. Ursula was unequivocally loyal to her son; she believed him, and never faltered from this view, though the evidence mounted over the years that Josiffe was telling the truth.

Thorpe pondered his options. If he did nothing then Norman would regard it as a sign of weakness and press on with his attack. If people ever believed that they had had an affair then his career would be over. He decided to silence Norman by using the law. He took out his House of Commons notepaper and outlined the letter that he would instruct his solicitor, Jimmy Walters, to send to Josiffe. This was an extraordinary document.[1] It revealed a man who believed that a lie could become the truth by force of will. He also believed that lies were more convincing if they were expressed in bizarre legal jargon:

We have been instructed by Mr Jeremy Thorpe to write to you both on his behalf and that of his mother, Mrs Thorpe, to whom you recently addressed an undated Letter marked 'Wednesday', bearing the address Dublin and received by her on Friday, March 21 1965. We are sending this Letter to Father Sweetman where we understand you are at present residing.

Although our client originally intended to answer individually the detailed allegations contained in your Letter, we propose at this stage to restrict ourselves to draw 2 main deductions as to its contents:

1. That you have alleged in your Letter to Mrs Thorpe that homosexual relations have taken place between yourself and her son on various occasions.

2. That having specified those persons to whom you have

so far restricted the publication of such a damaging allegation we suggest in the circumstances it was not appropriate for Mr Thorpe to send you immediately [the next word is missing].

In our view the contents of your Letter are in English Law a prima-facie case of blackmail, which you are no doubt aware is a serious Criminal offence. Our client says that it is his intention to take Legal opinion as to the position in the Criminal Courts of the Republic of Ireland since you are at present out of the jurisdiction.

Our client utterly rejects the damaging and groundless allegations which you have made against him and desires us to give notice that he will not hesitate to issue a writ, whether in the English or Irish Courts, claiming damages for defamation upon receiving the slightest scintilla of evidence that you have repeated this wholly obnoxious and untrue allegation . . .

Our client does not desire to enunciate the many occasions on which he has Tried to help you in the past. Suffice to say that you first approached him for help after having been discharged from receiving Mental Treatment and that he assisted you in obtaining 3 different jobs, one in London and two in Devon. More recently you approached him for help in regard to a job you had obtained in Switzerland upon which occasion the wife of one of Mr Thorpe's partners made 3 Telephone calls on your behalf to Switzerland whilst he advanced you £10 towards the incidental expenses of the trip. After you had terminated this job, almost immediately, Mr Thorpe subsequently contacted the Minister of State at the Foreign Office and the British Consul in Berne to effect the recovery of your luggage. Having failed to send this but having been assured that you had a job in Ireland and the necessary fare he advanced you £17 10s which he left with his Secretary, to enable you to purchase clothes for Ireland. From your Letter it is evident that it was not used for this purpose. Mr Thorpe heard from these latest employers you had walked out of that job shortly after arrival, claiming incidentally our Client was your Guardian and that your father was a wealthy Peer who had disowned you. Not least Mr Thorpe tried to assist you when the Police made extensive inquiries of you about the theft of a sheepskin coat and about

a horse allegedly stolen from Mr Van de Vater upon which
occasion he learnt that you also had a conviction for Theft
in the Juvenile Court where you were then residing at your
home in Kent. As a result of which he learnt that you had
been placed on probation.

In any event, although the contents of your Letter make it
abundantly clear that you are in desperate financial straits and
need money to buttress your failures our Client wishes to make
it plain that he would not now dream of giving any further
assistance whatsoever in the face of blackmail Threats and
after the allegations you have made against him and published
to his mother causing her great distress. Perhaps you would
indicate a firm of Solicitors to whom further correspondence
may be addressed.

On two accompanying pages Thorpe made further notes on Josiffe,
again written in the third person as though he were interviewing
himself. It began with the fiction that he had first met him at the
Commons rather than at the stables in Oxfordshire of his friend, the
multi-named Brecht Van de Vater. He also explained that he had
contacted a Foreign Office minister, Labour's George Thomson,
for help in locating Josiffe's suitcase, though it was curious that he
thought that this anecdote helped his case. Then he hesitated. He
decided that he ought to seek advice from his friend, Peter Bessell,
the Liberal MP for Bodmin in Cornwall.

The House of Commons has always attracted scoundrels and
rogues. They have seen the Commons as a way of making sexual,
financial or social conquests, which they would have struggled
to achieve without those magical letters, MP, after their name.
Peter Bessell was a member of this inglorious minority, though it
has to be said that he was also a conscientious MP for Bodmin
from 1964 until 1970. But he was also a hypocrite who could
not keep his hands off women, including prostitutes. He was a
dishonest businessman, whose ingenious schemes to make his
fortune always ended in failure. In his wake, he left a trail of
partners, whose abiding memory of him was the cheque which
came bouncing back from the bank.

One of his American partners, Eliot Steuer, said that Bessell
always gave the impression that he was 'loaded' yet never had
money in his wallet. Steuer always paid for everything when

Bessell visited New York to discuss the next multi-million-dollar deal. Bessell had expensive tastes; he was especially fond of the city's night-clubs, where he was entertained by young women with names like The Unique Monique and Bubbles. Steuer said, 'Let's put it this way. You go into a clip joint and you know you're going to be clipped. The same thing with Peter. I knew that I was being taken, but I really got a bang out of it. I knew he was a faker but I liked him. Do you know what I called him the end? Joe Disaster. Everything he touched was a disaster.'[2]

Shabby though he was, Bessell would not rate a mention in a historical study of the villains of Parliament; if he had not been involved with Thorpe he would have been forgotten by everyone, except the women he smooth-talked into bed and the business associates he cheated.

He first met Thorpe in November 1955, when he was 34 years old and fighting a by-election in Torquay, the genteel capital of the Devon Riviera. He had left school at 16 and was blessed with a deep matinée-idol's voice; he was charming and intelligent, which meant that women were willing to share his bed and businessmen were prepared to hand him large sums of money for his imaginative but doomed enterprises. Like many of the self-taught he was a show-off. He was always keen to demonstrate that he was an authority on music, religion, politics and history. Unfortunately he had often imperfectly digested what he had read, though he was so pompous that an audience usually assumed that he must be right. He was an astute observer of people and a fluent liar. This combination of talents meant that it was impossible to know when he was telling the truth.

Even as a young man his face was crinkled but, as he aged, he became increasingly distressed whenever he looked in the mirror: 'As I grew older, the lines on my face deepened until it began to look like a badly tessellated pavement. I took comfort from the fact that I did not have to look at it except when shaving. But Jeremy and others did. On at least half a dozen occasions he asked if I could not do something. "Couldn't you rub some cream in?" he said once. He also told me: "If only you could have your face ironed!"'

His clothes veered crazily as he sought a profitable identity; one day, the bespoke dark suit and cashmere overcoat marked him out as a classy entrepreneur, the next day, kitted out in a garish blue lightweight suit, he was the deal-maker who shopped hurriedly in the concourses of airports between flights. Russell

Johnston, the Liberal MP for Inverness, said, 'He was a conman of major proportions. He was like one of those American pulpit-bashers who's always screwing women. He was a great fantasist and loved to see himself as a wheeler-dealer of major proportions.'[3]

Thorpe, on the other hand, was the product of Eton and Oxford, those academies of the Establishment, was dedicated, or so his admirers thought, to the Liberals and was not interested in such ephemerae as women and money.[4] But they were actually very similar. This was a relationship between two men who fed off and understood the other's amorality; Bessell basked in Thorpe's political fame while Thorpe valued him as the fixer who could be relied upon to deal with an embarrassment. Bessell said:

We were a natural team. We were roughly the same height and build, with dark hair and narrow features. But it went deeper than any physical similarities or our showmanship, identical sense of humour and political philosophy. We were both wilful, quick to take offence, capable of arrogance, incurably sentimental, frequently devious and, because of the way we lived, highly vulnerable. My promiscuous womanising was less dangerous than Jeremy's homosexual affairs, but the driving force was the same and neither of us paused to consider the consequences. Politically I could not influence Jeremy, but in personal matters, recognising it is easier to deal with other people's problems than one's own, I took over Jeremy's. He was equally willing to help me. We also had many common personality traits, but none was more significant than our deliberate habit of compartmentalising our lives. This applied not only to obvious things like politics, sex or business, but even to our relationships with those closest to us.

It was never easy to unravel truth and fiction in Bessell's life. He constantly amended his curriculum vitae to maximise his chances of pulling off a business deal or luring a woman into bed. When he was trying to convince a potential investor in New York that he was a man of substance he would wave a photograph of a mansion in the English countryside and claim it was his home; if he was chasing a woman he would offer marriage once his divorce had come through. Sometimes he modified his c.v. for political purposes; according to Tom Dale, who was Thorpe's personal assistant when he was leader, Bessell would shape a speech to suit his audience. He was a gung-ho, no-nonsense right-winger if he was addressing conservative Liberals and a radical if he was talking to Young Liberal firebrands.[5]

He was born on 24 August 1921 and educated at Lynwyd School, Bath. His parents were divorced when he was 5 and he grew up with his father, J. Edgar Bessell, and his 'gentle but strict Victorian' grandparents. He was privately tutored until he was 7. He was then enrolled into an ordinary school, where he remained an undistinguished pupil until he was 16.

Then he became a Congregationalist lay preacher, which led to him registering as a conscientious objector. His father, who ran a ladies' tailoring business and, as Bessell grandly called it, 'an investment brokerage', died in 1940. Bessell later claimed that he expanded the businesses and sold them in 1948 for a handsome profit. He tried to de-register as a conscientious objector but, when he was finally cleared to fight, he was directed to the Ministry of Information, where he became a lecturer. In 1942 he married a young woman called Joyce Thomas; she died of tuberculosis in 1947.

The following year he married Pauline Colledge and moved to Paignton, a satellite of Torquay, on the Devon coast, where he launched a tailoring business. In his book *Cover-Up*, Bessell was so verbose that he could spin out the events of a few hours into a whole chapter – sometimes it seemed that the only detail missing was the brand of toothpaste he used – but he was reticent about his shop in Paignton, probably because even he could not make a tailor's shop in a sleepy Devon town sound high-powered.[6]

He joined the local Liberal Association, more for the social life than the politics. In 1953, Coronation Year, he organised, as he put it self-effacingly, 'an elaborate pageant of Britain's history' which produced a handsome profit for charity. Two years later destiny beckoned: 'When the Liberal candidate withdrew on the eve of the 1955 general election the Torquay Liberal Association turned to me because of my local fame as an amateur pageant producer,' he wrote.

Bessell came third in the poll and contemplated withdrawing from politics, but six months later the Conservative MP died. He decided to fight the by-election, with the help of big-name Liberals such as Jo Grimond and a rising star called Jeremy Thorpe. Despite their help – Thorpe drove through the town in an old van equipped with loudspeakers, urging the voters to back Bessell – he was third again when the results were declared in December. He had always feared that Torquay would remain impregnably Conservative and decided to hunt for a seat which he had a realistic chance of winning. He chose Bodmin in south-east Cornwall and in 1956 moved Pauline and his children there, leaving behind in Torquay the distressed creditors who were the first victims of Peter Bessell, visionary businessman.

The alliance between Thorpe and Bessell grew in strength after their first meeting in Torquay in 1955. They enjoyed each other's company but, more importantly, they also needed each other. Thorpe was always surrounded by acolytes, who could be trusted to perform delicate tasks or share confidences, but Bessell was more than just a lackey. He looked as if he might make a great deal of money, some of which would undoubtedly slosh towards Thorpe, and was also a useful ally in the West Country. Bessell knew that becoming an MP would provide him with much-needed weight as a businessman; he once said that the letters 'MP' attached to a name were worth more than stocks and shares. He was not certain, though, that he would make it to the Commons, but he was convinced that Thorpe had been sprinkled with the dust of political good fortune and would not just reach the Commons but, once there, would rise fast. Hence, he resolved to stick close to him.

Meanwhile, he had two concerns: to make serious money and to win Bodmin. He expanded what he called his 'investment brokerage business' to the United States. His first sure-fire money-spinner, however, was a flop. He had dreamt of building a chain of motels across Britain, close to tourist centres. He formed a company, Travellers Inns Ltd, and told a credulous media that he was in the process of raising the necessary £1,600,000 (*1995 equivalent: £28,000,000*) in the States. He flitted back and forth across the Atlantic, the epitome of the man who was going places in the world. But the motel dream crumbled. Next, he turned to Heathrow, where he wanted to build a luxury hotel. Once again, the project came to nothing. There were many other 'solid and exceptional' ideas, including the manufacture of plastic egg-cartons, which foundered. He said that it was not his fault: 'I did not lack the ability to discern marketable projects. I lacked the capital to exploit them.'

While he struggled to make a fortune he also wooed the electors of Bodmin. He had the backing of Isaac Foot, then in his seventies, who had twice been Bodmin's Liberal MP before the war and whose popularity, based on honesty, Methodism and temperance, was undiminished. Foot told Bessell that he could rely on what he called 'the Bible Christian vote' providing he conducted himself in the correct manner. So Bessell spent his Sundays in Cornwall in church and chapel. When he was in London, however, and unknown to his prospective constituents, he relaxed with a new girlfriend. 'I accept that my attitude to sex would have been anathema to most members of my congregations, but the Christian Church is an imperfect instrument of its Founder's purpose,' he said.

To the Cornish Bessell was a successful businessman, devout Christian and hard-working Liberal candidate. It was not only the humble voters in the small towns and villages who were conned; he was embraced by the old Liberal aristocracy, headed by Viscount Clifden.

Like most heterosexuals of his generation Bessell assumed that every man found women sexually stimulating. But, in the eighteen months before the general election of 1959, Bessell began to suspect that there was something different about his new ally, Jeremy. Frank Owen, the former Fleet Street editor and failed Liberal candidate in the Hereford by-election in 1956, who had been lured into a business partnership with Bessell, was the first to express openly what was rumoured amongst well-connected West Country Liberals. He told Bessell that he believed that Thorpe was a homosexual and that, if this became generally known, it would severely damage his chances in the forthcoming election. Other Liberals suggested that young Thorpe should marry or, failing that, be seen to be sowing some healthy wild oats.

Bessell tucked away these little stories for future use and gathered his own intelligence:

Jeremy was now 30, medium height, slimly built and with thick dark hair. Although not good-looking in the conventional sense, he had strong expressive features which, combined with the warmth of his forceful personality, made him extraordinarily attractive. If he remained too boyish to seem ready to settle down to married life, this did not alter the fact that he was the kind of eligible young bachelor who is normally surrounded by equally eligible young spinsters. His most frequent companion was his mother and it was all too obvious that he had no interest in girls. This might not have mattered if he had not sometimes been accompanied by younger men who had no apparent interest in politics.

These were early days in Bessell's quest to discover if Thorpe was a homosexual. He continued to sniff for evidence during and after the 1959 election. He made a mental note, for example, when his wife, Pauline, told him about Thorpe's behaviour at a Liberal garden party at Viscount Clifden's home, Lanhydrock:

> Jeremy arrived with a young man whom he introduced as a friend from North Devon. Jeremy was off-guard, and as he walked round the fruit and produce stalls, he paid more attention to the young man than to Liberal workers and visitors. A number of people spoke to Pauline about it and after a while she took action. Pauline never minced words. She took Jeremy on one side and told him his relationship with the man was obvious. She was not criticising Jeremy's personal life but she said, 'You can do what you like in North Devon, but not in Bodmin. Please send that young man away.' Jeremy, who as a rule did not take kindly to anything that could be interpreted as criticism, unprotestingly did as Pauline asked and for the remainder of the afternoon behaved as though nothing unusual had happened.

But outside these Liberal circles Thorpe was still seen as a dashing young man who was sure to go far. Chris Drake, who later became a BBC correspondent in the Middle East, was a reporter on the *Journal Herald* in Barnstaple. He said, 'None of us had a clue that he was gay. There was just no hint of it and Devon was a small village in those days. I was stunned when it all came out. He was brilliant. Everyone down there loved him.'[7]

In October 1959 Bessell hugged Thorpe and congratulated him on becoming North Devon's first Liberal MP since 1935. Thorpe assured Bessell that he would shortly be joining him in the Commons. But, as they laughed and joked, Bessell knew by now that Thorpe had a potentially fatal flaw. He was not prejudiced against homosexuals; indeed, as a man who regarded sex as second in importance only to money he was sympathetic to men for whom sex, albeit of a strange variety, was also a dominant feature of their lives. But that was irrelevant. Homosexuality was illegal and a public figure who was exposed as a homosexual would be ruined. He also knew that Thorpe would need advice and protection. And who was better equipped to offer this than Peter Bessell? So he stuck close. As an MP Thorpe was 'desperately short of money' and was grateful when Bessell invited him to join his latest company, Manhattan Equipment Ltd, which sold felt-tip pens. Later, the two worked together at Drinkmaster Ltd, which distributed hot-drink vending machines.

Finally, in the general election of October 1964 Bessell acquired the invaluable letters 'MP' after his name. He described his victory with typical modesty:

> I fought an all-out campaign. My name was plastered on hundreds of billboards. The windows in thousands of houses displayed my picture. I barnstormed through the towns and villages making as many as twenty speeches a day from a gaudily decorated Land Rover, which at night was illuminated by floodlights. The Saturday before the election a cavalcade of hundreds of cars tied up traffic throughout the constituency. It was blatant showmanship, backed up by superb organisation.

Bessell quickly settled into the Commons. First, he decided that he needed a mistress. He boasted that he found one when he advertised for a secretary: 'Diana Stainton was in her early 20s with medium blonde hair, striking brown eyes and an expressively sensuous mouth. As we talked she crossed her legs exposing the top of her stocking and part of her beautifully shaped thigh. If she knew where my eyes had strayed she made no attempt to adjust her skirt. I engaged her instantly.' A few days later, Bessell bragged, 'She was like a small tigress in my arms and in a few moments we were in bed,' though it has to be emphasised, Stainton was a respectable woman and there is no evidence, apart from Bessell's own claim, that she had an intimate relationship with him.

For the benefit of people who were not endowed with his remarkable sexual energy he explained:

> My relationship with Diana was by no means my first act of marital infidelity, nor was it to be my last. Like Jeremy, my extraordinary physical and mental energy was coupled to a desire for conquest in many things. Politics was one, although

that had safe roots in ideals and principles from which I did not waver. But it also found expression in my irresistible desire to possess, often quite briefly, sexually attractive women, and the willing response of many of them flattered my ego. By most people's standards my conduct was grossly at variance with other aspects of my life and certainly with the public image I created. Yet it would be hypocritical to pretend I regret my behaviour or that I believe it was particularly immoral. For me, women were the most beautiful of all creations, and I adored them.

Bessell was determined to move even closer to Thorpe, who, by the spring of 1964, was obviously Jo Grimond's natural successor. So, he moved in for the kill: 'I realised Jeremy and I had never talked openly about sex and that gave me an idea. The best approach would be to rip aside my own defences. Then he might respond by telling me something about himself.' He steered the conversation to his new secretary, Diana Stainton. Thorpe asked, 'Is she any good?' Bessell replied, 'Yes, particularly in bed.' Thorpe laughed.

Bessell said that he was not sure how to raise the subject of homosexuality:

I could not risk a direct question which might end the conversation. So, I babbled on about myself. I said that sex was a hobby. I said that some people collected stamps, played golf or bred horses. I liked screwing. Of course, I said, when I was young it was more difficult. I told Jeremy, 'Years ago nice girls didn't get into bed with you unless you married them first.'

Thorpe took the bait. He asked, 'So what did you do?' Bessell admitted that he could have told the truth and let Thorpe wriggle free; instead he reeled him in and said, 'In those days I still had homosexual tendencies.' Then he concocted a story about his fictitious homosexual tendencies, which delighted Thorpe, who ordered port to celebrate the heart-warming admission that the Member for Bodmin also liked going to bed with men. Bessell continued:

It had come as a relief to him that I was bi-sexual, but he

hesitated to unmask the side of his life of which, I was eventually to realise, he lived in constant fear. He started cautiously: 'When I was at Oxford, I had homosexual tendencies. Of course that was a long time ago but I suppose people like us never quite lose it, do they?' Now I had broken through. He relaxed totally and leaned forward again. His eyes twinkled and he spoke in a half-whisper: 'Peter, we're nothing but a pair of old queens!' We lifted our glasses again, tapped them and drank. Immediately I regretted what I had done. I had achieved my objective but now I had to overcome my guilt for having extracted it from him by trickery.

'Tell me,' said Jeremy, 'what would you say you are – fifty/fifty?'

'No,' I said quickly. 'I would say more like eighty/twenty.'

'Eighty/twenty – which way? Do you mean eighty or twenty per cent gay?' The term 'gay' was hardly in use in those days . . .

'Oh, I mean eighty per cent – for girls.'

It was his turn to confide, to put me at ease. 'It's the other way with me. I'm eighty per cent gay.'

I was able to respond honestly to this by saying it did not matter anyway. Jeremy's mood changed instantly. He said it mattered a great deal. It was easier for me because I was married, but what would they say in places like Lostwithiel (a small Methodist town in Cornwall, where homosexuality was regarded as a hideous vice found only in ungodly places like London) if they knew he was gay?

I had to admit he was right. For most of the older Liberals it would have been regarded as the worst form of original sin. I said what made it ludicrous was that a man could have half a dozen mistresses and get away with it. Jeremy replied, 'They wouldn't like that either in Lostwithiel.' Again he was right. The most positive thing now was that we were both vulnerable. I began to feel better. Although I had deceived Jeremy I had also disclosed my own weakness. We were on common ground. I told him that the most important thing was that they should not find out about us.

He agreed: 'We've done pretty well so far. Nobody in the House knows about me.'

I asked, 'Would anyone here care?'

He said, 'Yes, neither of us could ever be Leader of the Party if they found out.'

I said firmly, 'Very well, we shall have to make sure that no one ever finds out.'

The effect of my words, implying as they did a pledge of total loyalty, was dramatic.

'You're right,' he said fiercely. 'And, by Christ, Peter, we'll see that they never do!

On a Monday morning early in April 1965 Thorpe telephoned Bessell in Mayfair, where he had rented what he called 'a suite of offices' and invited him to lunch at the Ritz Hotel, which Bessell thought was odd since they were both members of the National Liberal and Reform Clubs. But Thorpe said that he wanted to discuss a highly confidential matter and did not want to risk being overheard.

Bessell met Thorpe in the foyer and they strolled into the dining room, which overlooked Green Park. He ushered Bessell to an isolated table and they sat down. They ordered their food and then Thorpe handed Bessell the seventeen-page letter which Josiffe had sent Ursula Thorpe from Ireland. Bessell thumbed through it slowly, feigning horror at the allegations but privately thrilled that he was the confidant of Jeremy Thorpe, future leader of the Liberal Party. Bessell said, 'It was in many ways a pathetic document and was the sort of letter a jilted woman might write to her former lover; a mixture of reproach, sorrow and affection. But I read into it, correctly as it transpired, a potential threat.'

Bessell pressed Thorpe for background so he could decide the best course. First, he asked, had he slept with the man? Thorpe stared bleakly and mumbled, 'Yes.' Then he said that anyone would have been tempted by the sight of the young Norman.

Bessell understood perfectly: 'I was immediately aware that whatever he felt later, Jeremy had genuinely cared for Josiffe. I had experienced similar situations with women for whom I felt an instant passion, which translated as love until I regained my senses. Then came the difficult and delicate task of breaking-off the short-lived tumultuous romances while avoiding, as far as possible, hurting the girl.'

Then Thorpe showed Bessell his draft letter, which threatened Josiffe with legal action if he repeated the allegations of the Dublin letter. Bessell shook his head vigorously and said that on no account should Thorpe use the law. He reminded him of the fate of Oscar Wilde, who had brought a libel action against the Marquess of Queensberry in 1895 and had ended up being jailed for buggery. This little history lesson did not please Thorpe: 'Then, what the hell am I to do?' he said.

Bessell tried to be positive and said that it was the word of an MP against that of a man with a history of mental illness. Thorpe looked uneasy and said that he had written letters which might, possibly, be misinterpreted if they were published in a newspaper.

Secretly, Bessell was delighted. He was the one man who could save Thorpe's career, which offered mouth-watering prospects for intrigue and advancement for Peter Bessell.

Thorpe told him that Josiffe was living in Dublin with a busy-body Jesuit priest called Father Michael Sweetman. Bessell offered to fly to Dublin later that week. Thorpe nodded and instructed him to threaten Josiffe with criminal charges, perhaps for blackmail. At the same time he should tell Father Sweetman that Josiffe was lying. Bessell said:

> His reaction was extraordinary. My proposed trip was nothing more than a reconnoitre, but his edginess disappeared and he proceeded to turn his attention to lunch with all the enthusiasm of a weight-watcher who has been told to abandon his diet. He had ordered steak tartare. He mixed oil and vinegar vigorously for his salad and then, after stirring the egg into raw chopped meat, rapidly devoured the lot. That day at the Ritz I witnessed the element of the spoiled child which remained with him throughout manhood. Jeremy believed he no longer needed to worry about Norman Josiffe since he had passed the problem over to me.

A few days later Bessell telephoned Thorpe and told him that he was booked on an Aer Lingus flight to Dublin and that he would be staying at the excellent Intercontinental Hotel. After he had checked in at the hotel Bessell set off to confront Josiffe at Father Sweetman's home in Milltown Park. Sweetman came to the door himself and invited Bessell into the living room. Far from being doddering, other-worldly and easy prey Sweetman was 'in his late 40s, had clear steady eyes, and was obviously a man of

strong character and integrity'. Sweetman said that Josiffe was
no longer staying with him; he had found the poor lad a room
in an area called Ballsbridge. Bessell did his best for Thorpe; he
showed Sweetman the letter Josiffe had sent to Mrs Thorpe and
suggested that he was a fantasist. But Sweetman said that Bessell
was mistaken. And, if it was all rubbish, why had a busy Member
of Parliament flown all the way from London?

Bessell tried again. He said that the letter amounted to blackmail.
Again, Sweetman was not impressed. He said that, as far he could
tell, it was nothing more than the truth. Then, to Bessell's relief,
he said that he had told Josiffe to forget the past and start his life
again. The meeting had not gone as well as Bessell would have
liked – ideally Sweetman would have denounced Josiffe – but
he had been conciliatory and, most importantly, was counselling
Norman to forget Thorpe, which was excellent.

Bessell set off to track down Norman. He found the room in
Ballsbridge but Josiffe was out, so he left a note, asking him
to telephone the hotel urgently. At 3 a.m. that morning Bessell
was woken by Josiffe; Bessell said that it was imperative they
met. He said that he was catching a flight back to London in
the morning and invited Josiffe to breakfast at his hotel. That
morning in the restaurant Bessell was pleasantly surprised when
he saw the stooped six-foot figure; he had dark rings under his
eyes, looked like he needed a hot meal and seemed much older
than twenty-five. Josiffe was inexpensively but tidily dressed,
which pleased Bessell, who liked men who took pride in their
appearance. He had a clammy handshake, which was also good,
because it meant that he was nervous. Josiffe, for his part, thought
that Bessell was 'very dynamic' in his immaculate dark suit, with
matching briefcase.

Bessell took control immediately by telling Josiffe that he had
a plane to catch and that they would have to talk in the taxi. He
warned him to refer to Thorpe only by his initials, in case the
driver eavesdropped.

I told Josiffe that Jeremy had given me the letter Josiffe had
written to Jeremy's mother and that in my view it constituted
a blackmail threat. I said that blackmail was an extraditable
offence and if Jeremy or I reported the facts to Sir Frank
Soskice, the Home Secretary, which was the best course
for an MP to take, I had no doubt that he would order a

police inquiry which might result in an application to the Irish Courts for an extradition order.

This was rubbish but he hoped that Josiffe would be shaken. He was not and announced: 'Well, that's marvellous, I can come back to England and get the whole matter sorted out.' Later Norman explained what had been going through his mind: 'Perhaps I shouldn't have said that but it was a way of sorting out my Insurance card. I thought maybe I would have to appear in court but at least things would be done. I mean, I was so totally despondent about it, I had no identity.'

This was not the response which Bessell had expected. Then Josiffe said that he had over fifty letters and other documents. He said that many were in his suitcase, which was missing somewhere in Europe. The size of this documentary cache surprised Bessell, who had thought that Thorpe had only written a few easily retrieved letters. Then there was worse news; Josiffe added casually that he had given the police in Chelsea some letters just before Christmas 1962. This was the first Bessell knew of the police's involvement in the saga.

Bessell changed tack and became sympathetic. He said that he agreed with Father Sweetman; Norman must forgive and forget. He said that he would help recover the suitcase and Norman's Insurance card; he also hinted that, as a high-flying MP and businessman, he might be able to arrange a job for him in the United States.

As they arrived at the airport Bessell handed him £5 for the return journey into the city. Overall, Bessell thought, it had been a successful trip. 'I boarded the flight satisfied. As I told Jeremy later, I believed the situation was safely contained. Josiffe, who looked so pitiful when I left him, had learned his lesson and would cause no further trouble. I was fortified by Father Sweetman's determination to persuade him to forget the past.'

Thorpe was delighted with Bessell's intervention and, as a token of his gratitude, presented him with a handsome gold cigarette lighter.

Thorpe's celebrations were premature. Bessell had barely had time to unpack his overnight bag when a letter arrived from Josiffe, which he read with a sinking heart. Josiffe was not strong on punctuation or grammar but was obviously not going to be fobbed off with threats about extraditions or homilies about forgiveness. He wrote:

Dear Mr Bessell,
    I have been to see Father Sweetman, and he tells me you were on the telephone to him last Tuesday and had told him you would endeavour to have the luggage sent as soon as possible to Milltown Park – thank you so very much Mr Bessell, I do hope you realised on meeting me that my intention has never been to do Jeremy any harm, regardless of how it looks. But I was so worried and in consequence having tried everything else thought Mrs Thorpe would perhaps have helped – I really did think she knew.
    Please try to understand how very complicated my life is with this 'disease' and also that I would never have written to Mrs Thorpe had things been different. Once again I can only say I am terribly sorry but unless you know the whole story how can you believe me.
    When you had gone I felt so worried about the whole affair and also rather sick as I feel that, as I told you, if somebody tells you something viz: they do care for you (This looks so silly) then it is so much more of a shock when something like this happens. Jeremy once lent me a book called *Giovanni's Room* by James Baldwin – a passage in it reads: '. . . as likened to an electric socket, and a light. Contact and there is light remove the plug and the light goes out. When there is a fuse there is contact but no light.' This reads rather oddly but its how I felt on leaving you. For those five years I have *nothing* at all to show at all. My life is so meaningless and when I thought that you were going to take me back to England, I didn't care. I felt that once all the 'dirt' that people have whispered about me for these years was dragged out and given an airing then with a fresh start perhaps I could have made a go of life. Which after a doctors help may have been normal and Heterosexual.
    I want so much to forget the past. All the things that have happened I must forget or I have no chance. You spoke of going to the States and how you could arrange to get me there. Perhaps a fresh start in a New Country may not be a bad idea. Father Sweetman seems to think that from a basic religious point of view I should be as well off. Though I love

Dublin, and all that it has to offer. The one thing it's impossible to get is a job. This is so sad because I know I could have made a success of life here. As you know if one hasn't got a degree it's impossible to get any sort of job (impossible anyway here and in England) where one's talents can be usefully employed. The more mundane and ordinary jobs people look at you and say 'Oh but you wouldn't like that' or 'Oh no, I'm looking for someone younger or older' when all they mean is who is this chap and why is he looking for a job like this?

It's all so difficult. Equity always has the hardy perennial – don't ring us we'll ring you! So what will happen? I have moved into a flat which only costs £3.00 and have therefore reduced my living from £15.00 to about £7.00. If only something would turn up I would be able to manage, I know. Also that things can't go on much longer in this way. Could one advertise in the *New York Times* Educated English Man or what do you have in mind? Also you did say something with regard to a job in Cornwall. Though as I said to you I really would be happier in a 'Catholic' country.

Mr Bessell. I don't really know what you think of me. I know I'm very mixed up but I do so need a help and a start and would really work so hard given the opportunity. Therefore please believe in me and understand that I would never have wittingly caused all this trouble. Please forgive me for writing on this envelope but I am in the garden at Milltown Park and there is no more paper. I am going to try so hard to find something. If you do hear of anything please will you let me know. Father Sweetman is still giving me money and I feel so guilty . . . Also he told me yesterday that he was halfway through the 'Coffers' – So you see I must get something.

I'm so sorry with regard to all this 'mess'. But I don't really know what to do. Please excuse the 'paper' once again.
Yrs sincerely,
Norman (L.J.).

Bessell replied with the encouraging news that the suitcase was in the process of being retrieved from Switzerland. He repeated his offer to help Josiffe find a job but added: 'There is one thing I must impress upon you again, and it is that you must cease to talk in such nonsensical terms about your relationship with Jeremy

Thorpe. As I have told you, I cannot and do not accept your version of the story, whereas I am quite certain that Mr Thorpe's version of it is true.'[8]

Bessell calculated that this mixture of compassion and paternal rigour was exactly what Josiffe needed. He was mistaken. A few days later he received a letter from Sweetman: 'Josiffe is in real difficulties about his luggage, etc. I wonder if there is anything you can do about all this: I am at my wit's end and as you know have limited personal resources. He has had no success in finding work. I wonder what is to be the end of it!'[9]

Even Bessell, who had a high opinion of his abilities to sort out messes, was beginning to realise the problem. Josiffe was the human embodiment of a swamp; he seemed harmless until you moved close and found yourself being dragged under.

On 30 April 1965 Bessell dictated a letter to Diana Stainton, his secretary. He told Josiffe that he had to go abroad and added that Miss Stainton was 'fully conversant' with the missing suitcase, which was now, he had been assured, making its return journey from Switzerland. He enclosed a £5 note to help Josiffe until he started the part-time job with horses which he had said he had just found. Bessell flew off to New York in yet another attempt to placate the disgruntled creditors who could not see that visionaries like him always experienced minor setbacks as they marched towards fame and fortune.

Stainton now decided to join the Josiffe letter-writing society. The £5 note had gone missing and she enclosed a cheque to Father Sweetman for the same amount, adding, 'I hope by the time this letter arrives, Norman's luggage will also have arrived. I don't think you should have any trouble at the Customs, as they went through the suitcase with a fine toothcomb this end.'[10]

Bessell telephoned from New York, where he had just gone to bed with 'a girl of Lithuanian parentage of astonishing beauty and broad-based knowledge and intelligence', and told Stainton to collect the suitcase as soon as it arrived from Switzerland. When it arrived at Victoria Station she left a message for Thorpe, who called her back that night. She said, 'It was an unusual telephone call and Jeremy had never rung me before at my flat and, indeed, he never rang me on any other occasion at my flat or in my office. He started the call in an unusual manner by saying, "Diana, darling, are you in a gorgeous négligé?"'

Next day Stainton and Thorpe drove to Victoria and collected the suitcase. Then they went to his flat at Marsham Court where, to Diana's astonishment, he forced open the suitcase. Stuffed amongst an assortment of clothes were the letters, neatly tied in two bundles, which he had sent to Josiffe. He took them out and slammed the suitcase shut before disappearing into the bathroom.

Satisfied that the suitcase now contained nothing that could embarrass him, Thorpe drove Stainton to the Aer Lingus office. There, on 13 May 1965, she made out the labels to ensure that the suitcase would be reunited with its owner while Thorpe paid the air-freight charge of £3. 17s. 8d.

Norman was not happy when he opened his suitcase in Dublin: 'I was pleased to have all my possessions back. But when I looked inside the case all the letters and everything to do with my staying at Marsham Court, like shirts and laundry marks, had all disappeared. I thought someone had forced the lock and taken the letters. I was very worried because I thought it could be a blackmailer. I became terribly despondent again.'[11]

In London Bessell asked Thorpe if it was true that he had stolen Josiffe's letters; it was, he said, and he was glad that he had done so. Bessell frowned at the thought of someone's belongings being pillaged in this disgraceful manner, but then he smiled and decided that, on balance, it had been a jolly good idea because Josiffe now had no evidence to support his fantastic claims; he could say what he liked and no one would believe him.

But he overlooked one crucial fact: Thorpe could not forget Norman, any more than Norman could forget him.

CHAPTER SIX

A few days after Thorpe had ransacked Norman's suitcase, Bessell popped into his office at Westminster to gossip and plan their glittering future. He thought that Thorpe would be cheerful now that he had, finally, retrieved his love letters and rendered Josiffe harmless. But Thorpe told Bessell that there was a new crisis. He said that a Liberal activist in North Devon had tipped him off that the police in Barnstaple were investigating his relationship with Norman. Bessell was stunned. 'Christ Almighty,' he said, as his mind raced to absorb the implications of an inquiry by incorruptible policemen in the West Country.

Then Thorpe reluctantly volunteered more details about his friendship with Josiffe. According to Bessell, he admitted for the first time that in 1962 Josiffe had given police in Chelsea several love letters and The Postcard. 'It was the most alarming news Jeremy had given me: Norman Josiffe subjected to police interrogation; and a postcard involving members of the Royal Family. Jeremy said, "One of the letters was descriptive. I said how it felt to screw him. And that I cared a lot about him and that all I wanted was to spend the rest of my life alone with him on a Devon farm,"' Bessell said.

He told Bessell that they had to ensure that the police in North Devon did not find out about the letters and The Postcard which, he hoped, had been lost somewhere in the bowels of Scotland Yard. He waited for Bessell, the fixer, to come up with a solution.

Bessell pondered. Then he had a brilliant idea: George Thomas, Labour MP for Cardiff and a minister at the Home Office. Thomas, Speaker of the House of Commons from 1976 until 1983, was a Methodist and a former National President of the Brotherhood Movement, an interdenominational organisation in which Bessell was also prominent, despite his colourful private life.

Thorpe slapped himself with delight. Bessell said later, 'That decision was a watershed. In seeking Thomas's help I had in mind that the Home Office could stop the police inquiry and that was my objective. It was the first act in what is usually referred to these days as a "cover-up".'

Bessell wrote Thomas a note, asking if they could meet, but next day they bumped into each other in the Tea Room at the Commons. He did not tell Thomas the truth; he said that while Thorpe might, perhaps, once have been silly it would be a tragedy if the career of one of the Commons' soaring stars was wrecked because of a minor indiscretion many years ago. Ideally, Bessell would have liked Thomas to order the police to drop their investigation: 'I thought to myself: It's no good asking him to do that because I damn well know he will shit himself on the spot. I said to him, "Well, do you think it would be better if I saw the Home Secretary?" He agreed at once and said he would arrange that.'

Bessell thought that he had done well but Thorpe did not agree. He ranted that the Josiffe file had to be destroyed before the Conservatives, who, he said, hated him, returned to power and used the file to destroy him.

A few days later Sir Frank Soskice, the Home Secretary, met Bessell in his office in the Commons. This was unusual; Cabinet ministers rarely entertained MPs and, when they did, an aide always took notes of the discussion. But Soskice was alone that day, which Bessell thought proved that Labour rated Thorpe highly. Soskice was a former lawyer who also represented a Welsh constituency, Newport in Monmouthshire. He was not a well man but possessed an agile mind and was respected on all sides of the Commons. He favoured legalising homosexuality between consenting adults, which encouraged Bessell, given the nature of the problem with Josiffe.

Bessell explained the problem: Jeremy was being pursued by a ghastly man, who had written to Ursula Thorpe claiming that he had had a homosexual affair with her son. Soskice nodded sagely, which Bessell took as confirming that he had read the police file on Thorpe. They moved on to the investigation in North Devon, which Soskice said would not lead anywhere: 'Unless the police in Barnstaple find something to connect Jeremy with this creature Josiffe, it would be unusual for them to extend their inquiries. It is important to keep Jeremy apart from this wretched creature. Don't allow him to get a hold over Jeremy. Tell him to go to hell. Get rid of him.'

Bessell was heartened. Soskice was not promising anything but it was obvious that no one wanted to see the new Liberal star embarrassed by 'this nasty little homosexual'. Soskice added that it was vital that Thorpe had nothing more to do with Josiffe: 'If he doesn't do that, then there might be circumstances in which he couldn't be helped.'

The meeting had gone splendidly, yet Bessell was now beginning to fear that Thorpe was locked in some strange combat to the death with Josiffe.

Once again, Thorpe was not satisfied. He told Bessell that he had expected an assurance from Soskice that the file, containing the letters and The Postcard, would be destroyed.

Bessell decided that he would just have to lie to Thorpe to shut him up. After further brief talks with Soskice and Thomas, where both said that there was no need for Thorpe to worry, providing he kept away from Josiffe, Bessell announced that the file had been shredded. Thorpe beamed and said, 'Marvellous.'

Meanwhile, Bessell worked hard to destroy what remained of Josiffe's credibility. On 26 May 1965 he wrote to Father Sweetman after he had been sent a bill from the Iona Guest House in Dublin, forwarded to him at the request of the Honourable Norman Lianche-Josiffe: 'Further troubles over this wretched boy: as you will see from the enclosed, he is now trying to make me responsible for his debts. This coincides hideously with Mr Thorpe's experience, and I suppose it is only a matter of time before you or somebody else is placed in a similar position. Frankly, I have lost patience, and if you are managing to retain yours, then I think you should be canonised!'

A few weeks later Sweetman replied. He said that Norman had complained that important personal items were missing from his suitcase and asked if anyone had interfered with it *en route* to Ireland. Bessell was curt: 'I can hardly imagine my secretary rifling the contents of his suitcase, and I am sure he received it in exactly the same state as when it left Switzerland. I only hope that he will manage to keep a job of some sort, and that he will not leave too great a trail of victims in his wake.'

By the early summer Bessell was congratulating himself that Josiffe had been neutralised. Sweetman had lost patience with Josiffe and government ministers had assured him, albeit in code, that Thorpe had nothing to fear. Thorpe now told Bessell about another worrying development. He said that a Liberal supporter had been passing Barnstaple police station and had picked up some litter which had fallen out of a dustbin. Amongst the debris were the remnants of a police report on his relationship with Josiffe. This anonymous Liberal had pieced together the fragments of paper and deciphered a name, James Collier, the prospective Liberal parliamentary candidate for Tiverton who, with his wife Mary, had entertained Josiffe for several exhausting months in 1961 at Thorpe's request. Thorpe ordered Bessell to find out what the Colliers had told the police.

Bessell was not sure that Thorpe was telling the truth; in the space of a few weeks, various un-named Liberals in North Devon had apparently discovered that the police were investigating Thorpe and had then loyally tipped him off. But Thorpe was the future leader of the Liberal Party and Bessell was determined to remain the confidant whom Jeremy would have to reward because he knew so much. So, he headed off to the West Country to debrief the Colliers. They met in the Clarence Hotel, Exeter. He told them that Josiffe had written an unpleasant letter to Thorpe's mother but omitted to mention his visit to Dublin, the ransacking of Norman's suitcase and his chats with Home Office ministers. Nor did he tell them about the rubbish-bin tip-off. They did not say anything about the police and Bessell did not ask them, which was curious since that was the purpose of his trip to the West Country.

They were not sure why Bessell had wanted to see them so urgently but were left with the impression that he was asking them to lie about Josiffe. They did not care for this and, as a result, Jimmy Collier resigned from the Liberal Party. In a letter to his local newspaper, the *Western Morning News* in Plymouth, he said that he no longer had confidence in the two West Country Liberal MPs, Peter Bessell and Jeremy Thorpe. Mary Collier said, 'Jimmy was very upset about Josiffe. He didn't like what was happening. Lying didn't go down well with him.'[1] Collier's resignation made no impact on either the Liberal Party in London or the national press. But the forced departure of Peter Bessell, MP for Bodmin, from Parliament would have been a major story.

The Commons was preparing to adjourn for the recess in August when Bessell sat down and checked the accounts of his various businesses. He realised that he was facing imminent bankruptcy, though naturally he did not think it was his fault. This would be a grave setback to his hopes of becoming a millionaire but it would also mean that he would have to resign from the Commons, since bankrupts could not be MPs. He turned to Thorpe, who told him that it would devastate the Party if he went in such ignominious circumstances; he told Bessell that he would find a solution.

There was a sub-plot here, which had nothing to do with the welfare of the Party. There was a tacit understanding between the two men; Bessell knew too much to be dumped and Thorpe needed a fixer who could move quickly if Josiffe surfaced again. Bessell had dealt with Josiffe and now it was Thorpe's turn to save him. Thus Thorpe persuaded a wealthy Liberal, the Reverend Timothy Beaumont, later Beaumont of Whitley, to lend Bessell £5,000 (*worth about £50,000 in 1995*). Then, in the first week of August, as Londoners were grumbling about the heat that made it impossible to sleep at night, Bessell told Thorpe that he needed another injection of funds. This time he calculated he needed £15,000 (*equivalent to £150,0000 in 1995*). Beaumont reluctantly agreed to lend Bessell another £5,000, providing that he raised the other £10,000 (*worth £100,000 in 1995*) himself. Thorpe suggested that Sir Felix Brunner, a past President of the Party, might be sympathetic. Brunner was on a Mediterranean cruise with his wife and, coincidentally, was due to dock in Corfu on the same day that Thorpe was scheduled to begin his summer holiday on the Greek mainland.

Thorpe and Bessell flew to Corfu, where they persuaded Brunner to 'lend' £10,000 for the good of the Party. Bessell was safe now and the two men flew to Athens, where Thorpe was meeting his holiday companion, David Holmes.

Bessell liked what he saw when they had dinner in a restaurant at the foot of the Parthenon. He wrote:

Tall, slim, with almost black hair and quietly dressed, Holmes typified his profession, merchant banking. I liked his sense of humour ... It was obvious he and Jeremy shared an intimate relationship which they made no attempt to disguise. I welcomed it. He was the kind of man I had expected Jeremy would find attractive and, unlike Norman Josiffe, would certainly not endanger his career. He was quiet-voiced and apparently unemotional. His hobbies were music, particularly the operas of Mozart, and collecting small antiques. His youthful appearance owed much to his well-ordered way of life. He had no more than average intelligence and I thought would not be reliable in an emergency.

Next day Bessell headed off to Nice to collect his £5,000 from Beaumont. (Beaumont complained later that his loans were never repaid.[2])

A less determined and ambitious man would have been fatally distracted by rumours of police investigations, the limpet-like Josiffe and Bessell's overdrafts. But Thorpe forgot these problems as he pursued the prize that he had always craved: the leadership of the Liberal Party.

He knew that Jo Grimond's hold on the Party was weakening. Since the general election of October 1964, when the Liberals had polled over 3 million votes but won only nine seats in the Commons, the Party had slipped badly. David Steel had become the tenth Liberal MP when he won the Roxburgh by-election in March 1965 but that had been the only triumph; in other by-elections, local-government elections and in the opinion polls the Liberals were being squeezed as the country reverted to its usual two-party mentality. The Liberals had no money and were finding it hard to muster new bright candidates for the election which everyone assumed that Harold Wilson, the Labour Prime Minister, would have to call shortly in an effort to win a workable majority.

At the Party conference at Scarborough in September 1965 Grimond tried to give the Party a new direction when he said that he would consider a pact with Labour, providing they could agree long-term policies.[3] Many Liberals were outraged by the idea of a formal alliance with the devil socialists, which left Grimond wondering whether there was any point leading a party that would rather remain an irrelevant rump than sacrifice a sliver of its ideological purity.

As the Party tore itself apart over the proposed link with Labour Thorpe quietly pounced when he ousted the national treasurer, Sir Andrew Murray, a former Lord Provost of Edinburgh. Since the early 1960s he had been running his own secret fund, which he spent on constituencies which he thought the Liberals had a chance of winning; now, as treasurer, he was determined to extend that influence and prove that he was the man who could raise the money that the Liberals needed to fight the two giants on their own terms.

To the horror of the idealists he said that he did not care where the money came from; traditional Liberals thought that money

from big business was 'dirty' but Thorpe dismissed this as naive
nonsense and told Trevor Jones, later Sir Trevor, Liberal President
from 1972 to 1973, 'Give me dirty money and I will clean it.'⁴
After his first year as treasurer, cash from appeals and gifts had
jumped by over 50 per cent, yet expenditure had also risen by
virtually the same figure. This was the pattern of his career: he
was a brilliant fund-raiser but insisted that you had to spend big
to achieve anything. When he became treasurer he appointed four
unpaid deputies: Leonard Smith, a Party official who had once,
briefly, employed Josiffe; Hugo Brunner, whose father, Sir Felix,
had 'lent' Bessell £10,000; Stanley Brodie, the lawyer who had
been one of his close friends at Oxford; and David Holmes. Their
precise duties were unclear; in 1995 Brodie could not remember
anything about his fellow deputy treasurers or their work for the
Liberals.

Holmes was the most interesting of the four. Officially, he was
responsible for raising money in Manchester, where he had a
home, but his only contribution to the Party was to procure
new cut-price carpets for the Liberal headquarters in London,
courtesy of a business contact in the North West. Holmes was
born in 1930 in the Yorkshire mill town of Cleckhampton, the
son of a humble clerk and a mother who told him that, no matter
how poor you were, you had to be smartly turned out because a
man was judged by his appearance. He attended the local grammar
school where he was studious rather than clever; nonetheless, he
won a scholarship to Oxford to study Modern History. There he
met, and was entranced by, Thorpe. Gerald Hagan, a television
executive in Manchester who met Holmes in the early 1960s
and lived with him for thirty years, said, 'David and Thorpe
were interested in the same things. Politics. History. David was
politically uncertain at Oxford until he met Thorpe and became
interested in Liberalism.'

Hagan insisted that Holmes had never had an affair with
Thorpe: 'I would know if they had. They were friends and you
don't go around screwing your friends.' He said that, unlike many
homosexuals, Holmes had always been at ease with his sexuality:
'He never pretended to be anything he wasn't. But he wasn't part
of what was called the gay scene. He was a splendid man. He was
gentlemanly and civilized.'⁵

After Oxford, where he gained a poor degree, Holmes took a
postgraduate degree in education at Cambridge. When he was 23

he fell ill with cancer but fought his way back to health. He gave up the idea of teaching and returned to Manchester to try and make his fortune in business. Although he had no qualifications in his chosen field he exuded success, unlike Bessell, who looked as if spent too much time in front of the mirror arranging his hair. Holmes made his way steadily. He specialised in tax and finance and, at one stage, held twenty-four directorships. He also lived stylishly; there was a converted coach house in Salford and a flat in Belgravia. Hagan, however, insisted that there was no money behind the façade: 'We had splendid addresses but they were really just little houses and flats. People thought that we were rich but we weren't.'

By the mid-1960s Holmes was a regular member of Thorpe's entourage in North Devon and at Party conferences, driving him to meetings, barring entry to his hotel room and generally acting as if Thorpe wanted to be shielded from ordinary Liberals. The rank and file in the party could not understand why a wonderful man like him bothered with characters like Holmes, who wore expensive suits and did not have proper jobs.

Hagan was not thrilled by the relationship between Holmes and Thorpe, but he had his career in television and did not interfere. He was adamant that, unlike Thorpe, Holmes led a quiet sexual life. 'He was an intelligent and attractive man and did not need to root about for sex. And, anyway, he was too busy working for that.' This was certainly the impression that Holmes gave to his partner. But it was not the truth. Like Thorpe, Holmes had a taste for cruising the streets: he also went on holidays with Thorpe, where sex with young men was the main recreation.

In March 1966 the Liberals came a poor third in the general election, signalling the beginning of the end for Grimond, who was exhausted by the effort of keeping a semblance of order amongst Liberals who spent more time bickering amongst themselves than fighting the opposition.

Labour won almost a million more votes than in 1964 and now had 363 MPs, a huge majority of ninety-six. The Conservative vote had dropped by over half a million and left them with 253 MPs. The Liberals limped in with less than 2½ million votes, a drop of 700,000 in two years, but, by a quirk of the system, had twelve MPs, three more than were returned in 1964. They included two new boys: John Pardoe, who won North Cornwall,

and Richard Wainwright, who had captured Colne Valley. Thorpe
polled almost 3,000 fewer votes than in 1964 and his majority
had shrunk from 5,136 to 1,166. Bessell also just scraped home
ahead of the Conservatives. It was now only a matter of when,
not if, Grimond resigned. Thorpe consolidated his position as
heir-apparent when he acquired a new, high-profile brief as the
Party spokesman on Commonwealth affairs. This guararanteed
Thorpe as much media attention as Grimond since Harold Wilson
was battling with Ian Smith, Rhodesia's Prime Minister, who had
made his Unilateral Declaration of Independence in the autumn
of the previous year in an attempt to prolong white rule.

Then, uncharacteristically, Thorpe faltered at the Party conference in Brighton in September 1966. The conference was
dominated by two stories: the new militancy of the Young Liberals and Thorpe's extraordinary suggestion that the Government
should bomb the railways in Rhodesia to starve Smith of oil and
force him to negotiate a settlement. Both stories were welcomed
by the Party hierarchy, who were relieved that the conference was
front-page news after years in the publicity wilderness. Mike Steele,
who had just become the Liberals' press officer, was delighted that
the Young Liberals, otherwise known as the Red Guard, were
attracting so much attention, on the principle that any publicity
was better than none. But older Liberals did not agree. They were
appalled by the policies which the Young Liberals tried to force
the conference to adopt. These included motions demanding the
withdrawal of American troops from Vietnam and Britain from
NATO and workers' control of nationalised industries. This was
the start of the long and bloody war between the Young Liberals
and the Party leadership, which reached its height during Thorpe's
reign.[6] Until Brighton the young radicals had dismissed Thorpe
as an Old Etonian opportunist but they thought that his speech
on Rhodesia was splendid, unlike the Liberal leadership, who
wondered if he had gone mad.

Thorpe's acolytes said that this was his own brainwave; his
critics said that, if that was true, it showed that, without his
speechwriters and advisers, he had the political sophistication of
a first-year undergraduate at a bad university. Other Liberals,
however, said that Thorpe had been conned into floating the
idea by a South African agent. Roger Pincham, a successful
businessman who later became Liberal Chairman, blamed a
South African with 'charm and money', who was, he thought,

called Stein. Pincham said, 'He wined and dined people in the Liberal inner circle. Shortly before Thorpe made his speech at Brighton a group of people, including the South African, were in Thorpe's flat in London. He told Thorpe that he had to say something dramatic at the conference about Rhodesia, such as bombing the railways. Then it got late and people stared drifting home. But he stayed there with Thorpe, talking.' A few years later Pincham was told that senior Liberals had proposed Stein for membership of the Reform Club but that he had been deported before he could take his place.[7] But the media did not care who had dreamt up the idea; it was a welcome relief from dreary debates about taxation and the nuclear deterrent.

Thorpe's rivals in the Party were furious. They realised that, though the bombing plan was ridiculous, it had boosted Thorpe; while they toiled away anonymously, debating the future of Liberalism, his grinning face beneath his new nickname 'Bomber' was plastered across the front pages of every national newspaper. He was now the only Liberal anyone outside the Party had ever heard of, apart from Jo Grimond. And, when Grimond did go, it was to hard to see how anyone could stop Thorpe. It was a prospect that appalled many Liberals, who wanted to be led by an intellectual of integrity not by a flashy Old Etonian who had never read a serious book in his life. Even his supporters recognised his limitations. Roger Pincham had no illusions: 'He was certainly not an original thinker. He was a great performer but he needed other people to do his thinking for him, like many politicians. But I think that he was sincere in his own way about Liberalism – it would be quite wrong to see him as man who was just doing it for his glory.'[8]

The moment that Thorpe had dreamt about for so many years came shortly before 10 a.m. on 17 January 1967 when Jo Grimond announced that he was resigning as leader. By the low standards of politics this was not a dirty election. This was partly because the candidates barely had time to assemble their manifestos before it was over; it was called, fought and decided in the space of a day. But it was also gentlemanly because this was the Liberal Party, which attracted a higher proportion of honest, well-meaning characters than the two giants.

However, two Liberals rose to the occasion and behaved with their customary slyness: Thorpe and Bessell. Thorpe knew that the Party might be destroyed if he was elected since his private life was a catastrophe waiting to be exposed. But he did not care because he was determined to become leader. Meanwhile, Bessell weaved between the three candidates and the other Liberal MPs, who were the electorate, telling half-truths and downright lies because he loved deceit for its own sake.

He was beginning to tire of politics.[9] Once he had been sure that the magic letters 'MP' after his name would be worth more than a fat share portfolio; now he reckoned that the ethical constraints imposed by membership of the Commons were a handicap to a brilliant entrepreneur like himself. There were also the usual cash-flow problems; he had exhausted the small pool of wealthy Liberals, who had already lent him £20,000 (*worth £200,000 in 1995*), and now, to ward off bankruptcy, he turned to his elderly admirer in Cornwall, Everilda Agar-Robartes, Viscount Clifden's sister. Bessell tapped her for £15,000 (*worth about £140,000 in 1995*) but knew that, sooner or later, he would come crashing down. If he was still an MP when that happened he would be ruined; there would be so much publicity that no one would ever go into business with him again. Much better, he thought, to retire gracefully from the Commons, still solvent, and then have another crack at making a million.

The election was scheduled for the afternoon of 18 January, just over twenty-four hours after Grimond's announcement that he was quitting. Compared to the 1990s, these were uncomplicated times; the Liberals' new leader would be decided by the twelve MPs, employing the system of proportional representation which the Party had always demanded for general elections. This meant that each MP would vote for his (there were no female Liberal MPs) favourite candidate but would also mark his second and third choice. If no one won an overall majority, of seven, in the first ballot then the third-placed candidate would be eliminated and the second choices of his supporters would be transferred to the remaining two contenders.

Thorpe had two rivals: Emlyn Hooson, a brilliant 42-year-old Welsh lawyer who was on the right of the Party, and Eric Lubbock, the 38-year-old son of Lord Avebury who had won Orpington for the Party in 1962 in a sensational by-election victory. Thorpe was guaranteed the backing of Grimond, the old master; John Pardoe, the telegenic new Member for North Cornwall; and David Steel, the baby-faced Member for Roxburgh. He also thought that he could rely on Bessell, whom he had recently saved from bankruptcy.

But Bessell had doubts: Thorpe had been useful but Bessell was worried that he was doomed by his voracious homosexual appetites. He wondered whether he might be better advised to support Hooson, who was infuriatingly moral and would never use his influence to procure loans for him, but who might offer better, as yet undefined, chances for financial advancement. So, in the space of a few minutes, Bessell persuaded Hooson to stand by promising to back him but then he changed his mind and switched back to Thorpe, to Hooson's everlasting anger.

There were other difficulties. Rumours were swirling around the Commons that Thorpe was a homosexual. These were started and then denied by Bessell, who was testing a new chaos theory: create confusion and take advantage of the muddle. He had been active even before Grimond resigned. In August 1965, he had drunk rather too much at the home of George Mackie, the Liberal MP for Caithness and Sutherland who lost his seat in 1966, and told him Thorpe was a homosexual. In April 1966 another Scottish Liberal MP, Alisdair Mackenzie, who represented Ross and Cromarty, unwisely confided in Bessell. Mackenzie, a God-fearing farmer in his early 60s who was lost amid the spiteful intrigues of Westminster, said that one of his constituents had told him that a young man called Norman Josiffe, who worked with horses in Dublin, was claiming that he had had an affair with Thorpe. Bessell concocted an ingenious lie when he told Mackenzie that the only reason that Thorpe was still a bachelor was because he had fallen in love with Pauline, his own wife, but had honourably refused to steal her from him.

Bessell had also involved another Liberal MP, Richard Wainwright, the new Member for Colne Valley. But Wainwright was no Mackenzie; he was a youthful 47-year-old Yorkshireman and a partner in the blue-chip London accountancy firm, Peat Marwick. He listened carefully as Bessell explained that he was concerned about Thorpe's private life. A few weeks later Wainwright had independent confirmation of Thorpe's sexual leanings when a young man turned up at the Commons and demanded to see Thorpe. No other Liberal MP was available so Wainwright had to deal with the visitor, who was entertaining other visitors with stories about Thorpe's sexual activities. Wainwright recalled, 'A policemen told me he had been haranguing the queue waiting to get into the House alleging all kinds of homosexuality against Mr Thorpe. So I took the chap out at once and bundled him into a cab.'[10] From that moment he was sure that Thorpe was not fit to lead the Party.

Wainwright was not alone in opposing Thorpe. In London a group of heavyweights, including Michael Meadowcroft, in charge of local-government affairs at Party headquarters; Pratrap Chitnis, later Lord Chitnis, who headed the Party organisation; and Timothy Beaumont, later Party President, launched a desperate 'Stop Jeremy' campaign. But they had no time.

They tried to persuade Wainwright to run in the election, in the hope that he would unite the anti-Thorpe factions. But he refused. They also tried to mobilise opposition in the constituences but there was little that they could do in a day and, even if they had had more time, they would have failed because most activists thought that Thorpe was the kind of young radical leader that the Party needed. Although some of this group had heard rumours about Thorpe's homosexuality they insisted many years later that this had not been the main reason for their opposition to him. They said that, as good Liberals, they could not have allowed a man's sexuality to influence their view of him as a potential leader, which was laudable but naive.

Michael Meadowcroft said that he had never trusted Thorpe: 'He had no depth, no rigour and no passion. He was superficial. I did not like his style as treasurer. He was autocratic and tried to sack people, which was unheard of in the Party. There was an acknowledgement that he was probably gay but I was more worried about his style and intellect. But we failed to stop him. He never forgave any of us for opposing him.'[11]

Richard Wainwright, who voted for Lubbock, simply said, 'I felt he was not fitted to be leader.'[12]

Russell Johnston, the MP for Inverness, backed Hooson. He said, 'There were rumours then about Thorpe being a homosexual but that wasn't the main reason I did not support him. At the time we were much given to philosophising about Liberalism. We did not want the Party to be too closely identified with Labour, which is what Thorpe would have done.'[13]

Michael Steed, an academic in Manchester who became Party President in 1978, also heard reports about Thorpe's alleged homosexuality in 1967. Steed, who was happily married but also openly bisexual, said:

We took a liberated view of sexual conduct and said that it did not matter. So it wasn't relevant to us if he was gay. But we didn't like his style, which was autocratic. There was deep concern about whether he was suitable to be leader . . . There were things about him that weren't right. One can see with hindsight that it went back to his days at Eton, when he was a fag. His treatment of those who were junior to him, in age or in sexual roles, was all of a piece. One sees with hindsight how his upbringing was all about bullying. He just carried that over into political life.[14]

Despite proportional representation the election ended in stalemate: Thorpe had six votes and Hooson and Lubbock three each, which meant that there was no third-placed candidate whose votes could be transferred. Wainwright decided to act as honest broker. He asked Bessell for an assurance that the rumours about Thorpe's private life were untrue; Bessell cheerfully lied and told him that he would not have voted for Thorpe if they were. A few minutes later Hooson and Lubbock withdrew. Jeremy Thorpe was now leader of the Liberal Party.

Belatedly, Bessell re-discovered his conscience. He told Thorpe that he could have exposed his affair with Josiffe, and his other homosexual flings, but had not done so because he believed he could become a great leader. But he wanted Thorpe to promise that he would now lead a quiet and respectable life. Bessell said:

He gave me an unqualified assurance on all the points I had made and added that if the Josiffe matter or anything similar should ever be in danger of becoming public he would commit suicide. He said, 'I give you my word that if anything should become public I will blow my brains out.' I was positive he meant it. It was my opinion that having taken the leadership with what in those days was a disastrous weakness, and since death would be the only thing that would silence a scandal, he probably would have no option in the interests of the Party.[15]

It must have been a delicious scene: Bessell, the womaniser and cheat, who had just lied to his fellow Liberals to ensure the election of his ally, asking for a binding promise from Thorpe a man whom he knew would say and do anything to achieve power.

CHAPTER SEVEN

Jeremy Thorpe woke up on the morning of 18 January 1967 to the headlines which announced that he had fulfilled his destiny. He was leader of the Liberal Party at the wonderfully youthful age of 37. Most newspapers supported either the Conservatives or Labour but were generally sympathetic to the poor old Liberals, at least until they staged one of their periodic revivals, at which point the press always blasted them back into their accustomed place as also-rans. Jo Grimond had been solid but had not exactly oozed charisma and journalists were thankful for Thorpe, who would brighten up a dull political landscape that was populated by late-middle-aged men with paunches. So Thorpe enjoyed his breakfast that morning. One newspaper gushed:

> In the Commons his style is cutting and aggressive. He lacks the artistry and expression of his predecessor, but he has a quick eye for the telling phrase. He believes that Liberals should be in basic agreement on fundamental principles but that different interpretations are acceptable. All of which points to the conclusion that Liberal policies under Mr Thorpe may not be any more orderly, but they are likely to be as fascinating as ever. *Vive la différence!*

William Rees-Mogg, the editor of *The Times*, was able to take a detached view since his own newspaper did not care if politicians were entertaining: 'Thorpe was one of the great actor-managers of politics. He had a considerable histrionic gift but he did not have a big idea on how the country should develop.'[1]

The pro-Labour *Daily Mirror*, then a serious and influential newspaper, was superficially favourable. Under the headline: 'The dandy with a mission', the *Mirror's* political editor, John Beavan, later Lord Ardwick, echoed the other commentators when he talked about Thorpe's style epitomised by '150 neckties and a range of suits as sharp as Savile Row can bring itself to cut'. But Beavan also hinted that, had it not been for the British libel laws and good taste, he could have done more than describe Thorpe's wardrobe. He pointed out that the Young Liberals were unlikely to be wildly enthusiastic about an Old Etonian with a short temper and continued, 'Politics and the Liberal Party will be gayer for his leadership . . . And perhaps it's a good thing to have a leader who contrasts so vividly with the other two.' Beavan was no mere tabloid hack; he was a former London editor of the *Guardian* when its headquarters were in Manchester, had edited the *Daily Herald* and had first-rate contacts, which meant that he had probably heard the same rumours about Thorpe's sex life which had worried Liberal MPs in the past few months.

Thorpe was also being scrutinised by gay Liberals. The Sexual Offences Bill, which decriminalised homosexuality between adults in private, did not become law until July that year, but gays were beginning to emerge from the shadows, hopeful that at last society would treat them like human beings. Bernard Greaves was a leading Young Liberal in 1967 and became one of the key figures in the Liberals' gay-rights movement, despite Thorpe's attempts to drive him from the Party. Greaves, who came out in 1971, said, 'I had had a perception for a long time that he was gay. But no politician could admit that he was gay.' But, sex apart, Greaves simply did not like Thorpe: 'The closer you got to him the less you liked him. We wanted to press him to challenge the political system. He undertook to do a variety of things. But over the next year nothing happened and we all felt let down.'[2]

Mike Steele, the Liberals' recently installed press officer, did his best to please the new leader. But the two men quickly fell out. Steele said, 'Thorpe was always asking the Party to sack me. He was a vain, totally self-centred bully. I did not like him at all. He was a bastard. He was a tremendous snob who was always trying to attract smart people into the Party. He was very keen on being leader. But he had no idea where he wanted to take the Party.' But it never occurred to Steele that Thorpe might be homosexual.[3]

In fact, many Liberals were iritated by Thorpe's style; he had what Michael Steed called 'a court', who shielded him from the fellow Liberals who had been elected to the committees to which Thorpe nominally reported. Even his key aide, Tom Dale, did not care for friends like David Holmes, or Robin Salinger, an urbane businessman who was thought to be the leader's stockbroker. He

said, 'I didn't like Holmes. I thought he was creepy. I didn't want
to be left in the same room as him. Then there was Robin Salinger.
He made me cringe.'

Dale was brusque and protective: 'I answered all enquiries except
when they were made by his constituents or VIPs, like the Prime
Minister. I arranged his programme. I organised everything for
him. If anyone wanted to speak to Jeremy they came through me.
I represented him at Party meetings. The demands on him were
tremendous. Everyone wanted to speak to him because he was
the leader. No one was interested in the other Liberal MPs.'[4]

He also monitored the problem of Norman Josiffe: 'We knew
he was a nuisance. We knew he was saying that Jeremy had
stolen his Insurance card. As far as we were concerned he was a
dangerous nut. Lord Goodman [Thorpe's lawyer] would threaten
an injunction if anyone intended to publish anything. That always
stopped the story.' Dale also heard the gossip that Thorpe was a
homosexual: 'Of course we heard the rumours but it never crossed
my mind that he was gay. But he was very friendly to people and
would pick up hitch-hikers and not worry how it looked.'

There were always people, he said, who wanted to believe the
worst of Thorpe. He recalled that on one occasion he had escorted
him to Rochdale, where he was speaking that night with the local
Liberal MP, Cyril Smith:

> We stayed the night at the Grand Hotel in Manchester. Jeremy
> ordered a whisky at eleven-thirty and we went through his
> programme for the following day. At half-past midnight I left
> him and went to bed. Next morning we met for breakfast.
> A month later a chap was being tried in Manchester for
> burglary. He said that he couldn't have done it because he
> was in bed with Thorpe that night. That story appeared in
> the Manchester *Evening News* and when I saw it I checked
> in my diary and, blow me, we were in Manchester that night.
> I suppose it's conceivable that Jeremy went out when I left
> him and trolled the streets but I think it's very unlikely.

Victors in the game of power always want to erase the memory
of the vanquished. So Thorpe immediately decorated Grimond's
office and ordered new carpets. He also tried to be statesmanlike
but only succeeded in being boring. MPs who had had always
packed the House to enjoy his jokes now found it hard to stay

awake when he was speaking. Thorpe explained, 'I felt that with the press regurgitating these clichés rather like vomit – "the man is only an after-dinner speaker, an entertainer" – one had to live this down.' David Steel, the party's Chief Whip, was dismayed by Thorpe's new dull persona. 'He felt he had to move away from the image of the sharp witty debater. It was disastrous.'

Grimond looked on and did nothing. Although he had backed Thorpe in the leadership election he did not intend to help him because he wanted Liberals to realise that, though he had not brought them power, he had been a far better leader than they acknowledged. He said, 'Perhaps I should have done more to help Jeremy. I didn't for a mixture of good and bad motives. Having given up the leadership I didn't see why I should have to enter into controversy.' Thorpe felt that he was being undermined by nostalgia for Grimond: 'Some of the mythology put out about Jo was posthumous praise. He did have an intellectually fresh approach but some of his ideas were incomprehensible. I think it was rather like modern music: people thought they ought to admire it.'

Many Liberals were also uneasy that he was so keen on the social perks of leadership, such as attending black-tie receptions at Buckingham Palace. David Steel said:

> I complained to him at the time but he argued that it was necessary for him as Leader to maintain the position of the Liberal Party as the third party in the State. But some of his colleagues felt he was socialising too much. When they went to see him about Party problems he told them anecdotes about the previous day's beanos. He would say, 'Harold [Wilson] told me this,' or, 'I met So and So at the Palace last night.' It was balls-aching stuff. Grimond couldn't be bothered with all that flimflammery. He preferred to think.[5]

But Thorpe did not care. Grimond might have been clever but the Liberals had become a bankrupt shambles under him; the Party now needed discipline, money and glamour, which is what he would provide, whether the purists liked it not.

In March, two months after his election, Wilson appointed Thorpe as a Privy Counsellor, which meant that he had the right to be given 'classified information, should the need arise, on a matter affecting national security'.[6] He could also call himself 'the Right Honourable', which delighted him. He pointed out that Grimond had had to wait for five years for the honour; here was proof that, thanks to him, the Liberals were being taken seriously.

Marcia Williams, Wilson's less than universally popular personal secretary, who became Baroness Falkender in 1974, said, 'Harold thought it was dreadful that Jo Grimond had waited so long to become a Privy Counsellor. He didn't think it was right that a leader of a political party was treated like that.'[7] But she said that there were also practical reasons for the appointment: 'It was intolerable for Harold. He needed to be able to talk to the leader of the Liberal Party on Privy-Council terms about things like defence, Northern Ireland and Rhodesia.'[8] She insisted that MI5 had not briefed Wilson about Thorpe's homosexuality, and later suspected that this had been part of MI5's long-standing plot to embarrass Labour: 'MI5 knew about Thorpe but did not tell Harold because they wanted to destabilise us.'

But there was another reason for Wilson's generosity: he liked Thorpe, just as Thorpe admired him.[9] But sensibly neither man advertised this relationship. Wilson's opponents in Labour would have condemned him for hobnobbing with an Old Etonian snob while Thorpe's Liberal critics would have asked why he was close to a man who wanted to expand the power of the State and the unions. However, in the village that was the House of Commons, the friendship was certainly not secret. Tom Dale said, 'Jeremy was very close to Wilson. They liked each other a lot.'[10] Lady Falkender said that Thorpe always brightened up dreary official functions: 'Harold and I used to giggle at his impersonations. He was a colourful addition to any dinner party.'[11]

Superficially, the two men had nothing in common. Although Wilson dominated British politics for over a decade he remained the lad who enjoyed chips and brown sauce, his pipe, whisky and sparky attractive women. Thorpe, on the other hand, wore bespoke suits and handmade shoes and was a secret homosexual. Wilson was thirteen years older and came from the Colne valley, Huddersfield, Yorkshire; his family was, said one biographer, 'low church, low-living, lower-middle-class and proud of it'.[12] He was brilliant, a socialist (though he had been a Liberal when he was at Oxford), gruff and hated fancy food and clothes. He was a skilful operator in the sharkpool of the Commons, which ensured his survival as the Labour leader for thirteen years. But, paradoxically, he was also naive. He was an authority on the temptations of alcohol and women but, like many of his generation, it did not occur to him that respectable men like Jeremy Thorpe spent their leisure time cruising the streets in search of sexual adventures with other men.

He had won the Labour leadership in 1963, after Hugh Gaitskell, who had led the party since 1955, died aged 56 on 18 January, after a short mysterious illness. Gaitskell had battled the hard Left as he tried to steer the Party away from vote-losing socialism towards the kind of social-democratic ideas which, three decades later, were espoused by Tony Blair. Wilson was the Left's champion while the Right was represented by George Brown, who was 'passionate, ebullient and working-class'.[13] He was also an incorrigible drunk and flirt who was constantly disgracing himself in public. The choice, lamented Tony Crosland, one of Gaitskell's most talented acolytes, was between 'a crook and a drunk'. The following month 'the crook' won. But instead of heaving Labour Leftwards, Wilson moved towards pragmatic centrism. A small but influential circle of right-wing politicians, senior civil servants, intelligence officers, writers and journalists were furious that Wilson was performing so effectively. They were convinced that this was a sinister plot to lull them into a false sense of security; they believed that the KGB had killed Gaitskell to enable Wilson, a long-term Soviet agent, to take over the Labour Party and launch a Marxist revolution. They also spread the rumour that he was having an affair with Marcia Williams, which was absolutely untrue.

William Shannon, a 27-year-old homosexual who worked in an expensive shoe shop in Mayfair, was delighted when he read about Thorpe's appointment as a Privy Counsellor. Early in April 1967 Shannon sat down in his flat in the Upper Richmond Road, Putney to write and congratulate Thorpe and ask for money to decorate his new home. He remembered Thorpe as 'a very nice gentleman' who had picked him up twice in the King's Road and taken him to his small but tastefully decorated flat in Marsham Court, where they had slept together. He dated the letter 5 April. He wrote:

> I hope you will remember me; for you and I have spent two very pleasant nights together ... Before I go any further I would like to congratulate you on your new office as Leader of the Liberal Party. I know it's a bit late but I haven't seen

you for simply ages. November 10th to be exact. There is no need to worry either, no one knows about you and nor are they ever likely to. I have never mentioned your name to any one. It was a question you asked me when last we [met] . . . I shall say it's our secret!!!

Shannon said that he hoped to borrow £150 to refurbish his flat. Once that had been done, he said, then Thorpe would be welcome to visit him:

You could come here as a place of retreat from the world of politics and business. If you like you could have a key to the place. It would be super to see you whenever possible and it would be more discreet than your own flat. I want this purely as a loan from one friend to another, no strings attached. I can pay it all back by the end of October. It has taken me some time to ask this from you simply because I did not want you to get the wrong idea about it. I certainly did not want you to do something else. Please, Jeremy, help me to do this and I will be always grateful. Can you please let me have it in cash and, if possible, by the end of this week, but please as soon as possible. I did call at the flat to discuss this with you but you were [out] . . . I am prepared to give you securities if you want them. I must close now, so take care of yourself at all times. I sincerely look forward to seeing you in the very near future and to hearing from you sooner.
Always, Bill.
PS. I would have asked someone else but to be honest none of them could afford it which is why I am asking you.[14]

He signed the letter and set off for Marsham Court, where he handed it to the porter. Shannon was neither a prostitute nor a blackmailer. But he was young, attractive, camp and was used to being 'looked after' by wealthy older men.[15]

He first met Thorpe in the King's Road in autumn 1966. He was studying the display in the window of an antique shop when a stooped man in a stylish suit approached him and asked if he was looking for anything in particular. They chatted and then Thorpe suggested that they might be more comfortable if they had a drink in his flat. There, after a few drinks, they went to bed. After 'making love' Shannon was ejected, just like Norman

Josiffe, from the single bed on to a camp bed which was stored in a wardrobe. In the morning Thorpe gave him orange juice and asked how he liked his eggs cooked. Then he gave Shannon £3 for a taxi.

A few weeks later, Shannon was cruising the King's Road again. And, once again, Thorpe moved in. Shannon recognised him but Thorpe behaved as if they had never met, either because he had a poor memory for faces or because he was so promiscuous he could not remember who he had last slept with. They adjourned to Marsham Court again. Thorpe asked Shannon if he recognised him; Shannon said coyly that he was 'a very nice gentleman'. Thorpe smiled indulgently, pointed to the framed photographs on the mantelpiece and said that he was an important Liberal. Then they went to bed.

When Thorpe read Shannon's polite begging letter he turned to his fixer, Peter Bessell. He showed him the letter and shouted that Shannon, 'the little bastard', was trying to blackmail him. Bessell sighed and said that he would sort it out, which brought the usual grin of relief from Thorpe. A few days later Shannon was summoned to Bessell's offices in Pall Mall. He had his hair trimmed, dressed in his smartest jacket and trousers and headed off, thrilled that nice Mr Thorpe had not forgotten him. He told Bessell that he wanted to borrow £150 and offered jewellery which he had insured for £300 as security. He added that he planned to repay the loan, at £20 a week. Finally, he gave the names of two referees who would vouch for him. Bessell frowned since this was not how blackmailing prostitutes usually acted. But he ploughed on:

> I told Shannon that his letter was an obvious case of blackmail. I produced a copy of it and he agreed he had written it to Jeremy. I then outlined what Jeremy and I planned to do. I told him that he would be tried at the Old Bailey and that the trial would be held in camera because it involved Jeremy Thorpe. I told him it was a plain case of blackmail and I had deposited the letter in a place of safety. In this instance, I told him, neither Jeremy nor I would take any action, but if he made further attempts at extortion we would inform the Police, producing the letter as evidence. I heard no more of the young man and, to the best of my knowledge, nor did Jeremy.

Shannon hurried off, shaken and frightened: 'Can you imagine if
my affair with Jeremy Thorpe had come out when I was in a job
which brought me into contact with all sorts of powerful people?
The whole thing was very frightening.'[16]

Norman Josiffe, however, was made of sterner stuff. And, unlike
Shannon, he was not at ease with his sexuality. Since his meeting
with Bessell in Dublin in the spring of 1965 he had suffered a
number of professional and sexual setbacks. He was based in
Ireland, had branched out into modelling and had changed his
name from Josiffe to Scott, a surname which had been fermenting
in his mind since he had lived in Devon in the early 1960s, as a
neighbour of Lord Eldon, whose family name was Scott. But,
once again there had been an emotional crisis and he had fled
to a monastery in County Waterford. Unfortunately the monks
were unsympathetic and he returned to Dublin, where he embarked
on an affair with a married man in his mid-50s called Maurice
Dockerell.

This was not wise; Dockerell was a former Lord Mayor of
Dublin and was a well-known member of the Fine Gael Party. The
Irish authorities were not pleased that a respected public figure like
Dockerell was intimately involved with an effete male model. So
they decided to warn Norman. He was arrested at his home by
Special Branch detectives and deposited in a mental hospital in
the city. He might have remained there permanently but for the
intervention two days later of a friend, a woman who owned a
café; she told doctors that she would make sure that he would
not be a danger, to himself or anyone else, if they released him.

He was determined to start his life afresh. On Thursday, 20
April 1967 he sat down at his latest address in Kildare Street in
Dublin and wrote to Peter Bessell:

Dear Mr Bessell,
    It is with great regret that I write to you for I know you won't
want to remember me. The fact is I am to go to America on
July the third and have found that when I was upset over
Jeremy, etc. I burned my passport. It is so important to
me. I cannot tell the passport people here why and how I
destroyed it. Also as you may have heard I have been living
here in Dublin, and shall be going to America under the name
I have taken when I came out of hospital of Norman SCOTT.

This does I suppose confuse the issue, but I am now known and accepted as this person. Also the flight and everything has been booked in this name. So can you help me with regard to changing my name – legally? It's very short notice! But really it is so important. I have been doing very well here in Ireland, of all things as a male model!! Have done several TV commercials and also stills for magazines, also still have a horse and she is going well. Mr Bessell, I am sorry to ask for this, for I know you are busy but there is no other way. I hope you are very well.
Yours sincerely,
Norman *Scott*.
PS. I am coming to London on 2nd May.

Bessell was in South Vietnam on a fact-finding mission sponsored by the United States government when the letter arrived at the Commons, but had instructed his new secretary, Judith Crowsley, to watch for any communication from Norman Josiffe. She opened the letter and was baffled, until she realised that Norman Scott was the dreaded Josiffe. When Bessell returned to London he was delighted; it seemed that the nightmare was over. He told Thorpe that Josiffe had finally pulled himself together. He was modelling, owned a horse and, best of all, was thinking of going to the States. He added that he would arrange a new passport and visa. Thorpe grinned and said, 'Marvellous! Christ, what a relief!'

But it was not that simple. After writing this uncharacteristically upbeat letter Norman immediately crashed into despair again, as he explained in a further letter to Bessell in July, when he was staying at his brother's home in Kent. He began:

Dear Mr Bessell,
   You will be surprised to hear from me. I should by now be in America but I was rather ill and had to go into the Portobello Nursing Home where I was kept under sedation by Doctor Peter Fahq. As you know there is no National Health Service there [in Ireland] and my room per week was forty pounds two shillings! So all my savings for America went. Even still I only paid my room bills, and Doctor Fahq's bill of 10 gns. is still unpaid. However, the treatment did me no good. I was very despondent and at my wit's end, but a friend – Susan Halliman, the Irish actress – told me of

a wonderful man here in England called Brian O'Connell at St George's, Knightsbridge, their psychiatric unit. I came here to England on July 1st, but as I had no doctor (GP!) he couldn't see me, so I got one. Then Doctor O'Connell couldn't see me until Thursday the thirteenth – yesterday. Consequently I had to find somewhere to stay, so I came here to my brother who is not terribly well off and it caused him a lot of discomfort. Yesterday I went up to Doctor O'Connell. I told him everything about my life, my childhood, my going to approved school (for bringing two bales of hay for my pony!) . . .

Scott continued with this stream of consciousness until he ended with this threatening plea:

I shall try somehow to get to America where I have many friends who still feel that I would do very well there. The situation is serious the more so because my brother cannot keep me here very much longer. Is there anything you can think of. I have no money left now. I cannot model because my nerves are so shot to shreds that I soak everything I put on. I can't showjump because I have no riding kit, it's all sold. I have no real qualifications, I am still on a vast amount of drugs which means I'm not too strong. But wonder, no not wonder, beg you to try to think of something. I need so much to be doing something. I've had so long to think. Is there no way of working my way to America? I cannot come up to London for I have no money. So I beg you Mr Bessell to help somehow. Doctor O'Connell of course will tell nobody. What I said to him but it had to be told don't you understand. It's not been fair to me all these years. I am truly sorry to write but I so need someone's help and you said long ago you would.
yours sincerely,
Norman.

Bessell and Thorpe could have ignored the letter. If they had then they would have been rid of Norman, who would, doubtless, have persisted with his campaign to retrieve his Insurance card and expose Thorpe. But no one would have believed him and he would probably have ended up in an asylum. Thorpe had destroyed the evidence of the affair when he had ransacked the suitcase in the spring of 1965, though he was haunted by the fear that Norman had a cache of love letters somewhere, which he would use one day to ruin him.

Thorpe could not let go. He ordered Bessell to check whether O'Connell was discreet; Bessell trudged off and returned, saying that the doctor had not liked his suggestion that he gossiped about patients. Once again, Thorpe should have relaxed. But he could not; he decided to seek advice from the country's most influential solicitor, Arnold Goodman, who had just been ennobled by his friend and client, Harold Wilson, for his services as adviser to the rich and powerful. It was absurd for the leader of the Liberal Party to seek legal advice from the country's most feared lawyer over unsubstantiated allegations by a young man with a history of mental illness, but Thorpe was still convinced that Norman possessed demonic powers of destruction.

Goodman read the letters that Scott had written to Ursula Thorpe and to Bessell and asked what Thorpe wanted him to do. He suggested that Goodman should write to Scott and warn him that he could face charges of blackmail. Goodman did not think that this was a good idea. He said that a letter from him might provoke Scott into further epistolary activity which would not help anyone. It would be better to encourage Scott to leave the country. Thorpe smiled with relief, as if Goodman had solved the problem.

Two days later Bessell was pressed into service again. On Wednesday, 2 August 1967 Scott arrived at Bessell's office in Pall Mall to discuss his future. He was thin, scruffy and shaking. But he was determined to claim his birthright: 'I was in a bad way but it didn't stop my asking for my bloody National Insurance card.' By now, Bessell knew how to handle Scott; he needed sympathy and hope for the future. In other words, Bessell thought, he was like Thorpe, who believed that other people should take responsibility for his actions.

The National Insurance card was tricky. Scott needed one which was correctly stamped to collect unemployment and medical benefits. Unfortunately, he did not have any sort of card, stamped or not. Long ago, after Scott had fled, cardless, from the stables owned by Van de Vater, Thorpe had obtained a temporary card and promised to pay for the necessary stamps, which had made him, legally at least, Norman's employer. But Thorpe had either lost or destroyed that and a new card, which

was posted to Scott, had also gone astray. Scott had never applied
for another one because, in his mind, Thorpe was his employer.
This meant that there was a stamp-free blank in Scott's life of
about five years. Bessell wondered whether he should try to
persuade Thorpe to clear the five years by posting a cheque to
the Department of Health and Social Security. But that would
not work because Thorpe would be filed officially as Scott's
employer.

Then he toyed with the idea of Scott simply applying for a new
card. But, again, there were difficulties. If he did that then Scott
would blame Thorpe for the five stampless years, as he made clear
to Bessell during their meeting: 'I pointed out to him there was
a real problem. I would have to state on my application form
that Jeremy had been my employer and had refused to send it to
me when I left for Ireland. They would want to know about the
nature of my employment with him. I was not going to lie.'[17]

Bessell was stumped. So he told Scott that he would pay him a
'retainer' of £5 a week while he sorted out a new National Insurance
card. These weekly 'retainers' lasted for eighteen months and were,
in reality, hush money. The sums varied from £5 to £7, were
always accompanied by short notes, usually signed by Bessell's
secretary, and were paid out of the petty cash of his company,
Peter Bessell Inc. Thorpe repaid half the total of between £600 to
£700. Meanwhile, Bessell endeavoured to procure a new Insurance
card for Scott without implicating Thorpe. If Scott had been willing
to lie about the missing card it would have been easy, but he was
not and it was, therefore, impossible. He wanted his original card,
with five years of stamps bought by Thorpe. That was his identity
and he would settle for nothing less.

Having assured Scott that he would receive a weekly retainer, in
lieu of the state benefits that he deserved, Bessell tried to interest
him in the hamburger business. He said that he would shortly be
opening a chain of hamburger restaurants in Britain and suggested
that Norman should travel to the States, where hamburgers were
an art form, to learn the trade; then he would be able to return to
Britain and take up a senior position in Bessell's new restaurant
chain. Scott was not much of a traveller – he had lasted only a
couple of nights with Dr Choquard in Switzerland, which was
his first and last foreign foray – but told Bessell that hamburgers
sounded challenging and fun. But nothing came of this. This time
Scott could not be blamed. Bessell's scheme collapsed amid the

usual excuses about treacherous investors and, in any case, he had never had any intention of helping Scott obtain a visa to the States. If he had done that, he reasoned, then he would have been implicated in the chaos and disasters which Scott would inevitably have exported to America.

Bessell did, however, obtain a new passport for Scott. Bessell, not Thorpe, signed the back of Scott's passport photographs, which showed that, belatedly, Thorpe realised that he ought to distance himself from Norman. In mid-September 1967 the passport arrived at Bessell's office in Pall Mall. By that time, however, Norman had forgotten about a new life in the States and was back in London, where he vowed that he would become a famous model.

Meanwhile Thorpe was heading off for a welcome break in the Greek sunshine. On Friday, 4 August, two days after Bessell's meeting with Scott, he strode imperiously through the passport-control desk at Heathrow. He flicked open his passport and looked impatiently into the distance as the officer studied the entry: in front of the name Jeremy Thorpe someone had scribbled 'Rt. Hon.'. The officer asked who had written that. 'My secretary,' said Thorpe, although she had not. The officer pointed out that only the proper authorities could alter the details in a passport. Thorpe replied, 'Yes, but they are not always competent.' He was airborne when the news agencies who were based at Heathrow circulated this amusing story to Fleet Street. Mike Steele, the Liberal press officer, fielded the subsequent enquiries as best he could; he checked with Thorpe's secretary, who denied altering the passport.[18]

In Greece Thorpe met his old friend David Holmes and two young women, one of whom was the future Mrs Thorpe. Her name was Caroline Allpass. She had been introduced to Thorpe by Holmes, was 29 years old, and was the daughter of Warwick Allpass, who owned a chain of furniture stores in London. She had been educated at Roedean, and had worked in London and New York for Sotheby's. One friend described her as 'a laughing, brilliant girl'; another said that she was 'attractive, sweet and shy' but added that she had a steely core and high standards, which men found hard to meet.[19]

Thorpe later gave journalists a heart-warming, but entirely untrue, account of the holiday. He said it had been a contest between Holmes and him for Caroline's heart, which was nonsense since Holmes was living happily with Gerald Hagan. Thorpe, however, told newspapers: 'I passionately wanted my own children. I decided that this lonely bachelor should get married. A friend and I went on holiday and joined two girls in Greece. One I knew already. I wondered whether I might marry her. I decided I wanted to marry the other. So did my friend. So we said, "Right. Queensberry Rules. Whoever wins, the other is best man." I won. He was the best man.'[20]

He did not, however, mention the adventure that he had had on the beach with Holmes and a male prostitute. This little encounter had unhappy repercussions; they both returned to London with gonorrhoea.

Predictably, Thorpe asked Bessell for help since he could not risk finding a doctor himself. Bessell recalled:

A few weeks after his return Jeremy asked me to come to his room in the House. He looked ill and drawn. Jeremy told me that while they were in Greece he and Holmes had picked up a male prostitute and taken him to a beach. Jeremy had anal intercourse. Holmes had done likewise and the prostitute had anal intercourse with Jeremy. I do not think Jeremy said whether the prostitute had anal intercourse with Holmes. In consequence of this episode Jeremy and Holmes had contracted Gonorrhea. Jeremy was unable to go to his own doctor since it would have been obvious that he had contracted the disease in consequence of a homosexual relationship. He asked me what I could suggest.[21]

Bessell asked a friend, Dr James Pencheon, a consultant psychiatrist at St Lawrence's Hospital in Bodmin, for advice. Pencheon recommended a doctor in Goldhurst Terrace, Hampstead, who later examined Thorpe, diagnosed gonorrhoea, prescribed the necessary drugs and told him to abstain from sex until the symptoms had disappeared.

John Fryer, then a young, openly gay writer, who later became a close friend of Thorpe, said that many homosexuals of the pre-Wolfenden era sought sex abroad:

He went to places like Greece and America for sex. When he was in London he loved the danger. That was half the attraction of it all. He had an enormous thirst for getting into really tricky situations. But there was a sense, I think, of liberation in going abroad. People don't know you and you are a long way from home.

It was quite usual for university chums to go off and carouse abroad. It was like two heterosexuals going off to Bangkok for girls. Jeremy wanted adventures with people whom he would never meet again.

Sex was a diversion for Jeremy. It was great fun and it was satisfying. But it was something to get over with so he could get back to being a politician. If you are homosexual or bisexual then you can't slam the door on it. You see someone on the tube and you think: Cor! He got an enormous amount of adrenalin from politics but there were times when he wanted to let his hair down and say why the fuck am I doing this, when there's a whole world of lovely warm bodies out there?[22]

Thorpe had always known that one day he would have to marry. He did not relish the prospect but it was his duty, like opening fêtes in North Devon. He was almost forty years old and needed a wife if he wanted to silence his enemies who were whispering that there was something not right about him. There is no doubt that he genuinely cared for Caroline Allpass, though his homosexual friends thought she was so trusting and naive that she did not realise that he had a dark secret life.

Their courtship was formal. Caroline told her friends that they did not sleep together because Jeremy was old-fashioned about sex before marriage. The press speculated feverishly that one of the country's most eligible bachelors was about to be snared but Thorpe would not be drawn; a few days before they announced their engagement he told the *Daily Express* that the reports that he intended to marry were 'ridiculous'.

Then, on 2 April 1968, *The Times* ran a front-page story which said that Thorpe had just proposed to Caroline Allpass on the top of the Post Office Tower. Inside was this regal paragraph: 'The engagement is announced between the Rt. Hon. Jeremy Thorpe, son of the late J.H. Thorpe, K.C. and Mrs J.H. Thorpe of Stonewalls, Limpsfield, Surrey, and Caroline, daughter of Mr Warwick Allpass of 3 Beeches Wood, Kingswood, Surrey and Mrs A.B. Williams of Court House Farm, Great Coxwell, Faringdon, Berkshire.' This was a marvellous story for the press: dashing politician falls for beautiful young woman. Thorpe's closest friends, MI5, Special

Branch, Liberal MPs, some journalists and a variety of other people, including dozens who had met Scott over the years, knew or suspected that Thorpe was a homosexual but there was no hint about this in the press; instead there was sycophantic drivel.

The *Daily Mail* carried an interview with Thorpe under the headline: 'The perfect wife, by the most eligible bachelor'. He emerged as a man who had been pursued by countless attractive women but who had simply been too busy saving his party to become involved. He said, 'One can't say whether bachelorhood is better than marriage, until one has experienced both. And then it's too late for regrets. But it can be a lonely life, you know, as a bachelor in politics. Going to official functions will be far more fun when one has a beautiful wife to share it all with.'[23]

Mike Steele was appalled when Thorpe asked him whether it would help the Party if he got married: 'He asked me how many points it would be worth in the polls if he was married. I said, "Oh, about two." Thorpe slapped himself and said, "No, five at least!"'[24] Bessell was also shocked. He knew that Thorpe had to marry for the sake of his career but he was annoyed by the thought of Caroline being taken to bed by a man who found women sexually repellent. Bessell was not strong on morality but this offended him.

He winced at the memory of a conversation that he had once had with Thorpe:

In blunt language, he described how he felt about the difference between a male and a female body, adding that he was 17, and had failed – the basic problem being his inability to tolerate a feminine aroma. I understood. Like Jeremy, I was highly sensitive to odours. I had always known that a homosexual relationship would be impossible for me because I disliked the smell of male bodies. Smell plays a vital part in the mating of most animals. Jeremy and I were sensuous men and, as this conversation showed, he reacted like me as an animal to scent.

However, Bessell remembered, Thorpe had been determined to overcome this repulsion: 'It's a bloody bore, but if it's the price I've got to pay to lead this old party – I'll pay it.' But John Fryer thought that Bessell had over-simplified Thorpe's sexuality: 'It is quite wrong to think of him as a gay man who lived out a lie when he got married. He was bisexual and fancied women. I know that he was in love with Caroline and found her attractive.'[25]

On Thursday, 30 May Thorpe married Caroline in the private chapel at Lambeth Palace. The Archbishop of Canterbury, Michael Ramsey, emphasised Thorpe's national stature by blessing the couple. Apart from a few relatives there were only two guests, Lillian Prowse, Thorpe's faithful agent in North Devon, and David Holmes, who was best man. Although Thorpe had insisted that this would be a private ceremony, details of it leaked to the media, enabling fashion writers to rave about Caroline's stunning outfit (champagne-coloured dress, matching organza coat, standaway collar). Next day, the couple departed for their honeymoon at a mystery location, the island of Elba in the Mediterranean.

However, many Liberals did not wish Thorpe well as he flew off with his adorable new wife. They thought that he was taking the Party in the wrong direction, towards Labour, because that is where he thought there were spare votes. Other Liberals had been disgusted by the wedding, which showed, they complained, that he was a Tory masquerading as a Liberal. The wedding reception promised to be even more offensive. Thorpe had booked the Royal Academy in Burlington House, Piccadilly for 27 June and had invited 750 people; indeed, Liberals grumbled, he seemed more interested in the dignitaries who had accepted his invitation than in Party business.

His most vocal critics were the Young Liberals, with whom he had been feuding for months. They saw him as an Establishment snob, dedicated to the preservation of the corrupt status quo; he dismissed them as scruffy, muddle-headed revolutionaries who should have been staging sit-ins on university campuses rather than wasting his time with their interminable policy statements. The Liberal Party's files in London already bulged with acrimonious exchanges between the Young Liberals and the leader. On 9 February 1968 Louis Eaks, the Young Liberals' vice chairman, who later died of AIDS, had launched this attack on Thorpe: 'We are increasingly impatient with the failure of the Liberal Party to provide a dynamic and principled leadership. We demand a sustained attack on the hypocrisy of Harold Wilson's government – yet it is well known that Mr Thorpe refuses to do this.'

Amongst the increasingly vocal gay community in the movement there had been considerable amusement at his marriage, as Bernard Greaves recalled: 'A Young Liberal produced a satirical poem on the marriage. A lot of people thought that it was in bad taste. It didn't actually say Thorpe was gay but that was what was behind it.'[26]

On 1 March Thorpe had refused to speak in Peterborough on behalf of Bernard Greaves, who had been adopted by the local association to fight the seat in the next election. Then, On 27 May, Thorpe had attacked again: 'We are not helped by the antics of that small minority in our midst who believe that the British electorate want Marxism in a new dress – what they call "non-state socialism". In so far as they are noticed they play into the Tories' hands by making the progressive side of politics seem absurd.' Next day the Young Liberals, including Bernard Greaves, had fought back. They said that Thorpe should either apologise for calling them Marxists or resign.[27]

Towards the end of the second week of his honeymoon news of the plotting by the disparate forces in the Party, who agreed on little except the need to remove Thorpe, leaked to the press. On 11 June the *Daily Mail* ran this front-page headline: 'Liberal move to oust Thorpe'. In Elba the couple refused to abandon their honeymoon. Instead, Thorpe called a meeting of the Party executive for 28 June, the day after his reception at the Royal Academy.

Thorpe returned two days early, to great sympathy, claiming that he had run out of money because of restrictions on taking currency out of the country. Newspapers were supportive and said that it just wasn't right to plot a coup against a man when he was on his honeymoon; Thorpe played on this shrewdly and said, 'They wait until I go away on my honeymoon and then attempt the palace revolution. I thought: This really is outrageous. My wife said, "Darling, is it always like this?" I said, "Only sometimes."'

Caroline was also wheeled out. She gave a long interview to the *Daily Mail* on 20 June:

What a rotten trick it was. Everybody had their say and Jeremy could do nothing. But I suppose in politics they always wait until you aren't there and can't defend yourself. It's a lot of nonsense, this talk about Jeremy being a socialite. From the moment I met him I was impressed by the wide variety of friends in his life. He likes people and is interested in them. If he gets friendly with some ambassador and is photographed with him it gets in the papers and he is called a socialite. He likes going out and being sociable, so why not? And if he didn't get invited and accept invitations, what would people say? They'd say the nastly little Liberal Party, they're just not fit to ask anywhere. It isn't really a quarrel over the leadership. It's much deeper. It's about the party they want. Jeremy is a true Liberal. He believes in Liberalism. He would never lead a party which was not truly Liberal. He would rather resign.

Then there was the personal touch. She said, 'Most politicians marry young and have their houses and families established before public life is important. So they have got the time. But we've married mid-stream. We've got to find a house and have a family. I could go out and double up for him. I could be reading his speeches all over the country and we'd cover it in half the time. But Jeremy is good at public life by himself.'

The day after the wedding reception at the Royal Academy Thorpe routed his opponents. At the meeting of the Liberal Executive Committee he talked about Party unity, saying disloyalty and dissension only comforted the Party's enemies. Then he demanded a vote of confidence and won it, sixty-two to two (Bernard Greaves, who had refused to be cowed by Thorpe, was one). Richard Moore, Thorpe's political adviser, said, 'The plotters were very stupid. By attacking Jeremy on his honeymoon, the silly idiots played straight into our hands. We could immediately bring into play their bad behaviour.'

Mike Steele said, 'Thorpe defended himself fiercely. That meeting was one of the nastiest I've ever sat through – almost fascistic in the way the loyalists attacked anyone who had criticised the leader.'

A few days later the Thorpes celebrated their wedding and his victory over the rebels at a reception for 700 people in Barnstaple, where he announced, 'We are two very happy people. We shall, at the very earliest possible opportunity, buy a house in the constituency and live here.' Caroline, who looked ravishing in a white mini-skirt, told journalists that Jeremy's flat in Marsham Court was too small for a family – and here she giggled – and she was trying to persuade him to buy a house south of the Thames, where prices were more reasonable. (Thorpe refused to live in such an unfashionable part of town; they moved to a larger flat in Ashley Gardens, Westminster). She was also keen, she said, to find a home in North Devon. She said that they were not rich but that they hoped to find something; they eventually bought a cottage in the village of Higher Chuggaton, just outside Barnstaple.

Early that summer, 1968, Thorpe thought that life was sweet. He had a lovely wife, who would for ever stand as evidence that he was not homosexual. He had defeated his enemies in the Liberal Party. The possibilities seemed limitless. But it was an illusion because Norman was still watching and waiting.

CHAPTER EIGHT

The Norman Scott of spring 1968 was a new man. The previous summer he had been a dishevelled wreck who was falling off the edge of life but he had clawed his way back from the abyss and was now clean and alert.

In April 1968, when Thorpe was finalising plans for his wedding and the glittering reception at the Royal Academy, Scott asked to meet Bessell at his office in Pall Mall. He was still scruffy but the dark rings of despair around his eyes had gone, which was a relief to Bessell, who had only seen him when he was on the brink of collapse. He said that he had decided to have another crack at modelling. But he needed money for clothes and the photographic portfolio that was a model's calling card. And, of course, he required help to buy food and pay the rent while he established himself. Bessell said that he was delighted that he was so positive about life but asked for a breakdown of his estimated start-up costs.

A few days later Scott wrote to him. He calculated that he needed about £200 while he was waiting to be paid for his first assignments: clothes would cost £40, photographers' fees £28, £15 for a model book, £15 for a bag, £40 on rent and £37 for food, gas and electricity. Bessell thought that this was excessive. On 16 May, as he was leaving for the States to tend to his perpetually tottering business empire, he dictated a letter to his secretary, Sheila Skelton, who signed it in his absence:

Dear Norman,
    My reason for doubt about spending as much as £200 is that it does not guarantee a future and what I am anxious to do is make certain that your future is secure. However, I think you ought to be able to cut down your requirements to about £75 and I do not see any reason why this sum should not be advanced. If at the end of the year you are not able to

make a go of things in London I would still be prepared to consider assisting you to go abroad.

It is up to you – £75 to get started now in London with no further commitment for twelve months. If you do not succeed then we can talk again.

Bessell could not remember whether he paid the £75. He was also not sure what happened to the weekly 'retainers' after this letter but there was no doubt that, whatever the source of his funds, Scott prospered for a few months in 1968. In early summer he was interviewed by the Bonnies model agency in Kensington, who told him that he had potential. He bought suits, shirts and ties and had his hair styled. Then he had a session with a portrait photographer. The result was impressive. The cover picture on his Bonnies portfolio was moody, menacing and macho: he was wearing sunglasses and a black polo-neck jumper and smoking a cigarette. Inside there were other versions of Norman, including Country Man, with two whippets on a leash. Bonnies also included his personal details, which were vital for prospective clients: 'Height 5' 11". Chest 38". Waist 30". Hips 36". Inside leg 33". Collar 15". Shoes 9. Gloves 8½. Blue eyes and brown hair.' These details were repeated in French for the overseas market.

Scott's lifestyle was hardly that of a man who had no regular income and who was fixated on his missing National Insurance card. His days were a preparation for the night's activites: cocktails, then the theatre, ballet or opera, followed by dinner and a party. One of his new friends was a young woman, the daughter of a policeman in Dorset, who shared a seven-bedroom flat in Earls Court Square with Susan Myers, who was passing her time as an art restorer at the Tate Gallery while she waited, or so her parents hoped, to meet a nice young man.[1]

One night he was introduced to Conway Wilson-Young, whose mother Charlotte was godmother to the daughter of the late Lord Beaverbrook, the Canadian press baron who had owned the *Daily* and *Sunday Express*. Wilson-Young was an 18-year-old Old Etonian who was the classic spoilt rich kid; he lived too hard and fast and died, aged 35, his body pumped full of cocaine, in his New York apartment. Scott recalled, 'Kath and I went to drinks at Conway's house and then we went to the ballet. Then I went back to his house and stayed the night with him. Oh God! He was very young and very bright but was very tense and difficult.

He was moody and intolerant and was always used to getting his own way.' Next morning Scott returned to the flat in Earls Court Square, where he met Susan Myers. Then he began an affair with her.

But that was not the end of Conway-Wilson. Scott shuttled between beds in Earls Court and Belgravia while his new boyfriend had a string of one-night stands with other men. Although Scott insisted that he loved Wilson-Young, money was the foundation stone of their relationship. He was impressed by the house in Chester Square, Belgravia, which Wilson-Young sold in 1973 for £286,000. Scott gushed, 'He would just go out and buy a Mercedes if he felt like it. He used to hold amazing parties. We flew to Austria to the opera at Salzburg. It was all amazing.' He glowed with pride when Conway-Young introduced him to Dame Margot Fonteyn, who, even young Norman knew, was a world-famous ballerina. In between the crowded nights of parties, drugs and men Conway passed a few pleasant hours by attempting to make a film on Fonteyn, which, Scott simpered, meant that he was a talented artist.

But Wilson-Young's parents loathed Scott, who symbolised everything that was wrong with their son's lifestyle. Philip and Nell Myers were also not impressed and were appalled when their daughter said that she had fallen in love with Norman. Nell was a wealthy Australian who had bought the family home, Partney Grange, a fine Queen Anne house at Spilsby in Lincolnshire. They had lavished money and time on their three daughters and hoped that they would marry well, and Scott was certainly not their idea of a good catch.

Thorpe's unmitigated joy over his election to the leadership and his marriage did not last long because, yet again, he was becoming agitated about young Norman. Then Bessell mentioned that Scott had once told him that he had kept 'a few' love letters from Thorpe. Bessell did not think this was important because the old bad Norman Josiffe was dead and buried; Norman Scott was a busy male model who wanted to get on with his life. Thorpe glowered at Bessell, as if he was somehow responsible for this appalling development. He told Bessell that he had to recover these letters, no matter what it cost. Bessell should have told him to sort it out. But he did not because Thorpe was the leader of the Liberal Party and he was determined to stick closely to him.

Bessell had a brainwave: they could ask a friend to pose as a journalist and approach Scott: 'Much to my shame, I proposed an imposter could tell Scott that he had heard about his affair with Thorpe and offer to purchase any documentary evidence of it for a story. It was shabby but Jeremy enthusiastically took up the idea.'

Thorpe paced around the room. He said that David Holmes would be perfect. Bessell protested that Scott might check Holmes's identity; Thorpe roared with laughter: 'He'll say that he's from *Der Spiegel*. Scott wouldn't know how to check that.' Bessell asked if he was sure that Holmes would help. Thorpe roared, 'He'll do anything we ask. He loves being around us. Tells all his friends in Manchester he's going to London to see the Liberal leader.'

A week later Holmes travelled to London. Their talk marked the beginning of the conspiracy which ended seven years later on a wild October night on Exmoor, when an airline-pilot-cum-hitman called Andrew Newton aimed a gun at Scott's head.[2]

That day, however, Thorpe did not suggest that Scott should be killed. He told Holmes that he wanted him to find out if Scott had any evidence of their relationship; he assured him that it would be easy to persuade him to hand over the letters. Bessell said, 'He told David to start chatting to Scott, inviting him for a drink and letting him know he was gay. He said he might even have to take him to bed to get hold of the letters.'

Then they debated money. Holmes and Bessell thought they should offer £200 for the letters; Thorpe thought that £25 would be enough. Holmes suggested a compromise of £100, to which, reluctantly, Thorpe agreed. They finalised the plan. Bessell would invite Scott to his office in Pall Mall. Holmes would position himself outside to 'gauge the sort of person he was dealing with' and would approach Scott when he left.

The sting was arranged for the following week. But it set the tone for the future conspiracy by going hopelessly wrong. Scott arrived punctually at Bessell's office. But this was a new Norman. He was carrying a leather briefcase containing photographs of himself as a model. Bessell was stunned by the transformation; Scott did not look the sort of man who would hawk homosexual love letters around Fleet Street. But he knew what had to be done to satisfy Thorpe, and so, rather half-heartedly, asked Scott about the letters. Scott looked blank and said that he had burnt the letters and his passport when he was 'upset' over Thorpe.

Bessell decided to abort the sting. As soon as Scott left the room he leapt to the window and signalled to Holmes to come up immediately. He told him that the crisis was over; Scott was working, had no further interest in Thorpe and had destroyed the letters. Holmes beamed and said that he had been dreading his assignment as a *Der Spiegel* journalist. He added, 'I must say, when I saw Scott I didn't think much of Jeremy's taste.'

Holmes returned to Gerald Hagan in Manchester and Bessell resumed his ceaseless quest for the funds to save his companies and launch new ones. Thorpe, however, knew that Norman had not finished with him.

Predictably, Scott's life began to fall apart. His affair with Conway Wilson-Young collapsed. He moved into Myers' flat in Earls Court Square but did not have the emotional or sexual maturity to cope with a monogamous relationship with a woman. He hopped from one male bed to another but could not understand why Susan always became upset when he updated her on his sex life. By November 1968 he had reverted to the old Scott, a wretched, whining character who blamed everyone but himself for his problems. He wrote to Bessell, explaining that he had no work, no money and needed help. Bessell was sympathetic and promised that he would reinstate the retainer, at £7 a week.

A week later Bessell broke the news to Thorpe in the Commons that Scott was floundering again. Thorpe's face darkened. 'Blast, I thought we'd heard the last of him,' he said. Bessell recalled, 'He said the Scott affair was like a black cloud hanging over him – that at night he sometimes dreamed that it would eventually destroy him. His sense of foreboding was real and I felt moved by it.'

The bell sounded to warn them of the impending Ten O'Clock Division, the voting which usually marked the end of the day's business. The Commons was in a state of high excitement that December – Wilson's government was battling to save the pound against the onslaughts of the City and the speculators – but Thorpe could only think about Scott.

After they had voted they returned to Thorpe's office. Bessell said later, 'Jeremy was convinced that Scott would ruin not only him but bring the Party to its final nadir. That was his overriding fear. People would no longer want or vote for Liberal MPs if there was a homosexual scandal over its leader. And the scandal would have a knock-on effect throughout the country, where Liberals had been elected to local, city and parish councils.'

The conversation between them after the vote was one of the key episodes in the trial at the Old Bailey in 1979. Since no one else was present that night it is impossible to be sure who was telling the truth. But the balance is tilted heavily towards Bessell. Bessell said:

Jeremy was adamant that he must stop Scott going to the authorities for an emergency National Insurance card. I remember him telling me, 'Heavens! I'd have a lot of explaining to do in Whitehall if that ever happened!' He was terrified and becoming more depressed by the minute. He asked me if I had any idea what a predicament and black crisis he faced every minute of his life. Then he told me, 'We've got to get rid of him, it's the only way.' I tried to persuade him that now he was married to Caroline, and with Scott trying to resume his modelling career, the danger he represented was gradually evaporating. He made a half hopeless wave towards the darkened window and his shoulders tightened into another gesture of despair.

Thorpe reached into the drinks cabinet and poured himself a whisky. Bessell asked if he was thinking of murdering Scott: 'He was wearing that Mandarin expression of his and rose to his feet before saying, "Oh yes, of course, it's the only way, it's the only solution. If I don't this man is going to haunt me all my life. It is no worse than shooting a sick dog." He said nobody could have any conception of what it was like to be pursued by Scott and vowed that he would kill himself if their relationship ever became public.'

Bessell protested that shooting Scott would be noisy and messy; there was also the problem of the body. Thorpe suggested various schemes, such as throwing the corpse in a river. Bessell volunteered that it could be tossed down one of Cornwall's many disused tin mines, which Thorpe thought was a good idea.

Bessell feared, however, that this was not a late-night, whisky-driven fantasy: 'I had to reach a very difficult decision. If I had said, "Jeremy, put this whole idea out of your mind, it's crazy, it's the most irresponsible thing I've ever heard. How can you talk like this?" If I had done that then Jeremy would have never talked to me again about Scott. So I thought I would play along with him. Then I would know what was happening.'

Thorpe said that, obviously, he could not kill Scott; nor could

Bessell, since everyone knew that they were close friends. He smiled and said that there was only one person whom they could trust and who would be prepared to risk everything for him: David Holmes. Bessell argued that Holmes was 'too wet' but Thorpe insisted that, providing he was properly briefed, he was just the man for the job.

Bessell hoped that Thorpe would forget the whole ridiculous scheme. He had quite enough problems – apart from the usual cash-flow difficulties, Pauline was showing signs of impatience with his philandering – without having to organise a murder for the Party leader. But in the New Year of 1969 Thorpe announced that Holmes would be arriving shortly in London to discuss his role as an assassin. Once again, the debate on Scott took place in Thorpe's office in the Commons; the discussion before Christmas had been bizarre but the conversation that day would have been hailed as a work of black-comic genius if it had been enacted on stage. There was Thorpe, the famed wit and leader of the Liberal Party, calmly running through the most efficacious way of killing his erstwhile lover with Peter Bessell, the womanising Liberal MP for Bodmin who had decided to leave politics before politics left him, and David Holmes, the fastidious homosexual who was devoted to Thorpe.

Thorpe's first idea was that Holmes should pose as a *Der Spiegel* journalist, as he had almost done the previous summer, and lure Scott to Cornwall. There, in some suitably deserted spot, he could break Scott's neck. He demonstrated how this might be accomplished, when he twisted Bessell's neck upwards, rather as if he was a Special Air Services instructor. But Bessell and Holmes pointed out that Scott would probably not sit quietly while his neck was snapped. Shooting was also ruled out, as Bessell noted; 'I said it was impractical because of the noise of the gun, the blood and the effort required to carry the dead body to a mine shaft without leaving a trail for the police or anybody else to follow.'

Thorpe tried again. He suggested poisoning Scott in a pub in Cornwall and throwing his body down an old mine shaft. Bessell stared in disbelief at Holmes: 'David's sense of humour overcame him and he commented, "Wouldn't it look rather odd if Scott fell off the bar stool – stone dead?" At this point I couldn't prevent myself from laughing uncontrollably.'

Honest men would have told Thorpe that he was mad and left but neither was prepared to risk losing his patronage. Bessell offered this pathetic excuse: 'I was deeply attached to Jeremy but my overriding consideration was to do nothing that would cause him to cease to confide in me. I regarded myself as responsible for his election as leader and it placed me under an obligation to keep myself informed of any aspect of his personal behaviour that might harm the Party.' Holmes's explanation for humouring Thorpe was just as feeble. He said:

> The situation was impossible because we who were Jeremy's friends had to accept the burden of trying to help him. If we had simply said no he might have gone elsewhere – and that might have led to even greater disaster. My feeling was that newspapers were unlikely to publish Scott's ravings so we had to allow the thing to die a natural death. But to keep Jeremy happy Bessell and I went through the motions of seeming to do something.

Later Bessell and Holmes had a cup of tea in one of the Commons' restaurants. They agreed that the best tactic would be to stall but Bessell admitted later, 'Neither of us realised that Jeremy had become so obsessive about Scott that he had trespassed beyond the boundaries of rational decision-making.'

Then in May 1969 Scott telephoned Bessell's secretary with the astonishing news that he had just married. Bessell and Holmes were ecstatic; Scott was now a married man and was trying to put his past behind him, thus relieving them of the onerous responsibility of killing him. But Thorpe was not sure. He agreed that the murder plot could be shelved but added that it might need to be reactivated one day because that was the best or, as he put it indelicately, 'the final solution' to the problem.

On Tuesday, 13 May 1969, Scott married Susan Myers at Kensington Register Office. It was not a joyous occasion. Her parents were appalled that their lovely daughter had fallen for a man whom Captain Myers described as 'a well-known poofter'. Mrs Myers refused to attend the ceremony. Also absent in protest were Susan's sister Belinda and her brother-in-law, the actor, Terry-Thomas, who did, at least, offer the newly-weds the use of a cottage at Milton Abbas in Dorset.

Captain Myers made no attempt to disguise his loathing for Scott, who had made his daughter pregnant two months earlier. At the wedding reception at a restaurant in the Old Brompton Road he said that the marriage was doomed, which was an unusual tribute from a bride's father. As Susan left he hugged her and said, 'Oh my darling, I wish you were coming home with me instead of to that dreadful homosexual.' Myers was still seething a quarter of a century later: 'The marriage disturbed me very considerably. My wife and I were very upset about the whole damn thing. We did everything to try and prevent it but if you try to stop a girl in that situation they usually go head-on and ignore you. Scott knew I couldn't stand him. He was the last person you would want any relative of yours mixed up with. I hated that man.'[3]

Scott revelled in the drama:

> I was exactly what they didn't want for Sue. They represented the last bastion of respectability. Before we were married, when Sue and I lived together in London, her mother was exceedingly disapproving. At our first Christmas at the family home in 1968 she placed a Christmas present on my plate at the breakfast table. I unwrapped it and found it was a personalised mug. Emblazoned on it was one word: 'Strychnine!' She hated me.

Two weeks after the wedding he moved to the cottage in Dorset while Susan worked at the Tate. But she found the strain too much and joined her husband to prepare for the birth in November. Then she discovered that, while she had her own, correctly stamped National Insurance card, she required Norman's to claim full maternity benefits. And, as he kept telling her, he did not have it because Thorpe had betrayed him. By now they were almost broke. Scott's modelling 'career' had always been a hobby, which gave him credibility with Conway-Wilson's friends but little money. The tenants who had moved into Susan's flat failed to pay the rent and she was too proud to ask her parents for money. So they had to beg and steal food. Neighbours recalled watching Scott scavenging in the fields, like an animal.

His humour was not improved when he opened his newspaper early in July; there, beaming out of the page, was Jeremy Thorpe, at the christening in the crypt of the House of Commons of his son, Rupert. When Thorpe had announced that Caroline was pregnant the previous autumn he had asked for privacy from the media for what was a 'domestic event' but now he wheeled out young Rupert to reinforce his new image as the responsible, but still dashing, family man. He was wearing a morning suit and a high-starched wing collar and posed for photographers with baby Rupert while Caroline hung around in the background with David Holmes, the baby's godfather.

Newspapers fawned:

Politicians and gurgling babies are quite a well-worn combination. But the occasion is rather different – well, there isn't an election in sight as far as Jeremy Thorpe is concerned. It is rather a special occasion, though – the christening of the Liberal Party leader's son Rupert. The baby was nattily dressed in the Brussels lace gown in which his father was christened. And from the happy way he lay in his father's arms afterwards it was obvious that Mr Thorpe had won a notable vote of confidence.

Incensed by the sight of the man who had ruined him prospering in this way, Scott turned again to Bessell and demanded action to obtain his National Insurance card. Bessell sensed that this time Scott was not just seeking attention or money; he was desperate and was close to cracking.

Bessell leapt into action. He contacted David (later Lord) Ennals, the Minister of State at the Department of Health, and told him about Thorpe's role in a 'muddle' over Scott's Insurance card. But Ennals could not provide Scott with what he wanted: an Insurance card that had been stamped by Thorpe. Bessell recalled, 'Ennals made the unhelpful suggestion that Scott should apply for an emergency card at his local social security office in Weymouth. That was the last thing I wanted. If he did there was the real danger he would spill out his story to the first civil servant he met. Jeremy would have exploded if that had happened. That flashpoint could have led to his ruin.'

On 27 August Scott lost patience. He telephoned Bessell and threatened to take his story to Fleet Street. He said that Bessell's promises were worthless and slammed down the phone. Then he called the Department of Health in London and demanded to be put through to David Ennals. He spoke to Ennals' private secretary, Kenneth Marshall, who tried to reassure him that his case was being examined urgently.

Bessell did not believe that any newspaper would touch the story but he did not think it would be helpful to the Liberals, Thorpe, or indeed himself, as the man who had paid the 'retainers', if Scott was let loose on the media. So, that day he wrote to Scott:

Dear Mr Scott,

I can understand your feelings and your anxieties, and I wish very much that you would believe that I am anxious to do all in my power to help you.

I do not think you appreciated that, although you have already been through the motions with two Ministries, following my representations you can start all over again with the assurance that you will get immediate help. Surely it is worthwhile to go to Weymouth and call the Department, having first made an appointment by telephone, and to say that I have told you that they will issue an emergency card on which you can claim benefits temporarily. You can then go to the Employment Exchange, hand them your card, and register as an unemployed person. You would not get unemployment pay as such, but once you have registered you would then get assistance from the Department of Health and Social Security.

Regarding your cards, I know your anxiety about this. I have done all in my power to hurry matters along, but miracles cannot be achieved in five minutes and it will take all the tact and persuasion of which I am capable to arrange for a card to be issued to you, properly franked, so that you can obtain benefit for your wife during her period of confinement. It would be a great mistake if you jeopardised this in the way you suggested to me on the telephone, and I hope, for your own sake, and in spite of your anxiety, you will accept my advice and guidance.

I have spoken to Jeremy Thorpe and put him in the picture regarding the present position.

Yours sincerely,

Peter Bessell.

Bessell thought that he covered himself neatly in this letter; as a caring MP he had been concerned about Scott, but had made it clear that he was not prepared to abuse his position to help him. In his haste, however, he had blundered; for the first, and last, time he had linked Thorpe's name to Scott in writing. Then he hit the phones. After a flurry of calls he persuaded social-security officials in Weymouth to visit Norman and Susan, to make sure that she received the minimum benefits for expectant mothers.

The new Mrs Scott was also busy on the phone. Norman was disintegrating and could only talk about that wicked man Jeremy who was to blame for everything. She decided to telephone Thorpe and find out how he intended to save Norman, herself and their unborn baby. She telephoned the village of Higher Chuggaton, where the Thorpes had just bought a cottage. She spoke to Caroline, who was looking after Rupert, and said that they were starving because her husband refused to accept responsibilty for Norman's Insurance card. Caroline was unmoved. Thorpe had already warned her that he was being pursued by a lunatic called Norman, who fantasised that they had had an affair. She told Myers that she would pass the message on to her husband and put down the phone.

But that was not the end of the telephone communications between Milton Abbas and Higher Chuggaton. Urged on by his wife, Norman decided to challenge Thorpe, to whom he had not spoken for almost five years. He said:

> I telephoned Thorpe, standing in the window at Stone Lodge with Sue behind me. We didn't want to do it but we were desperate. Caroline Thorpe answered. I just asked her to intercede. I told her, 'I don't know if you know but I have to get back my Insurance card.' She said, 'Why should Jeremy have it?' And I said well, he was my employer. We were lovers. You have a baby and you know what it must be like for my wife with no money. There was silence. Then she said, 'I don't want to know anything about it. It's disgusting.' Perhaps she said 'nauseous' and that was that. Then she said, 'I'm sorry,' and put the phone down.[4]

Scott now appealed to the social-security office in Weymouth and, predictably, told a baffled official there that Jeremy Thorpe, the MP, was to blame for everything. Over the next few weeks the Scotts received two social-security cheques for £15. But it was too late; Susan left for her parents' home in Lincolnshire, where it was at least warm and where there was hot food to sustain her during the final weeks of pregnancy. Norman returned to the flat in Earls Court Square, where he evicted the Czech and Iranian students who had been living there rent-free.

The next year was a blur of one-night stands with men whom he picked up in Earls Court and of reconciliations and rows with Conway-Young and Susan. After their son, whom they named Benjamin, was born on 18 November 1969 she returned to London to try and make the marriage work. But Scott could not be saved.

Thorpe, however, was pleased with life. His faithful friends, Bessell and Holmes, were handling Scott, who was like a sick animal which had to be put down because it was the kindest thing to do. He believed that he had made a crucial breakthrough because, for the first time in living memory, the Liberals had real money. The Conservatives had big business and Labour had the trade unions to provide the resources that were required to run a modern political party: the researchers, advisers and public relations wizards at headquarters, the agents in the constituencies and the expensive advertising agencies to ram home the message during election campaigns. But, until 1969, the Liberals had been virtually bankrupt. They had bumbled along from one terminal overdraft to another, well-intentioned but shabby, the also-rans of politics. Thorpe was determined to change that and drag the Party into the twentieth century. Then he found Jack Arnold Hayward, a 46-year-old multi-millionaire who lived in the Bahamas.

There were many colourful characters in the Thorpe–Scott saga but Hayward was certainly the most endearing; with his unkempt shock of white hair, untidy clothes and pockets stuffed with bits of paper and bills he looked more like an absent-minded retired geography teacher than one of the richest men in the world. He was so patriotic that his nickname was Union Jack. He flew the flag from his Rolls Royce, drank tea at 4 p.m. every afternoon and had introduced red double-decker buses and red post-boxes to the Caribbean. He told his friends that his guiding motto in life was: 'Keep all things bright, beautiful and British.' Despite his wealth he was utterly without side, disliked spending money on himself and gave away millions to good causes.

He was born in Wolverhampton. His father Charles, later Sir Charles, had been a circus performer (his act was known as 'the Living Head' because, thanks to strategically placed mirrors, he appeared to be disembodied) before making his first fortune

manufacturing motor-cycle sidecars. He went bust in 1929 but
bounced back and made a second, much larger fortune with his
engineering company, Firth Cleveland, which he sold in 1972 for
£26 million.

Jack had gone to the United States in the mid-1950s to
expand his father's businesses there. In 1956 he heard that an
American entrepreneur called Wallace Groves had approached
the government of the Bahamas; Groves wanted to lease 50,000
acres of land, equal to about a third of the island of Grand Bahama,
and construct a giant tax-free industrial complex, centred around
the harbour, Freeport. The government agreed, in return for a
guaranteed slice of the expected revenues. Hayward realised that
the possibilities were limitless and persuaded his father to invest
£1 million in Groves' scheme. His instincts were right; Freeport,
tax-free, stable and sunny, boomed and by the mid-1990s was
worth hundreds of millions. (Hayward and his partner of thirty
years, a barrister called Edward St George, bought out Groves
in 1978.)

In April 1969 he was at home in the Bahamas catching up on
news from the motherland in his overseas edition of the *Daily
Telegraph*. He noticed a heart-warming story about three West
Country MPs, Jeremy Thorpe; Peter Mills, Conservative MP for
Torrington; and Dr David Owen, Labour MP for Plymouth,
Sutton, who had shelved petty political difference to launch a
fund-raising crusade to save Lundy Island, a wildlife sanctuary
twelve miles off the North Devon coast in the Bristol Channel.
Lundy, 3½ miles long, with a permanent population of just ten
people, plus six lighthouse-keepers, no telephones, a pub which
only closed after the last customer fell off the bar stool and tens of
thousands of birds and animals, was being sold by the family of the
late owner to pay death duties. It was feared that it would be sold
to Americans, who wanted to turn it into a gambling complex, or
to Scientologists, who wanted to 'rehabilitate psychiataric patients'
there. The National Trust was willing to run Lundy but did not
have the necessary £150,000 to buy it.

Hayward did not like the sound of Lundy falling into the hands
of the foreign enemy. He said, 'I had never been to Lundy but I
had always been intrigued by it, a great lump of granite out there
in the sea. I was terribly impressed that these three MPs had got
together to try and save a bit of Britain. I had a bit of spare cash
at the time so I thought I would offer to help.'

He telephoned Thorpe's home in Ashley Gardens, London. It was late at night and Caroline answered and said that her husband was not at home. Hayward said, 'If I had got a snooty reply, which I might have done from certain English women, especially at that time of night, I would have called the whole thing off. But Caroline was sweet. She probably thought I was a nutcase and asked me to phone back, however late, because Jeremy was out at dinner.'[5]

When Hayward telephoned again Thorpe was in bed with his wife. Hayward said that he wanted to help with the Lundy campaign and asked Thorpe how much he needed; he replied that £150,000 would probably be enough. Hayward told him that he thought he could manage that:

> Jeremy told me that they had everything in place except the money. But I am sure that he thought that I was a nutcase. After we had finished speaking he telephoned someone who had once been my neighbour in England and asked if he had heard of someone called Jack Hayward and whether he was the sort of chap who would give away £150,000 to save Lundy. My friend told Jeremy, 'Yes, that's just the sort of stupid thing Jack Hayward would do.'

On 23 May Hayward and Thorpe were front-page heroes for saving Lundy from the depredations of American gangsters and religious fanatics. Thorpe elbowed Peter Mills and Dr David Owen out of sight and talked as if he was singlehandedly responsible for persuading Hayward to hand over the money to allow the National Trust to purchase Lundy. Hayward, meanwhile, made a few genial remarks to the press: 'My wife Jean is also a great believer in preserving Great Britain. She would like everything to stay exactly as it is – green, beautiful and lovely.'

That summer he was invited to Lundy as the guest of honour at a thanksgiving service. He said, 'I was very impressed at the way Jeremy had organised everything. I whispered to him in church, "God, Jeremy, you should be Prime Minister." He said, "My dear fellow, it's on the cards but I might need some help." He said that his party had an overdraft of £100,000 which had to be cleared.'

By now Mills and Owen had been forgotten. Hayward was charmed by both Caroline and Holmes: 'They were both delightful. It didn't occur to me at the time that Holmes was homosexual but, looking back, I can see that he had a bit of the woman in him, like many of these chaps. I wasn't a Liberal but I did feel sorry for them. They were the underdogs, after all.'

In fact, Hayward had nothing in common politically with Thorpe: 'I told him that I hated Europeans. But he said, "My dear fellow, we are so adept at diplomacy. Europe will be another British Empire." It was all a con but he was very charming.' Thorpe asked him if he would consider helping the Liberal Party; like all very rich people Hayward was used to fighting off people who wanted his money but he said that he would consider it. Once again, Peter Bessell, soon-to-be-ex-Liberal MP, conman and Thorpe's trusted friend, was drafted into service. Armed with a memorandum from Thorpe and the Liberal treasurer, Sir Frank Medlicott, he flew to the Bahamas to see Hayward. He left with the promise that a cheque for £150,000 would shortly be sent to Thorpe.

Hayward's cheque, for £150,000 (*about £1.2 million in 1995*), made out personally to Thorpe, arrived in London months later, in May 1970 and signalled the beginning of a vicious battle within the Liberals over who should control Hayward's money: Thorpe or Party officials. Thorpe believed that this was his money and he was determined to prevent anyone in the Party discovering how much Hayward was donating. A few senior officials, such as Sir Frank Medlicott, who suggested that the money should be administered in a conventional fashion, were brushed aside by Thorpe; he regarded them as mediocrities who would fritter away the money on such irrelevancies as staff salaries or running constituency offices. It was up to him, as leader, to decide how to spend the money and if Party functionaries did not like it then they would just have to lump it because, without him, they were nothing.

His main opponent was Medlicott, who thought that it was ridiculous that the Liberals had so many accounts, few of which came under the control of the treasurer, who was theoretically responsible for Party funds. Like many Liberals, Medlicott thought that it was time for these various funds, which had grown haphazardly over the years with the Party, to be unified. There was only one account over which he appeared to have undisputed command: the Liberal Party Organisation Fund, which paid Liberal staff and maintained links with the rank and file around the country. This was permanently short of money and Thorpe had no intention of allowing his Hayward money to go anywhere near it.[6] There was the Liberal Central Association Fund, which supported parliamentary candidates and MPs. Its treasurer reported directly to Thorpe. The General Election Fund handled donations from supporters in the run-up to an election but Medlicott, who was supposed to be responsible for it, complained that he did not have full control. Then there were Thorpe's secret accounts which were used to fight seats where the Liberals felt they stood a real chance of winning; Medlicott knew nothing about these. There was a Party Leader's Account, too, which Thorpe ran. Finally, there was another account, which Thorpe called the Liberal General Fund, which gobbled up most of the Hayward money.

The dispute between the two men about money had been bubbling for weeks before the arrival of Hayward's £150,000 but it came to a head that day. Medlicott wanted to use the money to pay off debts and suggested setting up a trust to make sure that the money was wisely spent. Thorpe was outraged; this was his money and he was not going to let a nobody like Medlicott tell him how to spend it.

Harold Wilson, Prime Minister for almost six years, called an election for Thursday, 18 June 1970, having been seduced by the opinion polls which showed that he would win comfortably. But, not for the first or last time, the polls were wrong. Thanks to Hayward's money, the Liberals were able to compete on equal financial terms with the big two, but it did not help because the Party was a shambles. Many voters confused the adult Liberals with the noisy Young Liberals, who disrupted cricket matches with South Africa. The Party was also weakened by internal feuding over whether it should embrace the new philosophy of 'community politics', whose exponents argued that the average voter would take more notice of Liberal candidates if they concentrated on local rather than national issues.

Thorpe, meanwhile, behaved as if he was taking part in a presidential battle, not a British general election, which history suggested would be decided by a complex interaction of local and national concerns, not by the personalities of party leaders. His advisers coined the slogan 'Faith, Hope and Jeremy', and whisked him around the country by helicopter, to conjure up the image of an energetic, high-tech leader. He also leapt hundreds of fences, shook thousands of hands and performed well in countless interviews. But it did no good.

The election result was one of the most surprising this century.[7] Labour's majority of almost one hundred was wiped out when Heath's Conservatives won 330 seats, 77 more than in 1966. The Liberals came limping in, a disastrous, humiliating third, with only six seats, half the number elected in 1966. Thorpe's own majority in North Devon was a wafer-thin 396 votes; and many commentators felt that he would have lost but for the beguiling presence of his wife Caroline. In Bodmin, vacated after six years by Peter Bessell, the Conservatives crushed his Liberal successor by almost 4,000 votes.

Thorpe was shattered. He searched for excuses – the Young Liberals, the distraction of 'community politics', the iniquities of a system that gave a party which polled over 2 million votes only six seats in the Commons – but, even for a man of his vast ego, he knew that he had to shoulder most of the responsibility. He had projected himself as the embodiment of the Liberal Party and he had been rejected. His mother had run the cottage in Higher Chuggaton while Caroline charged about the constituency and Jeremy zipped around the country in his helicopter. She said, 'I will never forget that ghastly election. They had to stay on and thank everyone who had helped them. I cooked some food for them and came back home. Caroline was marvellous to him.'[8]

Then Thorpe had to face the consequences. He had spent a fortune – it was estimated the campaign had cost the Party over £100,000 – and now Sir Frank Medlicott wanted to know how he intended to rectify the financial mess that his extravagance had caused. Thorpe responded by blaming Medlicott for the haemorrhage of Hayward's money and then proceeded to top up accounts that he controlled with the little money left in other funds. The scene was set for a major confrontation, which might have fatally wounded Thorpe. Then, on 29 June, Caroline was killed and Party finances were forgotten, at least for a few months.

That morning the Thorpes had packed their car at the cottage in Higher Chuggaton for the journey to London but they had so much luggage that they had decided that it would be sensible if Jeremy and Rupert travelled by train. Caroline dropped them off at the station, returned home to pick some white carnations and set off. Two and a half hours later, as she approached Basingstoke, forty miles west of London, her green Anglia estate car inexplicably veered into the path of a lorry and crashed into a car behind. The Anglia somersaulted into the air, leaving a trail of carnations across the road. By the time she was cut free and taken to hospital she was dead. Thorpe was in the Commons, for the customary tributes to the re-election of the Speaker, Dr Horace King, when he heard the news. He drove to the hospital to identify the body and then headed back to Higher Chuggaton.

The Queen and the Prime Minister, Edward Heath, sent telegrams of sympathy. Harold Wilson said, 'The news of the death of Caroline Thorpe was utterly devastating. It is a tragedy for Jeremy and their baby and a great shock for all who knew her.'

At the coroner's inquest several weeks later, Stephen Blythe, a passenger in the truck which she ploughed into, said, 'Mrs Thorpe seemed to be looking straight ahead of her. She did not seem to know where she was going. I said at the time that she was day-dreaming.' Yet the driver of the truck, Brian Knock, believed she was 'looking down at the inside of the car', which suggested that she had been trying to retrieve some luggage from the floor.

Caroline's death introduced a new and ugly element into the battle between Scott and Thorpe because Thorpe's friends claimed that Scott was responsible for the accident. They alleged that he had gone to the cottage the day before she set off for London and said that she was so upset by this that she crashed the next day. Scott denied this story; he said that he had only spoken to Caroline once – the previous summer – and that he had been in the flat in Earls Court Square, sedated because of another emotional crisis, when she died. Unknown to him, however, his estranged wife Susan had telephoned Caroline a month or so earlier from her parents' home in Lincolnshire and begged her again to help sort out Norman's Insurance card. Caroline said she could not help and put down the phone.

Next, there was the impact on Thorpe. He said:

I forgot about the electoral disaster. It just blurred. I suppose that, for a year, while I did everything I had to do – took Party meetings, did my constituency work, laid the wreath on the Cenotaph – I did it mechanically. Unless you believe in the Resurrection I think the whole of this life is a very bad joke . . . Separation in this life, compared to eternity, would be like a postage stamp on Cleopatra's Needle. People are not just snuffed out. There must be a further purpose.

He became obsessed with creating a grand memorial for her and eventually decided on a crafted column of Portland stone behind the cottage in Higher Chuggaton. He said:

> It involved getting permission from the Ministry of the Environment, getting the Ministry of Defence to take down a look-out post, getting Clough Williams-Ellis [the Welsh architect] to design what I thought Caroline would have wanted, choosing just the right piece of stone, arranging for Moura Lympany to play and the Archbishop of Canterbury to officiate.

Indeed, he spent so much time on this that John Pardoe, the Liberal MP for North Cornwall, wrote to him and said that, if did not have the energy to be leader, he should step down.

Then in December 1971 the work was finished. Thorpe said:

> The service was organised like a military operation. Land Rovers to get 200 people up the hill; 150 umbrellas if it rained. Blankets if the cold was bitter. It was like a miniature Taj Mahal. It's there for ever. When people see it rising into the sky they will think of Caroline Thorpe and the sunshine she brought with her during her tragically short stay in North Devon. I think I determined to do it on the day of her funeral. With its completion I was able to disengage from my total absorption.

CHAPTER NINE

Thorpe's enemies whispered unkindly that his public display of grief was a tasteless charade, designed to promote J. Thorpe. His friends insisted that he was genuinely distraught but were also embarrassed by his theatrical mourning. Peter Bessell, who knew as much as anyone about self-publicity, said that Thorpe could not help himself and was acting out a role, though this time it was as the distraught widower rather than the insouciant politician. But he also thought that it showed that Thorpe was 'morbidly obsessed' with death. This might sound uncharitable but the fact is that, while he was telling colleagues and journalists that he could only think about his dead wife, Thorpe was also managing to attend to a variety of matters, which had nothing to do with her, with his customary ingenuity.

First, he had to survive the assaults of his increasingly vociferous enemies within the Liberal Party. They thought that his presidential style, which implied that he *was* the Party, was disastrous; they said that Liberalism had always been about ideas rather than personalities and pointed to the awful results in the June election as proof that he should be dumped before it was too late.[1] At the Party conference that autumn in Eastbourne, a morose and poorly attended affair, the young radicals from the provinces allied with the rising stars of the Liberal establishment, including the future leader, David Steel and forced delegates to adopt the new 'community politics'. Thorpe did not like the sound of this since he was not interested in, and knew nothing about, such boring minutiae; some Liberals naively thought that he would resign in protest at this shift in policy but he had no intention of giving up the leadership on a matter of principle.

Thorpe had more luck, however, with Sir Frank Medlicott, who had had the effrontery that summer to argue that he should not have exclusive control of Hayward's money. When Medlicott confirmed publicly in Eastbourne that Hayward was

the Party's new benefactor Thorpe exploded with rage and claimed
that Hayward had requested anonymity, which was untrue. But
there was logic to Thorpe's ravings: he regarded Hayward as his
private piggy-bank and was determined that no one else should
have access to him or his money. Medlicott considered resignation
but hung on, out of loyalty to the Party, though he was broken by
the experience; a year later he was dead of a brain tumour. Thorpe
eventually replaced him with a friend from Oxford called Philip
Watkins. Watkins had been President of the Oxford University
Liberal Club in 1951 and had become a chartered accountant,
although he had fought – and lost – a series of general elections
in his attempt to become a Liberal MP. He was a quiet, reserved
man, who was rumoured to be a homosexual, but he was widely
respected in the Party for his honesty and accountancy skills.
Unlike Medlicott, however, he was totally loyal to Thorpe and
unquestioningly accepted that, as leader, Thorpe had the right to
decide how to spend the Party's money.

But it was his response to the news that Norman Scott's marriage
had collapsed that proved that he was not as preoccupied with his
late wife as he wanted people to believe.

Susan Myers had done her best but, just over a year after she
had ignored her parents' advice and married Scott, she admitted
defeat and told her solicitor that she wanted a divorce. During the
summer she had shuttled between their flat in Earls Court and the
family home in Lincolnshire, hoping that dear, hopeless Norman
would be so shaken by the prospect of losing her and their son
Benjamin that he would start behaving like an adult. But he could
not change. When she told him that she was having an abortion
because she could not face having a second child by him he sought
solace in bed with his rich young lover, Conway Wilson-Young:
yet he talked about this as if he had visited a marriage-guidance
counsellor: 'I rang Conway because I was depressed and he invited
me over to his house and I spent the night with him. The next day,
against my doctor's advice, I phoned Sue and told her that that
I had slept with him. Sue was very shocked and asked me why it
had happened and I told her I was so depressed.'[2]

She gave up. She returned to her solicitor and cited Norman's
affairs with two men, Wilson-Young and an interior designer who
worked at Harrods. She also described Scott's obsession with
Thorpe, but agreed that this was irrelevant to her petition for

divorce. Scott was puzzled and frightened when he received her solicitor's letter. It did not occur to him that he might, possibly, be responsible for the collapse of his marriage; instead, as usual, he blamed Thorpe.

He stormed out of the flat in Earls Court to instruct a solicitor to resist her demand for a divorce and, if that failed, to win custody of Benjamin. He was also determined to expose Thorpe; first, for turning him into a homosexual and, next, for wrecking his marriage by refusing to stamp his National Insurance card, which had made it impossible for him support his wife and son. As proof he carried the latest 'dossier' on Thorpe; this was much thinner than earlier versions, since he had either lost, destroyed or given away his revealing, intimate correspondence, and consisted only of the 'retainer' notes from Bessell, which proved nothing.

He walked into the first solicitor's office he saw and poured out his story to a senior partner called Cyril Lewis. Scott thought that Lewis was impressed: 'I told him about the whole of my relationship with Jeremy Thorpe and Mr Bessell and about my marriage to Sue and my association with Conway Wilson-Young. I told him the whole story because it was relevant to my divorce proceedings.' Two days later, however, Lewis wisely declined to become involved in this deranged young man's fantasies about one of the most respected and popular politicians in the country. Naturally, Scott was sure that this was another plot against him by the Establishment: 'Mr Lewis did not give any reason but I thought it might have been the political ramifications. It may be that he got in touch either with Jeremy Thorpe or Mr Bessell.'[3]

Exhausted and demoralised he spent the rest of the summer in a drugged stupor. In August Susan dispatched relatives to the flat to collect her belongings but he was in no state to stop them: 'I was full of drugs that day because my doctor had given me an injection. I woke up next morning to find myself in the room with no furniture or carpets. They had all been taken. Then I knew the marriage was over.'[4]

Predictably, he turned to Bessell, who, in Scott's addled mind, was the peacemaker who would effect a reconciliation with the man whom he both loved and hated. In October he telephoned Bessell's secretary in London and said that he was desperate because his wife was divorcing him. Bessell was horrified when he picked up the message: he feared that Scott would use a divorce hearing to denounce Thorpe. He thought that it was unlikely that the press would touch the story but they might be tempted since court reports were privileged. So he dashed to Thorpe's flat near Victoria Station. Thorpe, who was still insisting publicly that he was finding the loss of Caroline impossible to endure, told Bessell that it was vital that Scott should not be allowed to use the divorce to denounce him. Bessell agreed. It was curious that two intelligent, worldly men still could not grasp that Scott could say what he liked and no one would believe him. He had not seen Thorpe for over five years and no longer had any evidence to support his story of an affair. But that was too logical. So Thorpe agreed that they should persuade Scott to seek advice from a solicitor in London called Leonard Ross, who was a Liberal supporter and who had worked with them in various companies. Bessell promised that Ross would make sure that the divorce went through quietly, without publicity. But then Thorpe snapped, as if Scott was a bad tooth which could only be dealt with, once and for all, by extraction. According to Bessell, he said, 'Ross will do a good job for the moment. But it's got to be the ultimate solution. We daren't let Scott go near a court.'

Instead of telling Thorpe that he was mad and needed urgent psychiatric help, Bessell once more weighed up the idea, as if Thorpe had just proposed a new Liberal policy on taxation. He said that killing Scott in England might have unpleasant repercussions, since the police tended to disapprove of murder. Then Thorpe had a brainwave: he said that Bessell should lure Scott to the States with the promise of a job, where Holmes would kill him. Bessell said that this had potential; they debated various schemes, such as burying Scott's body in Florida, which Bessell explained was 'a big state, with a large central area that is deserted'.

Next day, they continued their discussion. Thorpe said that Scott should fly to Florida, where he would be met by Holmes, posing as his new employer. Having killed him, Holmes and Bessell would dispose of the body in the swamps, where alligators would consume it. Bessell said that this sounded splendid but added that he was so busy dealing with Scott's divorce that Thorpe would have to brief Holmes. Bessell moved smoothly into action on the non-violent problem of the divorce. He assumed the role of honest broker and persuaded Scott that Ross was an excellent lawyer who would be 'very tough with the other side'. Scott thanked nice Mr Bessell, who was always so helpful, and, in early November, made an appointment with Ross, who had offices near Regent's

Park. He dressed for the occasion in a flowered shirt and cream flared trousers but was pale and drawn from the strain of the past months, so that he looked like an ageing pop star who had fallen on hard times.

It was not a happy meeting. Scott blamed Thorpe for his marital difficulties and made it clear that he intended to use any hearing to expose him. He said, 'I made a statement to Mr Ross regarding my association with Thorpe and about his failure to stamp my employment cards which caused me to be in the present predicament about my marriage.'[5] If Ross had not been acting covertly for Thorpe he would probably have told this wretched, sweaty creature to leave but he was anxious to assist Thorpe and feigned concern. He explained to Scott that generally courts did not like awarding the custody of infants to men who were promiscuous homosexuals; this meant, Ross added gently, that it might be wise if Scott did not mention his affair with Thorpe. This was not what Scott wanted to hear and he stomped off to consider his position. Ross, meanwhile, scuttled round to Thorpe's flat to report that, in his view, Scott could be contained. He told Thorpe that, providing that Susan Myers did not cite him in her petition, he should be safe because a court would not listen to Scott's uncorroborated ravings.

A few days later Ross travelled to Skegness to consult with Susan Myers' solicitor, who agreed that Thorpe was not relevant to the proceedings. Ross returned to London, reported the good news to Thorpe and assumed, wrongly of course, that Scott would accept defeat gracefully. Early in December Scott arrived at his office, expecting to be told that the divorce would allow him to tell the world that Thorpe had wrecked his life; instead, Ross informed him that it was neither possible nor prudent to include Thorpe's name in any documents.

Scott might have looked like a broken man but, once again, at least as far as Thorpe was concerned, he showed that he had an unbending will. He informed Ross that he had no intention of following his advice: he said that he would seek Legal Aid and would include Thorpe's name in his application. He said:

> Ross asked how my relationship with Jeremy Thorpe could possibly be of interest to the Legal Aid people. He knew very well. The reason my wife was divorcing me was because our situation had become so intolerable through our straitened

financial circumstances. I mean, Sue would never have left me had we been able to afford to live together and I wouldn't have gone with the two men that I subsequently went with.

Scott accused Ross of working for Thorpe, which, for once, was not paranoia, and stormed out of the meeting. Later that day he telephoned and said that he would be instructing another solicitor, which was bad news for Thorpe. Once again, Bessell leapt into unctuous action. He telephoned Ena Josiffe, Scott's mother, and begged her to intervene with her son; he said that Ross was an excellent lawyer who just wanted what was best for him. She did not trust Bessell and hated Thorpe but, on the other hand, she did not want poor Norman to lose his son. So she did as she was asked and persuaded Norman to give Ross another chance.

After a quiet Christmas at home in Cornwall with his wife, Bessell set off in the New Year of 1971 for New York to bid farewell to his new girlfriend, Diane Kelly, and kill himself. As always, he had financial problems but this time he feared that he would not be able to wriggle free. He said:

> I faced the worst financial crisis of my life. On paper I owed half a million dollars. I persuaded myself that if bankruptcy became inevitable I would commit suicide. In the preceding ten years I had worked harder than at any time in my life. And, when I played, it was with the same intensity. Despite my slight build I had almost perfect health but I had used my capacities in a fight against what proved in the end to be impossible odds.

He said that he wanted to make his death look like an accident so that Pauline, who was marooned in Cornwall, would be able to claim on his insurance policies. After careful research he decided that a car crash in Florida would be best.

> I knew from dependable statistics that a particular form of collision over a certain speed meant instant death for the driver. I also wanted to kill myself in a climate where I could feel the warmth of the sun, listen to the sound of the ocean and see a velvet night. Throughout my life I had dreaded winter. Autumnal colours merely depressed me. Snow and chill winds

caused more than physical discomfort; they produced a sense of despair.

But he did not carry out his plan. After a passionate reunion with Diane he delayed his suicide and flew to the Bahamas to see Jack Hayward, ostensibly to brief him on Thorpe's recurring difficulties with Scott, but, in fact, to beg for money. Hayward had always liked Bessell, though he knew that he was a crook, and took pity on him; he 'lent' him £25,000, which he knew that he would never see again, and guaranteed his £10,000 overdraft at a bank in Plymouth. He said, 'Peter was desperate. He was facing his creditors. He was thinking of taking his own life. He had a wife and two children, and a girlfriend in New York. I felt sorry for him.'[6]

Bessell also claimed that he met Holmes in New York and in Florida to discuss Thorpe's murder plan. He said that they agreed that Holmes would tell Thorpe that they had planned the murder meticulously, as ordered, but that, unfortunately, Scott had failed to arrive.[7]

Bessell returned to London in mid-January, flush with Hayward's money and bursting with ideas for new business projects which would, finally, make him rich. He deputed Holmes to break the news to Thorpe that they had failed in their mission to kill Scott; meanwhile, he approached the problem with a new buoyancy. He asked Norman if he would like a job in the Bahamas with a wealthy entrepreneur called Hayward, who was a good friend. Scott did not, which was just as well since Hayward had already told Bessell that he did not have any openings in his tax-free industrial complex for a homosexual who loved animals. Then Bessell offered him a long free holiday. But Scott was not interested:

> Mr Bessell said I must have a holiday and wouldn't I like to go on a world cruise – for three months – the cost of which would be met by Jeremy Thorpe, himself and a philanthropic financier, Jack Hayward, who lived in the Bahamas. I said, 'Well, no, I wouldn't.' I then had a small whippet called Emma and he said, 'Well, if you want to you can take your whippet.' I thought this peculiar. You just don't take your dog on a world cruise. There are quarantine problems.

Scott had more important things to think about than jobs in

the Caribbean and cruises. On 13 January 1971 Ross wrote to him, promising that he would do his best to win him custody, or, failing that, regular access, to young Benjamin. But he also raised the subject of his own fees: 'Please let me know whether you wish me to obtain Legal Aid on your behalf. There has been some talk of your costs being paid by those who are interested in your future, but this is obviously a decision which you may wish to make yourself.' This little phrase was a rare acknowledgement that Scott might be telling the truth. Ross had been careful not to name Thorpe in his letter but his reference to anonymous benefactors was a useful addition to Norman's 'dossier'.

The letter also provoked another row. Scott had sent Ross a long statement, in which he described, in explicit detail, how Thorpe was responsible for his wife's unhappiness; yet, to his fury, Ross was behaving as if this was a routine divorce. He accused Ross of suppressing evidence and threatened to report him to the Law Society. Ross replied that he could not understand Scott's argument that Thorpe was central to the divorce and asked, 'How can your relationship with J.T. affect that issue?'

Then Scott seemed to lose heart. He appointed another solicitor but gave up trying to use the case to expose Thorpe; the marriage was formally dissolved in September 1972, granting him only four hours a year with Benjamin, in the presence of his ex-wife. Thorpe was not mentioned. Ross, meanwhile, spent many months chasing Thorpe for the money he was owed for his work on the divorce. Finally, in despair, Ross appealed to Bessell, who was trying to make his fortune in the United States, and asked him if he could remind Thorpe that he had still not been paid. On 27 April 1973 Thorpe sent Ross a cheque for £77.55.

As winter gave way to spring in 1971 Scott felt that it was time to return to the fresh air, animals and solitude of the countryside. The flat at Earls Court was empty, apart from the bed where he spent most of his time, drifting in and out of consciousness, and Sue and young Benjamin had gone and were unlikely to return. He spotted an advertisement in *The Times* for a cottage, costing £12 a week, in the village of Talybont, in Caernarfonshire, North Wales, an area where he had spent happy times with his disillusioned wife. He made a few rough calculations. The owner of his flat was offering him £1,500 to leave. Then there was Bessell, alias Thorpe. Scott still believed that Thorpe owed him a living and so, without the slightest embarrassment, asked Bessell for an advance on the rent for his new cottage. He said that he was thinking of setting up a stables and trekking business in Wales and would be in touch later to give Bessell details of the funding which he would require.

Bessell and Thorpe did not have to give Scott a penny but they did not see things like that; both were gripped by the fear that, if they did not continue to support Scott, he would wreak a terrible revenge. Thus, Bessell said that he was glad to see that Norman was not brooding on his failed marriage and promised to send Leonard Ross some money, which he could forward to Talybont. (A few days later he sent a cheque for £25 to Ross.)

Early in March, Scott set off, accompanied by an Afghan hound called Apple, two whippets, Kate and Emma, and a cat. He set up home in the cottage, a converted mill which gloried in the name Mill House. For the first time in his eventful but unhappy life he was well-off and could have afforded a new, low-key wardrobe but he kept his London suits and huge patterned ties, which he thought marked him out as a man of distinction. Locals, however, thought he looked as if he had escaped from a circus. For a few weeks Scott revelled in their attention, mistaking astonishment for admiration: 'I must have been the most exciting thing who had ever turned up in that village. My Afghan hounds and purple velvet suits and I don't know what.' He also took pride in two friends from London, Jack Levy, who designed record covers, and his wife, Stella, who worked in textiles; when they arrived at his cottage in a shiny BMW Scott imagined that the villagers would be impressed that he knew people like them.

The money drained away and inevitably the old insecurities returned, eating away at the self-confidence that had grown from the rare experience of having a full wallet. He staged another attention-seeking suicide and, as usual, people took pity on him. His latest saviours were Keith Rose and his wife, who owned a garage in the village. Once his head had cleared from the non-lethal overdose of sleeping pills he poured out his tragic story. The Roses clucked sympathetically at the way that poor Norman's life had been ruined by wicked politicians and corrupt policemen and said that they would help him fight for justice. He thanked them but said that he was travelling to London shortly to demand restitution from Mr Bessell.

The meeting in London went well. Bessell said that, unfortunately, money was short: Scott said that he, too, was experiencing

financial problems and demanded an immediate donation to cover
the rent of the cottage and about £5,000 to start a riding school. He
talked as if Bessell and Thorpe were a trust fund which existed to
support him: 'I was elated. I asked him would he please settle the
rent for the cottage and could he please let me have some money
to tide me over until they could let me have the £5,000. He said he
would send it straight away.'[8] He returned to Wales and informed
the Roses that he had won a famous victory. But Bessell did not
send the money and a few days later Scott telephoned him from
the Roses' garage, with Keith Rose listening on an extension as a
witness. Bessell grumbled about cash-flow problems but promised
to send 'five' to Scott, though he did not say whether that meant 500
or 5,000. On 7 April, however, a letter from Bessell plopped on to
Scott's doormat at the cottage, informing him that, sadly, he could
not raise any money and was leaving on an important business
trip to the States. Unwisely, he suggested that Scott should keep
in close touch with Leonard Ross, the solicitor who had sabotaged
his plans to expose Thorpe in court. Scott was furious: 'The rent
wasn't being paid and the people who owned the cottage were
getting very angry. I got more and more despondent as I realised
I'd been duped. One evening I told two or three people a little
of what had happened to me about Jeremy Thorpe. They were
disgusted.'

Rose was appalled by the duplicity of these smart people in
London and decided to protest to Thorpe. On 4 May he wrote:

> Mr Scott's financial situation is now critical. He is not without
> friends who are willing to help him, but obviously the situation
> must be resolved. It must surely be in your own interests to
> resolve it. I have nothing whatsoever to gain from this whole
> sorry business, or the knowledge of it. We should simply like
> to see Mr Scott settled into a reasonable way of life when he
> so obviously wishes this for himself.

Thorpe told Tom Dale, his loyal personal assistant, to tell this
strange Welshman that he was talking nonsense. Dale wrote
to Rose: 'As far as he [Thorpe] is aware he does not know
Mr Norman Scott. However, he believes that Mr Van de Brecht
de Vater [sic] knew a Mr Norman Josiffe, who may be the same
person. Mr Thorpe asks me to say he is under no obligation to
this gentleman.'

This was a stupid letter. Thorpe should have sent a curt one-line reply, denying that he knew a man calling himself Norman Scott. This would have been technically correct, since he had had an affair with Norman Josiffe not Norman Scott, and would have confirmed Rose's suspicion that Norman needed psychiatric help. But Dale's note, with its references to people with foreign names, suggested to Rose that perhaps Scott might not be mad.

Bessell, who was in New York at the time, was appalled when Thorpe told him about the letter: 'For the first time in six years Jeremy acted on his own to stave off a problem with Scott and the course he chose could hardly have been worse. It is difficult to fathom his reason for mentioning Van de Vater and, without explaining why, suggesting Scott might be Josiffe. The inescapable impression the letter conveyed was that Jeremy knew a good deal more than he was prepared to admit.'

Scott was not in a position to exploit Thorpe's misjudgement since, once again, he was penniless, homeless and depressed. He moved into a caravan and continued to bore villagers with his interminable stories about Thorpe. But there was one lonely soul who was flattered by the attentions of this handsome and sensitive young man. Her name was Gwen Parry-Jones, a wealthy widow in her mid-50s who had once run Talybont's sub-post office. She offered Scott the use of one of the cottages that she owned in the village; soon they were having an affair. Scott said:

> Gwen was obviously ripe for a friendship. She had the most wonderful eyes and a very good Modigliani sort of face. She was not a beauty but she was immensely kind. Everybody knew everything about everybody. It was obvious I was living with her. I think she was terribly proud that this young giddy poof had turned up in her life when she thought it was the end. She wanted to marry me although she knew it couldn't happen because of the way I was. But she laughed a lot when we were together.

She did not laugh, however, when Scott described how Thorpe had destroyed his life. She was a Liberal supporter and was shocked that the leader of the Party that represented honesty and decency in a wicked world could treat another human being so callously. She decided to intervene on Norman's behalf and wrote to Emlyn Hooson, the Liberal MP for the neighbouring constituency of

Montgomeryshire, whose father she knew. She asked him if he would investigate how a young man's life had been ruined by 'a leading member of the Party' and why a promise to give him the money to start a new life in Wales had not been kept. Hooson wrote back, saying that he would like to help but needed to know who she was talking about. She replied cryptically, 'Please tell Mr Peter Bessell that Mr Norman Scott is in a grave situation and if he has any decency he will fulfil his promise made to him immediately.'

Hooson was intrigued and invited her to meet him at the Commons the following week. Understandably, he assumed from her letter that Bessell was the villain who had abused this mysterious young man called Scott, which surprised him since he had always regarded Bessell as a womaniser; on the other hand, Hooson told himself, Bessell was such an immoral character that he probably slept with men as well as women. Hooson had represented Montgomeryshire since 1962. Although he was the undisputed Liberal intellectual at Westminster he had not risen as high as he had hoped, partly because his views on such matters as homosexuality were regarded as reactionary by Party activists and partly because he refused to cultivate allies in the tea rooms of the Commons. Parry-Jones' letter offered him the opportunity to make it clear that some Liberals still had moral standards, unlike those rowdy Young Liberals, whose idea of political debate was to scream clichés about oppression in the Third World, and to deal with the appalling Bessell, who had betrayed him in the leadership election of 1967.

Gwen Parry-Jones, the middle-aged widow, and her new boyfriend, young Norman, arrived at the Commons on the afternoon of 26 May, expecting to meet Emlyn Hooson. But Helen Roberts, his secretary, said that he had been summoned to an important meeting and wondered if they would make do with David Steel, the Liberal Chief Whip. As they made their way to Steel's office Roberts said that it was a pity that Mr Thorpe was abroad because Mr Hooson would certainly have wanted them to speak to him. Scott mumbled that it was probably just as well that he was not available.

This was the start of one of the most celebrated episodes of the Thorpe–Scott story: the Liberal Party's secret inquiry into Scott's allegations that he had been seduced and then ruined by Thorpe. In May 1971 only a handful of people knew about it but, a few years later, when Scott became front-page news, the politicians who were involved in it blamed everyone but themselves for their failure to establish the truth. Some pundits, notably Bessell and the investigative reporters, Barrie Penrose and Roger Courtiour, later declared that the inquiry had been a sophisticated cover-up because they mistook this long, unscripted black comedy for a British version of Watergate.

That afternoon in May 1971 Steel settled down and waited for Parry-Jones and Scott to confirm that he had been right to distrust Bessell who, during his mercifully short time as a Liberal MP, had had 'a string of ill-concealed affairs with his secretaries' while he lurched from one financial crisis to another. Then Scott poured out the story of the first meeting at Van de Vater's stables, the seduction at Thorpe's mother's house and his missing Insurance card. Steel was horrified: the accused was Jeremy Thorpe, his leader, not Bessell. Scott was gaunt, sweaty and spoke so quietly that it was hard to catch everything he said; Steel thought that he looked as if he was having a nervous breakdown. Although he was only 33 years old Steel had been an MP for six years and knew that the stars of the Commons such as Thorpe often became fantasy figures for society's flotsam. But he could not dismiss Scott because, laid out neatly on the desk, was the 'dossier' including the 'retainer' letters, which showed, at the very least, that Scott had had some form of relationship with Bessell or Thorpe. He told Scott that he should repeat his story to Hooson, as the recipient of Parry-Jones' original appeal and as an eminent lawyer, as soon as possible. Scott said that he would be happy to do so.

Her duty done, Mrs Parry-Jones headed back to Wales. Scott, meanwhile, spent the night with his BMW-driving friends, Jack and Stella Levy. As he was unwinding after the emotional exertions of the day, Steel was breaking the news to Hooson in the Commons: 'I called him into my room and unveiled the story. Emlyn said that I looked as white a sheet. "It's not about Bessell," I said, "it's about Jeremy."'[9]

Scott reported to the Commons the following day, 27 May. Hooson slipped into courtroom mode and gently probed Scott's story for weaknesses, while Steel listened and his secretary took notes. Even in normal circumstances Scott muddled fact and fiction, which gave the impression that he was a crude liar, which he was not. But now he was running on a lethal cocktail of adrenalin, anger and alcohol, which meant that his limited capacity for rational thought was further reduced. The story that he told Hooson was a jumble of exaggerations and half-truths, designed, subconsciously, to emphasise Thorpe's perfidy and his own misery. For example, he said that he had planned to shoot Thorpe in 1962 but had been arrested in the Commons before he had a chance to carry out his plan. This was the skeleton of the truth: he had, indeed, threatened to kill Thorpe but had done so in the privacy of a hotel bedroom, not the Commons, and had had a bullet but no gun. Anyone checking the story would have discovered that there had been an incident, just as Scott alleged, but that it was not as dramatic as he described. Nonetheless, Scott sensed that he was making an impact. He laid out his 'dossier' again, as if the 'retainer' letters from Bessell and other assorted correspondence, mostly concerning his divorce, proved his story. Hooson said that his file, far from showing that he had had an affair with Thorpe, suggested that he had been blackmailing Bessell. Scott was outraged. He said, 'I told them about the love letters from Jeremy. They asked me where they were and suggested I find them. I said Scotland Yard had some and I had left one with Major Shute in Gloucestershire for safekeeping. Then there were the bundles Jeremy had taken from my suitcase when I came back from Switzerland.'

Hooson and Steel stared in disbelief at the idea that they should set off, like muck-raking journalists, to obtain letters from the police and a mysterious major called Shute, in order to discredit their own leader. But they could not ignore Scott. If they did that then he would probably rush off to Fleet Street to complain about a cover-up, which would be embarrassing. They were also honest men and were determined to investigate his claims, painful though that would be. So they asked him to remain in London while they consulted colleagues. Scott was delighted. He returned to the Levys and waited, emotionally and physically drained, but sure that, at last, he would triumph. If he had been sensible he would have contacted Major Shute and asked for the love letter that he had left there; he would also have approached Scotland Yard for the return of the letters which he had given them in December 1962. But he did neither and just thumbed through his precious 'dossier'.

Emlyn Hooson, however, was more active. It was the Whitsun recess and Thorpe was in Zambia, combining private and political business. Hooson did not like or trust Thorpe but, on the other hand, he was the Liberal leader and it was essential to clear him of Scott's charges. So he talked to Mrs Parry-Jones, but she simply repeated what Scott had already said; he also traced Edward Smith, one of the detectives who had questioned Scott in 1962, who told him that Scott had alleged a homosexual affair with Thorpe and had given the police evidence which he claimed backed this up. But Hooson knew that none of this was conclusive; Scott's story was consistent but that did not mean that it was true.

But it was different when he telephoned Bessell in Cornwall, who was on a rare excursion from New York. He told Hooson that Scott was telling the truth. He said that he had given Scott a great deal of money over the years to buy his silence but added gloomily that he had known that always the truth would come out one day. Since Bessell assumed that all politicians were as amoral as he (and Thorpe) he expected Hooson to congratulate him on a well-organised cover-up and to agree that Thorpe had to be protected from the vengeful Scott. But Hooson was not like that and snapped, 'Jeremy will have to go. He'll have to resign as leader and he'll probably have to resign his seat as well. I'll be asking David [Steel] for a meeting of the parliamentary party so we can discuss the whole business.'[10] Bessell did not like the sound of this. He had enough problems with his failing businesses, without being dragged into a homosexual scandal. He was fond of Thorpe but, more importantly, needed him to remain the leader of Britain's third political party because that conferred respectability and opened doors. So he moved into damage-limitation overdrive. He telephoned Ursula Thorpe, who said that her son was returning the following day from Zambia. Bessell asked if she would tell Jeremy to call him urgently.

Next day Bessell broke the news to Thorpe: Hooson knew about Scott. Even worse, Bessell confessed, Hooson had caught him off-guard and he had, he was sorry to say, confirmed that Scott was telling the truth. But Bessell reassured him that they could fight off Hooson, providing they kept their nerve. They set out to isolate Hooson by giving the impression that he was only interested in discrediting Thorpe. First, Bessell lied about his conversation with Hooson. He told Steel that Hooson must have misunderstood; he had only told Hooson that Scott fantasised that he had been Thorpe's lover, not that it was true. Thorpe, meanwhile, also feigned outrage that his colleagues were siding with Scott against him. It was true, he said, that he had met Scott

many years ago at a stables in Oxfordshire. Scott had asked for
help over a missing National Insurance card but he had been so
busy that he had passed the case to Bessell. Thorpe then suggested,
with his usual loyalty to friends, that Scott might have blackmailed
Bessell. Thorpe also protested about Hooson's approach to the
police. He said that it was disgraceful that he had gone behind
his back in this way; he said that the police had no right to
release information on their cases to people like Hooson, who
only wanted to cause trouble, and he intended to protest to Sir
John Waldron, the Commissioner of the Metropolitan Police.

To their credit, Hooson and Steel did not buckle under this
barrage of lies and threats; they insisted that the Party hold a
formal inquiry so that it could not be accused of a cover-up. But
they promised that it would be secret.

On the afternoon of 9 June 1971 Scott was ushered into the office
in the House of Lords of Frank Byers, the Liberal leader in the
Lords, who had been chosen to chair the inquiry. He was flanked
by Hooson and Steel. Byers was a vigorous 55-year-old former
MP for North Dorset. He had won an athletics Blue at Oxford
and had had a distinguished war. He was a widely respected figure
in the Lords but he was probably not the best choice to lead the
interrogation of Scott. Even his friends conceded that he could be
brusque and insenstive, which were not the qualities required to
massage the truth from a man who was tottering permanently on
the edge of a breakdown.

The interview began badly. He fired questions at Scott, demanding places and dates. Scott always found it difficult to organise
the events of his life in chronological order but now, sweating
and shaking, everything became a blur. So he poured out the
usual litany of complaints about the seduction at Ursula Thorpe's
house, his missing National Insurance card and Thorpe's promise
that he would take care of him.

Byers growled. Over the years Scott had exasperated many far
more patient people and that day he was at his infuriating best.
He whined, sobbed, kept changing his story and blamed everyone,
except himself, for his miserable life. Byers made it clear that he
found Scott disgusting and added that, even if he had once slept
with Thorpe, he did not see why he should support him now.
Scott started to cry. Byers lost his temper and told him that he
was a common blackmailer, which was silly since Scott would

hardly have complained to the Liberal Party, and brought the 'retainer' letters with him, if he had been guilty of this. But, like many people before and after, Byers imagined that there was a logic to Scott's actions, which must have had something to do with money, when, in fact, Norman only wanted revenge.

Steel and Hooson tried to calm Scott but it was too late. He picked up his 'dossier' and fled. He said, 'Lord Byers looked at me as if I was absolutely loathsome. He was not at all affable and he didn't offer me a chair. I felt like a boy at school up before the headmaster. I told him, "I have been morally blackmailed. Through my loyalty to Jeremy I kept quiet. I did nothing. I have no Insurance card. And I have lost everything." I also told Byers that he was a pontificating old sod.' Byers snapped back that Scott needed psychiatric help.

Outside the Lords, as he dabbed at the tears, Scott realised belatedly that no one would believe him until he recovered Thorpe's love letters, which he had given the police in 1962. He telephoned Scotland Yard and asked where a nice man called Sergeant Edward Smith, whom he had met in Chelsea nine years ago, was working now; the Yard said that he was now Detective Inspector Smith and was based at Southwark, a short walk over the Thames from Westminster. He called Smith and arranged to meet the following day.

Meanwhile, Byers had also requested an audience with Smith. Next day, 10 June, Smith was quizzed by the panel. But it was a waste of everyone's time. As a result of Thorpe's protests to the Commissioner, Smith had been assigned a minder from the Yard, who was there to make sure that he did not say anything that would further annoy Thorpe. So Smith limited himself to non-controversial, monosyllabic answers. Yes, he said, Scott had once threatened to kill Thorpe but he had not been charged, and, yes, he had given the police certain letters but, again, these proved nothing. Byers nodded, satisfied that he had been right about Scott.

Shortly after Smith had returned to his office in Southwark Scott arrived to demand the return of his letters; instead he found himself treated like a criminal, as Smith and a colleague tried to establish whether he was a blackmailer. But after five hours they had to concede that there was no evidence to support this and had to be satisfied with yet another long statement, in which Scott described how his life had been ruined by Thorpe. It was dispatched to Special

Branch at Scotland Yard, and then to MI5, where it was added to what was, by now, a thick bundle of statements by him which spanned a decade.

Hooson, meanwhile, was not satisfied. In mid-June he wrote to Parry-Jones:

> Obviously my concern, and that of Mr Steel, is the very serious allegations made against one of our colleagues in an eminent position which are strenuously denied by that person. On the other hand, the young man tells a very convincing story and is obviously in a very distressed state, so that the question of corroboration is very important.
>
> With regard to the welfare of the young man you will appreciate that, even if his story is correct and is provable, then he does not appear to have a legal claim of any kind against Mr T. That there would be a moral obligation if the story is correct is undoubted. However, it is vitally important for me and my colleagues to clear away any suspicion of blackmail and this we are proceeding to do.

But Thorpe was moving fast to consolidate his victory. He wrote to the Conservative Home Secretary, Reginald Maudling, and Sir John Waldron, the Metropolitan Police Commissioner, saying that Hooson was still 'muck-raking' and that Byers felt that the only way to shut him up would be for them to clear him of wrongdoing. Thorpe did not ask them whether Scott's central allegations were true: that he, Thorpe, had had a long affair with Scott and that he had been involved in paying Scott to remain silent about it. Instead, he asked them whether specific claims about him were true; this was a stroke of genius because Thorpe had dreamt up many of these allegations himself. Naturally, Maudling and Waldron replied that, as far as they were aware, the charges that Thorpe outlined in his letters to them were false. Thorpe then presented their replies to Byers as if they had cleared him of any involvement with Scott, which they had not.

Maudling and Waldron knew from Special Branch and MI5 that Thorpe was a promiscuous homosexual but, officially, these files did not exist and could not, therefore, be discussed. The files also indicated that Scott had probably had an affair with Thorpe but that could not be proven beyond doubt and, in any case, this was no longer a criminal offence. On the other hand, Maudling and Waldron knew that Thorpe was not an honest man and could, and should, have refused to help him clear his name.

But there was another crucial factor, which had nothing to do with members of the Establishment looking after one of their own: Byers, Steel, Maudling, Waldron, and Hooson were heterosexuals who knew nothing about men like Thorpe and Scott, who married and had children but who were also homosexuals. Senior Liberals, such as Steel, had heard rumours about Thorpe's colourful private life but dismissed them as vicious gossip, of the sort that always swirled around successful politicians. Even if they had investigated the rumours they would not have found out much because the gay Liberals who knew about Thorpe would never have betrayed him in 1971. But a few gays were beginning to have doubts; they wondered why they should continue to protect a man who refused to acknowledge what he was, which was an insult to gays who had come out at great cost to their careers.

CHAPTER TEN

Norman lurched away from Southwark police station sobbing that life was unbearable. He had failed to destroy Thorpe. He had not even managed to recover the love letters which proved that he was telling the truth. He spent two nights in Hyde Park, pondering his future: 'Nobody believed me. I had to live but I still did not have my bloody Insurance card. And who was responsible? Jeremy Thorpe.'[1] After two nights on park benches, however, he decided that he might as well be depressed in comfort, so he returned to Bloomsbury to his friends, Jack and Stella Levy, and had a hot bath and changed his clothes.

That evening Leslie Ebbetts, a journalist who wrote about fashion for the *Daily Mirror*, came to dinner. Norman, bathed and wearing a crisp new outfit, had recovered from his brief experience as a down-and-out and was back on form. He introduced himself to Ebbetts by explaining how Jeremy Thorpe, the leader of the Liberal Party, had seduced him and ruined his life, which was how he usually opened conversations with strangers. She listened politely as this strange young man, who would have been handsome but for the sly eyes and feminine pout, talked in a barely audible voice about pots of Vaseline, handmade shirts, lost Insurance cards and cover-ups. She decided that he was probably mad but, on the other hand, Jack and Stella liked him and they were sensible people.

She told him that this was fascinating but said that, as an expert on hem-lengths and that summer's hot colours, she was not really equipped to tackle a story like this. But she thought that Jill Evans, who was an experienced news reporter on the *Mirror*, would know how to proceed. A few days later, Scott visited Evans at her flat in North London and repeated his astonishing story. But she was not interested either, though she was too diplomatic to say so; instead, she said that it was all too complicated for a tabloid newspaper like the *Mirror* and suggested that Norman should talk to an experienced investigative journalist. She said that she knew just the man: Gordon Winter, who freelanced for newspapers in Britain and South Africa. Norman was grateful: 'She said that Winter was a real investigative journalist and a very nice man who would sort out my problem. I felt happy and made an appointment to see him. By talking to a journalist I felt that I would gain protection if anyone tried to harm me while we sorted out my Insurance card problem.'

On the afternoon of Wednesday, 16 June 1971 Norman and Emma, his whippet, took a taxi from Bloomsbury to Pont Street, off Sloane Street, where Winter rented a flat. Norman had dressed for the occasion: he was wearing cream trousers, a hand-knitted sweater and an expensive snakeskin jacket. With Emma under his arm, he rang the bell.

A few minutes later Winter opened the door. He was in his mid-40s but was tanned and lean and looked younger, despite his thinning blond hair. Jill Evans had warned him that Scott was an unusual character. He said:

> Scott was outlandishly effeminate, but his face was ruggedly masculine with a deeply dimpled chin, strong sensuous lips and a large, slightly bent nose. His bush of black curly hair was carefully styled to look as though it had not been combed, and, all considered, he could have been taken for a monied pop star. But not when he opened his mouth. The timbre of his voice was soft, even musical, and his cultured English accent was such that he sounded like a duke, which was the kind of rank he felt he should have been born with.

He invited Scott and Emma into his living room. Winter began the interview gently: 'I asked him whether he was a member of the Liberal Party and if he knew any top Liberals. Then I said that I had once met Mr Thorpe, and Norman let out a high-pitched strangled scream and said, 'Oh my God, how can I trust you?' He managed to calm Scott by offering him a cup of tea. He also provided a saucer of milk for Emma, which reassured Norman, who judged people by their attitude to animals. Having decided that he could trust Winter he launched into his Thorpe story, which he had told countless times over the years. 'I was deeply in love with Jeremy. I thought our relationship would last for ever. But then he discarded me. That's why I loathe him now,' he said. Winter nodded, to encourage Norman to keep talking. He checked that the tape recorder on the table was working, though he had another as a back-up, hidden in a cupboard.

Beneath the charm and concern for small thirsty animals Gordon Winter was an unscrupulous man who would do and say anything for money. He was born in Yorkshire and, after a short spell as a burglar, which ended in jail, he emigrated to South Africa in 1960, where he persuaded the *Sunday Express* in Johannesburg to hire him as a crime reporter. He enjoyed his new career because he understood the criminal mind. Unfortunately, he grew too close to his sources and, after a local mine owner was murdered by London gangsters whom Winter knew, he was arrested, detained for two months and then deported.

When he arrived in Britain he claimed that he had been thrown out of South Africa because he was an incorruptible reporter who exposed injustice, which was his passport into the anti-apartheid movement. In fact, he had done a deal with BOSS. In return for a regular tax-free salary, paid in cash by contacts at the South African Embassy, he had agreed to become a spy in London.[2]

Over the next five years he became a respected commentator on organisations that opposed apartheid; yet, while he was writing stories that were critical of the South African government, he was secretly providing BOSS with information on Pretoria's enemies. He boasted, 'I was a fully fledged spy. I had eight filing cabinets next to my desk, crammed with records. I had 80,000 negatives cross-indexed. Everybody I had ever ever met, when I met them and where. I was a propagandist. My brilliance was negating enemies of South Africa.'

That Wednesday in June 1971 he sensed that Scott might turn out to be his finest coup. BOSS loathed the Liberals and would pay handsomely for a story that exposed the Party leader as a secret homosexual. So, he listened patiently as Scott talked for many hours about the physical and spiritual pain of homosexuality.

This meeting, which only happened because Jill Evans did not think that the *Mirror* would be interested in a homosexual, unemployed male model, thus introduced what became known as 'the South African connection' into the story. This caused tremendous complications a few years later, when Scott's allegations began to dribble into print. First, Thorpe used Winter's accidental involvement to accuse Scott of being a South African agent. Then Thorpe persuaded Harold Wilson that he was a victim of BOSS, which Wilson immediately believed, since he thought that he was also being smeared by the South Africans. Finally journalists, notably Barrie Penrose and Roger Courtiour, alias the intrepid duo, Pencourt, became obsessed with 'the South African connection' and spent many months investigating whether Scott was a creature of BOSS.[3]

Scott talked to Winter for hours. The essentials of his story were true but he also exaggerated; for example, he told Winter that he was at the centre of a major international conspiracy which involved 'top British VIPs and members of foreign royal families'.

By the end of the first week he trusted Winter sufficiently to let him copy his precious 'dossier' on Thorpe, the centrepiece of which were Bessell's 'retainer' letters, which, while they did not prove that Scott and Thorpe had been lovers, indicated that something odd had happened. Then, to seal their friendship, they went to bed. Winter explained that this was a routine professional chore: 'I would sometimes do this as part of my work. It's part of an agent's technique. I can walk into any restaurant and spot a homosexual. If he was of interest to BOSS I would behave as if I was a homosexual to get my grip on him.' Scott could not remember much about this episode apart from the fact that Winter had been, as he coyly put it, 'a very big man'.

After their night of passion Winter told Scott that he should return to Wales and wait for instructions while he investigated further. Scott was delighted that, finally, he had found a champion who would expose Thorpe and did as he was told; he thanked the Levys for their hospitality and headed back to Wales. He was still friendly with Gwen Parry-Jones but their relationship had cooled, which was not surprising after the strain of the Liberal Party inquiry and Norman's renewed interest in men. He moved to a village near Talybont, pottered around, schooling and selling horses and taking children on pony treks, and waited to be summoned back to London by that nice big man, Mr Winter.

Winter was also enthusiastic about Norman's story. He contacted BOSS headquarters in South Africa and said that he could destroy Jeremy Thorpe, the Kaffir-loving leader of the Liberal Party. But he was ordered to hold the story until the next general election: 'I was told that I should then hand the Thorpe–Scott file to a newspaper in London. Publishing it would bring down

Thorpe and the Liberal Party, split the Labour vote and ensure the Tory Party stayed in office.'

This was not a realistic plan. Although BOSS was, arguably, the most efficient intelligence organisation in the world it did not understand how the press operated in a democracy. No British newspaper would have printed a story about a former mental patient who claimed that he had had an affair with the Liberal leader. But BOSS officers were not journalists and did not understand these subtleties; Winter had no such excuse. He should have seen that there was only one publishable story: that the Liberal Party had secretly questioned its own leader about his alleged homosexuality. Newspapers would have run this as a legitimate news story, while insisting that Scott's allegations were baseless. But Scott would have been propelled on to the front pages, which would have been a triumph for Winter and a catastrophe for Thorpe.

In March 1972 Gwen Parry-Jones, the middle-aged widow who had had an affair with Norman and demanded justice for him from the Liberals, died. Her body was discovered at her home by a friend. She had been dead for a fortnight. Locals blamed Scott, who had toyed cruelly with her and upset her with his evil gossip about Jeremy Thorpe. Scott, however, insisted that she had killed herself because she despaired of the world after witnessing what had happened to him. He expanded this theory at her inquest in May at Bangor. The post-mortem showed that she had died of alcohol poisoning, although traces of aspirin and sedatives were found in her blood.

He told the coroner, E. Pritchard-Jones, that Parry-Jones often took sleeping pills, washed down with whisky. At first he was calm and rational but then began to sob and shake, which was the prelude to his standard denunciation of Thorpe. He said that dear Gwen had been 'a very good woman, very moral' and had been crushed by the 'corruption of politics'. Mr Pritchard-Jones frowned and said that he did not follow, so Scott ploughed on and explained how his life had been ruined by Mr Thorpe. Too late, Mr Pritchard-Jones realised that Scott was mad: 'When he started to make his strange allegations against Mr Thorpe I thought: I don't want to know about this. I thought: This fellow is a lunatic.' He told Scott that he had heard quite enough, told him to sit down and shut up and hastily delivered his verdict: 'Mrs Parry-Jones did have mental troubles. But I am not satisfied that there is clear evidence of self-destruction and the safest course is to record an open verdict.'

Scott's outburst would normally have gone unnoticed since even local newspapers do not bother to send reporters to routine inquests. But that day a journalist called Derek Bellis was in court, waiting for the inquest into the death of a well-known local skier. Bellis scribbled excitedly as Scott talked about his affair with Thorpe, and the subsequent cover-up, and rushed off to alert newsdesks in London. When they asked Thorpe's office to comment on claims that had been made at an inquest in Wales they were told: 'Mr Scott's allegations have been exhaustively investigated and there was not a scintilla of truth in them. He has a record of mental instability.' That was good enough for Fleet Street's news editors and not a word about Scott was published. Scott travelled to London to see if Gordon Winter had made any progress but he said that he was finding it harder than he had hoped to prove the story and told Scott to return to Wales. But the locals made it clear that he was no longer welcome there so he set off on his travels again; he found a job at a stud farm in Sussex but that only lasted a few months because he was 'depressed'.

Then his friends, Jack and Stella Levy, rescued him; they said that he could stay, rent-free, at a house which they had just bought in South Molton, a largish village south of Barnstaple in the heart of Thorpe's constituency. By now Scott had forgotten about his saviour, Gordon Winter. But Winter had not forgotten Thorpe and was still trying to think of a way to market the story. British Intelligence now began to take an interest in the activities of this prosperous freelance journalist who spent an inordinate amount of time with South African diplomats.

In November 1972 they moved against him. A man called Lee Tracey, who sold electronic bugging equipment, was asked by MI6, for whom he freelanced, to find out more about Winter. Tracey trailed him to a night-club, where he struck up a conversation about the latest developments in bugging and his work for MI6. When they met again Winter briefed Tracey on the Thorpe story, in the hope that right-wing elements in British Intelligence would leak the information to the press. If that happened, he calculated, then his masters in BOSS would be delighted: Thorpe would be disgraced and no one would be able to trace the story to South Africa. Tracey thanked him for the information, which he said would definitely interest MI5 and MI6. A few days later, however, he had bad news: British Intelligence already knew about Thorpe. He told Winter, 'They said to me, "You're behind the times, old boy. We've got a better file than this. We have known about this for a long time but it's not in our interest to do anything about it."'[4]

Winter was stunned; by trying to destroy Thorpe, he had exposed himself as a BOSS spy. A few months later he scuttled back to South Africa. But he deposited his file on Thorpe at a bank in London, just in case the story came to life one day.[5]

On the evening of Saturday, 24 February 1973 Thorpe told a meeting of Liberals in Barnstaple that he was remarrying in the spring. He said that his bride would be Marion, Countess of Harewood, former wife of the Earl of Harewood. His supporters gave him a standing ovation, delighted that brave Jeremy, who had lost his lovely young wife, Caroline, three years ago and been left to bring up Rupert, aged three, on his own, had found happiness again. His mother, Ursula, was also thrilled: 'I have just been lunching with Lady Harewood. She is absolutely charming. I am delighted for Jeremy. They have both been through so much and have been so lonely.'[6]

On Monday Thorpe and his fiancée, who was 46, three years older than him, held a press conference at his flat in London, still adorned with photographs and sculptures of his beloved Caroline. He had concocted a ridiculous story in April 1968 when he had announced his engagement to Caroline. This time he began with a fact: that he had been introduced to Marion a year earlier by their mutual friend, Moura Lympany, the concert pianist. But then he spoilt it by saying that it had been 'love at first sight' for both of them. Yet, though he probably re-married to boost his career, it has to be said he would have foundered without Marion; despite everything, she remained loyal over the years, in the face of revelations about her husband which would have driven most wives into the divorce courts.

To strangers she seemed cold and distant but friends said that this was no more than reserve; they said that she had had such a difficult life that she understood the pain of failure, which explained why she supported Jeremy as his life disintegrated. She was the daughter of Erwin Stein, who published music books in Vienna, and was named Maria Donata Nanetta Paulina Gustava Erwina

Norman Scott in 1968. He was 28 years old and trying to resurrect his career as a model.

Jeremy Thorpe cradles his son, Rupert, after the christening in the crypt of the House of Commons on 8 July 1969, watched by Caroline and David Holmes (behind Thorpe), the baby's godfather.

Jeremy Thorpe, the new leader of the Liberal Party, and his faithful friend, Peter Bessell, Liberal MP for Bodmin.

Jeremy Thorpe, the charismatic young leader of the Liberal Party, flanked by Edward Heath, the Prime Minister (left), and Harold Wilson, the Labour leader, at a memorial service at Westminster Abbey in 1970.

Jeremy Thorpe and Marion, Countess of Harewood, announcing their engagement in February 1973. They were married the following month.

Rinka, the Great Dane bitch. Scott tried to revive her with the kiss of life after she was shot by Newton on Exmoor in 1975.

Peter Bessell and Diane Kelly, his 38-year-old girlfriend and future wife, in their tiny home at Oceanside, California, February 1976. They adored each other and Bessell had never been happier. But the Scott affair was taking its toll.

Roger Courtiour (left) and Barrie Penrose (right), alias Pencourt, arrive at Minehead for Thorpe's committal in November 1978.

Marion leads her husband into the Old Bailey in June 1979 for another gruelling day. She always believed he would be acquitted and thought that he had been cruelly treated by the media.

John Le Mesurier, the carpet dealer who was accused of conspiracy to murder with Thorpe, David Holmes and George Deakin.

David Holmes, Thorpe's loyal friend, who organised the plot to silence Norman Scott.

George Deakin celebrates his acquittal at the Old Bailey in June 1979. His wife, Wendy, is more restrained.

Andrew Newton, the bungling hitman.

After his acquittal in June 1979 Thorpe and his wife Marion wave triumphantly from the balcony of their home near Hyde Park. His mother Ursula (left) always believed he was innocent.

Wilhelmina Stein. In 1939, when she was 12, the family, who were half-Jewish, emigrated to Britain to escape Nazi persecution.[7] They lived quietly and modestly in London. Marion blossomed into a beautiful and talented young woman; she was a brilliant pianist and seemed destined for a career as a concert pianist. In 1948, however, she fell in love with one of the most eligible men in the country, the Earl of Harewood, four years older than her, who was eleventh in succession to the throne.[8]

The British Establishment was not pleased when they announced their engagement in July 1949: she was foreign, a commoner and, worst of all, half-Jewish. But the public loved her because she was young, pretty and refreshingly unstuffy. She gave up her career and became a mother and charming hostess at Harewood House in Yorkshire and their London house, in Orme Square, overlooking Hyde Park. She was a patron of the arts and was always helping young musicians. The tabloids' 'experts' on the Royal Family said that the Queen adored her. But this fairy-tale marriage collapsed in 1962 when Harewood ran off with a young Australian model; they had a son two years later. In April 1967 Marion divorced him. She kept the house in Orme Square and a house called Curlews, near Aldeburgh in Suffolk. She also retained custody of her three sons, Viscount Lascelles, Robert and James, which was a comfort but later brought heartache when they became unruly teenagers.

Jeremy and Marion married quietly on 14 March 1973 at Paddington Register Office. There were three witnesses: Thorpe's friend and business adviser, Robin Salinger, Ursula, and Marion's eldest son. Then they drove to Westminster Abbey to celebrate Holy Communion and were joined by Rupert, and Marion's other sons. Afterwards they held a small party for forty close friends and then flew to Nice, for a two-day break, since they had to delay a proper honeymoon until the next parliamentary recess.[9]

Peter Bessell watched these developments with amusement. He was now based permanently in New York, where, as usual, he was lying and cheating in an attempt to avoid financial ruin. He maintained cordial relations with his wife, Pauline, who worked at the United Nations in the city, but was having a passionate affair with Diane Kelly. Although he had been furious when Thorpe married Caroline Allpass, he did not mind when Thorpe told him about Marion, who, he told himself, was probably too old to worry about sex.

In April the happy couple flew to the Bahamas, where they stayed in Jack Hayward's house, and then travelled to New York, where Hayward's partner, Edward St George, lent them his apartment. There, Bessell adopted the role of gnarled New York veteran and tour guide. He believed that Marion was just the sort of well-bred and intelligent companion Thorpe needed if he wanted to make the tricky transition from young iconoclast to mature leader. But he was shocked when Thorpe told him that he did not intend to give up men. Bessell said, 'I asked him if Marion knew about his homosexuality. He said that she did not and that it was a problem.'[10]

But they did not waste much time discussing sex. Thorpe told Bessell that Jack Hayward and his partners were toying with the idea of selling Freeport for about 100 million dollars and that he had offered to find them a buyer, which would, of course, involve a commission, which could be as much as 7 million dollars[11]. Bessell's weak heart pounded at this exciting news and he immediately offered himself as Thorpe's partner in arranging the sale. He said that a major American oil company, such as Mobil, would jump at the chance to buy Freeport, where it would be able to build its refineries without interference from idiots who were more worried about wildlife and clear blue seas than profits and jobs. And, Bessell boasted, he knew just the man who would introduce them to Mobil: George Lawrence, whose family owned a chunk of New York called Bronxville, which was worth an estimated 6 million dollars. Bessell leant forward, smiled and said that he was arranging the sale of the Bronxville property for a handsome fee, which was a not very subtle way of telling Thorpe that he, too, had some juicy deals in the pipeline.

They set off to Washington for exploratory talks with officials in the government. They were confident that they could find a buyer for Freeport but they also had to persuade the American government to guarantee the purchase, since a different Bahamian government might nationalise the land. They made little progress in Washington, however, and Thorpe had to return home. But, as he was leaving, he reminded Bessell that they had unfinished business in England: Norman Scott. Bessell nodded, as if he had expected this, but, inside, he felt queasy: the Freeport deal would make him a rich man but there was obviously a price, which was silencing Scott.

But Thorpe was too busy that summer to worry about Scott.

Instead of a traditional wedding reception he organised what he called 'A Musical Evening' at Covent Garden Opera House. Many Liberals were appalled when they heard that Thorpe had sent out invitations that were embossed with gold and carried what he called 'a crest', as if he was a member of the aristocracy.[12] But he did not care what these kill-joys thought. He said, 'I don't care a damn . . . One has to bloody well lead one's own life. It's my life and my wedding. If one cannot have a reception such as one wants, then to hell with them. One has made enough sacrifices in one's personal life. They can find another leader.'[13] He was invulnerable after two sensational by-election victories in July when the hitherto rock-solid Tory seats, Ripon in North Yorkshire, and the Isle of Ely in East Anglia, crashed to David Austick and Clement Freud.

Peter Bessell, ex-Liberal MP, however, was not interested in the Party's soaring popularity. He was in such trouble financially that, once again, he decided that he would have to kill himself to avoid dishonour. He still had his smart apartment and office in New York but he was actually broke and owed tens of thousands of dollars. He had staved off bankruptcy by sending post-dated cheques to creditors but knew that these would bounce, which meant that he would be prosecuted for fraud. He reflected, 'Mentally, I was exhausted. Years of struggle, during which, ironically, I found solid and exceptional projects that brought me within an inch of a permanent solution to my problems, had taken their toll. As before, I saw suicide as the means of relief I sought. Death offered the prospect of the peace for which I ached.'

On Wednesday, 12 December he flew to London to try and con money from business contacts. But they did not believe a word he said and he fled, in despair, to his house in Cornwall. There, as he wondered what it would be like to be dead, he decided to have one last crack: that Sunday he telephoned Jeremy Thorpe and begged for help. Thorpe told him to report to Orme Square as soon as possible. Bessell was so grateful that his old friend still cared about him that it did not occur to him that Thorpe had no idea how to raise the money. He gushed, 'It was Jeremy at his best: the man who reacted spontaneously . . . to any form of human need. His concern for me was totally devoid of selfish motives.'

On Monday he drove to Orme Square. After dinner Marion retired so that Jeremy and poor Peter, who looked so tired, could talk privately. Bessell said that he could think of only one solution: Jack Hayward and the Freeport deal. Thorpe said that he did not quite see this; they had not secured the guarantees from the American government that potential buyers wanted, which meant that there was no deal and, therefore, no commission for them. Bessell nodded gloomily and skulked off.

By Wednesday, however, Thorpe had changed his mind. He told Bessell that perhaps he was right; they could tell Hayward that everything was in place, that they had a buyer and a promise of a guarantee from Washington, but that they needed an advance against their commission of, say, $500,000 to pay various middlemen. Then they would divide the money and be rich. Bessell wondered what would happen when Hayward discovered that the Mobil deal was a fiction but Thorpe said that this was defeatist; he was sure that Mobil would buy Freeport and, if it did not, they would tell Hayward that they had been deceived by the middlemen. Bessell liked the idea although he could see that it would be cruel, even by his standards, to con Hayward, who had saved him from bankruptcy. But he had no choice. He said, 'Jeremy Thorpe, the Leader of the Liberal Party, a politician respected for his integrity on all sides of the House of Commons and by millions throughout the country, was going to lie to a man who trusted him implicitly. He was perpetrating an ugly deception on a man without whose financial help it was doubtful if Jeremy would still have been an MP. And I was participating.'

Hayward was in London that week. Thorpe called him, lied about Freeport and asked for an advance of half a million dollars. Hayward said that this seemed fine and promised to arrange for the money to be transferred to Bessell's bank. Then he departed for the Bahamas. But Thorpe underestimated Hayward. He liked, but did not trust, Bessell and had no intention of sending him one dollar, let alone 500,000. He admired and also trusted Thorpe and thought that he must have been conned by Bessell. So he returned to the Bahamas without arranging any payment to them.

The awful truth soon dawned on Bessell and Thorpe: Hayward was not going to send the money. So Bessell rushed back to New York to plead with one of Hayward's advisers. The man listened politely and told him that, in his view, the whole scheme stank and he would tell Jack that he should not hand over a cent. Bessell slumped back into depression and, yet again, began to plan his suicide. He decided that he would wait until the New Year because, as he put it, he did not want Diane and his family to associate Christmas with his death. But, of course, this was an excuse for not killing himself.

Thorpe was furious. His scheme to swindle Hayward had nothing to do with wanting to save a friend; he had dreamt it up because he wanted to make real money. Thanks to his marriage he was comfortable financially. Instead of a poky flat he now lived in an elegant London house. He had a country retreat in Suffolk as well as his cottage in North Devon. His wife was popular and well-connected. But this was not enough. He believed that a man like him, who had so much to offer the country, should not have to think about money; he should live stylishly, untroubled by such petty matters, so that he could concentrate on serving the people. More practically, he had just lost a large slice of his income after the crash that December of a company called London and County Securities, which dealt in second mortgages, finance, property and building. He resigned as a director shortly before it folded but many Liberals thought that it was too little, too late; they said that he had shown lamentable judgement by becoming involved in a company which the City had long suspected was heading for disaster.

Dick Taverne, Labour MP for Lincoln until he won it as an Independent in March 1973, had also been asked to join London and County. But he had refused: 'They asked me to join the board and were offering me a hell of lot of money. But I made enquiries and was told that it was crooked. But Thorpe was eager for money and indifferent to where it came from. All his financial dealings were shady.'[14]

Thorpe knew that he could not afford another scandal and resigned his other five directorships, which he could ill afford. The Young Liberals applauded his 'courageous move', which demonstrated that the Liberals would rather be poor than compromised, but inwardly he was fuming. Now, more than ever, he needed money.[15]

So when Bessell telephoned from New York and told him the bad news Thorpe told him to pull himself together; this was a setback, not a disaster. He told Bessell that they should meet after Christmas in Miami, fly to Grand Bahama and charm the money out of that 'fucking millionaire', Jack Hayward. They could not pull out now even if they wanted to because, if they did, Hayward would discover that they had tried to cheat him, which would be a calamity.

Thorpe spent Christmas with Marion in Suffolk and then flew to Miami to meet Bessell, who was with his girlfriend, Diane Kelly. Next day Hayward dispatched his private plane to ferry them to Freeport, though Diane had to take a scheduled flight due to space problems. Bessell was pessimistic. He had conned countless people over the years but was sure that a multi-millionaire like Hayward, who was surrounded by suspicious lawyers, would not believe their story about middlemen demanding huge advances. But Thorpe said that he was an internationally respected politician and no businessman or his lackeys would dare to accuse him of lying.

That night Bessell and Thorpe had dinner with Hayward, his wife, Jean, and his business partner, Edward St George. It did not go well. Hayward was 50 years old and St George four years younger. They were a first-class double act; Hayward pretended to be absent-minded and naive while St George said little and watched. This was an excellent method of discovering who was trying to cheat them because few people took any notice of the suntanned, silent figure who looked as if he might be Hayward's driver. St George said, 'Thorpe was very plausible. He was an important politician of apparently impeccable integrity. I accepted what he said. It was when I listened to Bessell that I started to worry.'[16] Hayward was charming but adamant: he said that they would have to convince Wallace Groves, the American entrepreneur and founder of Freeport who was still the major shareholder in the company.

Bessell and Thorpe retreated to their hotel, where Bessell told Diane that things were looking bleak. As usual he was disgusted by himself: 'I lay in bed realising the appalling levels to which Jeremy and I had degenerated. What made the scheme so ugly was that Jack Hayward had for years shown us nothing but kindness and generosity. If we should succeed I would be paying off my debts with stolen money. If we failed the Liberal Party would lose its largest financial contributor.' Thorpe, meanwhile, chose a different way to unwind after the strain of trying to cheat Hayward; he picked up two young men and took them to his room, where they made so much noise that Bessell took two Mandrax tablets.

Next morning, as agreed, they flew with Hayward and St George to meet Groves, who lived on a neighbouring island. But Thorpe was not feeling well after the night's excesses and was sick into his trilby.[17] Groves' home was the sort of house which Bessell dreamt of owning and was set in stunning semi-tropical gardens. The five men settled into chairs and Thorpe began to describe the marvellous deal that Bessell and he had worked out. He was talking about Mobil and the middlemen who needed immediate payment when Groves interrupted. He said that there was no question of any money until the American government formally guaranteed the purchase, and Mobil, or whoever, signed the contract. And that was final. He told Thorpe, 'If it goes through, we'll reward you beyond your wildest dreams. The Liberal Party will be the richest party in Great Britain and you can have champagne for breakfast, lunch and dinner for the rest of your life, if you wish.'[18]

Back in their hotel in Freeport, Bessell and Thorpe decided to appeal directly to Hayward, without St George's baleful presence. Hayward, however, insisted that his partner should be present. St George said:

I felt as if I was in the dock for having suggested that the leader of the Liberal Party knew about this attempt to cheat Jack. I thought: Screw it. Thorpe and Bessell said, 'We understand that you have suspicions about this.' I said, 'No, not suspicions. It's a con. You are trying to steal money from Jack. There is no deal.' Bessell said that this was a gratuitous insult and that he would have to consult his lawyer. I told him that he would need a lawyer because fraud was a serious criminal offence. Then he stomped out. Then Thorpe said, 'Do you really think that Peter would do this?' He dropped Bessell completely. But there was no doubt in my mind that Thorpe was involved.

Hayward, however, told St George that he was being too harsh. He could not believe that the man who led one of Britain's great political parties would try and cheat a friend and patron who had saved his party from bankruptcy.[19] St George sniffed and said that it was obvious that Thorpe thought he was 'an easy touch'.

In their hotel in Miami Thorpe agreed with Bessell that things did not look good. Bessell said that he had decided against suicide, which would upset Diane, his wife, and his children, Paul, aged 22, and Paula, aged 25, who ran his 'offices' in New York and London. It would be better for all of them, he said, if he disappeared quietly with Diane. He promised Thorpe that, before doing so, he would write to Hayward and apologise for trying to con him. He would also say that he had deceived Thorpe, who was innocent. Thorpe said that this was an excellent plan and thanked him in advance for taking the blame for the failed sting.

On 2 January 1974 the two men embraced and Thorpe returned to London. They next met at Minehead, in November 1978, when Bessell was one of the main prosecution witnesess against his old friend, Jeremy Thorpe. Bessell now organised his disappearance. He flew to New York and wrote letters to Hayward and Thorpe, confessing the attempted fraud; to creditors, apologising for letting them down; to his children, instructing them to close down his 'offices'; and to his prospective father-in-law, Fred Miller, asking if he would oversee the dismemberment of his business empire. Then, with Diane and two dachschund puppies, they flew to California, where Bessell lied to irate creditors, rented a car and set off to Mexico to begin a new life.

They checked into a cheap hotel in the dusty little border town of Ensenada, where Bessell took stock: he had come so close to making millions with his Bronxville–Freeport deals but now had $69 and had to depend on Diane to pay the hotel and car-rental bills. But beneath the despair he was unchanged: he *knew* that he was destined to be rich and that setbacks like this were inevitable when you were a brilliant and innovative businessman. So, after a few days sweating in his seedy hotel room, where he suffered a heart tremor, they headed back to California. They stopped at a small town called Oceanside, which they both liked and which later became their home, and the indestructible Bessell began to plan yet another comeback.

CHAPTER ELEVEN

Thorpe returned to London to a barrage of criticism from fellow Liberals, who could not understand why their leader had gone missing when the country was facing its most serious crisis since the war, as Edward Heath's Conservative government struggled to cope with soaring energy prices abroad and demands from workers at home, led by the miners, for massive pay rises. Cyril Smith, the heavyweight, outspoken MP for Rochdale, led the assault by writing an open letter to Thorpe, demanding leadership. But Thorpe lied his way out of trouble: 'If Mr Smith had made enquiries he would have found out that I had been away having private and political talks in the Caribbean and America.' He did not mention that he had, in fact, been with Peter Bessell, the bankrupt, womanising ex-MP whom the Liberals wanted to forget, trying to cheat Jack Hayward, who had given the Party £150,000, out of half a million dollars.

Every Western government was suffering after massive increases in oil prices by Arab states, which 'ended the era of cheap energy on which the West had prospered so complacently over the past half-century'.[1] The previous October most Western governments, including the British, had tried to remain neutral after surprise attacks on Israel by Egypt and Syria.[2] But it did not help: the Arabs pushed prices even higher.

Heath had the additional problem of a militant trade union movement, many of whose leaders were left-wing extremists, who thought that the unions had a political duty, to fight for socialism, as well as an economic one, to win pay awards for their members. The miners were Heath's main opponents. They demanded a 35 per cent pay rise, in recognition of the new importance of coal, and declared an overtime ban when the government refused. On 1 January 1974 Heath announced a Three Day Week to save fuel and tried to negotiate peace with the unions. But then the miners voted to strike, which gave him no choice: on 7 February he called an election for Thursday, 28 February. He explained on television: 'The issue before you is a simple one. Do you want a strong government . . . or do you want them to abandon the struggle against rising prices under pressure from one particular group of workers?'

At first, the pundits thought that Heath would 'win by a landslide' but it soon became clear that the country was more annoyed with him than with the miners, who evoked complex emotions amongst even middle-class voters who loathed the trade unions. The word 'miners' conjured up powerful images. They were men of unquenchable bravery who toiled in unspeakable conditions. They lived in tight-knit communities, where everyone shared and no one locked their doors and where there was a loyalty to family and fellow workers which had vanished elsewhere. They were Bolshy but they were good men who rallied to the flag in a crisis, as they had done in two world wars. It required a more ruthless leader than Heath to turn the nation against the miners. A decade later another Conservative Prime Minister, Margaret Thatcher, deployed the might of the State and the slick skills of friends in public relations against them and, after a year of bloody conflict, the miners had been turned from romantic heroes to far-left wreckers and their power had vanished for ever.

That did not happen in 1974. Heath believed in One Nation Toryism. He was conciliatory and reasonable but many voters blamed him for the confrontation, which was unfair. Meanwhile, Harold Wilson, the Labour leader who had been Prime Minister from 1964 until 1970, also struggled and seemed, so *The Times* thought, 'tired and ineffective'.

The Liberals sensed that this was their chance. Cyril Smith recalled:

It was time for all-out attack. We decided to field the greatest number of candidates this century – 517 – and were going for *power*. The euphoria wagon was not only dragged out of its stable, but was pushed off on a tearing, whooping, cheering downhill charge. Life aboard the wagon, in February 1974, was the most exhilarating period of my life . . . Jeremy Thorpe strode jauntily on to the stage. Compared with the other two wily old birds (Edward Heath and Harold Wilson), he was a veritable kingfisher, nattily dressed, his gold watch-chain swinging from his double-breasted waistcoat, his trilby at a jaunty angle. He led a magnificent election campaign, only to be robbed by the system . . . He wanted, like all politicians, power and influence. A fifth of the country wanted him to have it also.[3]

Thorpe fizzed. He stayed in his North Devon redoubt to defend his majority of 369 but, by accident, his absence from the daily press conferences in London worked to his advantage. He set up a television link between his headquarters in Barnstaple and the National Liberal Club in Whitehall so that he could take part, in a statesmanlike fashion, in the daily jousts with the media. One historian wrote, 'He came across as much the most vigorous and attractive of the three leaders. This had the unexpected effect that he appeared loftily detached from the dogfight being waged in London.'[4] He jumped over fences, cracked jokes and exchanged his usual trilby for a Russian-style white beaverskin hat. And, as the opinion polls indicated mounting disillusion with the two giants, he began to dream the impossible: that the Liberals would win the election.

Privately, however, many senior Liberals were less than thrilled with their leader's strategy. Trevor Jones, a plain-speaking businessman who was knighted in 1981, had been the Liberal Party's President in the year leading up to the election and was contesting the Toxteth constituency in Liverpool that February. He thought that Thorpe was behaving with inexcusable selfishness: 'Jeremy was so worried about his own seat that he spent £60,000 – which was a hell of a lot of money in those days – on his landline. It meant that the Party was struggling for money in the rest of the country.'[5]

On 28 February, the Liberals won 6,063,470 votes, 19.3 per cent of the total polled. This was treble the support that they had enjoyed in the election of 1970 and twice as many as 1964, the Party's best post-war performance.[6] Thorpe was flanked by his wife, Marion, and David Holmes when the results were read out that night at Barnstaple's Queen's Hall. His majority had swollen to 11,072. But it was not good enough because the Liberals had needed between 25 to 30 per cent of the national vote to gain 100 or more seats. So they returned only fourteen MPs, an increase of just three on the previous Parliament. The Conservatives had 297 seats and Labour 301, although Heath's team had polled more votes than Labour, 11,868,906 against 11,639,243.

That weekend it did not require a degree in constitutional law to work out that neither commanded a majority of the 635 seats in the Commons and would have to court the Liberals and a handful of Unionists from Ulster. Heath was determined to try to remain in power and summoned Thorpe to Downing Street. The Young Liberals and many Party activists, for whom Liberalism was a radical, left-wing alternative to socialism, were appalled by the sight of their leader hurrying to London to discuss a possible pact with the Conservatives, whom they hated, and warned him that there would be 'mass resignations' if he betrayed the Party to Heath.

Thorpe did not see it like that; he believed that the Party needed to be in government, even as a junior partner in a coalition, if it hoped to become a genuine alternative to the Conservatives and Labour, but privately, of course, he was also desperate for ministerial office. He spent two hours on Saturday morning at Downing Street with Heath, who offered him a seat in Cabinet and a Speaker's Conference to examine the Liberals' demand for proportional representation. In return, the Liberals would have to support the Conservatives. Thorpe said that he needed to consult colleagues.

Heath was only trying to cling to office, which most prime ministers would have done in the circumstances, but his offer to Thorpe was extraordinary. If Thorpe had accepted he would have had a seat in Cabinet, perhaps as Home Secretary, which would have made him titular head of MI5, which had a thick file on him, describing his secret life as a promiscuous homosexual. Yet Heath knew in general, if not sordid detail, about Thorpe; he had definitely been briefed about Thorpe's sex life by Lord Carrington, the Conservative Party Chairman and Minister of Defence, and probably by MI5. But he still offered Thorpe a senior job, perhaps in the hope that these reports were wrong.

That evening Thorpe returned secretly to Downing Street to see if Heath would commit the government to reform the electoral system, which was the cornerstone of Liberal policy; Heath would not budge since he knew that his own supporters would not accept proportional representation, which, for Conservatives and Labour alike, would have been tantamount to committing suicide.

On Sunday, Thorpe entertained David Steel, the Chief Whip, Jo Grimond, the former leader, and Lord Byers, the Liberal leader in the Lords, to lunch at Orme Square. Steel, who had been 'confused and irritated'[7] by the alacrity with which Thorpe accepted Heath's invitation, made it clear that, without a deal on proportional representation, the Party would not support a coalition. Thorpe nodded glumly and said that he feared that he was right. Next day, the fourteen Liberal MPs met and formally rejected Heath's offer although they did suggest that a government of 'National Unity' should be formed. But this was a publicity stunt, not a serious proposal, designed to show that the Liberals were more interested in the fate of the country than petty party politics. On 4 March Heath resigned and the Queen invited Harold Wilson to form an administration.[8]

On Sunday, 3 March 1974, the colour magazine that came with that morning's *Sunday Times* had a brilliant coup: a long profile of Jeremy Thorpe, the 44-year-old leader of the Liberal Party and the man who, that tumultuous weekend, held the destiny of Britain in his elegant Old Etonian hands. That day, instead of being just another hack politician, he was the most important man in the country. The magazine cast an unexpected and uncomplimentary light on the Thorpe who was so well-known to the public: the cheerful fella who was always jumping over fences and talking in funny voices. The Thorpe described by the magazine was a more complex man than this; he was troubled by his privileged background, the premature deaths of a doting father and an adoring first wife, and by a still-very-much-alive and domineering mother. He was also not popular in his own party. Un-named Liberals told the magazine that he was an autocrat and a snob whose dislike of the Tories was based on a personal grudge. 'Jeremy resents the fact that really grand country-house Tory society is outside his ken. He's a bounder. They would class him as not quite a gentleman,' said one anonymous Liberal with conspicuous disloyalty.

Other Liberals complained that he was a jackdaw, who repackaged others' ideas as his own. They said that, whatever the Party's faults, it had always been led by men of intellectual weight. The nineteenth-century Liberal colossus, William Gladstone, who had been Prime Minister for twelve years, had read 20,000 books, written fifteen and mesmerised crowds with rich sentences of 300 words, and relaxed by chatting about Homer for six hours.[9] But Thorpe's idea of a long read was a one-page brief from an aide and his contribution to political theory was the occasional polemical article in a newspaper.

This was splendid stuff. During the past month of electioneering Liberals had gushed about his brilliance; now the general public learnt that many did not like him very much.

The story, which included the most revealing interview ever given by Thorpe, had been researched and written before Christmas by a talented American journalist called Susan Barnes, who was also the wife of the Labour Party's Anthony Crosland.[10] The article was, however, most notable for what it did not say. Barnes had never heard of Norman Scott, Peter Bessell or David Holmes. She did not name Jack Hayward as the Liberals' main patron. And she did not say that Thorpe was a homosexual.

The article had been inspired by Harold Evans, editor of the *Sunday Times* since 1967, and by the magazine's editor, Magnus Linklater, one of Evans' protégés. Evans was a small, enthusiastic man from Manchester who had become a journalist when he was 16 years old. Since taking over the *Sunday Times* he had redefined Sunday broadsheet journalism in his own image: imaginative, fearless and unashamedly populist. He revelled in principled battles against government or big business which, by a happy accident, also increased circulation and enhanced his own stature as the most daring editor in the English-speaking world. He insisted that magazine articles which told suburbanites that their lives could be transformed, if only they shopped and exercised more energetically, should be balanced by investigations exposing the horrors of the modern world. His advertising department protested that the readers wanted to be cheered up, rather than depressed about the iniquities of poverty at home and the tragedy of the latest small war in the Third World, but he over-ruled them; the profile of Thorpe was an example of the journalism which made his magazine more than a vehicle for pap.

Linklater shared this commitment to serious reporting and had asked Barnes to 'look at' Thorpe in the autumn of 1973, when the Liberals seemed poised, not for the first time, to become a real third party rather than just an option for voters who were bored with Labour and the Conservatives. Linklater felt that there were fascinating angles here. For example, how would Thorpe cope with the radicals from the provinces, who saw the future of Liberalism in terms of 'community' politics? And what about Thorpe and the Young Liberals? They had calmed down a little since the late 1960s but Thorpe still did not care for them.

Barnes worked hard and talked to dozens of people about Thorpe's family, education, beliefs, personality and leadership style. But she also heard the same rumours which, three years earlier, the Liberal hierarchy had dismissed as malicious gossip when they held their secret inquisition of Scott. One friend, who was a successful writer and broadcaster, told her that Thorpe was a well-known figure in London's homosexual community and had a weakness for rent boys, which often ended in blackmail or robbery.[12] But she did not think it was her job as a serious writer to dig into a public figure's sex life, which was what grubby hacks on the *News of the World* did, and she told him that she was not interested: 'I said that I did not think it was relevant to look at a politician's sexual peccadilloes. My source said that you had to know about these things because they affected the way a politician performed in office.'[13]

If she had shown any interest in her friend's tip about Thorpe he would have told her to speak to a homosexual journalist called Oleg Kerensky, the grandson of Alexander Kerensky, Russia's last prime minister in 1917 before the Bolsheviks took power. Kerensky was born in London in 1930. He studied at Christ Church, Oxford and was an active member of the Union at the same time as Thorpe. Then he became deputy editor of the *Listener* and ballet critic of the *Daily Mail, International Herald Tribune* and *New Statesman*. He was also an open homosexual; he once said that he had only become involved in politics at university because it was the next best thing to embracing a fellow male student. He was renowned amongst his friends in London and New York for his voracious sexual appetite before he died, aged 63, in New York in July 1993 of what newspapers called 'an AIDS-related cancer'.[14]

The friend who told Barnes about Thorpe said:

Oleg Kerensky was my closest gay friend. He had a gargantuan sexual appetite and from what he told me so did Thorpe. Oleg gave up his life to his sex life. He did everything you could imagine and more. Toilets, everything. He said that Thorpe was doing the same and getting into the most terrible messes. Thorpe would pick up rent boys and then they would steal stuff from his flat. If he tried to get it back they would blackmail him. Oleg thought that Thorpe enjoyed playing with fire. He was like a child who would go on until he was slapped down. Oleg was quite specific about this. Until then I had never thought of Jeremy as homosexual. It just hadn't occurred to me. But then my generation didn't think of things like that. Then it seemed to make sense. He had always had this overweening ambition and drive and a very powerful libido would fit into that. His sex life seemed to have been fast and furious.'[15]

Others who inhabited London's political-media world, where gossip was exchanged over expense-account lunches, had heard the same stories from Kerensky. They included an MP, who had also known Thorpe at Oxford. He said, 'Oleg told me that Jeremy was picking up rent boys. He was very surprised that a man in Thorpe's position was behaving like this. Oleg said that Thorpe had managed to get one of these boys a job in the House of Commons. Oleg thought that he must have liked taking risks.'[16]

But the article in the *Sunday Times* did contain clues about Thorpe's secret life as a homosexual. Thorpe told Barnes, 'People think that what I expose is the whole. But there are things one passionately wants to keep private, things that are no one's business. What isn't realised is how professionally I don't expose what I don't want to.' He added that he knew that some people could not understand why someone of his age should have such a close relationship with his mother: 'The conventional bourgeoisie think this distinctly odd. They think you must be a raving queer,' he said, as if he was making a private joke to those trusted fellow homosexuals who knew the truth.

Norman Scott was in no state to enjoy the *Sunday Times*'s revealing profile of his former lover. When it was published he was in bed in a rented 'bungalow' in the village of Simonsbath, north-east of Barnstaple, on the edge of Exmoor. He was not looking well. He was emaciated because he had been living on vegetables, which he picked from the nearby fields, and was semi-conscious after his usual late-night feast of whisky, tranquillisers and sleeping pills. He knew that something was wrong but the details were hazy. He recalled that he had been visited a few days earlier by his doctor, Ronald Gleadle, who had taken possession of his precious 'dossier' on Thorpe. In return, the doctor, who had been so understanding over the past year, had told him that he no longer needed to worry about money because he now had £2,500 in his name at a local branch of Lloyds Bank. Scott did not know it that Sunday morning, as Thorpe tried to persuade his Liberal colleagues over lunch in London that they should enter into a coalition with the Conservatives, but his 'dossier' was now a pile of ashes in the Aga at the home of Michael Barnes, Thorpe's solicitor in Barnstaple. This was the result of an extraordinary transaction involving Gleadle, Barnes, David Holmes and Jeremy Thorpe, the man who was on the brink of a senior job in the Cabinet.

The loss of his 'dossier' that February in 1974 was the climax of a busy year which made Scott's earlier life seem rather dull. When he had moved to South Moulton, courtesy of his friends, Jack and Stella Levy, he had been given yet another opportunity to sort himself out; he could have given up drugs and alcohol, found a job and, most importantly, forgotten Jeremy Thorpe, whom he had last seen eight years earlier. But, of course, he did not do this.

He found a new confidant: Dr Ronald Gleadle, who practised at the South Molton Health Centre. Gleadle prescribed large doses of Librium, to calm Scott, and Mogadon, to help him sleep, but soon realised that drugs would not solve his new patient's problems. Scott, meanwhile, proudly showed Gleadle his 'dossier', as if this explained why he could not cope with life. He said, 'I was obviously very, very tense and very, very nervous and I explained what happened in great detail. In fact, I took my file with me and told him everything.'[17] Then, to try and convince Gleadle that he meant business, Scott took out his razor blade and etched 'incurable' on his arm. He said, 'It was the homosexuality which was incurable. And Thorpe was responsible for that. I don't understand why people couldn't always see that.' But he spoilt everything by immediately summoning Gleadle; a few minutes later he was grimacing and sobbing as the doctor stitched the wound in his kitchen. After this the Levys decided that it would be best if their house guest moved on. Scott headed back to the moors, where he rented what he called a 'bungalow' on a farm owned by Graham and Hazel Leeves, with whom, naturally, he soon fell out.[18]

Gleadle, meanwhile, decided that he had a duty to inform the Liberal Party that one of his patients was making serious allegations against their leader. He contacted Lord Banks, a former President of the Liberal Party, whom he had met when they attended the same church in Harrow. Banks listened patiently as Gleadle outlined Scott's story and promised to investigate. In turn, Banks spoke to Lord Wade, a senior Liberal peer from Yorkshire; he told Banks that the Party had heard all this before, had investigated Scott's story and decided that he was a liar. Wade, however, told Thorpe, who then reassured Banks that Scott was a lunatic who was fixated on him. But Thorpe added helpfully that, if this chap Gleadle was worried, he could always talk to his solicitor Michael Barnes, who lived in Barnstaple and knew the whole story about the mad and dangerous Scott. Banks thanked Thorpe, passed the message to Gleadle and returned to his hobbies, listening to Gilbert and Sullivan and studying Clyde river steamers.[19]

Gleadle now wondered whether poor Norman might benefit from spiritual cleansing, rather than further huge doses of drugs, and recommended the Reverend Frederick Pennington, Vicar of the All Saints' Church in North Molton, who ran 'hypnotherapy' sessions in the South Molton Health Centre, designed to draw out neuroses from a patient. Scott thought that this was a marvellous idea because it would give him a chance to explain to a stranger how Thorpe had ruined his life. So he made an appointment to be hypnotised by Pennington. He saw the vicar six times. He responded well to hypnosis and impressed the vicar, who tape-recorded Scott's ramblings. He said, 'I heard his life story and I took it for granted that everything he told me was true. One does, you know, when they are under hypnosis because they are re-living certain experiences.'[20]

Early in 1974 Pennington decided to confront Thorpe at his constituency surgery in Barnstaple. Thorpe was furious that, once again, Scott had resurfaced, but Pennington mistook this for the anger of an innocent man and retreated to North Molton. However, back at home, Pennington brooded that even an hysteric like Scott could not have lied under his expert spell. He felt morally obliged, therefore, to fight for Norman and decided to enlist the help of the local Conservative candidate, a farmer called Tim Keigwin. He told Keigwin and his agent, Robin Nelder, about Scott and they, in turn, promised to alert Conservative Central Office. Nelder sent a report of their conversation with Pennington to Party headquarters in London but no one wanted to know about a hypnotising Devon vicar who had talked to a lunatic who claimed that he had slept with Jeremy Thorpe.

Scott did not stop with Pennington. He read a story in his local newspaper that an author and playwright, Ronald Duncan, who lived outside Bideford in North Devon, did not think much of

Thorpe. Scott invited Duncan to his 'bungalow' and poured out the familiar story. Duncan said that the house looked like 'a chemist's shop' but was sufficiently impressed to travel to London to suggest to *The Times* that they should investigate further. But the newspaper was not interested and he returned home.[21]

On Saturday, 12 January, Scott was given fresh ammunition when a helicopter landed near his 'bungalow'. He said that two men jumped out and ran towards the house: 'I was frightened so I cowered behind the door in order not to be seen through the window. They were hammering at the door, shouting for me to come out. One of them was very burly. I remained quiet until I heard the helicopter roar its engines [sic] and fly off across the moor.'[22] It is possible that he imagined the whole episode but that was irrelevant; Scott believed that Thorpe had hired thugs to beat him up or kill him and was determined to broadcast the incident.[23] So, having calmed himself with whisky and pills, he telephoned Tim Keigwin. He told Keigwin that his life was in danger and that he had to talk to someone whom he could trust.

Next day Keigwin and a local solicitor, John Palmer, spent several hours at the 'bungalow', listening to Norman's setpiece story about Thorpe. Scott gave them a statement, which he had scribbled out the previous night, and showed them his 'dossier', which consisted of his 'retainer' letters from Bessell and the papers on his divorce. Keigwin was a man of principle and dispatched Palmer to Conservative Central Office in London to brief Lord Frazer, the Party's deputy chairman, and Sir Richard Webster, the director of the Conservative Party Organisation. They thanked Palmer for his trouble and told him that they would be in touch; they passed the file to Lord Carrington, who glanced at it and decided that the Party wanted nothing to do with filth like this. Carrington mentioned the story to Edward Heath, who agreed, and, as a result, Keigwin was ordered to forget Scott and to fight the coming election with Thorpe on the issues, which most certainly did not include Thorpe's alleged homosexuality.

Finally, there was Gordon Winter, the journalist-cum-BOSS spy who had debriefed (and slept with) Scott in 1971. According to Winter, BOSS told him to travel to Britain as soon as Heath announced the election and sell the Scott story, which would, so BOSS hoped, discredit the Liberals and, possibly Labour, and boost the Conservatives. Winter claimed that he slipped into Britain in February, unnoticed by MI5, and approached the *Sunday People* and the *Sunday Mirror*. But they were not interested in the ravings of a man called Norman Scott, who was obviously deranged, that Jeremy Thorpe, who looked as if he would hold the balance of power in the next Parliament, was a secret homosexual who had stolen his ex-lover's Insurance card.

Winter scuttled back to South Africa, without bothering to tell Scott what had happened. The episode revealed him to be a fool as well as a crook. A trainee journalist on a local newspaper would have told him that no newspaper, let alone two national tabloids, would touch this story.[24]

With so many people, including vicars, doctors, writers, parliamentary candidates, senior Conservatives, spies and journalists trying to win justice for Scott or have him consigned to an asylum, it was inevitable that Thorpe would hear that his former lover was making an unwelcome impact. So he instructed Holmes to seek guidance from his legal adviser, Lord Goodman. Holmes said, 'I told Goodman what Scott was doing in North Devon and said that Jeremy's agent was worried about the effect that this might have on the campaign. Very wisely he advised us to ignore the man.'[25]

But Thorpe could not do that. He ordered his solicitor, Michael Barnes, to warn Keigwin that he would be sued if he mentioned Scott during the three weeks of electioneering and, to emphasise the point, told Barnes he had to attend – and make sure that he was seen – at Keigwin's major meetings. This was foolish and unnecessary: Barnes' baleful presence was bound to attract attention and Keigwin had no intention of defying Party headquarters. Predictably, journalists covering the campaign leaked the story, albeit in a garbled form, to *Private Eye*, which fuelled Thorpe's fear that, as he stood, poised on the brink of political greatness, Scott would destroy him.

Then Dr Gleadle intervened. He approached Barnes and said that the Liberals might want to buy some letters in the possession of one of his patients which, if they were published, might damage the Party. This was an extraordinary act which Gleadle never explained satisfactorily: 'My principal reason for doing so was that, at the time, Mr Scott had become obsessional about these matters and I felt it would assist me in treating him if I could discover whether the allegations were true or whether they were fantasies which he believed or had made up.'[26]

Barnes enlisted Holmes, who was staying with him, since

Thorpe's cottage was full (Thorpe, Marion, Ursula, Rupert, a nanny and a cook). Holmes sought instructions from Thorpe, who ordered him to 'look into it'. So he met Gleadle, who asked for £25,000 for the letters, which belonged to a man called Norman Scott who hoped to open stables. Holmes knocked Gleadle down to £2,500, which he said he would have to pay by cheque, since the Liberals were not wealthy and did not have instant access to cash. Gleadle grumbled but said that, since they were all men of their word, that would have to do. In return, Holmes told him that he required a guarantee that these were the original letters, that Scott had not made any copies and that Scott would never discuss the transaction.

On the evening of Wednesday, 27 February Gleadle drove to Scott's 'bungalow'. As usual, Norman was in bed in a drug- and alcohol-induced stupor. Gleadle took the 'dossier', left a note explaining the terms of the sale, and hurried off. As agreed, he handed the letters to Holmes and pocketed the cheque. Then Holmes and Barnes drove south, to Thorpe's cottage at Higher Chuggaton. Holmes said:

We took the letters to Jeremy's home. Jeremy read through every one and we discussed them until three in the morning. When Barnes and I got back home I burnt them in his Aga cooker. The following day Jeremy said it must have been the most expensive bonfire ever. Certainly, every step I made in the negotiations with Dr Gleadle was made after discussion with Jeremy and with his authorisation.[27]

Having grabbed a few hours' sleep after these exhausting discussions, Thorpe emerged from his cottage, immaculate and beaming, to face the waiting press and head off to vote in the election which would, he hoped, propel him to power. Yet it had all been a waste of effort and money: the letters that they had bought and burnt were worthless, since the most that they suggested was that Scott had been blackmailing Bessell. Next, Scott had given Winter and the Liberal Party inquiry copies of the 'dossier'. Finally, and most importantly, the fact that Holmes, his best friend and godfather to his son, had purchased them with a traceable cheque was a catastrophic mistake because it proved that Thorpe, not Bessell, was buying Scott's silence. He did not know it but he was now doomed.

CHAPTER TWELVE

After the Liberals' failure in February's election and the purchase of Scott's 'dossier' Thorpe felt that everything was slipping away and told himself that he would only be free when Scott was dead. To be fair, any Liberal leader would have struggled to maintain the momentum of the New Year, when the country had experienced one of its periodic bouts of disillusion with the two squabbling giants of politics. It did not last and by spring 1974 Labour and the Conservatives had recovered their poise, which left the Liberals grumbling, as usual, that it was unfair that they did not have more MPs. Thorpe had not helped himself by his negotiations with Heath because he was now seen as just another power-hungry politician. He was also losing his touch politically and made a series of uncharacteristic mistakes by, for example, continuing to talk about the need for 'a government of National Unity' which was yesterday's idea, born of the confrontation between Heath and the unions. It also angered the Young Liberals, who believed that Thorpe was turning the Party into a rump of the Conservatives, because Labour had made it clear that they would never join a coalition government.[1] Friends, like John Pardoe, could not understand what was going wrong. But the reason was simple: Norman Scott.[2]

It is impossible to date precisely the moment when Thorpe decided that Scott had to be silenced permanently, 'the final solution' which he had first discussed six years earlier with Bessell and Holmes in his office in the House of Commons. But the evidence suggests that, by spring 1974, he had the outline of a plan that required large amounts of untraceable money. On 10 April he wrote to Jack Hayward in the Bahamas.[3] It was a long, chatty and thoroughly deceitful letter. He told Hayward that he was still trying to persuade contacts in Washington to guarantee the sale of Freeport, which was true, and that he was making progress, which was a lie. He apologised for 'that bastard Bessell', who had tried to cheat them both, which was also a lie since he had been a partner in the attempted sting. Then he moved to the main point.

He asked Hayward for £50,000, £10,000 of which would be used to settle what he called 'election expenses'. He said that, because he had fought North Devon as well as lead the Liberals, there had been 'an overlap on expenditure which I would prefer not to argue about'. This was potentially disastrous, Thorpe wrote, because 'each candidate is limited to a total sum for his individual campaign and if he exceeds it by one penny he can be unseated!'. He asked Hayward to send £40,000 to the Liberal Party General Election Fund but said that the remaining money, to cover 'election expenses', should go to a man called Nadir Dinshaw. He wrote: 'Dinshaw is Rupert's godfather and is conveniently resident in Jersey. He has agreed to settle bills which fall into this ambiguous category.' He added that this would allow him to 'clear up everything *safely*'. Dinshaw was a God-fearing businessman who had been born in Pakistan and had become a British citizen in the late 1950s. He had met Thorpe in 1969 on a bus at Heathrow and shortly afterwards became Rupert's godfather.[4]

After the election in February Thorpe telephoned him in Jersey and asked for a small favour; he said that Jack Hayward would shortly be sending send him, Dinshaw, £10,000 to settle Thorpe's outstanding 'election expenses'. Thorpe added that Dinshaw should give the money to Holmes. Dinshaw knew nothing about the regulations governing election expenses but trusted Thorpe and agreed to help, providing that there was no publicity, since he was a shy man who did not want to be bothered by reporters. Thorpe assured him that the transaction would be confidential and that, in any case, it would not interest the media because it was just a tedious piece of book-keeping.

Dinshaw received a cheque from Hayward, dated 3 May 1974 and drawn on Protocol Trading Corporation (Exuma) Limited's account at Barclays Bank, Haywards Heath, Sussex. Dinshaw wrote a cheque for the same amount and sent it to Holmes. Holmes said, 'Naturally I had to account for this money to Jeremy. With Jeremy's full knowledge I also got the £2,500 back which had been used for the Bessell letters.'[5] He claimed that he used some of the money to settle unspecified election debts but this was a lie; Thorpe's agent in North Devon, Lillian Prowse, was efficient and honest and, if her candidate had inadvertently overspent during a campaign, which he had not, would not have allowed an outsider like Holmes to pay off the debts surreptitiously.

The fact is that Holmes kept the remaining £7,500, though he did not know how Thorpe intended to use it. He certainly did know, however, that Thorpe was pathologically obsessed with Scott, who had reneged on his deal with Gleadle and was running around North Devon, telling anyone who would listen that Thorpe had wrecked his life. Holmes said:

> Jeremy's agent and Liberal sympathisers were always ringing up or sending notes about this terrible man making horrid remarks. Several of Jeremy's friends wanted to find out what Scott really wanted. Everybody wanted to help get the pressure off Jeremy. But Scott's only desire seemed to be to cause trouble. All this gave Jeremy a sense of permanent persecution and a feeling that he would never be safe with that man around. I received endless phone calls from Jeremy which were full of panic and despair. All through 1974 he was on the phone to me about it twice or more a week. He became as obsessed with Scott as Scott was with him. It was silly of us to expect Scott to shut up after getting the £2,500. We talked continually about what we could do and he returned to the theme of killing Scott. It was more a general thing. Like Henry II said of Thomas à Becket: Who will rid me of this turbulent priest? Whether he would have gone ahead if I had found someone prepared to do murder, I don't know. We never got to that stage because there was no way that I was looking for an assassin.[6]

Gerald Hagan, Holmes's live-in companion, became increasingly irritated by Thorpe: 'David was constantly badgered by him. David felt that Thorpe was going out of his mind. But I only knew this man Scott was pestering Thorpe. If I had known what was really going on I would have told David that Thorpe should sort it out himself.'[7]

In September Harold Wilson called a general election for 10 October. Thanks to Hayward the Liberals were better off than usual but, instead of using the money to bolster the Liberals in constituences where they stood a real chance of winning, Thorpe spent a fortune on himself, since he was convinced that he *was* the Party. He splashed out on a hovercraft, which ferried him dramatically along the coast until it was damaged as it sped up a beach in Devon. Then he hired a helicopter and dashed from one marginal Conservative seat to another. He hoped that he would be seen as a high-tech leader of the future but journalists covering his campaign thought that it was desperate stuff and disrespectfully dubbed his helicopter 'Jeremy Thorpe's Flying Circus'. The Liberals fielded a record number of candidates but polled almost 1 million fewer votes than in February and ended up with only thirteen MPs. Thorpe's majority in North Devon was slashed by 4,000. He blamed the voting system again but senior Liberals had heard all this before and told each other quietly that, perhaps, it was time for Jeremy, who had almost achieved the impossible, to step down and let a younger man, with fresh ideas, have a crack.

Meanwhile, Scott was restless. He had £2,500 in the bank and a man with big money like that needs more than a rented 'bungalow' on a farm. So he headed for the brightish lights of Barnstaple. He brought a car, ultra-fashionable clothes, which did not go down well in a small conservative town, gallons of alcohol and was indiscriminately generous to 'friends', who always seemed to pop up when Thorpe did the decent thing and looked after him financially, as he had promised he would do after he had seduced him all those years ago in Ursula's house in Surrey. He worked, for nothing, in a boutique called The Hunky Dory, and went out briefly with Lucia Potter, the daughter of a prominent local Liberal. And, naturally, he talked about Thorpe.

When his money had almost run out he remembered that he had lost his 'dossier', which was a disaster because it was, in his mind at least, the equivalent of a personal pension plan. He blamed Gleadle and decided that, far from trying to help him, he had, in fact, been trying to poison him with lethal doses of drugs. Now that he had located a new villain, who, he suspected, was in league with Thorpe, Scott decided to instruct a solicitor to fight for justice for him. He chose Jeremy Ferguson, who was based in Bideford, near Barnstable. He treated Ferguson to his standard denunciation of Thorpe and gave him details from his bank, proving that Gleadle had paid him £2,500. In December 1974 Ferguson wrote to Gleadle and demanded the return of his client's 'dossier' but Gleadle replied, truthfully, that he did not have it and suggested that Ferguson should contact

Michael Barnes, a solicitor in Barnstaple, if he required further details. Ferguson skimmed the letter and filed it, unaware that it was destined to become one of the key elements in Thorpe's downfall because it proved that his solicitor had been involved in the purchase of Scott's documents.[8]

Scott was now doing what he did best: spreading confusion. He acquired a new psychiatrist, Douglas Flack, a consultant from Exeter who ran an out-patients' clinic in Bideford. In February 1975 Ferguson and Flack exchanged earnest letters on the best way to put pressure on Gleadle to return Scott's property. They agreed that Scott was sane but highly-strung and deserved help because Gleadle had behaved badly. Flack thought that they should, perhaps, approach the Medical Defence Union in London. Ferguson thought that this was an excellent idea because he did not want the case to go to court since that would be distressing for his client.

But they did not understand Scott. He wanted to retrieve his 'dossier' but he wanted publicity even more because that would destroy Thorpe. So he told Ferguson that he was not impressed and was going to sell his story to what he portentously called 'a foreign publication'.

A new group of characters now became involved in trying to 'deal with' Scott by threatening him, stealing his files, beating him up and finally by shooting his dog. But, far from convincing him that it would be best if he forgot Thorpe, the unprecedented attention inspired him to new heights of indignation. This was the most chaotic episode in the drama. It opened ominously for Thorpe in November 1974 when workmen who were decorating Bessell's former offices in Pall Mall found a battered briefcase in a hidden cupboard; inside was a packet of photographs of nude men and a file marked 'The Property of Mr Jeremy Thorpe'. There were dozens of letters, including Scott's letter to Thorpe's mother, written in March 1965, Thorpe's draft reply and Bill Shannon's request for money to the 'nice gentleman' who had picked him up in the King's Road. The workmen thought that it looked 'like a blackmail dossier against Mr Thorpe' and were tempted to sell it to a newspaper abroad which, they thought, would pay about £15,000. But they were not sure if this would be right or legal so they handed it to the *Sunday Mirror*. The newspaper read it and paid them £200 as a 'gratitude gift'. The editor, Robert Edwards, consulted Lord Jacobson, the chairman of the *Mirror* Group, who had already turned down Gordon Winter's scoop on Scott. They decided that this this was not the sort of story a family newspaper should touch and sent the file to Thorpe. But, just in case, they also copied it and deposited it in a safe in their legal department. Thorpe did not know this, though, and wrote an unctuous little note to Jacobson, whom he knew socially, thanking him for his discretion. But privately he was seething and told Holmes that Scott had to be eliminated before it was too late. He also wrote to Hayward again because he needed to finance the plot against Scott. He asked for £17,000 to settle 'election bills' but Hayward did not respond.

Holmes was not sure how to proceed. Bessell was carving out a new life on the West Coast so he turned to one of his dubious 'contacts', an amiable, large man in his mid-40s called John Le Mesurier, who sold cut-price carpets near Bridgend in South Wales. Le Mesurier, who was born in Southampton, had served in the Royal Air Force before launching into the carpet business. But he had not been successful and knew that his current venture, the Pyle Carpet Discount Centre, was his last chance. Le Mesurier said:

> I had never seen David so worried. I asked him what was the matter. He told me about Norman Scott. He said that Scott had made Thorpe's life a misery. Thorpe had tried everything to silence Scott. He'd tried setting him up in a job. He'd tried paying him a weekly retainer. He'd tried buying him off with £2,500 for his letters but soon after the money was paid Scott was flashing copies of the letters around in the same threatening way. He had gone to live in Thorpe's North Devon constituency where he could shoot his mouth off all over the place. The gossip was getting worse all the time. David told me that Thorpe was so obsessed by the threat posed to his political career by Scott that he had conceived an almost manic desire to have Scott killed. I could see that David was at his wit's end and he was immensely relieved when I said I'd help.[9]

Le Mesurier thought that Scott 'needed to be taught a lesson' and turned to one of his own 'contacts', George Deakin, who sold slot machines and pool tables in South Wales. He was not an impressive-looking character: he was 34 years old and was small, sandy-haired, and wore dazzling suits. But he had made a fortune, symbolised by large cars with personalised number plates, a mock-Tudor house and a blonde wife, in a business dominated by hard, unscrupulous men. So Le Mesurier thought that he would be able to advise Holmes on the best way to handle Scott. Deakin was thinking of buying a house abroad and Le Mesurier said that he knew just the fella to advise him on the tax implications of this: David Holmes.

But when they met they did not spend long discussing the problems of a holiday home overseas. Deakin clucked sympathetically as Holmes told him that a friend was being blackmailed; a woman had already killed herself and a child's life was being threatened. (This was a reference to young Rupert Thorpe; absurdly, Holmes thought that Scott might kidnap him.) Deakin assumed that the 'friend' was Holmes and said that the blackmailer should be taught a lesson. Le Mesurier asked if he knew someone who could handle 'a frightening job'; Deakin said that he would think about that. Thorpe, however, wanted immediate action. Le Mesurier said, 'He was pressing David very hard. He told David, "Let's get on with it! Let's get on with getting the bloody man killed!"'

There was no reason for Le Mesurier to become involved further but he was genuinely anxious to help Holmes, who was 'an old and well-tried friend'. So early in February 1975 he moved into action. With a friend, whom he never identified, he posed as a German journalist (hence, Scott's boasts to his solicitor about selling his story to a 'foreign publication') and arranged to meet Scott in Barnstaple, where he stole his briefcase. A few days later they returned and beat up Scott outside a pub. Scott was inspired now. He was rushed to the local casualty department, where he sobbed that his life was being threatened by Jeremy Thorpe. After being patched up there he begged his psychiatrist, Douglas Flack, to admit him to his mental hospital, where he would be safe. Flack refused because he did not want Scott to upset patients and staff with his stories about being buggered by one of the country's leading politicians. Scott was furious: 'In the past doctors had found me mentally ill. Yet when I wanted to get into hospital to protect myself from people who wanted to harm me I was turned down. Of course it was Thorpe I feared. I just knew he was behind the men who beat me up.'[10]

Having been refused sanctuary in a mental hospital he hid in parks and public lavatories. He said, 'I was frightened because my file had gone and without it I could not prove my story.' Then he pulled himself together and drove to Higher Chuggaton in his ageing Morris 1100, which he had bought with Gleadle's money, to confront Thorpe, who had ruined him. He negotiated his way safely through the narrow lanes leading to the cottage and parked the car. But Marion Thorpe was not pleased to see him and said that her husband was not available. Scott choked back the tears and got into his car. But he was so upset that he missed a gear change and slid into the garage doors. He asked Marion if she would help. She sighed, got in and drove the Morris into the lane. Scott mumbled his thanks and headed back to Barnstaple: 'It had been a waste of time. I still had no Insurance card and my file had gone.'[11]

Then he remembered that Gordon Winter had a copy of his 'dossier'. He wrote to the Johannesburg *Sunday Express* asking if he could please have it back. A few weeks later Winter invited Scott to visit him: 'You are most welcome to stay in my spare bedroom. I am quite sure that I can break the story from this end. This will make the UK press very much interested.' But Scott did not want to travel to Africa and said that he only wanted his files. Late in May 1975 Winter replied, saying that he had arranged for Scott's file to be copied and posted to him. Thus, Scott was reunited with his 'dossier'.

There were two new elements by spring 1975 which added to the muddle. First, Cyril Smith, who had just become Chief Whip, was told that Thorpe was bound to be exposed as a promiscuous homosexual, which would ruin both him and the Party, and, second, Holmes and Le Mesurier had hired an airline pilot called Andrew Gino Newton to deal with Scott.

The warning came from Bernard Greaves, the gay Liberal, who was so worried about Thorpe's behaviour that he made an appointment to see Smith on the afternoon of Wednesday, 30 April. Greaves said:

> I told Cyril that Thorpe was behaving recklessly in West London pubs and clubs. I had this from a variety of sources. He was being recognised. He was picking up strangers, not people who were introduced to him. Now, lots of gays did that but he was the Party leader and a married man and he

was taking a major risk. Cyril was grateful and said that he would get back to me if need be. But he didn't contact me again.[12]

Smith did not say anything publicly but, as Chief Whip, which made him the Party's intelligence officer responsible for preventing damaging scandals, quietly noted Thorpe's private life was a disaster waiting to happen.[13]

Thorpe did not know about Greaves' visit to Smith but he was aware that finally Holmes was making progress over Scott. This meant that he needed more money. On 5 March 1975 he had written to Hayward again, asking for £17,000; and, as before, said that he needed to cover fictitious election expenses by channelling £10,000 to Dinshaw. But Hayward did not reply. So Thorpe tried again on 6 July. This time he asked Hayward for £19,000. Hayward now sent £9,000 to one of the funds that Thorpe controlled, The Liberal Party Direct Aid Committee, but did not authorise the balance of £10,000 to be transferred to Dinshaw in Jersey until 24 November. This caused difficulties because Dinshaw made a series of payments, in cash, to Holmes during the year and became anxious when Hayward's money failed to arrive.

Dinshaw did not know it but the money that he gave to Holmes had been earmarked to finance the 'final solution' to the Scott problem. The recipient was Andrew Newton, who had been recruited in Blackpool on 26 February 1975 at a drunken dinner. He had been introduced to George Deakin by a mutual friend, David Miller, who ran a printing shop in Cardiff, and was told that he was required for a 'professional frightening job'. Newton thought that this sounded good fun and agreed, providing the money was right. Deakin said that he would be paid between £5,000 and £10,000, which Newton thought was about right.

Newton was 28 years old and had been brought up in Chiswick, West London. His father, a Polish-American called Niewadomski, left his Italian mother Maria when he was three; she changed her name to Newton and opened up the house to lodgers. Andrew became a commercial pilot when he was 24 and by 1974 was a senior first officer with British Island Airways. He was not an intellectual but he was cunning, good-looking and had a string of attractive girlfriends. He also wanted to be seriously rich, which he knew would not happen on his salary of £6,000 (*about £30,000 in 1995*).

In the following years, as details of the plot to 'deal with' Scott leaked out, Newton, Le Mesurier, Holmes and Deakin squabbled about what had really happened in 1975. Holmes and Le Mesurier admitted that they hired Newton but insisted that they had only asked him to frighten Scott. Deakin said he knew nothing. Newton, however, protested that he had been recruited to kill Scott and pointed out that they would hardly have paid him so much – the figures varied between £10,000 and £20,000 – just to scare someone. It does not matter now who was telling the truth although the balance is tilted towards Newton because Holmes and Le Mesurier already knew that Scott could not be frightened into silence. Everyone involved in this preposterous plan agreed, however, that Thorpe told Holmes that Scott had to be killed and that he used Jack Hayward's money to finance the plot. It is also undeniable that Holmes and Le Mesurier underestimated Newton; if they had been professional criminals they would have ensured that he did not know their names or why they wanted him to scare / hurt / kill Scott. But Newton persuaded them both to meet him, which was a disastrous breach of security.

Newton was also keen to find out more about Scott, the man whom everyone wanted to silence, on the principle that it might be more profitable to blackmail Holmes, who seemed to have real money. So, in between his flying duties with British Island Airways, he tried to tempt Scott to meet him in London and then Bristol with various unlikely stories about possible modelling jobs. But Norman refused to leave the relative safety of Barnstaple.

On 12 October 1975 Newton broke cover. He met Scott in Barnstaple, introduced himself as Peter Keene and claimed that he had been asked by 'a friend' to protect him from an assassin. Scott said, 'He told me, "You're in a great deal of trouble. You're going to be killed. A man has been paid a five-figure sum to kill you."' They adjourned to the Imperial Hotel for a drink where Norman sobbed out the usual story about Thorpe. He also showed Newton his 'dossier' which, while it proved nothing, suggested to Newton that Scott might not be as mad as he seemed. He scribbled notes on the back of a pink airline roster he found in his pocket and gulped when Scott mentioned The Postcard and Lord Snowdon. He thought now that he could not lose; he would be paid a great deal of money for killing Scott but that would only be the start because so many important, rich people were involved and they would have to pay for his silence. His first job as a hitman would set him up for life.

He drove north and told Holmes that they had to talk. They met at Manchester's Piccadilly Station, where Newton told Holmes that Scott had a dangerous bundle of documents. Holmes turned white and said that he had to move quickly, before Scott caused any more damage. There was a discussion about money, the details of which they later disputed: Newton said that he was paid a few hundred pounds as an advance against the agreed fee of £10,000 for murdering Scott while Holmes insisted that he paid him nothing and that the total involved was only £1,000, to scare, not kill Scott. It must be said, though, that Holmes certainly had the kind of money which Newton claimed that he was offered; the £7,500 from Jack Hayward's first payment had been topped up by regular cash payments from Dinshaw, who was still waiting to be reimbursed.

Newton headed off to London, to borrow a gun from a friend, a temperamental Mauser pistol, which had been made in 1910. Meanwhile, Holmes was briefing Thorpe: 'I told Jeremy that I was actually doing something and that allowed him to relax a little because he could convince himself that the problem was being attended to.'[14]

On Thursday, 23 October, when Newton was between flights at Glasgow Airport, he telephoned Scott, who was house-sitting for friends in Combe Martin, a few miles north of Barnstaple, and arranged to meet the following day. On Friday, Newton, aka Peter Keene, Scott's protector, set off from Blackpool in a Ford Escort owned by his girlfriend, Eleanor Rooney. As agreed, he met Scott at six o'clock that evening outside a hotel in Combe Martin but there was a hitch: a Great Dane bitch called Rinka, who was Scott's latest canine companion.

Newton, who was terrified of all dogs, from dachshunds upwards, thought that Rinka looked like 'a donkey' and told Scott that he did not want her in his car. But Scott said that he would not go anywhere without her so, reluctantly, Newton agreed. They set off to Porlock in Somerset, 25 miles to the east on the A39, where Newton said he had to meet a business contact. He deposited Scott and Rinka in a hotel in Porlock. Shortly after 8 p.m. he picked them up and they headed back towards Combe Martin. They climbed on to the moor and then the car began to stray across the road. Scott said that he would drive if Newton was tired; Newton thanked him and pulled over.

Scott told Newton to move across to the passenger seat 'to stop Rinka jumping out and making the car all wet'. Scott opened the door, bent his head against the wind and rain, and ran around the front, picked out by the headlights. But Newton had misunderstood and had also got out, to be followed by Rinka, who thought that she was going for a run. Scott grabbed her lead and tried to calm her. He told Newton, 'I'm sorry. I meant, just move over and then she wouldn't get out.' But the sight of a highly excited Rinka, pulling and jumping and wagging her tail, was too much for Newton. He shouted, 'Oh no. This is it.' He killed her with a shot to the head.

Scott could not understand why Rinka had collapsed. He bent down and tried to revive her. Then he realised that she was dead. He screamed at Newton; 'You've shot my dog. Oh no, not my dog . . . You can't involve Rinka. You can't involve the dog.' As he was crying, Newton grabbed him and pushed something hard against the back of his head. Then Newton swore, 'Oh fuck, oh fuck,' and released Scott, who turned and saw him crouching by the headlights, examining what appeared to be a gun. Scott ran a few paces and then turned, so that he could be close to his beloved Rinka when he died.

But Newton was still having trouble with the gun, which had jammed. He was shaking after almost being devoured by Rinka, the man-eating donkey, and could not free the firing mechanism. So he decided to abandon the mission. He got into the car and drove off, leaving behind him the great unanswered question of the whole story: What would have happened if his gun had not jammed? Would he have fired around Scott (which would have been dangerous since he was not a marksman and could easily have hit Scott) or would he have deliberately killed him?

Scott was hysterical. He stood in the road sobbing and waving. A few minutes later Edward Lethaby, an off-duty AA scout, saw a figure in his headlights and pulled up. Scott ran to the car, shouting, 'Oh please, someone's shot my dog and someone's tried to shoot me.'

Newton drove at top speed to David Miller's offices in Cardiff. He let himself in and sat down to see why the Mauser had malfunctioned. Around midnight Miller, who often bedded down there, arrived and found Newton upstairs, cleaning a gun. Newton told him about the débâcle on the moor, when he had had to shoot a dog which was going to chew off his head, and complained that he was working for 'a bunch of amateurs'. As he talked, he fiddled with the pistol and said that the firing pin was faulty. Next morning he cleaned the car, which was splattered with Rinka's blood, and hid the gun in a cupboard without telling his host.

Then he suggested that Miller might like to join him and Rooney on an exotic holiday, which would not cost much because, as a pilot, he could wangle cheap tickets. Miller said that sounded fun. Newton was in a good mood that morning as he drove out of Cardiff. It did not matter that Scott was still alive because Holmes would have to pay the promised £10,000, or else. He was going on holiday with his girlfriend and a mate. Life could not be better. But he had forgotten Norman Scott, who was determined to avenge Rinka.

CHAPTER THIRTEEN

If Andrew Newton had driven a few more miles that Friday night in October 1975, and back into Devon, Detective Chief Superintendent Michael Challes of the Avon and Somerset police would have enjoyed a quiet weekend, pottering around his home in Taunton. Instead, he was propelled on to the national stage after a lifetime of honest and unspectacular service and almost destroyed, emotionally, physically and professionally.

A few hours after Newton murdered Rinka, Challes was telephoned at home by the duty CID officer at Bridgwater police station, 30 miles south-east of Porlock, and told that there had been a shooting on his patch. This was the West Country in the 1970s and few criminals used guns, even to kill dogs, so he would probably have been briefed on Monday. But there was a special urgency that night that demanded the attention of Somerset's most senior detective: the incident involved Norman Scott.

While Newton was in David Miller's office in Cardiff, dismantling the ancient Mauser to try and discover why it had failed him, Scott was in a state of hyper-indignation. He was treated for 'shock' at a hospital in Minehead and sobbed to doctors, nurses and police that it was all the fault of Jeremy Thorpe, who wanted him dead because he knew too much. After several years drifting around Devon, telling anyone who would listen that Thorpe was a wicked man who had ruined his life, he had become a well-known anti-hero; even police officers who had never met him knew that it would definitely not help their careers to become entangled in his crazed campaign to ruin the MP for North Devon and leader of the Liberal Party. So the CID officer at Bridgwater immediately passed the Scott buck to Challes.

Challes had a gut instinct, born of over twenty years as a policeman, that this case was bad news. Although Rinka had died in Somerset Scott lived in Devon so Challes telephoned his counterpart in the Devon and Cornwall force, Detective Chief

Superintendent Proven Sharpe, who groaned when he heard that the ghastly Norman had almost been shot. Sharpe had dealt with him the previous year, after the police had been tipped off that he might be blackmailing Thorpe, and had not enjoyed the experience. He had questioned him in Barnstaple and had become so exasperated that he had banged Scott's head against a cell wall. But Scott had just laughed and said, 'You can go on doing that for ever. I won't change my mind.'[1] That Friday night in October 1975 Sharpe told Challes that, having met the man, he was sure that he had staged the shooting on the moor to publicise his lunatic claims.

Next day they agreed to divide the work: Challes would probe the death of the Great Dane while Sharpe would collect background information on Scott. They also agreed that it would be best if the press were not told anything since it would not help anyone if Scott's distasteful stories about the Liberal leader were plastered across the newspapers. They kept Scott happy by asking him to give a statement. He looked terrible – he was skeletal and sweaty and was so nervous that he looked as if he would implode – but he always enjoyed denouncing Thorpe. Thus, he had no difficulty gathering his thoughts when a detective from Bristol arrived at Combe Martin to interview him; four hours and nineteen pages later the officer staggered away, feeling as if his brain had been scrambled.

It did not take long for news of Rinka's murder to leak, despite the efforts of Challes and Sharpe. The story was a welcome relief from the usual diet of local news, such as the row at the parish council about the state of the public convenience in the park and a burglary at the sub-post office, where stamps and pension books were stolen, and the *West Somerset Free Press* went big on Rinka. It headlined its report: 'Mystery of the dog in a fog', and said:

Police are believed to be still investigating at press time a mystery as impenetrable as moorland fog, in which a self-described political writer is said to have claimed that an attempt was made on his life. Police at Bridgwater refused to confirm or deny a story that had gained circulation – that the killer of the pet also tried to shoot a man, but that the gun jammed. Neither would say whether the dog owner is a Mr Norman Scott, of Park Lane, Combe Martin. Press reports claimed that Mr Scott had left the West Country for South Africa.

This final sentence was a reference to Scott's long-standing fantasy that he was writing a book, which would be published in South Africa. This was a piece of classic Scott mischief; it seemed harmless at the time but quickly grew into a fully grown fact, when it was plucked by journalists and cited as proof that BOSS was responsible for everything. In fact, the 'manuscript' that Scott carried everywhere with him was no more than his handwritten version of the many statements he had given to the police over the years. It had as much chance of being published as a book, even in South Africa, as Norman had of being adopted as the Liberal candidate in North Devon.

Thorpe laughed when the *West Somerset Free Press* telephoned him for a comment on Rinka's death: 'Are they hunting dogs on the moors these days?' he said. This was not a wise joke because Auberon Waugh, who wrote for *Private Eye*, lived in Somerset and subscribed to the *West Somerset Free Press*. Waugh had never trusted Thorpe and was offended by his tasteless quip about the death of a Great Dane. He made a mental note to follow developments.

Curiously only the *Sunday Express*, a newspaper not renowned for its investigative zeal, dug further. The *Express* usually served its readers in Middle England a diet of stories about the Second World War, pets and gardening, and thundered in its editorial columns about the need to defend the standards that had made Britain Great. But, on 2 November 1975, Michael Dove, the chief reporter, was set loose on the mystery of Rinka. His story, headlined: 'Exmoor riddle of frightened man and a shot dog', revealed that a Great Dane had been shot and that her owner, Mr Norman Scott, claimed that the killer was a private detective who would also have murdered him if his gun had not jammed. Dove then said that it was curious that Detective Chief Superintendent Michael Challes, who was a very senior officer, had been assigned to such a minor incident; Challes would only say, however, that he had been asked to handle Rinka's murder because of 'the ramifications of the affair', which raised more questions than it answered. Dove also approached Thorpe, who said, 'I have been aware of this man Scott. He once presented himself at the House. I did not see him. I made a report to the Home Secretary and this would be about three years ago.' The rest of Fleet Street ignored Rinka that Sunday but news editors clipped the *Express* story and circled the names Scott, Thorpe, Challes and Rinka, and assigned reporters to see what they could find out, just in case there was something in this nonsense about a dead dog.

David Miller, meanwhile, had locked up his printing shop and set off to London with a small bag of lightweight clothes for his trip to Pakistan with Newton and Eleanor Rooney. He also had the Mauser which Newton had hidden in his office, though he was not happy about carrying a gun on a train. They flew from Heathrow on 31 October for a break which Newton thought he thoroughly deserved. Thorpe and Holmes, however, were not so relaxed. Holmes said, 'Newton called me and said that everything was OK. But I was appalled at the thought that he had shot a dog and left a hysterical Scott weeping by the roadside.'[2]

The police soon identified Newton. One of Scott's friends in Barnstaple told them that she had been suspicious about a man, called Peter Keene, who had visited Scott a fortnight before Rinka was killed, and had written down the registration of his yellow Mazda. Even in this pre-computer age it only took a few hours for the Devon police to track down Newton, who had hired the car in Blackpool. On 18 November Challes' oppos were waiting at Heathrow when Newton returned from Pakistan with Rooney and Miller. He was arrested and driven to Somerset.

His friends called him 'chicken brain' but he was cunning and, by the time he was sitting in the interview room in Bridgwater police station, had concocted a cover story which, so he thought, would keep him out of prison and ensure that he was paid a great deal of money by David Holmes and his rich friends. He said that he had met Scott after he had sent a nude photograph of himself in response to an advertisement in a sex-contact magazine. He said that, of course, he had thought that he was writing to a woman and had been horrified when Scott had turned up in Blackpool and demanded a monthly payment of £4 in return for not sending the photograph to British Island Airways, his employers. He said that he had hired the Mazda and driven to Barnstaple a few months later to try and persuade Scott to leave him alone. But Scott had only wanted to talk about Thorpe. So, Newton continued, he had borrowed a gun and returned to Devon, intending to scare Scott by shooting around him; but it all went wrong. He hated dogs and had shot the Great Dane. He aimed the gun at Scott, intending to fire a few bullets around him, but the gun had jammed.

Challes' team were not convinced. Why had Scott bothered to travel from Barnstaple to Blackpool, which was a long, expensive journey by train, to demand a few pounds a month? Why had Newton driven to Devon twice, which must have cost him a year's blackmail money? Why use a gun, rather than his fists, to frighten Scott? But, on the other hand, the police thought that Scott had blackmailed Thorpe and so they concluded that, perhaps, Newton was telling the truth.

Challes and Sharpe were also under pressure from their superiors to make sure that Scott did not use the incident to embarrass Thorpe; thus on 20 November Newton was charged with having possession of a firearm with intent to endanger life. Police searched his mother's house in Chiswick where the Mauser was found, together with the notes that he had scribbled on his pink airline roster when he met Scott, including the reference to The Postcard and Lord Snowdon. Then Newton was released on bail.

The West Country police were also given a not very subtle hint that it would be best for everyone if Thorpe's name was kept out of the investigation when Sharpe and a colleague, Detective Inspector Ivan Pollard, visited Special Branch at Scotland Yard. Pollard said, 'We got nothing from them. They were very cagey. We thought that they knew about Thorpe's homosexuality but they didn't show us their files.'[3]

Norman Scott now had a new ally in his campaign to ruin Thorpe: Andrew Newton, who was determined to extract as much money as possible from his involvement in Rinka's killing and did not care who suffered as a result, providing that it was not him.

He saw Holmes half a dozen times over the following weeks. He saw himself as a hot-shot gangster so they met in ludicrously melodramatic circumstances in churches and railway stations; they even whispered to each other from adjoining telephone boxes, like characters in a B-film. Thanks to Jack Hayward and Nadir Dinshaw, Holmes had ample funds and gave Newton £400 in cash, with the promise of £5,000 after his trial, on condition that he kept his mouth shut. He did not care for Newton, whom he thought was a spiv, but assured him that he had powerful friends, who would make sure that he did not go to prison. Holmes said, 'All this was agreed in advance with Jeremy. We were in regular contact and he was consulted on every detail.'[4]

Thorpe assumed, rightly, that the police would not want to dig too deeply into the circumstances surrounding Rinka's murder but in mid-December he had a terrible shock when he read *Private Eye*.

Auberon Waugh did not share the police's respect for the leader of the Liberal Party and wrote:

> West Somerset is buzzing with rumours of a most unsavoury description following reports in the *West Somerset Free Press* about an incident which occurred recently on Exmoor. Mr Norman Scott, a thirty-five-year-old writer, of Combe Martin, North Devon, who claims to have been a great friend of Jeremy Thorpe, the Liberal statesman, was found by an AA patrolman weeping beside the body of Rinka, his Great Dane bitch, which had been shot in the head. Information about this puzzling incident has since been restricted on Home Office orders, but a man [Newton] arrested at London Airport on a firearms charge will be appearing shortly before Minehead magistrates on 19 December, when we may learn more. My only hope is that sorrow over his friend's dog will not cause Mr Thorpe's premature retirement from public life.[5]

There were other worrying developments. David Miller, Newton's chum from Cardiff, smelt money and sold photographs of Newton to the press. Then Newton held what he called a press conference, though it was, in fact, a reminder to Holmes and Thorpe that he expected to be rewarded for his discretion. He had been charged, which meant that newspapers could not publish anything which touched on Rinka's death, but that did not matter because he knew that Thorpe would understand the implicit threat of this aside: 'I think it is wrong for Mr Thorpe to be dragged through the mud by men of straw . . . I have never met Thorpe or Wilson and Scott is a petty, vindictive man.'

After Newton was committed to stand trial at Exeter in March 1976 Thorpe told Holmes that they had to prevent Scott, who would be the chief prosecution witness, from using the case to publicise his horrible allegations. Holmes told him that he was worrying unnecessarily: the judge would tell Scott to shut up if he started to talk slanderously about a distinguished public figure who had nothing to do with Rinka's death. But Thorpe was convinced, as he had been for many years, that Scott possessed demonic powers and that he would, somehow, contrive to repeat his monstrous allegations in court.

He told Holmes that Peter Bessell, who was living quietly in California, might provide the solution. Bessell could write a letter saying that Scott had been blackmailing him and that, in desperation he, Bessell, had bought the file containing the 'retainer' letters in February 1974. They could show Scott's solicitor this letter and say that they would hand it to the police if his client mentioned Thorpe during Newton's trial; blackmail was a serious offence and Scott would be so frightened that he would do as he was told. Holmes was so pathetically in awe of Thorpe that he did not tell him what he really thought: that this was a ridiculous idea. He could not see why Bessell would want to confess that he had been blackmailed by a neurotic homosexual, which would not do much for what was left of his reputation.

But even if he was foolish enough to sign a letter like this, Holmes thought that a 'confession' by Bessell would be exposed immediately as a bizarre hoax. Bessell had been in California, not Devon, in February 1974 and had never heard of Dr Ronald Gleadle, who had bought the letters. Gleadle had negotiated with him, Holmes, and Michael Barnes, Thorpe's solicitor, and would, presumably, say so if the police asked him. There was also the undeniable fact that Gleadle had banked a cheque for £2,500 drawn on the account of Mr David Holmes, merchant banker and godfather to Rupert Thorpe. And, finally, Scott's solicitor, Jeremy Ferguson, had been told by Gleadle that he should contact Barnes if he wanted to find out what had happened to his client's letters. But Holmes said nothing and nodded limply when Thorpe instructed him to ask Lord Goodman for his opinion; Goodman said that, legally if not morally, Bessell could say what he liked.

Peter Bessell was happy. He was living in a tiny 'cottage', which some people would have called a hut, on the beach at Oceanside. He was broke but he had his beloved Diane, a stunning young woman who adored him, his faithful dachshunds, the sun and the sea. He remained optimistic. He was writing a children's book, which, he told Diane, would be a great success, and made regular forays to Los Angeles to meet 'business associates'. She knew in her heart that nothing would come of any of this but did not care; Peter was tanned, relaxed and had recovered well from his heart attack although she was concerned about his lungs, which were ravaged by decades of chain-smoking. She was not pleased when he told her that Holmes would be on holiday in the States in January and was planning to visit them; she warned him not to become involved again with Thorpe, who had brought him only heartache. But Bessell assured her that she should not worry; this would be a purely social visit and, in any case, he no longer had anything to offer Jeremy.

On 19 January 1976 Bessell met Holmes and his lover, Gerald Hagan, at San Diego Airport. Holmes had already told Hagan that he had some confidential business to discuss with Bessell so Hagan checked into a local hotel, while Bessell and Holmes drove north to Oceanside. *En route*, Holmes said that Scott was still causing serious problems, which surprised Bessell, who had assumed that Norman had long since perished in a haze of alcohol, drugs and self-pity. Holmes ploughed on and said that Scott had been blackmailing an airline pilot called Andrew Newton. Bessell said that this did not sound like the Scott whom, unfortunately, he had once known well; awful though he was, Bessell continued, Scott had not seemed the type of man who would resort to blackmail. But Holmes ignored this and described how Newton had become so exasperated with Scott, the blackmailer, that he had shot his dog on Exmoor.

Bessell had led a stable, if impoverished, life with Diane in California, far from Scott's rantings and Thorpe's lies, and wondered if Holmes was telling an elaborate joke. He later wrote:

> It was all laughable. I was fond of dogs so I asked David what the breed was. He replied impatiently that he had no idea, but it was a big animal. I said heartlessly, 'Perhaps the pilot intended to kill Scott and just shot the dog by accident.' I was joking but David said that Newton had told the police that he did not give a damn about the dog and would shoot Scott next time he saw him. I chuckled and said, 'That should make a good headline for the *North Devon Journal*!'

Holmes did not find this funny. He insisted that Scott would use Newton's trial to attack Thorpe. There was only way to stop him: Bessell had to write a letter describing how Scott had blackmailed him. Bessell was stunned but Holmes said that he had taken advice from Lord Goodman, who thought that this was a solid idea and would certainly not endanger Bessell. He said that the letter should be addressed to a solicitor called Michael Barnes, who, he lied, represented Andrew Newton. Bessell was baffled by this; surely, he asked Holmes, he should address the letter to Scott's lawyer? No, said Holmes, it would be better to tell Newton's solicitor.

Then he told Bessell that, in any case, the letter would never be made public. Bessell nodded but, as a veteran liar himself, sensed that he was not being told the truth.

As they reached the motel in Oceanside, where he was staying that night, Holmes confessed that there was another problem: he had paid £10,000 to Scott for the 'retainer' letters. (He had only paid £2,500; this was a pointless lie because Bessell did not know that Jack Hayward had sent £10,000 to Holmes, via Nadir Dinshaw in Jersey.) Bessell gasped and said that he must have been mad; he pointed out, correctly, that the letters had been worthless but that Holmes had now invested them with a new and dangerous importance. Holmes told him that he had had no choice; they could have been used, he pointed out, to embarrass him as well as Thorpe. Bessell now felt guilty and said that, of course, he would help.

Although Bessell had many faults he was sentimental about his old friend, Jeremy, with whom he had once dreamt of power and glory; he also thought, genuinely, that it would be wrong if Thorpe's career was wrecked because of sexual weakness. After all, Bessell told himself, the only difference between them was that he liked to go to bed with women while Thorpe preferred men. He was also flattered that, even now, as a penniless and discredited ex-MP, who lived in a beach hut on the West Coast, Thorpe, the leader of a great political party and a Privy Counsellor, needed him.

So he agreed to write the letter. But he modified Thorpe's draft significantly. Thorpe had wanted him to say that he had bought the 'retainer' letters, using money from Diane's father, but Bessell said that it would be wrong to involve him. He also watered down the allegations that Thorpe had wanted him to make against Scott. He wrote that, at first, he had given money to Scott because he felt sorry for him but that Scott had then threatened to expose an affair with a secretary. But, Bessell continued, he only paid Scott 'a few pounds' and they soon lost contact. Even if this had been true, which it was not, this hardly constituted blackmail; from this letter Scott emerged as a pathetic character who deserved help, not imprisonment. But Holmes seemed satisfied and telephoned London. Thorpe was not at home so he asked Marion to tell him, 'Mission accomplished.'

Next morning, 20 January, they drove back to San Diego to collect Hagan. Bessell had been brooding about the letter and told Holmes that, frankly, he thought that he was lying. Holmes stuttered that he was right. But he still did not tell the whole truth; he admitted that he had recruited Newton to kill Scott but did not say that Michael Barnes represented Thorpe, not Newton, nor that Thorpe was planning to sacrifice Bessell to save himself.

They collected Hagan and headed for the airport to catch their flight to San Francisco, where they were going to resume their holiday. Hagan listened, appalled, as Bessell and Holmes gossiped; just like Diane, who had feared for Peter, Hagan was worried that his own partner, David, was being manipulated again by Thorpe. Hagan said, 'Bessell was very indiscreet in the car and I found out about the letter. I was very sad that David was involved in something that had nothing to do with him. But Bessell was overjoyed to see someone from his former life and wanted us to stay. He was obviously missing Westminster and hated the isolation of California.'[6]

Thorpe, meanwhile, had been busy lying in London. He told Cyril Smith that 'a hothead' called Scott would shortly be appearing as a witness in the trial of a man accused of shooting a dog. Smith stared and wondered if Thorpe had gone mad. Thorpe continued softly, as if he was outlining a new strategy on education: 'Scott is going to allege that he had a homosexual affair with me and that I paid to have his dog shot as a warning to him to keep his mouth shut.'[7]

Smith recovered his poise and said that, surely, no newspaper would publish rubbish like this. Thorpe scowled and said that he was simply taking the precaution of warning his Chief Whip about a possible public relations problem. Smith remembered that Bernard Greaves had told him the previous April that Thorpe was a homosexual, whose reckless promiscuity could cause irreparable damage to the Party. So, he made some discreet enquiries. He spoke to David Steel and Emlyn Hooson who revealed that Scott had appeared before a secret Party inquiry in 1971 but had not produced any evidence to substantiate his claims. Smith decided that, in view of this, he had to make absolutely sure that Scott was lying and asked Thorpe if he could run through the story once more. But Thorpe was not pleased by the tone of his Chief Whip's questions and said that it was outrageous that Smith was taking the wretched man seriously; he said that Scott had psychiatric problems and ordered Smith to tell the police in Devon about this. Smith was 'thoroughly concerned' now and decided to seek the advice of Roy Jenkins, the Home Secretary, who had access to police files on Scott. Jenkins said that he could not, of course, interfere in a criminal investigation but added that he would alert the police in Devon to Scott's background.[8]

Unfortunately for Thorpe, Norman had made his own plans. Late in January 1976 Michael Barnes heard that Scott was due to appear in court in Barnstaple on the 29th, charged with dishonestly obtaining social security benefits totalling £58.40 in June 1975. Scott was looking forward to the hearing and told friends, 'I committed fraud quite deliberately in order to get caught and appear in a public courtroom.'[9] An enterprising news agency tipped off Fleet Street that it would be worth covering the hearing. This was Norman's big moment, which he had been dreaming about for many years, and he rose to the occasion magnificently. The magistrates in Barnstaple suspected that something was wrong because the press benches were packed with expensively suited reporters who obviously did not work for the local newspapers.

The case began quietly, as the prosecution lawyer, Michael White, described how Scott had fraudulently claimed supplementary benefits. This was not very exciting and the reporters from London wondered why they were wasting their time here. Then Scott burst into action. He started to sob and shake and shouted, 'It has been fifteen years. I really would like to get this matter cleared up. It has become so sick. I am being hounded all the time by people just because of my sexual relationship with Jeremy Thorpe. It gets worse and worse. I am sorry but I must say it. I am so tired and upset and that is why all this has happened.'[10] There was pandemonium. The clerk of the court told him to shut up. But it was too late: the press had scribbled down the fatal quote, which was privileged and could not be censored by Lord Goodman.

Scott's solicitor, Jeremy Ferguson, apologised for his client's outburst: 'Mr Scott is young, excitable and anxious and he feels vulnerable. He has from time to time got into bad company. He has talked to the wrong people and has been given the wrong sort of help and advice. He needs assistance, not punishment.' Scott was put on probation for two years and ordered to pay back the money, which, he told the court, he had needed to finance the copying of a book that he was writing.

Then he pressed home his attack on Thorpe by holding a press

conference at Gloucester Cottage, his temporary home in Combe
Martin, which, by a delicious irony, had once been the offices of the
local Liberal Party. He said, 'I really didn't want to hurt anyone. I
am sorry all this had to come out. I don't like to blacken anyone's
name. I think I shall have to leave the country now because people
around here are hostile to me.' He provided journalists with useful
background:

> I came to Devon in the first place to help Jeremy in his
> constituency work. We got on famously. Jeremy took a
> room for me in Draycott Place, Chelsea, a house owned
> by a Mrs Flood [sic]. This was my home for three months.
> Jeremy used to come and see me there. Sometimes we went
> to Devon and other times we went to Stonewalls, his family
> home. I have not seen or spoken to Jeremy for a long time. I
> do not expect that we shall meet again, except by accident.

He also gave them selected highlights from his 'dossier'. He told
them about Tim Keigwin, the Conservative candidate who had
been warned by his own party not to mention Scott during the
election campaign in February 1974, and about someone called
'Van de Brecht de Vater', the riding ace who owned a stables
in Oxfordshire where he had first met Thorpe. This was good
stuff, because there were leads for reporters to follow. They
would be able to check with Liberals in the West Country,
to see if they remembered Norman and with Mrs Flood, of
Chelsea, who would surely recall an hysterical homosexual called
Norman whose boyfriend wore Edwardian suits. There was also
Tim Keigwin and the man with the long foreign name.

But reporters did not have time to probe further; they had
deadlines and filed their reports to London. It was not easy,
though, for news editors there to get a reaction from Thorpe,
whose office was already being swamped with calls from the
press after the publication that day of a Department of Trade
investigation into the collapse of London and County Securities
in 1973. Thorpe had been a director, earning £5,000 a year,
with assorted perks, until he resigned, just as the company fell
apart, leaving debts of £50 million. The DTI report acquitted
him of malpractice but said that he should not have lent his
name to a company like this. It said that, in future, politicians
had to be certain that companies did not shelter behind the

respectability conferred by having eminent public figures on their boards.

Later that day Thorpe issued two statements through Lord Goodman's office. First, he dealt with the DTI report: 'I placed total reliance and faith in quarters where it is now, alas, all too clear that confidence was wholly misplaced.' Then he moved to Scott: 'It is well over twelve years since I last saw or spoke to Mr Scott. There is no truth in Mr Scott's allegations.'

Thorpe's denial shocked his gay friends in the Liberal Party; they did not expect him to come out, since that would have been professional suicide, but did not see why he had to talk as if homosexuals, like Scott, were sub-humans. John Fryer said, 'He saw his homosexuality as a problem and started fabricating all sorts of things. A lot of us were furious when he denied a relationship with Scott. Yes, I believed Scott.' Michael Steed, the Liberal from Manchester who later became Liberal President said, 'I always assumed that Scott was telling the truth. But, by denying it, Thorpe made it an issue of his veracity rather than his sexuality. I remember thinking that it was remarkably like Watergate, in that Thorpe gave the impression that there was a plot, even if there wasn't one.' Bernard Greaves thought that Thorpe's reaction to Scott proved that, apart from being an egomaniac, he was a liar. Then Cyril Smith contacted him. Greaves said, 'He asked me if I knew anything about Scott. I said that I didn't. I just passed on the gossip about Thorpe.'[11]

Harold Wilson, however, was convinced that Thorpe was the victim of a smear campaign, organised by the South Africans, who hated both the Labour and Liberal Parties. Wilson had long been sure that, as Prime Minister, he had been subjected to a variety of dirty tricks over the years by assorted far-right forces, including MI5 and BOSS. He believed that the same sinister organisations were using Scott to destroy his friend Jeremy, who loathed apartheid, just like him. So, encouraged by his faithful secretary Lady Falkender, who said that he had to 'save' poor Jeremy, he told Thorpe early in February that he knew that he was innocent. Thorpe was thrilled and told Cyril Smith, 'It will be pushed on to the South Africans. The Prime Minister thinks that there are South African influences at work.'[12]

Wilson should have known better than to nail himself so firmly to Thorpe's decidedly shaky mast. But, whatever his knowledge of Thorpe's sexual past, he now ordered further checks. He asked Barbara Castle, his Social Services Minister, to discover who had ordered the prosecution against Scott, hoping, no doubt, for clues leading to MI5 and Pretoria. Castle had to disappoint him when she reported back a few days later. She described his reaction in her diary:

> Harold's face dropped a bit when I told him that Scott's file seemed to show Jeremy's relationship with Scott had been longer and more domesticated than he had so far admitted. My aim is to warn Harold against going overboard for Jeremy too recklessly. He has already made a rather hysterical attack on the press for 'hounding' Jeremy . . . He really is an incredible mixture of caution and recklessness.[13]

Journalists were also digging. The *Daily Mirror* revealed that Gordon Winter, a South African reporter with links to BOSS, might have orchestrated the whole affair; this introduced a glamorous dimension to what had been, until then, a sordid story about dead dogs and homosexuals. This was an unfortunate development because 'the South African connection', as it was dubbed by over-excited journalists, did not exist.

Other newspapers came up with hard facts rather than speculation about international conspiracies. Scott revelled in the attention and leaked more information from his 'dossier'. He told the London *Evening Standard* about Bessell's 'retainers' and the purchase of his files for £2,500 by Dr Ronald Gleadle. Then Cyril Smith, who was besieged by reporters, mentioned that Bessell had written an affidavit, accusing Scott of blackmail. This was now the hot story of the week and the Sunday newspapers deployed their top investigative reporters to unravel the mystery of Rinka, 'retainers' paid by a Liberal MP to a homosexual, BOSS and much else besides. Unfortunately, they could not find Bessell, who had disappeared many months ago.

That Sunday he was minding his own business in Oceanside, tinkering with his book of children's stories and taking his arthritic dachshund for a spin on the beach in the trolley he had constructed for her. Then David Holmes called. He explained that there had been a small problem: Scott had appeared in court and denounced Thorpe and next, the press knew about Bessell's 'affidavit'. But Holmes insisted that none of this mattered because the story was dying. This was untrue, as Bessell's solicitor in London pointed out when he telephoned Oceanside: he said that every newspaper in the country was desperate to speak to Bessell.

Bessell suspected now that Thorpe had set him up to take the blame for Scott and went to bed seething. Next day, Monday, 2 February, was worse. The *Daily Mail* had discovered where he lived and telephoned the beach hut; the *Mail* said that they could send their West Coast reporter to Oceanside immediately. Then Thorpe called, begging him to say nothing or to lie. Bessell was thoroughly confused. He adored being centre stage again. But he did not want to be portrayed as a crook who had been blackmailed by a homosexual, which would not help him relaunch his business career in California. He was still fond of Thorpe but thought that it was a poor show to blame him for Scott. He concluded that Holmes had bought Scott's 'dossier' as the first stage in the plot to murder him; if Scott was killed Thorpe had to be sure that the police would not find any letters linking him with Scott.

Protecting Thorpe because he had had an affair with Scott was one thing; it was quite another to become involved in a murder plot. So, on Tuesday, 3 February the *Daily Mail* carried the first major interview with Bessell. Headlined: 'My part in the Thorpe affair', it explained that Bessell was living in California and had not, after all, been blackmailed by Scott. Other newspapers read the story, decided that Bessell knew much more than he had admitted so far and dispatched reporters to confront him in Oceanside. There, they camped outside his hut, demanding answers from him. Under pressure from Thorpe, who telephoned constantly, he kept changing his story; one minute he said that he had been blackmailed by Scott and the next that he had not. Bessell said:

For two years I had lived a life of seclusion with Diane. Slowly, with Diane, without whose love it would have been impossible, I had built a new life in California. Now, without warning, I was being thrust back into a past I had intentionally sealed off for ever. Reporters were no doubt surprised by me: a former Member of Parliament living with an attractive woman in a miniscule clapboard cottage. The job of these reporters was to flush out the story and not to waste energy considering the effect on my business, family or friends. i had disappeared in questionable circumstances so I was dubbed 'the runaway MP' who had deserted his wife and children.

He could have refused to say anything but vanity overcame caution
and he talked – and lied – at length. But he conceded that he did
not handle the press with his usual aplomb:

> I had become used to dressing informally in California and
> received the journalists in a polo-neck sweater and slacks. It is
> valuable to remember that, if one wishes to be treated with any
> respect by British reporters, one must dress formally, avoid
> the use of first names and severely limit the time you spend
> with them. Throughout the crisis Jeremy did well with the
> Press, largely by keeping reporters at arm's length, exercising
> authority and rarely answering questions.

On Tuesday he changed his mind again. Thorpe told him that he
would have to justify himself to his fellow MPs and senior Liberal
lords the next day and urgently needed Bessell's support so, once
again, Bessell lied to save his old friend. He now 'confessed' to
reporters in Oceanside that Scott had been blackmailing him:

> My reputation had been irretrievably damaged and I had little
> to lose. But if Jeremy was forced to quit the leadership, the
> Liberal Party would be split asunder and that was something
> that had to be prevented. I had earned the contempt of
> everyone. The evidence against me was damning. I had no
> one to blame but myself that the new life that Diane had
> begun to build had now taken its place among the ruins of
> the past.

Thanks to Bessell, Thorpe survived his grilling by the Party on
Wednesday, 4 February. He lied fluently and, by the end of the
meeting, had convinced everyone that Bessell, not him, should be
explaining himself. But it was only a reprieve. Four days later he
was questioned by Detective Chief Superintendent Proven Sharpe
about Rinka's death and Dr Ronald Gleadle. He said little but
promised Sharpe 'a comprehensive account' as soon as his legal
adviser, Lord Goodman, was available; but naturally he never
wrote it. He remained in regular contact with Bessell; he thanked
him for his help and promised that Scott would soon be forgotten.
Bessell said that he would continue to protect him but warned that
he expected support in return; it should have been clear now to

Thorpe that Bessell was not enjoying his role as fall-guy and that he was edging towards a public confession.

But, back in London, Cyril Smith thought that they had weathered the storm: 'We were allowed a month of comparative peace and hopes began to rise that the affair really was over – Jeremy's side. Letters poured in by the hundred, a few critical, but the vast majority expressing support.'[14]

This was an illusion. Newspaper editors and their senior executives, who belonged to the same gentlemen's clubs as Thorpe, dismissed Scott as a 'nauseous, erratic and desperate man', but reporters who had followed the story had different ideas: they did not like Scott but, on the other hand, their research showed that much of what he told them was true, such as his claim that Dr Ronald Gleadle had paid him £2,500 for his 'dossier'.

Late in February, David Holmes panicked and threw himself on the mercy of the Director of Public Prosecutions. He confessed that he had, in fact, bought the letters because he had wanted to protect the Liberal Party. Holmes said that the DPP was 'very helpful' but wanted him to run over his story with the police, which worried Holmes, who seemed to think that, because he was a gentleman, the DPP would simply forget the whole affair. Holmes said, 'I was not happy but I saw Detective Chief Superintendent Sharpe in a private room at the Reform Club. Again, I did not involve Jeremy. Sharpe was not pleased that I would not make an official statement.'[15]

On Friday, 5 March the storm broke when newspapers telephoned Cyril Smith and told him that David Holmes, Thorpe's best man and godfather to young Rupert, had paid £2,500 for Scott's letters. Holmes blamed the police for the leak, although there was no proof of that, and issued a futile statement, through his solicitor, David Freeman, saying that he had acted alone, to save the Liberal Party from embarrassment. But no one believed him. Thorpe asked Smith that night where he now stood; Smith said, 'In a bloody mess.'

Next day's headlines were a nightmare for the Liberals. The *Daily Mirror*, which had led the way in the investigation, declared: 'I paid £2,500 to Norman Scott, says the godfather'. Senior Liberal MPs such as Emlyn Hooson and Richard Wainwright, who had had private discussions with Bessell over the past weeks in an attempt to discover the truth, were convinced now that Thorpe should resign. David Steel was not certain, until he had dinner a few days later with Nadir Dinshaw, who was a good friend.

Dinshaw had been horrified by the press's revelations about Holmes and told Steel that he was concerned that the money that he had received from Hayward and passed to Holmes, at Thorpe's request, might have been used to pay for Scott's letters. He said that he had paid Holmes £10,000 by cheque and £7,500 in cash, which disturbed Steel: 'My concern was, who had paid Newton to shoot Scott's dog? An appalling possibility presented itself: Was it David Holmes? I now had information which finally convinced me that Jeremy ought not to remain as Leader.'[16]

The Liberals seemed to be imploding. Cyril Smith admitted, 'There are things going on I know nothing about,' and indicated that he might not be able to continue as Chief Whip. Thorpe, however, was still fighting: he announced that he would resign the leadership at the Party assembly in September and seek re-election, under new rules, which meant that the rank and file, rather than MPs, would elect the leader. Liberal MPs were appalled by this; they knew that ordinary Liberals still adored Thorpe because they did not know the truth.

Then Harold Wilson stepped in. He shrugged off Barbara Castle's protestations that her research in Whitehall's files showed that Thorpe had lied about Scott – Wilson would only concede, grudgingly: 'I dare say there may have been something at some time.' But the important point now, he said, was that Thorpe was being destroyed by South Africa. So, during Prime Minister's Questions, he said, 'I have no doubt at all that there is a strong South African participation in recent activities relating to the leader of the Liberal Party.' He talked about 'massive resources of business money and private agents of various kinds and various qualities' but said that he had no evidence that the government was involved.

Emboldened by Wilson's support, Thorpe tried to finish Scott off, before he could launch another attack the following Tuesday at the trial in Exeter of Andrew Newton. He summoned Harold Evans to his home in Orme Square and gave Evans a point-by-point rebuttal of Scott's claims, vetted by Lord Goodman. This was a pack of lies. He also gave background material to Evans, which was completely untrue. On 14 March the *Sunday Times* ran a front-page headline: 'The lies of Norman Scott, by Jeremy Thorpe', backed up by a long story inside the newspaper, written by the crack investigative unit, Insight. This blamed Bessell and Winter for the mess that was threatening to destroy the Liberals.

This marked the end of Peter Bessell's support for his old friend. When he read the *Sunday Times* in Oceanside he was furious: 'The main purpose of the articles was to shift the burden of responsibility for Scott from Jeremy to me and to a lesser extent to Gordon Winter. I made the decision to abandon the personal support I had given him in the matter of Scott since 1965.'

On 16 March Newton's trial opened at Exeter Crown Court. The journalists who had been assigned to the case settled down to report what they thought would be the big story of the day; they were not pleased when they heard that they had been knocked off the front page by two huge news events – the announcement by Buckingham Palace that Princess Margaret and Lord Snowdon were separating after sixteen years of marriage and Harold Wilson's resignation as Prime Minister.[17] But the death of Rinka was such a fascinating story that newspapers still gave the trial generous space that week.

Scott was the star of the proceedings and managed, despite the efforts of the judge and prosecution lawyers, to repeat his allegations about Thorpe. By his standards he was calm and controlled: 'Mr Thorpe said when I first went to live with him – I know it sounds unwholesome, but these are his words as far as I can remember, "I don't want you to have to worry any longer about money." In other words, I was supposed to live with him and be cared for by him for the rest of my life.' He denied blackmailing Newton or Bessell and insisted that nice Mr Bessell would tell the truth one day, a remark which brought an uncharacteristic lump to Bessell's throat in Oceanside when he read it in his airmailed newspaper.

The judge had more luck, however, with the two pieces of pink paper that Newton had made notes on when he had met Scott in Barnstaple. Scott had told Newton about The Postcard and Snowdon and Newton had duly scribbled down this information but the judge had no intention of allowing Scott to drag a member of the Royal Family into a case involving contact magazines, nude photographs and an hysterical homosexual and would not allow any discussion of Newton's note.

Newton, however, played the buffoon brilliantly; in between idiotic jokes he changed his story so often that, by the end of the trial, he was dismissed as a congenital liar. But that did not mean that people thought that Scott was telling the truth about Thorpe; on the contrary, it was felt that Newton and Scott deserved each other and that it did not matter why Newton had killed Rinka. Patrick Back QC, who was defending Newton, caught the mood of the court when he said that many homosexuals had 'a terrifying propensity for malice'. He continued: 'Do you remember how Scott started with a soft effeminate voice and a sort of false humility and, at the crucial moment, came the tears. Then they were gone and we had the charade of fear, the shaking of the hands and the stuttering of the tongue. Do you think that was real?'

On 19 March Newton was sentenced to two years in prison, which shocked him, since Holmes had assured him that 'powerful friends' would make sure he was acquitted. Scott was also not happy. The press turned on him and described him as 'a spiteful blackmailer, eaten with hatred'.

Thorpe believed that he had escaped and told friends that he had the three most important people in Britain on his side: Harold Wilson, Lord Goodman and MI5 [sic]. But he had forgotten Bessell, who was determined now to force Thorpe to resign as Liberal leader. There were a number of reasons for this. He thought that Thorpe had betrayed him to the *Sunday Times* in March. He was convinced that 'the Establishment' was protecting Thorpe, which offended his old Liberal instincts. He thought that it had been wrong to try and kill Scott. He was also worried that the Liberal Party would be destroyed if Thorpe remained as leader. He had been touched by Scott's statement that he was, at heart, a truthful chap. And, finally, he wanted to be at the centre of intrigue, for the last time.

So he began to unburden himself to Richard Wainwright, the Liberal MP for Colne Valley; Richard Rowntree, who was Wainwright's business partner and a former Liberal candidate; and Emlyn Hooson. He told them everything, apart from the fact that Holmes had recruited Newton to kill Scott. Yet he was still agonising: 'I explained that I had been tormented for three years by this fact: Jeremy had taken me into his confidence and sought my help in containing the Scott problem on a basis of absolute trust. I said that to destroy his political career by use of the knowledge I acquired because he trusted me would ordinarily be utterly unthinkable.' In one letter Bessell declared that Thorpe was 'a sick and frightened man'. He wrote: 'Those of us who worked for the success of his candidature in 1967 did not give Jeremy a licence to use the Party for his own ends . . . Jeremy is ill because he has been haunted by the spectre of revelation.'

He arranged to meet Rowntree and Wainwright in New York to discuss how Thorpe could be dislodged without further damaging the Party, but on 1 May Scott, backed by the *Daily Mirror*, announced that he was suing the Metropolitan Police for the return of the letters which he gave them in 1962. Goodman promptly demanded the letters, too, since they had been written by his client. The news provoked the final flurry of activity. Bessell decided that he had to save the Liberal Party from the potentially fatal embarrassment of a scramble between Scott, Goodman and the police in the courts over the ownership of Thorpe's love letters by giving yet another exclusive interview to the *Daily Mail*. This time he told almost the whole truth. He did not reveal that Holmes had told him that Newton had been recruited to kill Scott but, otherwise, he was frank.

On the evening of 5 May Thorpe was tipped off by the *Sunday Times*, which was still a firm ally, that Bessell had talked to the *Mail*. Thorpe was incandescent and ordered Holmes to contact Bessell and demand that he retract everything that he had told the *Mail*. Bessell refused. On Thursday 6 May the *Mail* published its Bessell scoop: 'I told lies to protect Thorpe.'

Harold Evans was beginning to suspect that he had been conned. He spoke to Thorpe, who said that, of course, he had not known about Holmes's visit to California to collect Bessell's 'affidavit' accusing Scott of blackmail. He said that Holmes must have acted independently, which struck Evans as odd since Thorpe also admitted that he had been in touch with Holmes that day. Evans told his Insight team: 'It creates a serious doubt in my mind about the honesty of Jeremy Thorpe . . . I said that we would want to talk to him in some detail about what had happened and he agreed. His last remark was that Bessell was a Judas.' The *Sunday Times* tried to persuade Bessell to talk to them but he did not trust them; he agreed, however, to meet Tom Mangold, a sharp-witted BBC reporter who had followed the saga closely.

Thorpe and Holmes were still fighting to shut Bessell up. Holmes telephoned Oceanside again and begged him to issue a statement, saying that it was all a terrible mistake, but Bessell told him that he intended to give the whole story to the BBC. They never spoke again. Holmes reported to Thorpe, who was terrified: Bessell was now out of control and might well reveal the truth about Rinka, the late Great Dane. So Thorpe tried to regain the initiative by approaching the *Sunday Times*.

Goodman had obtained copies of the letters that Scott had given to the police in 1962 and offered them now to the *Sunday Times*. Evans agreed to use them on condition that they were published in full, including Thorpe's damning aside, 'Bunnies can (and will) go to France.' A senior journalist on Insight also interviewed Thorpe and believed that it was significant that Thorpe refused to deny that he had once had 'homosexual tendencies'. But Evans refused to include this in the story, arguing that he had promised Goodman that he would not present the letters 'in a hostile way'.

On 9 May the *Sunday Times* published the letters. Most people thought that they showed that Thorpe had lied about his relationship with Scott but the newspaper still could not believe that Thorpe, MP and PC, was a liar and that Scott, a sweaty and neurotic homosexual, was telling the truth. So the newspaper advised its readers:

> The central question about the Thorpe–Scott letters is whether or not they prove that Thorpe has been lying in denying a homosexual affair with Scott 15 years ago. They are clearly in terms more affectionate than most men would use to another man; but they are also wholly consistent with the record of Thorpe and his family trying to revive the spirits of a man in distress. But are they the record of a love affair? . . . It is clear that they do not constitute proof of a physical relationship.

But it did not matter what the *Sunday Times* thought; like most people, senior Liberals were certain now that Thorpe had lied about Scott. The Liberals prided themselves on their tolerance; homosexuality was not a crime, even for a Party leader, but lying and organising a cover-up certainly were and Thorpe had to go. Thorpe clung on for a day, trying to lobby support, but friends told him that it was over. On Monday, 10 May he wrote to David Steel, the acting Chief Whip, and resigned. But, even now, he lied:

> From the very beginning I have strenuously denied the so-called Scott allegations and I categorically repeat those denials today. But I am convinced that the campaign of

denigration which has already endured for over three months should be drawn by me as an individual and not directed at Liberals collectively through their Leader. No man can effectively lead a party if the greater part of his time has to be devoted to answering allegations as they arise and countering plots and intrigues.

It was 8 a.m. on Monday in Oceanside when Mangold broke the news to Bessell. They had spent the previous day recording a ninety minute interview, during which Bessell revealed everything, except the murder plot, but Mangold now needed a short snappy quote from him for the news bulletins which covered Thorpe's resignation. They filmed that and then set off for the airport. As they were driving there Bessell was overcome by an uncharacteristic urge to tell the simple, unqualified truth. He told Mangold, 'Jeremy persuaded David Holmes to hire Andrew Newton to murder Norman Scott.' Mangold gulped and asked how they could prove this. Bessell sighed and said, 'We can't. David Holmes will admit nothing and it's only my word against Jeremy's.'

CHAPTER FOURTEEN

He had lost the leadership, which was a terrible blow, but had become the Liberal spokesman on foreign affairs, which was not a bad consolation prize. There were big issues here, which were more interesting than the future of rural bus services in the West Country. He was a man of vision who needed a large canvas; the wickedness of apartheid rather than the iniquities of social security payments to single parents.

Scott was a busted flush and Newton was in jail. Thorpe was sure Bessell would continue to lie because it was expedient. (This was a fatal miscalculation because Bessell was dying and dying men often try to rectify past errors rather than plan future triumphs.) Holmes had been a fool to admit publicly that he had paid Scott £2,500 for the 'retainer' letters; but Thorpe was confident that this problem, too, could be contained because Holmes was pathetically loyal and would never betray him.

Then Harold Wilson, Thorpe's friend, stepped in and wrecked everything. On the evening of Wednesday, 12 May 1976 Wilson stood in his shirtsleeves in the drawing room at his home in Lord North Street, Westminster, and spent ninety minutes with two young journalists from BBC Television called Barrie Penrose and Roger Courtiour.

This was the start of the baking summer which emptied reservoirs, cracked house foundations and left the British grumbling that they only wanted rain, but Penrose and Courtiour were wearing heavy, dark suits. They thought that this was only right since they were being granted an audience by a man who had retired formally as Prime Minister the previous month after dominating British politics for over a decade. Neither had ever spoken to Wilson; they were humble journalists and interviews with prime ministers were conducted by the stars of the BBC. (Penrose had once yelled a question at him from the middle of a pack of pressmen, which Wilson had refused to answer.) That morning Penrose had been pleasant suburb south of London where you could buy a detached house for the same price as a two bedroom flat in the city centre, and been invited to meet Wilson privately that evening. Penrose was baffled: he was one of dozens of television news reporters and was hardly the obvious choice for an ex-prime minister to summon for an exclusive chat. Nonetheless, he alerted the BBC newsroom and asked for a camera crew to be on standby that evening, in case Wilson changed his mind and wanted to give a formal interview.

Then Penrose called Roger Courtiour, an old schoolfriend who was a researcher in the Corporation's current affairs department, and suggested that he might like to join him for the meeting, on the assumption that, whatever Wilson said, it would probably be strong enough for a punchy story on the news and a longer report on a current affairs programme. Neither had any idea why Penrose had been selected by Wilson or what he intended to talk about.

It was a pity that they were not allowed to film him that evening because they would have had a sensational story. As Courtiour scribbled in his notebook, desperately trying to keep up with Wilson, Penrose sat there, sweating in his suit, wondering if this was real; it was clear that either Wilson was paranoid, which was a good story, or that the most terrible things had happened when he was Prime Minister, which was even better. Although Courtiour's notes were the only evidence of that conversation Wilson did not dispute their record, which must rank as one of the most astonishing outbursts by a senior British politician this century.[1]

He opened by asking if they had read his speech that day to journalists in the Commons press gallery on South African interference in British politics. They had not, though they were too embarrassed to say so. He did not wait for a reply and carried on: 'I think that democracy as we know it is in grave danger. Anti-democratic agencies in South Africa and elsewhere put all our democratic futures at risk. I think you as journalists should investigate the forces that are threatening democratic countries like Britain. I think you will find an investigation rewarding. I will help you although for the time being I cannot speak too openly.'

They realised now that he had chosen Penrose because he had been trying over the previous weeks to substantiate the allegations that Wilson had made in the Commons that March about South Africa. Courtiour had also been toiling to turn these theories into broadcastable stories but had only managed to piece together an inconclusive story about corruption in a South African multi-national. But then no one else had made much progress; the media had only managed to unearth a few low-key stories about South Africans, a con here, a dubious deal there, which did not amount to the sinister masterplan that Wilson had said was waiting to be exposed.

If Wilson had stopped with South Africa that evening Penrose and Courtiour would not have had much of a story. Then he moved into top gear. He said that MI5, Britain's spy catchers, had plotted to discredit him, his political secretary, then Marcia Williams, and senior Labour figures. In the summer of 1975 he heard that MI5 was spreading rumours that he was a communist who headed a 'secret cell' at Downing Street: 'They were saying that I was tied up with the communists. The link was Marcia. She was supposed to be a dedicated communist. They were so blinkered they believed that socialists were another form of communist.' He called in Sir Maurice Oldfield, the head of MI6, and Sir Michael Hanley, the Director-General of MI5, and demanded an explanation. Both confirmed that a small group of officers in MI5 were unhappy with his premiership but neither told the whole truth: that a number of senior officers in MI5 and MI6 believed that he was a KGB agent.

Wilson said that he heard nothing more from Oldfield or Hanley. So he carried out his own checks. He used a friend, George Weidenfeld, who had published his memoirs in 1971, to ask the Central Intelligence Agency in Washington if they knew anything about South African and/or right-wing infiltration of the Labour and Liberal Parties. As a result, in March 1976, George Bush, the new head of the CIA, flew to London to assure him that the agency was not involved in any plots to destabilise him and to offer any assistance he might need in the future to curb the renegades in British Intelligence. Penrose hoped that his face did not betray his excitement as Courtiour's pen flew across the notebook; he prayed that his friend's speedwriting was not buckling under the strain of so many red-hot revelations about British Intelligence.

Secrecy still enveloped Britain in the 1970s, like a black cloud. The CIA was listed in the telephone directory and competed on university campuses with law firms, banks and oil companies to recruit the cream of the country's youth. Prospective directors of the agency were grilled publicly before congressional committees about their political allegiances, sex lives and financial affairs. In Britain, however, governments of both parties refused even to confirm that MI5 and MI6 existed.

Wilson now moved to Norman Scott, who was, he revealed, an agent of the South Africans. He puffed on a cigar (this was another, minor scoop; Wilson only smoked a pipe in public) and advised them to investigate Peter Bessell and Gordon Winter, who were also part of the international conspiracy against Thorpe. He said that they should start with a file on Scott which had gone missing from the Department of Health and Social Security office in Chelsea. If they could trace this they would find the first documentary link with South Africa. In his mind everything was linked and nothing was an accident. He said that this would become Britain's Watergate, which obviously appealed to him because he would be vindicated, and secondly, because, like every recently retired occupant of Downing Street, he was missing the adrenalin of publicity.

Now it was up to Penrose and Courtiour to find the connections. Wilson said that this would be difficult and would take months of hard research but he told them they could call at his house at any time for guidance. When they had cracked the story he would give them an exclusive interview and demand that a royal commission be set up to investigate the whole affair. He paused and offered this surreal analysis of his role: 'I see myself as the big fat spider in the corner of the room. Sometimes I speak when I'm asleep. You should both listen. Occasionally when we meet I might tell you to go to the Charing Cross Road and kick a blind man standing on the corner. That blind man might tell you something, lead you somewhere.'

As he escorted them out he emphasised that they should tell no one, apart from their editors, that they had met; nor should they trust the telephones or the post. He ushered them into the living room on the ground floor and stopped by a cupboard. He opened the doors and stood proudly to one side, like a small boy showing off a new train set, and pointed to a 7-foot-high safe. He said that he had bought it after a series of burglaries on himself and his staff and added that he could now sleep soundly at night. He offered this advice: 'Make sure your own security is as good.'

Outside Penrose and Courtiour stared at each other in disbelief.

Then Courtiour, a quiet and reserved man, staged an impromptu impersonation of Fred Astaire on the pavement. Penrose muttered that he was worried that the story would be snatched away from them by their senior colleagues in the corporation or that it would leak to newspapers, who would scoop them. But they knew that if they boxed cleverly they would be famous.

Journalists have never enjoyed a very high reputation. Public opinion polls always show that they rank alongside politicians, used-car dealers and double-glazing salesmen. In the public mind they wear raincoats, drink too much and peer through letterboxes trying to persuade some poor soul cowering inside to open the door. Yet only a tiny proportion of journalists are reporters; the majority work in offices, commissioning, editing and administering. In television and radio the ratio of office-bound staff to reporters is even higher. Like the Army, where fighting troops are outnumbered by support staff, every frontline hack with a notebook or microphone is supported – and often undermined by – the team in head office.

Penrose and Courtiour – later dubbed 'Pencourt' by *Private Eye*, a half-complimentary, half-mocking Anglicisation of the Watergate duo's nickname, Woodstein – were unlikely partners. They were in their early thirties and had known each other at grammar school in Surrey. But, apart from that, and their tax status, they had little in common.

Both men were freelances, at least as far as the Inland Revenue were concerned. This was not unusual. Many journalists in the BBC, including newscasters, were either on loose contracts or worked casually from week to week, to avoid the high tax rates, National Insurance and pension contributions that accompanied staff status. Until they met Wilson this was unimportant; but BBC executives found it useful a few months later when they decided that Pencourt were causing too much trouble and should be dumped.

After school Penrose went to the London School of Economics but he dropped out and sought adventure in Paris. He drifted into journalism there and became a writer on art for the *International Herald Tribune*. After a year there he returned to London to fight his way into the major league of national newspapers.

Most reporters do as they are told by their editors; Penrose, however, had a rare knack, which cannot be taught, of being able to find original stories; he was also exceptionally competitive, even by the cut-throat standards of journalism. After four years freelancing for the *Observer* he joined the BBC in 1970 as a reporter. He worked as a freelance on the new late night current affairs programmes, where the traditional ethos of the BBC, that the Corporation reported the news, objectively and without comment, was being challenged by a more aggressive style of journalism. These new current-affairs reporters were encouraged to be opinionated and to break stories, rather than just follow the agenda set by newspapers. This was anathema to the Old Guard within the BBC, who felt that the Corporation was jeopardising its reputation for balance by allowing these young men, and a growing number of women, to parade their beliefs on air. It was also simplistic since the old BBC had embodied just as many prejudices: for example, that the Empire and the class system were good and that socialism and egalitarianism were bad.

But they were right when they alleged that there was a leftish bias to these programmes. This was inevitable, however, since the most talented reporters saw the world in terms of cover-ups and conspiracies, exploiters and exploited; journalists who thought that the world was basically in good shape did not want anything to do with the polemicists in current affairs.

Roger Courtiour came from a military family and was self-effacing and unusually tidy as a boy. He decided to skip university and do some good by working in a United Nations refugee camp in Greece, where he became fluent in Greek. In 1970 Penrose heard that a programme in current affairs was looking for a Greek speaker to help research a story and suggested Courtiour. It was an ideal job for him. He had no desire to be on television, unlike most of his colleagues, who were desperate to appear in front of the camera, and enjoyed preparing material for a reporter. So, he would arrange interviews, organise briefing notes and suggest possible shots for camera crews. He was methodical and was renowned for his well-ordered filing system, which he told colleagues was the key to successful investigatory journalism. While a reporter would dream about presenting a peak-time programme Courtiour only wanted to be a producer, though he was too modest to talk in such nakedly ambitious terms. He was the epitome of BBC man; hard-working, discreet and loyal. He had always accepted that it was not his place to argue with his superiors, at least until he became entangled with Wilson.

This combination of talents – Penrose's energy and guile, Courtiour's patience and organisation – was precisely what was required to unravel the Scott–Thorpe saga. Indeed, without Courtiour's cross-referenced notes and transcripts it is doubtful whether they would have been able to navigate their way, albeit inadequately, through the morass of the Thorpe story.

On Thursday, 13 May 1976, Pencourt described their mind-bending interview with Wilson to a junior executive, Bob Kearsley, the News Intake Editor. They were still flushed with excitement but Kearsley did not share their enthusiasm. He thought that 'manage-ment could get a coronary' and told Pencourt that he would have to pass the story to Andrew Todd, Editor of Television News. With the gloomy resignation of a man who understood the ethos of the BBC Kearsley predicted that Todd would seek guidance from the Director-General. Later that morning Penrose was ushered in to meet Todd and his deputies. (Courtiour was excluded because he worked for Current Affairs, a rival department.) But they were even less impressed than Kearsley; indeed, they behaved as if he was, somehow, conspiring with Wilson to embarrass the BBC. They told him that only the Director-General could decide how they should handle Wilson. This decision was in the great tradition of all bureaucracies: play safe by passing a controversial buck upstairs.

There were a number of forces at play here. If Pencourt had been working for a newspaper or an independent television company their only problem would have been fighting off other reporters trying to clamber aboard their exclusive. But they were at the BBC, which had more in common with the Civil Service or the Army than commercial news organisations. The officers and gentlemen were the editors, who ran the departments. Above them were the tiers of bureaucrats, the controllers, managing editors and many others with impressive titles but ill-defined roles, stretching up to the Director-General, Sir Charles Curran, and beyond him, to the Board of Governors. These were distant figures, who were rarely seen by ordinary journalists and programme makers; they inhabited offices on the top floors of Broadcasting House, near Oxford Circus, and Television Centre, in West London, where they tried to make sure that nothing was broadcast that would jeopardise the continued funding of the Corporation through the licence fee.

The story that Wilson was offering was unwelcome because, merely by taking his claims seriously, the BBC would be making a political statement. This did not appeal to executives in a corporation which had a quasi-governmental atmosphere and which allowed a representative from MI5 to sit in the basement of Broadcasting House to ensure that political extemists did not infiltrate it. Todd and his acolytes would have been happier if Wilson's allegations appeared in a newspaper; this would have been news, which the BBC could have reported. They were worried, too, about Wilson's motives. In the spring of 1971 David Dimbleby, one of the BBC's stars, had interviewed Wilson about the money that he had earned from the serialisation of his memoirs in the *Sunday Times*. Wilson was incensed by Dimbleby's suggestion that he was making quick, easy, money out of his premiership and threatened legal action against the BBC. The BBC apologised but neither side had forgotten the incident, which left executives that morning wondering why Wilson had chosen Penrose.[2]

After the meeting with Todd, Penrose and Courtiour headed off to begin their investigation. They went to the Department of Health and Social Security office in Chelsea, where Wilson had told them to begin their search for Scott's 'missing' file. This was the first of dozens of expeditions which Pencourt made in the following three months as they tried to prove the unprovable: that Norman Scott was a stooge of the South Africans who was lying to discredit Thorpe.

The following day the BBC tightened its grip on Pencourt. They were told that Sir Charles wanted to meet Wilson. A few hours later Pencourt were travelling in Curran's limousine towards Lord North Street. Pencourt were flattered that the Director-General was taking a personal interest in the story and thought that this boded well. But they were quite wrong; he wanted to stamp his authority on the investigation immediately, before Pencourt's enthusiasm threw up unpleasant revelations which the Corporation would not want to broadcast.

Curran was 54 years old and had joined the BBC in 1947 as a talks producer in radio but had fallen out with his editors and had gone to Canada, where he became assistant editor of *Fishing News*, which was his one and only excursion into print journalism. He returned to the BBC in 1951 as an administrator. He was a natural bureaucrat and climbed the BBC ladder steadily and in 1969 was appointed Director-General. This was similar to making a non-driver the head of the Automobile Association or appointing a pacifist as commander of the SAS. Pencourt should have realised that Curran had a different agenda when he turned to them in the car and told them that they must not listen if Wilson talked about security matters since that would be a breach of his oath as a Privy Counsellor.

They were greeted by Wilson, who ushered Curran upstairs for a private conversation. A few minutes later Pencourt were summoned to hear their fate. Curran seemed keen. He told Pencourt that they should continue to meet Wilson and 'exchange confidential documents'. These meetings would be secret and both sides would deny that they were happening if there were any leaks to the media. The investigation would focus on South African interference in 'British political life'. It would be 'a slow burner' and would take months of meticulous research; when this was completed Wilson would give an exclusive interview to Pencourt. They would work in a 'Special Unit', reporting to a producer called Gordon Carr, who would have access to Curran or other very senior executives. In the meantime, if Wilson was approached by other BBC journalists on routine matters he would handle these enquiries in the normal way. But he would only talk to Pencourt about the real story.

But there were ominous signs. Curran repeated his pronouncement that Wilson would not, of course, 'reveal information on matters covered by his Privy Council oath or about high-level security matters'.[3] Wilson and Pencourt nodded, although they did not know what he meant since everything revolved around intelligence agencies in Britain and overseas. Next, Curran was only interested in 'the South African dimension'; he seemed to think that Wilson's other allegations, which were actually stronger stories, were irrelevant or must not be pursued because he should not have mentioned them in the first place. Finally, as he climbed into his limousine, he started muttering again about Wilson's motives, which showed that he was just as worried about why Wilson was talking as whether he was telling the truth. But Pencourt were delighted. They now had the unequivocal backing of the greatest broadcasting company in the world to get stuck into what would surely be the best story of their lives.

For the next three months Pencourt worked tirelessly. They kept a daily diary of interviews, phone calls, theories and doubts. They called this *The Red File*, because it was in a red folder, and dispatched regular updates to Curran. They were worried that it might be stolen and never let it out of their sight; they also used a not-very-clever code to disguise the names of the main players. (AA was Curran; Wilson was The Source or SM, which was short for Spider Man.) It was a fascinating but depressing document. Pencourt were dogged but ingenuous; as they dug out the truth about Scott and Thorpe they failed to notice that the BBC, the organisation in which they had such touching faith, was preparing to sabotage them.

They did not know, for example, that on the weekend in May before their first meeting with Wilson another BBC journalist, Tom Mangold, had met Peter Bessell in California. Bessell had given a long, frank interview about Scott and Thorpe, though he omitted a few important details. No one will ever know if this interview would have been broadcast (though, judging by the BBC's general approach towards the Scott–Thorpe story, it seems certain that it would not have been shown) because Thorpe resigned as Liberal leader as Mangold was preparing to fly home with his red-hot exclusive. He was told to forget about Norman Scott and to ask Bessell for a short assessment of Thorpe, the leader. That was broadcast but his earlier interview with Mangold, where he had talked so frankly, was consigned to the BBC basement.

Meanwhile, Pencourt were given an office in the BBC building in Lime Grove, Shepherd's Bush. They had a safe but no telephone, which was a problem since they did not want to use the phones in other offices and risk being overheard. Journalists love gossip and the installation of Penrose and Courtiour in their own room, complete with a safe (they preferred to keep their files and tapes at home and the safe remained empty), provoked a flurry of speculation. No one asked them directly what they were doing but colleagues probed gently, in the hope that Pencourt would give them a clue, which they did not. Only Mangold seemed to know that they were working on a story which was, somehow, linked to Thorpe. He told Penrose that he had asked Bessell to help them; Penrose, who had no intention of breaking cover, nodded non-committally and hurried off.

Pencourt had a team leader, a producer called Gordon Carr, a Yorkshireman who had carved out a comfortable niche on 'Special Projects'. He was supposed to liaise with Curran but he left Pencourt to their research and they rarely saw him in Lime Grove. They were anxious, however, to keep him fully briefed, which was not easy as he spent much of the summer renovating a house in Yorkshire.

They met Wilson throughout the spring and summer and were given a small tape recorder, which cost the-then enormous sum of £700, by Carr to ensure that they could keep an indisputable record of their conversations. *The Red File* showed how hard they toiled from May until August 1976. Penrose often stayed up throughout the night at home to talk to Bessell in California; slowly, bit by bit, he cajoled the story from him, of the affair between Scott and Thorpe, the weekly 'retainers' and Thorpe's demands that Scott should be killed. Pencourt also interviewed Scott in London. From what they had read in newspapers and been told by Wilson they expected Scott to be cunning and calculating. He was a South African agent and a blackmailer and it was their task as professional journalists to prise the truth from him. But this was not the man whom they met at a hotel near Victoria Station. He was a physical and nervous wreck but would not break under interrogation. He insisted that he had had an affair with Thorpe, though he added that he knew that no one believed him. He was not interested in money, which was strange for a seasoned blackmailer, and handed his precious letters and documents to Pencourt without asking for money or even a receipt. A week later Pencourt travelled to Scott's cottage at Combe Martin, Devon, to film an interview with him. Once again, he told the same story.

They returned to London and were greeted by the unwelcome news that elderly supporters of Thorpe had seen them filming Scott. Thorpe had alerted his legal adviser, Lord Goodman, who had protested to the BBC that it was outrageous that the Corporation was taking Scott seriously.

Pencourt were almost alone now. The media has a short attention span and, by the summer of 1976, Scott and Thorpe were yesterday's men. This was the media's view: Scott might have had a one-night stand with Thorpe in the early 1960s; he had blackmailed Bessell over his extra-marital affairs, and then Newton, who had shot Rinka in an attempt to scare him off; Holmes was a buffoon who had bought the 'retainer' letters out of misguided loyalty to the Liberal Party and Thorpe had resigned as leader and deserved to be left in peace.

There were a few journalists, however, who believed that

nothing in life was this straightforward. This brave little band included Auberon Waugh of *Private Eye*. He might have seemed like a caricature country pub bigot, who was for ever complaining about the eating habits, dress sense and unpleasant odours given off by the working classes, but he was also an excellent reporter and had always suspected a scandal behind Rinka's death.

He had also never liked Jeremy Thorpe. In 1967, when he was political correspondent for the *Spectator*, he had watched Thorpe in the Commons:

My unease was explained by the double-breasted waistcoats. It is a curious fact that these unusual and slightly absurd garments were worn as a badge of office at the public school in Somerset where I boarded. Moreover, Thorpe, as leader of the Liberal Party, had an unmistakably prefectorial air about him which I mistrusted. It would be absurd to pretend that all prefects at my school were hypocrites, sodomites or criminal psychopaths, but enough of them seemed to have tendencies in one or more of those directions to put me on my guard against anyone who retained the uniform and mannerisms of a public school prefect in later life.[4]

Most people, however, thought that Waugh and Pencourt were trying to dig out a non-existent conspiracy. They told each other that Britain was not a banana republic and that public figures such as Jeremy Thorpe did not behave in the disgraceful manner alleged by these unpatriotic, muck-raking journalists.

Pencourt plodded on. They had no idea where the story would lead but they kept digging, ignoring the rumblings of disapproval from their masters at the BBC, who did not want an investigation into South Africa's alleged interference in British public life to turn into a probe into Jeremy Thorpe's private life. They spoke to key witnesses, including Emlyn Hooson, David Steel, Barbara Castle, Jack Straw, Dr Ronald Gleadle and the Rev Frederick Pennington. They tracked down Tony and Donald Johnson, the decorators from Essex who had discovered a cache of letters written by Scott and Thorpe in an envelope marked 'The Property of Mr Jeremy Thorpe', when they had been working at Bessell's former offices in Pall Mall in November 1974; they told Pencourt that they had handed them to the *Sunday Mirror* and had heard nothing more.

Pencourt were edging slowly towards the conclusion that Thorpe had lied consistently about Scott. However, this was not what the BBC wanted to hear. Curran was now so alarmed that his 'Special Unit' was running out of control that he banned Pencourt from approaching Thorpe in an attempt to prevent further damage.

Unfortunately, Pencourt also thought that South Africa was central to their investigation, which meant that they saw the story in terms of an international conspiracy rather than a tragi-comedy of sex, fear and ambition. On 1 July, Pencourt summarised their ideas in the top-secret *Red File*. They headed their notes: 'The South African Dimension: Points to Consider to Date'. They said that they were 'only in the fifth week of the investigation' but had already made some startling discoveries. They outlined their theories about MI5, MI6, the CIA, BOSS, the Rhodesian intelligence services and corrupt British civil servants and politicians in what they obviously thought was a sombre and authoritative fashion. But it read like the opening chapter from a bad airport thriller and BBC bureaucrats thought that it was ridiculous and dangerous rubbish.

Thus, on the afternoon of Friday, 2 July, Pencourt were summoned to meet Desmond Taylor, an abrupt Ulsterman who basked in the title of Head of BBC News and Current Affairs, and Peter Hardiman Scott, Curran's 'Chief Assistant' who was the BBC's former political correspondent. It was not a happy discussion. For three hours Pencourt were attacked by Taylor, watched by Hardiman Scott and Gordon Carr, the not very loyal supremo of the 'Special Unit', who said nothing as he weighed up whether to distance himself openly from his team. They were told that they were deliberately defying the Director-General, which, in BBC terms, was like a couple of parish priests saying that they did not think much of the Pope. Sir Charles had ordered an investigation into South African interference in Britain, not an inquiry into Jeremy Thorpe's sex life. Pencourt were behaving like policemen and it had to stop. As a former political correspondent Hardiman Scott was incredulous that Pencourt were wasting BBC money on the preposterous claim that Mr Thorpe had planned to kill Norman Scott.

Pencourt were chastened by this savaging and filled three pages of *The Red File* with plaintive protests that they had not set out to investigate Thorpe's homosexuality. They remained BBC men, who only wanted to work for the Corporation and, like all journalists, craved the approval of their editors. For a few weeks there was an uneasy truce. But, as Britain sweltered in the hottest summer in living memory, it became clear that Pencourt were still irritating important people, who did not care for these impertinent young journalists. In late July David Ennals, the Social Services Minister, was furious when Pencourt pestered him for an interview. (This was a legitimate enquiry since Bessell had asked him in 1969 if he would look into the problem of Scott's Insurance card.) Ennals met Curran and, as a result, Peter Hardiman Scott was allowed to read the Ministry's file on Scott; he reported, 'Jeremy Thorpe was never the employer of Norman Scott.' He advised Curran that there had been no cover-up and that 'nothing is to be gained or discovered by pursuing this line of enquiry further'.

Hardiman Scott was a respected and experienced journalist and was quite capable of reading and accurately summarising a government report. The file should have shown that Thorpe had stamped Scott's card when he was working as a canvasser for the North Devon Liberal Association in 1962. But this information was not included in the file that he was given; it is possible that this was an accident but civil servants do not usually misplace documents and it is more likely that someone had filleted it to remove all traces of Thorpe. But Pencourt could hardly accuse Ennals or his staff of lying; they were having enough trouble at the BBC without suggesting another conspiracy.

So they concentrated on South Africa, as Desmond Taylor had ordered them to do. Once again, *The Red File* showed how hard they worked; painstakingly, and with Wilson's help, they drew up lists of extreme right-wing organisations, such as the racist and anti-Semitic National Front, which might, somehow, be involved in this non-existent plot. Naturally, they could not find any link between these brutish, but ineffectual, groups and Wilson and Thorpe. The only common factor was Gordon Winter, the freelance journalist whom they thought worked for BOSS. Tuesday, 6 July was a typical day for Pencourt:

Lonhro Report published with possible links for our story. Meeting with G. Gable at Grosvenor Hotel at 4.30 p.m. Talk for just over an hour and a half. Main points: National Front in the two '74 elections and put up approx. 200 candidates. The cost of this was £200,000. Where did this money come from? At this time George Young (ex-Deputy Director Intelligence)

left the Monday Club and said that he would be taking
with him source of funds. Dr H. (South African) came to
England twenty years ago. National Front candidate for City
of Westminster. Owns house in Teddington. Richard V. –
wealthy parents in Hove ... V. may have been appointed
to see that funds from South Africa are well spent.[5]

They carried on like this throughout July. They tracked down a man
in Brighton who was 'suspected of being a channel for slush funds
from South Africa', investigated the Anglo-Rhodesian Society and
tried to establish links between far-right organisations in Britain
and mercenaries who had fought in Southern Africa. On Tuesday,
13 July they travelled to the South Coast again in a doomed attempt
to implicate National Front activists in the conspiracy against
Wilson and Thorpe. They reported that a couple in Brighton
had 'received monies from South Africa and whilst it is shown
as dividends on investments it could be that the money is part
of the slush funds referred to in Parliament'; that an accountant
in Worthing, a few miles along the coast, handled the affairs of
people who had 'South African interest'; and that a design firm
in the same area had business links with South Africa.

But, once again, they were hammered by their superiors at the
BBC. On Thursday, 15 July they were grilled by Andrew Todd, the
Editor of Television News, who said that he could not understand
their obsession with Thorpe's private life. Penrose pointed out that
they had spent the past few weeks trying to establish 'the South
African dimension'. It was hardly their fault, he said, that they kept
returning to Thorpe. This did not satisfy Todd, who said, 'You've
produced extraordinary information. But you're like puppy dogs
who keep bringing back sticks. But these sticks always seem to
have some connection with Scott.' Time was running out rapidly
for Pencourt but they could not see it; Todd was offering them a
chance now to back off, admit the error of their ways and do what
they were told. But Pencourt were not sensitive to these nuances
and imagined naively that they were taking part in a lively debate
with Todd. So he threatened them. He said that they would be
receiving contracts shortly, which would formalise their role as
members of a 'special unit'. But Pencourt were stubborn: they told
Todd that they would not become involved in a 'cover-up'. Todd
scowled and decided that they needed to be taught a lesson.

After the meeting Alan Protheroe, a Welshman who was Deputy

Head of Television News and later rose to become Assistant Director-General, told Pencourt that he was worried about the BBC's attitude: he said that he would be depositing a letter with his bank, describing the way that they had been treated. (He told Pencourt later that he had decided against this because the bank wanted to charge him for a safe deposit box.) He added, 'I want to make it absolutely clear that I want to press on with the story whatever others may feel. The story can and must be made public by the Corporation.' Then Gordon Carr warned them that their contracts would be 'tough and brutal'.

A week later Pencourt received the promised contracts at their homes. They were worse than they had feared. In return for six months' work in the 'Special Unit' they would have to sign away all rights to the story; if the BBC chose not to broadcast their material they would not be able to publish it elsewhere. A normal contract would have said that the BBC expected first and exclusive use of any information that they collected but that they would be free after that to use it as they wished; this was the formula that allowed journalists to turn stories into books. But the contracts offered to Pencourt had been specially drafted by the Corporation's resident lawyers and meant that they would be barred, for ever, from saying or writing anything without the BBC's permission.

The Red File described their final sad weeks at the BBC. They continued to probe the Thorpe–South Africa story, as if, by ignoring the ultimatum over their contracts and working conscientiously, the problem would go away. But they remained blind to the realpolitik of the situation and hammered the final nail in their own coffin when Penrose telephoned Bessell in the early hours of Thursday, 22 July. He obtained the most detailed description yet of the conspiracy to murder Scott and was so excited that he telephoned Carr at home; unfortunately Carr fell and gashed his head when he staggered down the stairs to answer the phone. Then Penrose drove to Courtiour's home to play him the tape recording of his conversation with Bessell.

This was not a dispute about money. Pencourt were asking for the not very princely sum of £4,000 each for six months' work. But they were worried that the contracts were designed to ensure that their investigation would never be made public. On the other hand, neither wanted to leave the BBC. This was both practical and sentimental. They needed the facilities and expenses of the Corporation: most importantly, working for the BBC gave them access to people. They knew that they would struggle as freelances. They would have to pay for everything, such as phone calls, clippings from newspapers, hotels and meals. Penrose would have to return his office car. And they feared that no one would want to speak to them if they lost their BBC identities.

Reluctantly, they began to organise an escape route. They had already talked to a publisher, Tom Rosenthal, managing director of Secker and Warburg, about writing a book. But they had assumed that this would be a spin-off from a BBC film, not a substitute. Rosenthal was a respected figure in London publishing. After Cambridge and National Service he had moved into publishing, where he demonstrated a flair for both the business and literary sides of the trade. He was 41 years old and was a big man, physically and in terms of his personality. His entry in *Who's Who* made him sound like a typical member of the Establishment – he enjoyed opera and was a member of the Garrick Club and the MCC – but, as Pencourt discovered, he had more appetite for a tough investigation than their bosses at the BBC. He offered Pencourt an advance against royalties of £10,000.

They were still trying to convince the BBC to compromise. Then, on 4 August, Desmond Taylor, Head of BBC News and Current Affairs, lost patience with them, as Pencourt noted gloomily in their *Red File*: 'He told us we had been fucking about and getting away with murder. He said, "You must realise you have had enough time. Either you sign the contracts or you are no longer working for the BBC." He gave us until 11 a.m. the next morning.' They retreated and again poured out their hearts to *The Red File*: 'We have not been asked to take part in a dialogue but have been given a take it or leave it ultimatum which reflects no credit on the BBC.' They made a final despairing plea to Curran, but he refused to speak to them. So, on Friday, 6 August they signed a contract with Secker and Warburg, which both sides agreed should remain confidential, given the nature of Pencourt's enquiries.

The BBC now tried to lure Courtiour away from Penrose, who was regarded as the real troublemaker. The following Monday BBC executives told Courtiour that he ought to return to the *Tonight* programme, where he might find himself offered 'a more permanent arrangement' than he had previously enjoyed. But Courtiour refused. At the end of August Penrose prepared for life after the BBC. He bought a car, a battered old Volkswagen Beetle, and held a planning conference with his partner. It had been easy over the past few weeks to say that they would rather leave the BBC than concede control over the investigation; but it was different now that they had actually done that. The future did not look bright. The advance from Secker and Warburg would barely pay normal living expenses for six months, let alone fund an investigation which required expensive phone calls and trips around Britain and abroad.

Their reserves were further depleted when they splashed out on a large portable photocopier. Pencourt were sure that this was a sensible investment, since documents were the key to the story. This was the era before every self-respecting newsagent had a photocopier so they needed their own machine when they visited sources. It ran off the Volkswagen battery, was slow and required constant topping-up with chemicals, which burnt the skin; but it served them well and Courtiour's files grew fatter every day with photocopied documents. They also bought a briefcase and installed a tape recorder inside it so that they could secretly record future interviews. Like their mobile photocopier this was primitive; the recorder inside clunked loudly when it was running and had a tendency to chew up tapes. Yet no interviewee ever suspected that there was something odd about a briefcase that emitted such strange noises and which Pencourt would fumble with every hour. (They became expert at surreptitiously changing tapes by pretending to search for papers.) It took another chunk out of their cash reserve but they calculated that they had to have an indisputable record of their interviews to stand any chance of publishing a book. They believed, rightly, that most of the people whom they met would refuse to let them take notes or would deny that they had ever spoken; hence, secret recording was the only solution, though, as ex-BBC journalists, who had always observed the Corporation's strict ethical code, they were uncomfortable that they had to resort to these tactics. But the recording briefcase meant that they had an unchallengeable record of all their interviews; critics could dispute their conclusions but could not accuse them of fabricating quotations. They also began to squabble. Penrose resented the fact that Courtiour could not drive and smoked heavily, which made him feel sick. Courtiour, for his part, said that he felt that he was in 'a state of limbo' without the security of the BBC.

There was also an unspoken fear: although both men believed that there was an important book to be written about Wilson and Thorpe neither was sure what it would say. Over the past three months Courtiour had organised his files with his customary efficiency but the cross-referenced notes and transcripts did not add up to a book. The more they read what they had amassed the more confused they became; they were not sure whether their proposed book would expose a plot by various intelligence agencies, including MI5, to smear Wilson and Thorpe or whether they would be revealing a conspiracy to eliminate Scott. Because of Wilson they still believed that these two stories were linked, but, despite their probing of far-right groups in Britain, they had failed to establish any definite connection. And, even if they did concentrate on Thorpe, they would have to convince Secker and Warburg's lawyers that the book was not libellous. From the safety of his home in California Bessell could say what he liked about murder plots but Pencourt knew that they could not simply quote him in their book. They had to prove what he told them. This was a daunting prospect since it did not seem likely that the conspirators who had wanted to dispose of Scott would want to confess to two ex-BBC journalists. This was not a promising start to their new life as co-authors of the book that would blow open Britain's Watergate.

Meanwhile, Gordon Carr remained the head of the 'Special Unit'. Curran wrote to Wilson, explaining that Pencourt had not been suitable. He offered two staff journalists as replacements; Wilson refused to meet them and continued to see Pencourt, to the fury of BBC executives. Carr soldiered on and spent the next three months trying to prove that Thorpe was the victim of a South African plot (he failed and the unit was shut down).

Then BBC staff leaked a jumbled account of Pencourt's departure to *Private Eye*, which gleefully portrayed them as a couple of hustlers who had been wasting the Corporation's money on an investigation that was going nowhere. But a magazine which employed Auberon Waugh as its chief satirist was not going to be conned into thinking that this was the whole story; the *Eye* reported, for the first time, that Pencourt had been meeting Wilson regularly. This suggested, the magazine added, that perhaps Pencourt were dumped by the Corporation for reasons which had nothing to do with their productivity.[6]

The BBC moved into disinformation overdrive in an attempt to prevent the rest of the media examining more closely what had gone wrong with the 'Special Unit'. The press office issued this statement, designed fatally to damage Pencourt: 'The BBC has withdrawn its offer of contract work to two freelance journalists who approached the BBC in May claiming to have special information about the allegations of South African interference ... Given the costs of present-day journalism, whether in newspapers or in broadcasting, the expenditure has been modest.' Journalists at the BBC knew that Pencourt were being cruelly traduced but said nothing for fear of losing their jobs. Many years later Alan Protheroe, who had privately encouraged them, said, 'I was one of the few executives to back Pencourt. The BBC wasn't in favour of investigative journalism. The governors did not want it. They didn't want to rock the boat. There was a feeling that British institutions were under threat. The BBC didn't want muck-raking journalism. It only wanted to protect British institutions.'[7]

CHAPTER FIFTEEN

In October 1976 Pencourt decided to invest a large chunk of their rapidly shrinking advance from their publisher in interviewing Peter Bessell in California. They could not afford the trip but they were desperate. They knew him only as a voice which boomed interminably at great expense over the phone to Penrose in the small hours. He had talked for many hours about Thorpe's affair with Scott, the 'retainers' he had paid, the plans to dispose of Scott in a disused Cornish tin mine and Holmes's role as conspirator-in-chief. This was fascinating but without corroboration it was useless. Pencourt did not know what Bessell could add but they had to do something to prevent their project falling apart. So, on 14 October they slipped away from their base in Surrey for their make-or-break interview in California. If they had still been working for the BBC they would have travelled in style but they were freelances on a tight budget so they ended up in the economy section of Air New Zealand, where the seats seemed to have been designed for legless midgets.

After twelve hours they arrived, exhausted, in the evening in Los Angeles, where they were met by a tanned Peter Bessell. He looked as if he was prospering on the West Coast; he was 56 years old but seemed younger, despite a face that was more crinkled than ever after its battering by the sun. He was thin, with delicate, bird-like hands but his voice was deep and rolling and seemed to have been transplanted from a sturdier frame. He was as pompous in the flesh as over the phone and made it clear that they were in California to listen, not debate, which was fine by them, providing that he gave them the evidence they needed to take the story forward.

He suggested that they should stay in his favourite motel on Sunset Boulevard in Hollywood and drive to Oceanside the following morning. He talked as if this was a discreet, stylish establishment, which high-flying businessmen like him preferred to vulgar five-star hotels, but it turned out to be a dive, where prostitutes entertained clients whom they picked up in local bars.

They checked in, but Bessell did not sign his own name; he said that, for security reasons, he always called himself Dr Paul Hoffman when he was staying in LA. He said that he had to be careful because he knew too much; there were people who would willingly stump up the $2,000 it cost in California to hire a professional hitman. Normally Pencourt would have pushed Bessell for more details on this threat to his life, which would have been a terrific story, but they were so tired that they did not care whether he thought that he was Donald Duck and was being stalked by Mickey Mouse, and trudged off to their rooms to sleep off jet lag.

Next morning Bessell was in a half-jaunty, half-confessional mood. He said that he would be totally frank with them but demanded that they sign a legally binding agreement which would prohibit them from using any of the information he gave them; they refused and it was not mentioned again. As they drove to his home in Oceanside, he said that he loved America and would never return to England, though he was also worried that he would be extradited on a conspiracy-to-murder charge. He moved to his health; he smoked too much, his lungs were in a shocking state and his doctor did not know how long he would live. Then he brightened up and said that his girlfriend Diane Kelly wanted him to forget Thorpe and get on with life. His 'cottage', as he liked to call it, had a small living room, where he displayed the trophies of Peter Bessell, Liberal MP for Bodmin and international statesmen. Even these were bogus, like the man; scattered amongst the pictures of a young Bessell were photographs of world leaders, which gave the entirely false impression that he had known them well. His new companion, Diane, was seventeen years his junior. She was a divorcee, whom he had met in New York, and was tall, with a shock of auburn hair, and radiated West Coast energy. Her father, Fred Miller, a wealthy, retired company executive, had already saved Bessell from disaster with loans.

They settled down to discuss Thorpe. Courtiour arranged his files, containing the cream of the transcripts, letters and assorted documents that they had amassed in the past three months. Bessell had his own neat files and stacked them in front of him. They eyed each other's collection of papers suspiciously and lit the first of hundreds of cigarettes. Bessell was a showy smoker, who flicked ash constantly and flourished the cigarette for dramatic effect, like a character from a 1930s Hollywood film, whereas Courtiour was workmanlike and puffed seriously as he sorted through his notes. Penrose, meanwhile, cursed the luck that had united him with a co-author and a key source who were both chain-smokers.

Bessell had already talked at length to newspapers about what he portentously called the 'cover-up' to protect Thorpe but Pencourt were certain that he knew much more; and, as they settled down to begin the interview, they could only hope that he would tell them the whole story.

They spent four days at Oceanside. Bessell would not allow them to take notes but they had their briefcase, which secretly recorded every word. A more modest man would have suspected that it was strange that two journalists, who had flown halfway around the world to interview him, did not mind that they were not allowed to keep a record, but he was so vain that he assumed that they were just glad that he had agreed to see them.

The days followed a pattern. Bessell talked about Thorpe, his eyes misting with the memory of a once-precious friendship, while he fussed his three dachshunds. Courtiour arranged his files and handed Bessell documents to authenticate with his signature. Sometimes, as a special treat, he let Courtiour examine his own files. Penrose was always anxious to escape the fug inside the cottage so would volunteer to find a photocopier when Bessell said he was willing to release documents. (California was in the forefront of photocopying technology and Penrose never had any trouble finding a machine.) Bessell drew heavily from a closely typed 100-page document which he called his *aide memoire*. He had written this shortly before Pencourt arrived and told them that it was his 'affidavit', which he intended to deposit with a lawyer in case anything happened to him. At first, he refused to read from it but then hubris overcame him and he began to quote chunks. Diane was furious. She reminded him that they had agreed that he would not become involved again with Thorpe; he had been called a liar, a hypocrite and a Judas and knew that the Establishment in Britain would destroy him if he threatened Thorpe again. But he would not listen.

He read slowly, oblivious to Penrose's briefcase by his feet which made strange clunking noises. He began:

Aide memoire: Peter Bessell's involvement with Norman

Scott [Norman Josiffe] and related matters. Prepared by Peter Bessell, September – November 1976. Copyright Peter Bessell. This is not prepared as a carefully constructed account for publication. Its primary purpose is to put on record, as accurately as memory will permit, the details of a series of events in which I was either personally involved or about which I was dependably informed by one or more of the persons principally involved . . .[1]

And so it went on, hour after hour. He left nothing out. He described the suitcase which had gone missing in Switzerland, the retainers and the whisky-sodden plotting with Thorpe and Holmes on how best to dispose of Scott. Then, on page 58, he described Holmes's visit to California in January 1976:

Holmes said, 'Newton was hired to kill Scott.' I believe I said, 'Oh Christ, David,' and added that I thought that all ideas of that sort had been abandoned years ago. I asked where Jeremy had found Newton, since I naturally assumed that it was Jeremy who had hired him. Holmes said, 'Jeremy didn't find him. I did.' Then he said something to the effect that he knew we had always worked together to stop Jeremy putting his murder plan into action but that after 1974 he had agreed with Jeremy that it was the only way. I said something like, 'David, I am appalled. I never thought you would be party to that. Thank God it failed.'

He thought that 'the first major acts in the cover-up of the Jeremy Thorpe affair' began in 1965. He argued that the whole affair was really about class and snobbery: 'The law in Britain operated in different ways for different people. By achieving prominence one automatically acquired a measure of immunity denied to those perons who had not sought or achieved a public position. That is, of course, indefensible and the whole history of the Thorpe affair is evidence of that inequality.' He said that the Establishment, already battered by a series of scandals, could not risk the public-relations disaster of an old Etonian politician being exposed as a lying bugger. Then there was the fact that homosexuality bound the governing elite; if Thorpe was exposed then other eminent men would be threatened. Finally, there was The Postcard, which Josiffe had given the police in Chelsea in 1962 and which suggested, wrongly, that Antony Armstrong-Jones, Princess Margaret's new husband, was involved. The *aide memoire* was Bessell at his fluent, persuasive best, but it also revealed him as a womaniser and a crook.

After four days Pencourt had everything that they needed. They told Bessell that it was one thing for him to sit in California, out of reach of the British libel laws, and quite another for a publisher in London to bring out a book containing these allegations. He wished them luck but said that he had no intention of returning to Britain to support them: 'I could be extradited if the police in Britain ever took the Scott investigation seriously. But the Establishment don't want the real story to come out. It's all dead. Everyone has lost interest.'

Then they made a fatal mistake; they told him that they were stopping in Washington to check leads that Wilson had given them. Bessell could not resist the opportunity to show off and scribbled a note, addressed it to a man called Dave, sealed it and handed it to Penrose. This was unfortunate. Pencourt did not want to believe they were investigating a straightforward story of love and revenge, albeit one with complex sub-plots involving such unlikely characters as a paranoid ex-prime minister, a hypnotising vicar and a solicitor who paid £2,500 for letters and then burnt them in his cooker. They were convinced that they were unravelling a complex, international conspiracy so, as they flew to Washington, they decided that Bessell's note to Dave proved that he had high-level intelligence contacts in Washington. Thus in mid-air they came up with a number of eccentric theories, in the style of Harold Wilson, their prize source; for example, they thought that Bessell might be working for American Intelligence and was deliberately steering them away from South Africa for reasons which were known only to his CIA masters. Thus, they believed that everyone whom they met in Washington over the next few days was working for the CIA, MI5, MI6 or BOSS. They recorded every conversation and wasted countless hours in the States – and back at HQ in Surrey – discussing the possible roles of the Western and South African intelligence services in the Thorpe story.

They returned to Britain, their briefcases crammed with tapes of conversations which meant nothing and their heads spinning with bizarre theories which distracted them from the main task: proving that Thorpe had had an affair with Scott and had then tried to kill him.

*   *   *

The elation of Oceanside soon dissipated in Surrey as Pencourt began to sift through their transcripts of the *aide memoire*. They listed the people whom they should approach and the incidents which had to be confirmed. As always, Courtiour was filer-in-chief but it was up to Penrose, the reporter in the team, to devise a strategy that would yield a publishable manuscript rather than just more interviews.

Then *Private Eye* unhelpfully revealed that Pencourt had seen Bessell: 'The inimitable duo who are "following up" Harold Wilson's allegations about South Africa have spent what by all accounts was a fascinating three days with Peter Bessell, the former Liberal MP for Bodmin and a friend of Jeremy Thorpe.'[2] The *Eye* had an advantage over Pencourt and the mainstream media because it did not care whether it was sued for libel; indeed, it thrived on libel actions because they justified its reputation as a fearless satirical magazine and, in any case, the costs of court actions were usually covered by appeals to readers. So the *Eye* pressed on, in a manner that no newspaper or television station could have done, and said that Pencourt were 'sniffing around Liberal contacts in the West Country'.

BBC executives were also concerned by these developments. Gordon Carr was still in charge of the 'Special Unit', with a brief to prove that Thorpe was innocent and had been smeared by the South Africans. But he was not making much progress, which was not surprising since this thesis was untrue. When these executives read *Private Eye* they realised that Pencourt had not been eliminated, which was worrying. If, by some horrible accident, Pencourt turned out to be right about Thorpe there would be awkward questions about the way that the Corporation had handled the story; so they decided to scupper Pencourt.

Early in November 1976 the BBC dispatched Carr and Mangold, the journalist whose interview in the spring with Bessell had been dumped in a basement, to Oceanside. They had an unworkable brief: to persuade Bessell to allege publicly that the South Africans were behind the allegations against Thorpe. Carr told Bessell that the BBC wanted to use an interview with him as a lead-in to a studio discussion with Wilson and Thorpe, in which he could take part via satellite. Carr added, 'It would do you good to appear with them, you know.'

Bessell stared in disbelief and told Carr and Mangold that they knew that 'the South African dimension' did not exist. Bessell said, 'Carr listened quietly. When I had finished he turned to Mangold and said, "You were right." Mangold replied, "I told you Peter would have nothing to do with another cover-up." They had fulfilled their instructions but made no attempt to disguise their relief at my response. Carr said cheerfully that the BBC would probably have to abandon the project.'

While Bessell was rejecting these advances from the BBC Pencourt were unsure how to proceed. So they turned to Harold Wilson. When they visited him at Lord North Street on 16 November 1976 they required an emergency transfusion of common sense but Wilson made matters worse. He said that they were on the right track which was understandable since he still believed that everything – MI5, BOSS, the CIA, Thorpe, rumours about Wilson's affair with Marcia, Princess Margaret's divorce and much else besides – was one huge conspiracy.

Pencourt could have dropped Thorpe and concentrated on Wilson and his allegations about MI5, which was a more marketable story. But they would not abandon Norman. So they set off, more in hope than the expectation that it would yield anything, to confront David Holmes in Manchester. But he was not at home and his partner, Gerald Hagan, said that he did not know when he would be back, which was not good news for Pencourt. They told Hagan the name of the hotel where they would be staying and retreated to assess their position. Then they were given a much-needed boost. A prominent solicitor in London called D.J. Freeman, whose clients included Harold Wilson, telephoned their hotel in Manchester and told them that he represented David Holmes and that Holmes was prepared to meet them.

On 15 December Pencourt met Holmes for the first time at Freeman's offices in London. He laughed when they summarised Bessell's allegations and dismissed him as an attention-seeking fantasist who felt that he had been forgotten in California. But Pencourt were sure that he was lying, though they could not prove it. Nonetheless it was encouraging: Holmes was clearly panicking now, which meant that Thorpe might also lose his nerve.

Scott, meanwhile, was back to his familiar self. During the latter half of 1976 and the New Year of 1977 he shuttled around the West Country, spreading chaos. He had a new, semi-permanent partner, a quiet young woman from Northern Ireland called Hilary Arthur, whom he had met when she was working in Barnstaple. In May 1976 she had given birth to a daughter, whom they named Briony. Scott said, 'Hilary was a kind and intelligent person. She was in love with me and was very supportive.'[3] But, like his ex-wife Susan Myers, she was exasperated by his obsession with Thorpe and his daily confessions that he was sexually attracted to men.

In the autumn of 1976 he was still living in Combe Martin. Hilary preferred not to live with him, but remained nearby. By now, she had become involved with a religious sect, which was not surprising after the emotional buffeting she had suffered with Norman.

His cottage had been lent to him by a journalist called Brian Cook, who worked for the *Western Morning News*, the West Country's regional newspaper, based in Plymouth. Cook had known Scott for a year and, like many people, had taken pity on him: 'Initially I was pretty sceptical when he told me about Thorpe. Then I spent time talking to him and looking at his documents and I thought that he was telling the truth.'[4] However, that was his private view and he did not share his thoughts with readers of the *News*, a conservative newspaper of record which left investigative journalism to the hot-shots in London.

Pencourt were also sympathetic. They believed that he was telling the truth, which Scott, who was used to being dismissed as a liar, appreciated. He had no telephone in the cottage so they sent him telegrams when they wanted to check facts with him, asking him to contact them urgently. His stockpile of documents was much depleted but occasionally he stumbled across an interesting titbit; for example, he was delighted when he found a letter from the National League of Young Liberals, dated 12 March 1976, which informed him that he had been nominated as Honorary President of the League. The letter said that, while the post was honorary, 'the President has often proved a useful link between the Young Liberal Movement and the Party'.

Then he tired of Combe Martin and found a house close to Dartmoor in the village of Teigncombe, in mid-Devon, where Hilary thought that they might be able to repair their relationship, in the kind of isolated, self-sufficient existence which Norman thrived on. He still had no job, no income and no National Insurance card but was, by his standards, almost happy with his animals, his girlfriend, and daughter, whom he adored.

He enjoyed Pencourt's occasional visits. He liked discussing the minutiae of their investigation and was touched that they often bought food for the household from the village shop. But, grateful though he was for their support, he was blunt about their prospects; he told them that Thorpe had 'got away with it' and that they should give up. But they knew that, in his heart, he wanted them to destroy Thorpe.

They pressed on. They drove to Cardiff to interview Dave Miller, the printer who had introduced Newton to George Deakin as the ideal man for a professional 'frightening job'. Miller had satisfied the press with his dramatic description of how Newton had arrived one night in October 1975 at his shop in a bloodstained car complaining about the gun that had jammed on the moor. But after this flurry of publicity he had been forgotten. Pencourt cultivated him over the following months, teasing little facts from him, such as the telephone number of a man in Barnstaple who, they discovered, was Thorpe's solicitor. Miller also used them; by helping Pencourt he was trying to ensure that, if they ever wrote their book, he would be portrayed as a man who had done nothing wrong. But he also wondered if he could make some money from the story without risking prosecution.

Pencourt decided now that they had to reach Andrew Newton, the airline pilot-cum-hitman who was in jail in Preston for shooting Scott's Great Dane. He had been a model prisoner and was due to be freed in four months. Unfortunately he had not shown any desire to discuss his short, unsuccessful career as a gunman with them and had failed to respond to their requests for an interview.

They approached a young woman called Eleanor Rooney, an Irish air hostess who lived in Blackpool and who had gone out with Newton before he was jailed. She said that Andrew did not want to discuss Scott with anyone but did give them a copy of the statement he had made to the police after he was arrested for shooting Rinka. Pencourt were excited and intrigued when they read this. Newton had told the police that Scott had talked to him about Lord Snowdon but when they checked the reports on Newton's trial at Exeter in March that year they saw that Snowdon's name had not been mentioned in court. They decided that this was further proof of a conspiracy to protect the Royal Family.

Pencourt were determined to meet Newton and so they headed off to Blackpool to try and persuade Rooney to help. She agreed that Penrose could accompany her on her next visit to Newton but said that it was up to him to arrange the necessary Visiting Order, which was a problem since VOs, as they were known, came from prisoners. On 21 December he telephoned A Wing at Preston and told a warder that it seemed as if his VO from Newton had been delayed in the Christmas post. The warder said that, as it was Christmas, he would bend the rules.

Later that day Rooney and Penrose, wearing a dark suit and carrying a briefcase, which, happily, made him look like a solicitor, drove to Preston prison. They were nodded through the gate and into the visiting room, along with wives, girlfriends and children who wanted to exchange festive greetings with their loved ones.

Newton scowled when he saw Penrose. He pointed to the magic briefcase and snapped, 'Has that been checked by the screws?' Penrose knew that if Newton saw the tape recorder inside then the interview would be over and that he might well be in serious trouble; so he bluffed and started to fiddle with the catch. Newton was not pleased, 'Don't open it, for God's sake,' he said. 'They'll think you're passing something to me.'

Penrose explained that he was researching a book and asked if Newton had any theories on the death of Rinka. Newton had vowed to himself that he would not say anything, lest he should forfeit the money Holmes owed him for the expedition to Exmoor with Scott, but he could not resist, 'There are people who are very interested in my story not coming out. But there are also people interested in the truth. Watergate was just dealing with breaking and entering and lying. If I said anything it would wipe out one political party.'

He was circling the bait but Penrose had to make him bite. He told Newton that, obviously, it had all been a charade, which had been designed to frighten Scott. Newton took pride in his abilities as a professional assassin and did not like being portrayed as a buffoon; so he said that he knew who was feeding Penrose this nonsense – David Holmes. He told Penrose that Holmes should understand that it was not a joke to plan a murder. 'He wants to advise himself on the laws of conspiracy. Mr Holmes is pretty naive. This place is full of prisoners. You've only got to talk about robbing a bank and that's conspiracy.' He was in full flow now and suggested that Penrose should ask Thorpe for his views on the death of Rinka and remind him that 'certain arrangements' had to be honoured. Then he slumped back in his chair as he realised that, having decided that he would say nothing that might lead the police or the press to the men who owed him a great deal of money, he had done precisely the opposite. It was the last time that he spoke to a reporter without demanding payment.

Pencourt were delighted when they hunched over their tape recorder in their hotel. To people who knew nothing about the death of Rinka the interview would not have made any sense but Pencourt were ecstatic; after months toiling to prove a link between Newton, Holmes and Thorpe they knew now that there was a connection. Holmes had always insisted that he had never met or spoken to Newton; they had established that this was a lie.

However, their euphoria soon evaporated. They realised that they still did not have incontrovertible evidence that Holmes and Thorpe had planned to kill Scott. If they had been working in America, where the press could say virtually what it liked, they could have quoted Newton and accused Thorpe and Holmes, but this was Britain, where the media were hamstrung by the toughest libel laws in the world.

CHAPTER SIXTEEN

Jeremy Thorpe was in fine form in spring 1977. Marion was supportive. Peter Bessell was dying slowly in California. The BBC had shut down the 'special unit', which he had once feared might dig up muck from the past. Those disrespectful young reporters, Penrose and the other chap, with the funny French name, were presumably scratching a living in local television. He relied on Lord Goodman, the most feared solicitor in the country, to make sure that the press never mentioned Scott. If a newspaper dared to ask his office about this odd fellow who lived on the moors in the West Country Goodman leapt into action; he would telephone the editor and point out that his client was an honest man and that Scott was a proven liar. If they were stubborn he fired off letters threatening terrible consequences if his client, the Rt. Hon. Jeremy Thorpe, MP, PC, was accused of anything.[1]

But his fatal error was to dismiss Pencourt. Wilson was still talking to them although they did not tell him that it looked as if he had been conned by Thorpe since he might have terminated his relationship with them. So, when he suggested that it might be better if they used his loyal secretary, Lady Falkender, as an intermediary they were enthusiastic. This would avoid an unpleasant meeting, when they would have to tell a former prime minister that he had made a fool of himself by accusing the South Africans of framing Thorpe.

On Tuesday, 22 March they arrived at her home in Wyndham Mews, near Oxford Street. She had been Wilson's 'private and political secretary' since 1956 although she was still only 45 years old.[2] This title might have sounded pretentious but it actually understated her role as supreme confidante. She had been at Wilson's side throughout his eight years in Downing Street, enjoying an intimacy with him which enraged ministers, civil servants and assorted advisers, especially Joe Haines, Wilson's press secretary for seven years.

Haines came from the East End of London, had left school
when he was 14 and had fought his way into newspapers. He was
abrupt, short-tempered and, like Falkender, had a high opinion
of his own talents; they had a tempestuous relationship but both
thrived on the constant bickering and plotting of Downing Street.
Haines savaged her in his memoirs. He said that she had a
first-class brain but added that she was selfish, manipulative,
and spiteful: 'Everyone at Downing Street feared and loathed
her. Her influence was all-pervasive ... many went in dread
of her ... by the time Wilson went out of office there were
only two views about her held by the staff, and they were both
unprintable.'[3]

She was born in Northamptonshire, the daughter of a builder
called Harry Field, who was a staunch Conservative. She won
a scholarship to the local grammar school, where she was
one of the star pupils; her teachers wanted her to apply to
Oxbridge but she insisted on going to Queen Mary College,
London because she wanted to be as close as possible to the
centre of political action. She dreamt of becoming a Labour
MP but then she fell in love with, and married, Ed Williams,
an engineer who was chairman of the college's Conservative
Association.

In 1957 he went to Seattle to work for Boeing, met another
woman and told Marcia that their marriage was over. They
divorced in 1961 and, like many people who have been wounded
in this way, Marcia threw herself into her work. Her relationship
with Wilson was complex; while his wife, Mary, gave him a
loving home she offered intellectual companionship and a shared
fascination with politics.

When Pencourt arrived at her home, carrying three leather
bags and a suitcase, stuffed with files, she was finding it as
hard as Wilson to adapt to life after Downing Street. She
was on a committee examining the state of the British film
industry, had picked up a few directorships and had dabbled
in journalism, but this was dull compared to life as a prime
minister's trusted aide. She ushered Pencourt into the living
room, escorted by her sister, Peggy Field, who shared the house
and who had been Mary Wilson's secretary. Courtiour unpacked
his files as Penrose explained that they had a problem; they had
discovered that while Wilson was right about MI5's smears it
looked as if he was wrong about Thorpe. She agreed that this

presented difficulties: 'Harold certainly won't be happy to hear that,' she said.

They talked for thirteen hours. Pencourt read extracts from their files, including Scott's statement to the police in Chelsea just before Christmas 1962, and Bessell's monologue to them in California. They also outlined their theories on dirty tricks against Wilson by MI5 and BOSS. Many people would have keeled over with this mind-numbing detail, much of which had nothing to do with anything, but Falkender was a receptive audience.

They revealed that they had guaranteed outlets for their material. They told her about their contract with Tom Rosenthal at Secker and Warburg, which they had not mentioned to Wilson in the interests of security. They also said that the *Observer* had just bought the serialisation rights to their book and, finally, best of all, that the newspaper's editor, Donald Trelford, was so excited by Wilson's allegations about MI5 that he wanted to publish them before their book was finished. Falkender said that it was marvellous that a newspaper intended to expose the right-wing extremists in MI5 who had plotted against a great prime minister.

As the hours slipped by, with Courtiour marshalling the files which were spread out on the carpet, Penrose decided that Falkender would turn out to be an even better source than Wilson. He rambled but she shot poison-tipped darts; he soon tired but she had apparently limitless powers of concentration. She casually tossed a scoop to Pencourt, the first of many which she gave them over the following months, when she revealed that Buckingham Palace had asked Wilson to time his resignation to coincide with the announcement that the marriage of Princess Margaret and Lord Snowdon was over. Pencourt rose wearily and promised to keep her informed on their progress; in return she said that she would be diplomatic when she broke the news to Wilson about Thorpe.

The deal with the *Observer* relieved the psychological and financial pressures on Pencourt. They were grateful to Tom Rosenthal but he was a publisher and they were journalists who craved recognition from their colleagues. It also provided a much-needed influx of cash because the newspaper agreed to pay £50,000 for exclusive first rights to the book.

Pencourt returned to their research with renewed vigour,

teasing more quotes from sources and trying to locate new ones. They made regular sorties to the West Country. Scott had moved again, to an isolated cottage on Dartmoor, near to Chagford, west of Exeter, where he was happy with Hilary Arthur, his daughter, Briony, and his goats, chickens, ducks, pigs and dogs.

They also decided to pick up what journalists call 'colour' in Higher Chuggaton, where Thorpe owned a cottage. They did not plan to approach him but thought that it would help the book if they could describe the village and collect quotes from locals. They made a discreet reconnaissance. He lived just off the main road which ran through the hamlet. There was a cottage, an annexe, which had once been a barn, and a garage. There were also high, solid gates which Thorpe had erected the previous year when the media were hounding him about his alleged relationship with Scott. Pencourt sat in their car, making notes, when they spotted Thorpe striding towards them, his famous trilby perched on top of his head. He shouted, 'Are you lost? Can I help?' Pencourt thought that they should introduce themselves, got out of the car, told him that they were Barrie Penrose and Roger Courtiour and wondered if he would answer a few questions. He backed off, arms flailing like a windmill, and said, 'You have already had a writ for criminal libel.' Penrose replied that, as far as he knew, they had not heard from his lawyers, but Thorpe was already retreating to the sanctuary of his home. It was the first and last conversation between hunters and hunted.

On 6 April Newton was released from prison. Pencourt tracked him to Hampshire, pursued by a small band of Fleet Street reporters who, unlike their editors, also believed that there was a cracking story behind the death of Rinka the Great Dane. But Newton refused to say anything.

Then there was a crisis that demanded Pencourt's immediate attention. On 5 May, Falkender invited them to Wyndham Mews. After dinner, served by two Filipino maids, she said that Wilson was not pleased at the direction of their investigation and found it 'difficult to accept' that Thorpe had lied to him about Scott. But that was just the start. The previous night he had seen Thorpe, who had suggested that he should talk to Lord Goodman. She said that Goodman had advised Wilson that it would be 'better' if he did not speak to Pencourt again. She told them, 'Arnold [Goodman] asked where you two were getting your resources from after you parted company with the BBC. He asked if Harold had considered the possibility that funds might be coming from South Africa.'

Pencourt were furious. They had risked everything and now they were being accused of being South African agents, which was an appalling calumny. It also jeopardised their book. They knew that it would be disastrous if Wilson publicly distanced himself from them. True, they had their tapes, which proved that they had quoted him accurately, but they knew that they would not win a public scrap with a former prime minister. It was vital, therefore, that they reassured him as quickly as possible. They were baffled by Goodman's role. He was Thorpe's legal adviser and had tried to protect his client from their enquiries. On the other hand, he also advised Wilson, which should have meant that he supported the campaign to expose MI5. He was also chairman of the *Observer* Editorial Trust, the newspaper which had acquired the serialisation rights to their book.

They told Tom Rosenthal that he had to assure Falkender and Wilson immediately that they were independent journalists who were writing a balanced book. On 10 May, Pencourt and Rosenthal visited Falkender. Rosenthal insisted that none of them were working for the South Africans, which she already knew. Pencourt also reassured her by saying that they would not just be writing about Thorpe; they said that they would also be exposing South African interference in British politics, which was what Wilson wanted to read about. She nodded but added astutely that, from what they had told her, they had such excellent material on Thorpe, which had nothing to do with South Africa, that they would obviously concentrate on him in their book. She was a veteran in the game of politics, the first rule of which was never to take responsibility unless necessary, so she passed Rosenthal on to Wilson. But she did have the grace to apologise: 'I try desperately never to cross Goodman. All the people involved, Harold, Jeremy, everyone, is represented by him,' she said.

A week later Rosenthal saw Wilson at his new flat in a mansion block in Ashley Gardens near Victoria Station, where Thorpe also had a home. Pencourt waited nearby in Westminster Cathedral and knew that the future of their book depended on Wilson backing down; Rosenthal and the *Observer* would have to dump them if their key source denounced them now. It only required a short statement from Wilson to the Press Association, probably issued by Lord Goodman's office, saying that he did not trust two journalists whom he had been meeting privately, and they would be finished. Then Rosenthal appeared in the cloisters. Mass had just begun so he had to whisper: 'I gave Sir Harold all the assurances that were necessary. Arnold Goodman is apparently adamant that he shouldn't see you again. But Sir Harold said that you could keep in indirect touch with him through Lady Falkender.'

They adjourned to a café, where Rosenthal tucked into a fried breakfast. He said that Wilson had not discussed Goodman's theory that they were South African agents and had only been interested in the likely repercussions of the book. 'He is very, very worried and is frightened that he's started something that is bigger than he can control,' said Rosenthal. He added that Wilson felt guilty about Thorpe:

> He said that Jeremy was a friend. I told him that I appreciated that but pointed out that this was a man who was a Privy Counsellor and who had offered himself up as Prime Minister. I said that people like this had to lead rather more strictly regulated lives than the rest of us. He said, 'Yes, yes, quite right.' [Rosenthal added that Wilson was still obsessed with security.] He said that he hoped that I had taken precautions against burglars. I said that I didn't have anything in my house. He said that wasn't what he meant. He said that he was worried about the proofs for the book being stolen.

Pencourt smiled at each other; they were still in business.

Donald Trelford was 39 years old and had become editor of the *Observer* two years earlier. He had worked his way steadily up the journalistic ladder after graduating from Cambridge in the mid-1950s; after learning the basics of the trade in Coventry and Sheffield he had moved to Malawi, where he edited a newspaper. Then he joined the *Observer* in London. The *Observer* had dominated the Sunday broadsheet market in the 1950s but had slipped to second place since Harold Evans had taken control at the *Sunday Times* in 1967. The *Observer* was still respected for its liberalism, its thorough reporting of foreign affairs, particularly in Africa, and its stable of elegant writers; but the *Sunday Times*, aggressive and populist, had more readers and was making more money.

Trelford was determined that the *Observer* would beat the

Sunday Times at its own sensationalist game. One way to do that was to buy 'properties': ready-made stories culled from books, which could be turned into front-page stories which would lead the weekend's television news bulletins and be picked up by daily newspapers. But there was an implicit problem with the Pencourt investigation, which neither Trelford nor Rosenthal had confronted when they shook hands on the deal. As an expert on Southern Africa Trelford was fascinated by BOSS but he knew that stories about South African spies did not sell newspapers. Nor was he interested in a sordid tale about a homosexual affair between Scott, who was a vindictive nobody, and Thorpe, who was yesterday's man.

Trelford and Rosenthal were friends. They belonged to the same clubs and often did mutually beneficial business. So, when he had been selling the Pencourt project, Trelford had made the requisite polite noises when Rosenthal talked about his authors' exciting revelations about Thorpe. But Trelford had made it clear, or so he thought, that he was only interested in Wilson's allegations about MI5. That was not how Rosenthal and Pencourt saw it. They believed that the *Observer* had bought the whole book, not just Wilson's easy-to-digest, explosive allegations.

Pencourt should have sensed that all was not well, however, when they went into the *Observer's* office to discuss their forthcoming story on Wilson. They were disappointed that a junior reporter, rather than one of the heavyweight stars, was assigned to debrief them and were surprised that he fidgeted so much when they opened their files and began to talk about Scott, Thorpe and 'the South African dimension'. Roger Courtiour uncharacteristically lost his temper during a conversation with John Cole, the deputy editor, who had only just been told by Trelford about Project Pencourt. (Cole was later the BBC's Political Editor and became a national celebrity, courtesy of his beguiling Ulster syntax.) He asked if Pencourt were claiming that Jeremy Thorpe, who was a personal friend, had stolen Scott's Insurance card. Courtiour exploded that not only had Thorpe done that but he had also ordered Scott's execution.

Penrose, who was by nature more suspicious than his co-author, wondered whether they had chosen the right newspaper; the *Observer* had strong links with the Liberal Party and Lord Goodman was chairman of its board. But Penrose told himself that he was being overly suspicious; after all, Trelford had bought their book and could not, surely, have serious reservations about it. Pencourt expected the *Observer* to move quickly on the Wilson story. But June came and went and nothing happened. Early in July they agreed that the newspaper needed reassurance. So they arranged for Trelford and his defence correspondent, Andrew Wilson, to meet Falkender, who would confirm that they had accurately reported Harold Wilson's views on MI5. The meeting took place at her home on 13 July. Superficially, it went well. Falkender told Trelford that Harold Wilson and she had spoken in detail to Pencourt about MI5's campaign against Labour. She said that, although she had had not read their manuscript, she trusted them.

But there were sub-plots to the conversation, which boded ill for Pencourt. Trelford said that he was worried that people might think that Wilson was 'paranoid'. He was also puzzled that Wilson had not ordered an investigation into MI5, and finally, wondered why he had chosen to talk to ordinary journalists like Pencourt, rather than to senior people, such as himself. Falkender was surprised by this; he had bought Pencourt's book which, or so she thought, meant that he was, in outline at least, sympathetic to what Wilson and she were saying. But she was diplomatic and explained that Wilson could hardly have asked MI5 or MI6 to investigate themselves. She told him: 'The only people qualified to present the evidence and present the case for an inquiry are the same people who are part of what is wrong. So how could a prime minister do that? You have got to use the system and you can't override them. You can't say, I will have my own people because I don't trust you.' Trelford nodded and hurried off to his engagement but the damage was done, although Pencourt did not realise it.

On Sunday, 17 July, the *Observer* ran a front-page story by Andrew Wilson, headlined: 'Wilson: "Why I lost my faith in MI5", and carrying the logo, 'World Exclusive'. Even by the unsentimental standards of Fleet Street, the *Observer* treated Pencourt shabbily. The newspaper stripped the Wilson story down to its sensational basics but gave the impression that Pencourt were hacks who had walked in off the street with unsubstantiated claims, which it had painstakingly checked. The *Observer* indicated, too, that it had strong reservations about Wilson. There were hundreds of photographs of him on file, in statesmanlike pose, but it selected one of him in sinister dark glasses and a dark baggy suit, which made him look like a Mafia don. The story suggested that Wilson had exaggerated the damage inflicted on him by MI5; the *Observer* did not actually say that he had gone mad but many readers might have thought that from the photograph and text.

Andrew Wilson opened his article by summarising his namesake's suspicions about MI5. He continued: 'Sir Harold's suspicions were voiced in a long series of meetings with two journalists, Barrie Penrose, 35, and Roger Courtiour, 36, who at the start of their meetings in May last year were working under freelance contracts for the BBC. They have since made available to the *Observer* their notes of these meetings and others they had with Sir Harold's political secretary, Lady Falkender.' The *Observer* claimed that it had launched an exhaustive investigation into Pencourt's claims, which was impossible since Trelford had only seen Falkender three days earlier. It added: 'We have painstakingly checked this material. While we cannot be certain whether Sir Harold was justified in his suspicions about MI5 or was merely over-reacting to a series of unconnected incidents, we are satisfied that the material does faithfully reflect the considered views of the former Prime Minister.'

On the evening of Saturday, 16 July Penrose and Courtiour drove to the *Observer's* offices by Blackfriar's Bridge, off Fleet Street, to collect the first edition of the newspaper. They stared at the front page and saw that they had been relegated to the status of tipsters. But then they shook hands and said, 'The show is on the road.' But they knew, in their hearts, that they had been humiliated. A year of non-stop work had been reduced to a few glib 'accusations' by Wilson, written in such a way that it sounded as if he ought to be locked up.

They did not want to antagonise the *Observer* and consoled themselves with the thought that the story was only a holding operation while they completed the book. They returned to their homes in Surrey and resumed the investigation. The manuscript was now comfortingly thick although they had not finished writing. Unfortunately, they were trying to combine three books in one, which was a recipe for disaster. There was the Thorpe–Scott affair, Wilson's and Falkender's allegations about MI5 and BOSS, and an account of how they, the authors, had tackled the investigation.

They had piles of documents, courtesy of their portable

photocopier, and scores of letters and transcripts from sources. When they first met Wilson he said that he was inviting them to investigate Britain's Watergate and they had taken him literally. British journalism was anecdotal and discursive but Pencourt thought that collecting facts and quotes was more important, just like American investigative reporters.

Any author would have struggled to turn their material into a readable manuscript which would satisfy the libel lawyers and shock and entertain the public but the task was beyond Pencourt. Courtiour was a conscientious and hard-working journalist but he was a researcher, not a writer; so, Penrose worked alone.

This was Penrose on Gordon Winter, BOSS super-spy:

> From a Machiavellian point of view it seemed clear that the knowledge gained by Winter and passed on to others could, if it were stored away quietly and added to, become the nucleus of a much bigger bombshell – either to be used as a tactical deterrent or exploded as the occasion demanded. In the cynical world of intelligence agencies, where the foibles of men can be exploited at times as a covert instrument of national and international politics, such excruciating conflicts between the individual's conscience and the laws of society are the spawning grounds of treachery. Jeremy Thorpe might well be viewed by BOSS, the CIA – or for that matter the KGB – not as a promising career politician serving his country but as just another potential victim who could possibly be used one day to weaken his country's government.

There were islands of coherence, when Penrose quoted someone, but these were surrounded by oceans of prose like this:

> They [Pencourt] also felt strongly that it was misleading to dismiss the idea that there had been foreign interference in British democracy. This idea too could be part of a cover-up. The further the reporters [Pencourt] advanced, the more it became clear that the three main British political parties and even such democratic institutions as the BBC had all become inextricably tangled up in the Thorpe–Scott affair. So was it very likely BOSS, and other foreign organisations which had a track-record for interference, had failed to exploit this embarrassing cover-up situation? If the doings of Norman Scott could have

an influence on the decisions of successive Prime Ministers, would a foreign Intelligence Service be so forbearing and turn its back on exploiting the obvious possibilities . . .

Penrose had opened *The Pencourt File* dramatically:

> No one would have guessed that this tiny incident of the shot dog was the key to why an established Prime Minister resigned when he did. That it was linked with Lord Snowdon's departure. That it would lead to the uncovering of one of the most cancerous political scandals of our time. That the affair had actually involved three of the world's most powerful Secret Services. And that it had undermined democracy and altered the course of British politics over most of the last two decades.

Four hundred pages later, however, he confessed that he was not really sure what it all meant, which was commendably honest but did not do much for the book's credibility:

> The reporters [Pencourt] were now becoming irritated by the smaller details of the story; they wanted to solve finally the most important riddles which still remained. Why, for instance, had Harold Wilson resigned at the time he did? Was the resignation linked with the wider implications of the dog-in-a-fog affair? . . . Were indeed the efforts in Britain and America to make the Scott story public hitting at the Labour Prime Minister where he was thought to be most vulnerable? Penrose and Courtiour agreed that this argument, implausible at the beginning of their investigation, now seemed increasingly possible . . . To the reporters the story had far too many political implications it seemed for some people in high places to want the truth to emerge. Ordinary justice, it seemed, had become dangerously entangled in a sinister web. Thus affairs of state had in that sense put democracy at risk.[4]

In Pencourt's defence, however, it must be said that the cleverest journalist in the country would have struggled to turn their material into a coherent book. The interviews with Wilson and Falkender were a particular problem because much of what they told Pencourt was unintelligible. Wilson had dominated British politics for over a decade; even his enemies, who condemned him as a cynical opportunist, conceded that he had a brilliant mind. Pencourt, however, often found it hard to follow him, as he drifted from one subject to another and made cryptic accusations about the sinister forces which had tried to ruin him. But he was a former prime minister and they did not think it would be proper to point out that they did not understand what he was saying, so they listened politely and followed up his ideas on how to develop their investigation by, for example, chasing Nazis who lived on the South Coast because he thought that they were part of BOSS's diabolical conspiracy.

Falkender was better, though she also believed in the right-wing plot to destroy the Labour Party. She was also a tremendous gossip and gave them a series of scoops of varying degrees of importance; unfortunately she talked in code because she did not want to be accused of giving away secrets to journalists. This was a tragedy for Pencourt because her coded tips were the agenda for the next decade of bestselling spy books, notably her revelation, expressed in triplespeak, that Sir Anthony Blunt, the former Surveyor of the Queen's Pictures, was the Fourth Man in the so-called Cambridge spy ring of Kim Philby, Donald Maclean and Guy Burgess. For Pencourt this was the journalistic equivalent of not bothering to check the National Lottery result and throwing away a winning ticket. But, to be fair, the Wilson–Falkender transcripts were so baffling that it was a miracle that Penrose managed to make any sense of them.

This was Wilson talking about burglaries:

I've had at least fourteen robberies and break-ins. Some of them concerned me directly; there were attempted break-ins at Marcia's cottage in the country. Other members of my immediate staff had burglaries. In the first three months of this year five of my staff have been burgled. One was burgled twice. The burglaries were from Highgate to Eton to Islington. I'm convinced some are connected with South Africa and others with intelligence-gathering by intelligence people here. I don't accept they're a coincidence. The coincidence is far too great. There have been far too many of them, far too many . . .

What I didn't tell you was that Marcia's cottage was broken into for a second time in the country a weekend before last. They stole a television set which they had done a year before.

Got in round the back: got through a window. A glazier in Great Missenden, near Grange Farm [Wilson's country home], who was in difficulties over being evicted and grateful for help I gave, checked the lock or something at Marcia's cottage. He saw the same footsteps as in an earlier robbery at Marcia's. He thinks he may have disturbed them by flashing his torch. This was more than just an ordinary robbery . . .

Here was Falkender describing George Wigg, who had once been Wilson's Paymaster General, with special responsibility for security:

Wigg was saying things to me like, 'Keep your voice down. This room alone – these rooms have at least five or six different sets of bugs in them.' And I said, 'Well, I am in the middle of Downing Street,' and he said, 'That is all the more reason why we have to whisper.' I mean, why do I want to whisper? This is the Cabinet Minister. If they had to do that right in the middle of Downing Street there was no hope.

This was how Falkender raised the subject of the Fourth Man:

He is someone who would make your hair stand on end. The Cabinet Secretary was called in after a very senior person went to the Ministry of Defence to provide information about the identity of the Fourth Man. It is now questionable whether John Hunt, the Cabinet Secretary, is aware of the terrible consequences there would be if anyone did suddenly identify this man as the Fourth Man. I think the whole fabric of the Establishment would collapse around everybody's ears. So Donald Beves [a senior civil servant who had just been wrongly identified by the press as the Fourth Man] was the perfect man to put up but was he put up because they wanted to draw attention away from the real man, or was he put up because they wanted everyone to know they were drawing attention from the real man so that they could become an issue and then reveal the real man. Do you understand? That is what worried me. Was the reason pure or was it even more sinister and complicated to make the revelation that much more awful when it emerged?

Finally this was her analysis of the Thorpe affair:

> What puzzles me in all of this is why would MI5 want to
> neutralise Jeremy Thorpe and want to get at Harold and
> myself. When they are getting rid of us ... mean, one of
> the stories is that I am an agent for the KGB ... Well, that is
> very common gossip put around by people who have access
> to your files and have vetted you and know all about you.
> So when they put it out they know they are putting out a
> deliberate lie. If they don't then what is it that stops them
> from getting to the information that clears you because they
> have access to your file, they know whether you are one or
> not. What makes them deliberately say the opposite of what
> they know to be the facts? Why do they concoct a story as
> MI5 contacts or MI5 people that they must know is not
> true? Or do they not know if it is true?
>
> They explain it all away by them – Marcia and Harold,
> poor souls – going off there to Russia together. Obviously the
> only place they could actually go together to be quiet and on
> their own and then get into a compromising situation. Well,
> you know only a nutter would say that because only nutty
> people, and you would have to be certifiable, would actually
> choose the Soviet Union. I mean it is such an uncomfortable
> place. I mean you have a lady on the corridor. You have
> umpteen people from different branches of their security
> forces ... apart from the fact that you are accompanied
> by a private secretary, the Foreign Office Private Secretary,
> half the FO are there with you. Even when Harold went into
> Opposition he was still being accompanied by God knows
> who and staying at the British Embassy and reporting on
> everything that had been said to him. Now how come that
> none of that had filtered through to MI5, and the security
> forces?[5]

Summer turned to autumn and there was still no urgency from
the *Observer*. Pencourt kept writing, believing that, sooner or
later, Trelford would send for them to discuss the serialisation
for which he had paid handsomely.

On Wednesday, 19 October 1977 Pencourt were scooped. The
Evening News, the now-defunct London newspaper, carried a
front-page story, headlined: 'I was hired to kill Scott. Exclusive:

Gunman tells of incredible plot – a murder contract for £5,000'. Pencourt felt sick when they read this. The *News* reported that Andrew Newton had been paid £5,000 to kill Scott, although he did not say who had employed him, not out of loyalty to Holmes but because the *News* had refused to pay him the £150,000 which he had demanded to name names. The newspaper also said that Detective Chief Superintendent Michael Challes, of the Avon and Somerset police, would investigate Newton's allegations, at the request of the Director of Public Prosecutions, Sir Thomas Hetherington. Hetherington the *News* explained, only became involved in cases when the police referred them to him for a ruling on whether there was sufficient evidence to launch a prosecution. But the DPP also intervened when issues of 'public interest' were raised and could even consult with the Attorney-General, who was, unlike the DPP, a political appointee.

Sometimes a story, dismissed by the media as boring, can instantly become fashionable; that is what happened when the rest of Fleet Street read the *News*. It was unfair on Pencourt but the fact was that reporters, who would have been ridiculed a few hours earlier by their news editors if they had suggested that they pop down to Devon to have a chat with Norman Scott, were ordered now to crack the story, no matter what it cost. The rest of the press tried to find Newton but he had disappeared. Thanks to Holmes and John Le Mesurier, who wanted him as far away from the press and the police as possible, he had set off to Rhodesia to begin a new life as a pilot. But he was arrested there and deported back to England. Le Mesurier said nothing at the time but later explained what had happened:

I handed £5,000 to Newton shortly after his release from prison on St Bride's Common near my home. By then I discovered that he was interested in getting a good deal more and with the newspapers after his story he had an exaggerated sense of his own importance. He said he needed another £12,000 to qualify as a jet pilot and then he would get out of our hair immediately.

I was sceptical and remember telling David [Holmes] that with Newton we had acquired an albatross round our necks far more dangerous than Scott had ever been. He was a crafty, conniving liar and was nobody's fool. In any event, David stumped up the money and I made the largest payment –

£12,000 in cash – at the Piccadilly Hotel in Manchester. Not long after that the idea came up we should try and arrange a flying job for Newton in Rhodesia to get him out of the country. It seemed a good idea as there was a lot of speculation, originally sparked off by Harold Wilson's statement in the Commons, about the possibility of Thorpe being framed by South African security services. With Newton safely out of the way in Southern Africa it might appear that the speculation was correct and divert attention from ourselves. Newton was agreeable so I got his ticket and expenses for the trip, which came to another £1,000. All the money came from David out of the funds directed to him by Thorpe.[6]

But that October the chasing pack of journalists, led by Pencourt, did not know about this.

Pencourt were still reeling from the shock of the Newton story when the *Evening News* hit them again. The front-page headline was: 'Former MP reveals murder plot. Exclusive: He must be bumped off.'[7] Pencourt could not believe it: Peter Bessell, whom they knew so well, had given the newspaper a child's guide to the conspiracy to kill Scott. The story did not identify any of the plotters, whom it referred to only as 'prominent Liberals', but Pencourt knew that they had lost the initiative. It was unbearable; they had known all this, and much more, since their trip to California a year ago.

Tom Rosenthal was not pleased that his book was being undermined by this flood of revelation and told his old friend Trelford that the *Observer* had to do something quickly. On Sunday, 23 October, the *Observer* carried Pencourt's report of their conversations with Bessell the previous October. They explained how a prominent Liberal called X (the British libel laws prevented them from naming Thorpe) had tried to persuade Bessell to organise Scott's execution. They also made it clear that Holmes knew more than he had so far admitted: 'Bessell has told us that the man we must refer to as X suggested to him that David Holmes be instructed to kill Scott.' Finally, they persuaded Wilson to give them this telling little quote: 'I had no idea that one of the outcomes of the investigation [by Pencourt] would be an alleged murder plot involving Liberals. When the enquiry began in May last year I wanted my South African allegations investigated. I only learned about an alleged murder plot some weeks ago.'

But Pencourt knew that they had come second and they did not like it. It was not entirely gloomy, however, because Thorpe was big news again. Yet the truth in all this was irrelevant; if one newspaper obtained a scoop with, say, Peter Bessell, that indicated that there had been a plot to murder Scott, then rivals would immediately adopt the opposite view since Fleet Street was about 'knocking down' the opposition's stories. For example, a few days after the *Evening News* and *Observer* stories, the *Daily Express* sent one of its top writers, Paul Dacre, to Oceanside to destroy Bessell. Dacre conceded that Bessell was 'a key figure in the Thorpe affair' who held the answer to 'more damning secrets than anyone apart from the former Liberal leader himself'. But that was the only semi-flattering comment. The overall tone of the article was summed up by the headline: 'Penniless, shabby, pathetic – the man nursing Jeremy's secrets'. Dacre fizzed with indignation. He said that Bessell was a rapidly ageing womaniser and self-confessed liar and gleefully quoted him: 'People in Britain think of me as a totally undependable liar or someone who has betrayed his friendship with Jeremy Thorpe. It's a heads you lose, tails you lose situation.'[8]

On Thursday, 27 October Thorpe succumbed to the ceaseless pressure from the media and called a press conference. Pencourt wanted to witness this historic occasion, although they did not need to attend since they were authors, not daily newspaper reporters. Along with almost a hundred journalists they arrived at the former New Scotland Yard building, which had been turned into an annexe of the House of Commons. Then they were told that there had been a change of venue and were directed to the Gladstone Library on the third floor of the National Liberal Club. But they were stopped at the door to the library and told that they were not welcome; they persuaded a colleague to take their tape recorder, so that they would have a record of Thorpe's historic speeech, and retreated. But they did not give up. They slipped back into the club, climbed into the rafters and descended so that they could listen to what promised to be a thoroughly enjoyable encounter.

Clement Freud, Liberal MP for the Isle of Ely, and Marion were on the platform with Thorpe, along with John Montgomerie, a partner in Lord Goodman's law firm. (Goodman could spot a lost cause and shortly afterwards told Thorpe that he should find a new legal adviser.) Thorpe began by reading from a prepared statement:

'I must stress that anyone expecting sensational revelations is likely to be disappointed . . . not a scrap of evidence has been produced to implicate me in any plot to murder Norman Scott.' Then Pencourt heard him slip effortlessly into lying mode. He said, 'Norman Scott is neither the only nor the first person I have tried to help. But a close and even affectionate relationship developed from this sympathy. However, no sexual activity of any kind took place.'

He turned to Harold Wilson's suggestions that he, Thorpe, had been smeared by South Africa. He said, 'I did not myself promote this belief and it is fair to say that Sir Harold has himself expressed his doubts.' Of Bessell, his erstwhile friend, he said icily that he would have preferred that he had spoken to the police rather than the press. He continued:

> It would be insane to pretend that the emergence of this story has not placed an almost intolerable burden on my wife, my family and on me. Only their steadfast loyalty and the support of my many friends, known and unknown, from all over the country, has strengthened my resolve and determination to meet this challenge. Consequently, I have no intention of resigning, nor have I received a single request to do so from my constituency association.

After a few relatively polite questions, Keith Graves, a burly BBC Television News reporter, who later became one of the Corporation's star foreign correspondents, said, 'The whole of this hinges on your private life. It is necessary to ask if you have ever had a homosexual relationship.' There was uproar. Marion Thorpe demanded that the culprit stand and repeat the question, which Graves did: 'Would you comment on rumours that you have had a homosexual relationship?' John Montgomerie, Goodman's representative, insisted that he 'could not allow' Thorpe to respond, for unspecified legal reasons and because it was 'improper and indecent' to ask questions like that of a 'public man'. Graves replied that it was a legitimate question because the whole story centred on whether or not Thorpe had slept with Scott. By now everyone was shouting and the press conference disintegrated.

Newspapers were not impressed by Thorpe's performance but the politics of Fleet Street dictated how the story was covered. Some editors had supported Thorpe so vociferously that they could not change direction now. *The Times*, which was edited by

William Rees-Mogg, Thorpe's rival in the Oxford Union, avoided the central issue, whether Thorpe was telling the truth, and debated sexual ethics: 'From a Christian point of view, homosexual affairs are likely to be less grave than adulterous affairs, because they are less likely to threaten the welfare of other and innocent people. The idea that "adultery" and homosexuality is not all right belongs to the cultural prejudices of the public house and to Christian ethics.'

The *Sunday Times* also found itself in difficulty. Like a supertanker, which cannot easily change course, it was still lumbering in support of Thorpe, though by now it knew that he could not be trusted. The newspaper declaimed: 'To ask a public man whether he has ever been a homosexual is as indefensible as to ask him if he has ever committed adultery. It scrapes the barrel of journalistic slime. Backwards and ever backwards the innuendoes go. That is the stuff of McCarthyism and its whispering agents deserve no honour.'

Pencourt raced to complete their book in the mistaken belief that, now that Thorpe was front-page news, the *Observer* would want to serialise their material as soon as possible. They continued to gather new information. This time, however, they did not dig up an esoteric new twist on the non-existent 'South African dimension' but a genuine scoop. Dave Miller, the Cardiff printer, had been shaken by the stories in the *Evening News* and the *Observer* and feared now that he was involved in something which might end in a prison sentence. So he decided to tell Pencourt the truth about the plot to kill Scott, which included the fact that he was innocent of wrongdoing. He said that he had become involved in the spring of 1975, when a friend called George Deakin, who was in the fruit-machine business, asked if he knew a 'tough guy'. Miller said Deakin and another man, called John Le Mesurier, wanted this 'tough guy' to help a pal, who was being blackmailed. Miller said that he had recommended Andrew Newton, who would 'do anything for a laugh'. Miller continued, 'The next thing I heard about it was when Newton turned up at my place on the night of the Scott shooting.'

Then Miller moved to early 1977 when Deakin had contacted him and said that Le Mesurier wanted to meet. At this point, he told Pencourt, he began to fear for his own safety because he knew so much; so he decided to start taping conversations. Le

Mesurier told him to pass a message to Newton assuring him that he would be paid. There were further conversations with Le Mesurier, all of which Miller recorded, as they planned the meeting at which Newton would be paid his fee of £5,000. On 18 April 1977, Miller said, they met at St Bride's Common, Glamorgan, and Newton was given his £5,000 by Le Mesurier, a handover which was photographed by a detective agency which Miller had hired. But Miller did not know – and neither did Pencourt – that Le Mesurier later paid Newton a further £12,500, which was the remainder of Jack Hayward's £20,000, to ensure that he minimised Le Mesurier's role in the conspiracy.

Then Pencourt confronted Deakin at his home in Port Talbot. He was frightened and insisted, 'I didn't know that there was going to be any murder attempt. It was just a question of a blackmailer being warned off. I'm pretty sick about how it all turned out.' Then they asked him if he would name the person behind the plot; he told them that David Holmes had masterminded the recruitment of Newton. He said, 'I suppose I was approached by Holmes because people in the one-arm bandit business get to know some pretty rough characters.' Deakin's solicitor, Barrie Stephens, gave Pencourt a short but conclusive statement: 'My client's one positive act was to put Mr Holmes in touch with Andrew Newton.'

Pencourt hurried back to Surrey. They now had 'indisputable evidence' that Newton had been hired by Holmes, via an odd collection of Welsh wide boys, to kill Scott. There were still many loose ends. Where had the money come from to pay Newton? Had Holmes discussed Newton with Thorpe? Why had Holmes and the Welshmen risked so much for Thorpe? But, as Pencourt returned to their typewriters, they were understandably delighted that finally they had cracked the mystery of Rinka. Unfortunately, they had almost completed the manuscript, which was already far too long. So they wrote about Miller and Deakin in an uncharacteristically succinct fashion, which was a shame since the information deserved space. They should have rewritten the entire book but they did not have time so they plopped their interviews with Miller and Deakin at the end of the manuscript. This was disastrous, since they had already devoted tens of thousands of words to elaborate theories about Rinka's execution, which their own research had just proved were wrong.

Tom Rosenthal deployed an editor to put the book into a publishable shape and length but she simply cut chunks, which further confused Penrose's tangled narrative. Rosenthal then dispatched the book to one of the country's most distinguished libel lawyers, James Comyn QC, who later became a High Court judge. Many lawyers would have killed it, on the assumption that it was bound to attract a string of writs, but Comyn thought this was such an important story that Secker and Warburg ought to take a risk. Having decoded the manuscript he wrote to Rosenthal:

> This proposed book, even in its heavily edited form, must be regarded as a fairly high risk from the legal point of view . . . The book evolves from and in many ways revolves around Harold Wilson. It has unexpectedly become, for the main part, the story of the Jeremy Thorpe–Norman Scott affair. In regard to that it follows two separate but linked themes: the alleged homosexual relationship between these two people and the efforts to frighten, injure and perhaps even kill Norman Scott.

Comyn paid tribute to Pencourt's diligence but emphasised the dangers if Thorpe chose to sue:

> I have no doubt at all the book alleges a homosexual relationship with Scott. Furthermore, it asserts aggravating circumstances – seduction by Thorpe, a prolonged living together and criminality . . . These are serious allegations but I strongly doubt that Thorpe would sue . . . although I cannot guarantee that. The only consideration I would put against this is my personal judgement that he may have gained some public sympathy of late and that feelings are now running his way against 'the over-persistent Scott' and 'the prolongation of this persecution'.[9]

Comyn said that he was 'far more worried' about the allegation that Thorpe had plotted to kill Scott, which, he said, 'we quite plainly cannot prove'. But he thought that Rosenthal should take a chance.

Pencourt expected that the *Observer* would now tear the manuscript from them so that it could plan the serialisation. But, once again, nothing happened. They could not understand the *Observer's* lack of enthusiasm. They knew that Thorpe was rattled because he had visited Rosenthal a few weeks earlier and demanded to see the manuscript; Rosenthal refused and told him that he would have to wait for it to be published. Once again, Pencourt were punished for the *Observer*'s indecision. The British tabloid press has many faults but it has always been more irreverent than the so-called quality newspapers. While *The Times* and the *Sunday Times* agonised about the morality of asking a Privy Counsellor whether he was a homosexual, the hard men of the tabloids, who were used to examining the seedy underbelly of society, were ordered by their news editors to start digging. They had a major advantage over their colleagues in the broadsheet press since they were able to offer sources large amounts of money.

Dave Miller, who had spoken so frankly to Pencourt, was still worried that he might be charged but he could not resist the opportunity to make a financial killing. He had a criminal record: he was convicted at Cardiff Crown Court in 1972 for unlawful and malicious wounding and for assaulting a police officer and, in December 1975 he was found guilty at Uxbridge Magistrates' Court of obtaining a pecuniary advantage by deception.[10] But that did not worry the *People* newspaper, which paid him £8,000 for his tapes and photographs of his dealings over Newton. On 13 November the *People* ran his story, together with a blurred photograph of Newton being paid his £5,000 'fee' by Le Mesurier the previous April. Pencourt were devastated. They had worked non-stop for many months to crack the story of Rinka but they were in danger of losing everything because the *Observer* would not take them seriously.

CHAPTER SEVENTEEN

Detectives in Bristol who had worked on the investigation two years earlier into the shooting of Rinka the Great Dane groaned at the news that Tony Hetherington, the Director of Public Prosecutions, had ordered an inquiry into Newton's claim that he had been hired to murder Norman Scott. They had not enjoyed the first inquiry into Rinka's death because senior officers, who did not normally bother with such minutiae, had made it clear to them, without actually saying so, that the case should be wrapped up quickly. In late October 1977 the prospects were even less promising. Journalists were crawling over the story and interviewing people whom the police had never heard of, let alone questioned. Detectives in Bristol knew how to nick villains but they were not strong on negotiating with the DPP, Scotland Yard's Special Branch, MI5 and defendants who were on first-name terms with prime ministers.

They had no idea where to begin. Newton had been convicted and was hardly likely to tell them the truth now; and, even if he did, could not be charged again. They could interview Scott but knew from their past encounters that he would explain in gruesome detail how Thorpe had ruined his life. They also suspected, rightly, that Scott did not think much of them after the less than sympathetic way that he had been treated during the Rinka investigation.

But they knew that Thorpe was worried. On 31 October, Daniel Farson, a television interviewer and author who lived in the West Country, described how Thorpe, who was a friend, had tried to use him to discredit Scott.[1] Farson told the police that Thorpe had first talked about Scott before Rinka was shot in October 1975: 'Thorpe said, "Have you heard about my nut in North Devon?" I didn't know what he was talking about. He said, "Norman Scott. The man who keeps persecuting me."' Later Farson met Scott in a local pub; Farson told Thorpe that Scott wanted to destroy his career 'for the sake of England'.

Farson next talked to Thorpe about Scott shortly before
Newton's trial at Exeter in the spring of 1976. Farson said:

> Thorpe expressed an anxiety that, when Newton came to
> trial, Scott would make an outburst in court that would
> cause him further problems. He told me something of Scott's
> background. He mentioned that he had been having trouble
> with Scott over some National Insurance contributions which
> Scott claimed Thorpe owed and he also said Scott was
> blackmailing an MP named Bessell over an affair that he'd
> had with a girl. I found all this incomprehensible. He also
> said that Scott had made an outburst in a Welsh court some
> time previously and was alleging a homosexual affair with
> him [Thorpe] which was not true.

In early May 1976 Thorpe contacted Farson again because he
wanted to stop Scotland Yard returning to Scott the letters that he
had written, including the one in which he declared, 'Bunnies can
(and will) go to France.' Farson said Thorpe drove from London
to have lunch with him:

> He said to me, 'I'm worried about two letters that I've
> written to Scott. They aren't bad news but they're not good
> either. Scotland Yard have the letters and they are going to
> be released.' He said that if the release could be avoided the
> whole affair would blow over in a couple of months. I told him
> that I doubted very much if that would be the case, because, as
> with Watergate, if people knew things were concealed it would
> never blow over. He said that he was thinking of resigning
> the Liberal leadership and fighting again under a new system
> which the Liberals were adopting. I was wondering where
> I fitted in to this and he said, 'I've had legal advice from
> Lord Goodman that if you made a statement saying that
> you'd heard Norman Scott threatened to destroy me then
> Lord Goodman would go to the police with this and that
> the file on Scott would not then be closed, but kept open,
> consequently the two letters would not then be released.'

But Farson refused to help. A few days later, Thorpe sent a message,
asking him to forget the whole matter.

This was interesting but did not lead anywhere. Then Detective

Inspector Don Taylor had a brainwave. He told his boss, Detective Chief Superintendent Michael Challes, that they should ask two journalists called Barrie Penrose and Roger Courtiour for help. Taylor said that he had read somewhere that Penrose and Courtiour were writing a book about the Scott–Thorpe affair and thought that, in the absence of leads, they might be able to help. (The Bristol police were not regular subscribers to *Private Eye* and had not heard the nickname Pencourt but, over the following months, they came to value the *Eye*'s libellous updates on the Thorpe story.)

Challes did not like the idea. It offended his sensibilities as a detective to ask anyone, especially journalists, for assistance. But he had to do something; this was a high-profile case and his superiors wanted action. So Taylor set off to Surrey to meet Pencourt. He spent three hours at Penrose's home. They gave him a child's guide to the conspiracy, minus their complex theories about MI5, the CIA and the South African dimension. They handed him the names and addresses of their sources, including the alleged conspirators, and showed him their files, which he thought were better than anything he had seen in the CID room at Bristol, and said that they would be happy to meet Challes to discuss the matter further.[2]

Pencourt put their professional necks in nooses by helping the police, who could now steam ahead with their investigation. No one could predict when someone would be charged but it was possible that, thanks to Courtiour's files, this would happen before their book was serialised or published. It did not occur to Pencourt that if anyone was charged – or if there was a likelihood of charges – then their story would be killed, stone-dead. The law was unequivocal on this: 'The laws of contempt lay down that where criminal charges are imminent (or made) any comment on a case in a newspaper (or book) may be judged a contempt of court.'[3]

In other words, they would be limited to stating the names and addresses of people who had been charged; they would not be able to write a word about Scott, Bessell, Wilson, MI5 or South Africa.

If they had only been concerned with making money then they would have refused to see Taylor. But this was no longer just a story to them; it had become a matter of honour, verging on obsession, to prove that they had been right about Thorpe. If

anyone had asked them to chose between a bestselling book and
Thorpe's conviction they might well have opted for the latter,
which was unprofessional but public-spirited; it was also bad
news for Thorpe because, without them, the police investigation
might well have foundered.

On 2 November Challes and Detective Superintendent Davey
Greenough, his faithful number two, travelled to Surrey to
meet Pencourt. Once again, Courtiour laid out his files on the
living-room carpet as Penrose outlined their findings. Taylor had
been given a beginner's version but Pencourt thought that, in view
of their seniority, Challes and Greenough could cope with a more
sophisticated analysis. Challes was taller than his oppo. He was
ruddy-faced and could have passed for a farmer on an outing to
the capital. Greenough was shorter, slimmer and, judging from
his flaired trousers, was more fashion-conscious. He also smoked
heavily, to Penrose's despair, and was always rolling tight little
cigarettes.

Pencourt began with Thorpe's seduction of Scott. Then they
moved to the 'retainers' that Bessell had paid, Thorpe's demands
that Scott should be thrown down a disused mine shaft in
Cornwall, Holmes's meetings with Bessell in the States and,
finally, the recruitment of Newton to dispose of Scott. They
explained how they had tracked people down and pieced together
the truth, while the two policemen sat there, delighted that they
had two sources with such splendid files and dismayed that they
needed the help of two journalists, which made a mockery of the
police. They were particularly interested in Courtiour's files on
Bessell. They said that Bessell seemed to be a vital figure, and
looked longingly at the folder which contained his *aide memoire*.
Then they asked Pencourt if they thought that Bessell would see
them in California. They said that they would ask him.

Challes and Greenough headed back to base, to file the names
and addresses that Pencourt had given them.

Challes was always uncomfortable about Pencourt and, at
one point, claimed that he did not even know that they were
journalists.[4] Yet over the next ten months his team often turned
to them for advice or help in locating people whom they wanted to
question. Sometimes the police were so desperate that they asked
Pencourt if they would approach a potential witness to find out
whether he would be prepared to see them and repeat what he had
already told them. (There were few women in the story. Marcia

Falkender was the only female with a starring part in the drama; the others, such as Diane Kelly or Newton's girlfriend Eleanor Rooney, had cameo roles.)

Thanks to Pencourt the police knew that they should start in Wales, with Dave Miller and George Deakin. Challes said:

> Miller was interviewed as many others were, as being a possible defendant, and he was subsequently interviewed on that basis [sic] and I made this plain to him and his solicitor, as part of my proper duty as a police officer. As late as April 1978 he was still regarded as a possible defendant ... I also went to see Mr Deakin at Porthcawl. I went to see him at his invitation on the 18th of November 1977. I believe that by this time there had been substantial press publicity. In any interview I had with Mr Deakin, he always answered the questions I put, in some manner. There was never an occasion when Mr Deakin answered with words of 'No comment' or 'Ditto' or anything of that sort.[5]

But a pall hung over the inquiry. Don Taylor thought that this was a repeat of the Rinka débâcle: 'I always thought it was good to arrest people and then ask them questions. But everyone was worried about political fall-out with this case. Challes and Greenough were in every day with the Chief Constable. I had the feeling that they were fed up with me.'[6] However, he had no further opportunity to protest about the conduct of the case; shortly before Christmas he was promoted and transferred.

Challes and Greenough experienced conflicting emotions when they arrived at Heathrow on Monday, 12 December 1977 for their flight to Los Angeles to interview Bessell. They were excited and proud. Detectives like them might occasionally wangle a trip to London, or if they were very lucky, to Paris, but a mission to the West Coast was unprecedented. On the other hand, they also had the problem of Pencourt, who had employed old-fashioned journalistic wiles after Challes had asked them to arrange an interview with Bessell. They telephoned him in California and said that, in their opinion, he should see the police, but they suggested that he needed independent witnesses, such as themselves, who would ensure that he was fairly treated and that there was no repeat of the 'cover-up' of the Rinka investigation. Bessell agreed and they passed the good and bad news to Bristol: yes, Bessell would see Challes but only if Pencourt were present. But Pencourt did try to minimise Challes' embarrassment. They knew that it might look suspicious if they flew out with him so, after they discovered that he had booked with Pan-Am, they bought tickets with British Airways. Unfortunately, police regulations stated that officers travelling overseas had to use a British carrier; so Challes and Greenough were transferred to the same BA flight as Pencourt. To make matters worse, there was a leak about their expedition to the *Daily Express*, who dispatched a reporter and photographer to Heathrow. Pencourt stayed in the shadows and boarded the flight quietly, while the detectives tried to ignore the press's impertinent questions and popping flashlights.

Twelve hours later Challes and Greenough (and Pencourt) arrived in Los Angeles, exhausted and sweating in their West Country winter suits, and were greeted by Bessell, doing his usual impersonation of a retired Hollywood matinée idol. They were also met by hordes of freelance American journalists, who had been instructed by newsdesks in Fleet Street to get the story, with pictures, of the arrival of the crack British detectives. But the Americans had no idea what was going on and fired off questions at anyone who looked remotely British. Unlike the policemen, Bessell loved the attention, which reminded him of the great days, when he was the high-flying MP for Bodmin and a future millionaire. He said that he had arranged a conference the following afternoon at his lawyer's office in Los Angeles, which was a relief to Challes and Greenough, who were beginning to have doubts about the wisdom of their trip, which was supposed to be secret but was turning into a pantomime. Then they were escorted to a local hotel by their minder, an FBI agent called Larry Campbell, who remained at their side during the next, trying five days. Pencourt, meanwhile, headed off for dinner with Bessell, who was so excited by the day's events that he looked as if he would burst with pleasure.

At 2.30 p.m. the following day Challes and Greenough arrived for the meeting with Bessell at the smart offices in Beverly Hills of his lawyers, Allan Susman and Steven Payne. But Pencourt were also there.

While Challes brooded about the presence of two journalists at what should have been a private discussion between two senior police officers and a witness and his legal advisers Greenough was rolling a cigarette. Smoking had not yet become a semi-criminal activity in California but it was certainly not fashionable. Greenough was oblivious to these niceties and carried on as normal, taping and licking the cigarette into shape. Susman and Payne were fascinated as he fumbled to construct what looked like a joint and decided that British detectives might look stuffy but were actually rather cool because they smoked dope publicly.

Then there was another unhappy misunderstanding, which was recorded by Pencourt's tape recorder. For once this was being used openly, though Challes was obviously not pleased about the machine whirring on the table in front of him. Susman turned to him:

Susman: Chief, do you gentlemen have cards?
Challes: Yes, indeed. Here you are. [Challes and Greenough gave him their warrant cards.] That's my identity card from the constabulary.
Susman: Do you have personal cards?
Challes: We don't have those . . . they are our personal cards.
Susman: Can we keep them?
Challes: Keep them? No, I'm afraid not!
Susman: [He got up and walked to the door.] Then, if you don't mind, I'll have these Xeroxed.

Susman handed the cards to a secretary and returned to his seat, unaware of the gravity of what had happened. Warrant cards were more precious than passports, or National Insurance cards, and policemen never gave them to anyone. Now Challes and Greenough had lost them and were crestfallen; they sat there, saying nothing, hoping that the cards would be swiftly returned. (They were.)

This lull in the interview allowed Bessell to draw his usual vivid character sketches:

Michael Challes was in his early 50s, heavily built and was far removed from the popular conception of a senior British police investigator. His informal manner was matched by a ready, open smile. But his most striking feature was his keen blue eyes. Naturally kind, when he was angry or suspected duplicity they became ice-cold and penetrating. Despite my earlier reservations and suspicions, I liked him instantly. His rich West Country accent, the fact that we were both born in Somerset and that he had begun his police service on the beat in my home town, Bath, demolished many barriers.

Davey Greenough was a small, compact man. He was also highly intelligent and likeable. As with Challes, unimportant bonds played their part in establishing our relationship. His love of dogs and consuming interest in wildlife were concerns to which I responded. In the months that followed I came to trust both Challes and Greenough implicitly and had no reason to believe my judgement was wrong.[7]

The meeting was also a forum for Bessell to explain, at length and without interruption, his theories on the delicate balance between public duty and the obligations of friendship, subjects on which, he believed, he spoke well and controversially. But Challes was more anxious to find out whether he was prepared to return to Britain to give evidence and so, when Bessell paused for breath, he sneaked in the question: Would Mr Bessell come back to Britain if necessary?

But that was far too straightforward for Bessell, who issued this agonised statement:

> I am not prepared at this stage to give any sort of undertaking that I will give evidence in Britain but, on the other hand, I don't want you to interpret that as meaning I will not do so because I would be guided very much by how events transpire over the next few months as your inquiry proceeds. If the situation arose where you felt you were able to satisfy me that unless I was in Britain and prepared to give evidence there might be, let us say, inaccurate justice in a sense that one who has responsibility might get away with something which we would all think was wrong then I might indeed be persuaded that my evidence was crucial and come back. But at this stage I want to keep my options open and I make no secret of the fact that this whole thing has been kept low-key and there has been something very close to a cover-up at a very high level and in those circumstances I am not prepared to make a fool of myself.

Poor Challes listened patiently as Bessell droned on and waited for a chance to show that, though he was only a policeman from Bristol, he understood the Big Issues raised by the case. He said, 'Perhaps a lot of what you tell us will fall into moral grounds or even political grounds and some will fall into criminal grounds, because the moral and political grounds are of interest to me because they show background. I am here seeking evidence for facts in regard to criminal activities, but I can't divorce the three.'

Then he turned to the investigation into Rinka's death, which, he confessed, had been unsatisfactory 'because we couldn't get the starts we wanted'. This time would be different: 'I'm looking at myself now and protecting myself. I am out to uncover what there is to be uncovered. If there's nothing under a stone when I turn it over, well, then there's nothing under it. I don't want another inquiry in three years' time by someone else. If there are criminal proceedings arising out of this involving others, well, I'm sorry, it's got to be aired.'

He was angry about the media and said that it would help everyone if Pencourt were banned from future discussions. He said:

I am making no statement whatsoever and when I was accosted at the airport I made it quite clear to them [reporters] because they were saying, Mr Challes, can we get together and I said look, I am not giving any interview, I am not giving any statements and any future statements that we decide to make will be issued through my press office in Bristol, England. Throughout this inquiry the press have tried to make this a public inquiry and I have tried to stop it being public.

Bessell nodded and said that he agreed, but, then again, he said that the media had a job to do. Privately, of course, he loved being the centre of attention but, to his credit, he said that he would not drop Pencourt now, since they had taken him seriously when everyone dismissed him as a fantasist:

I have worked together on this closely with them over the last year and they have been enormously helpful to me in giving advance warning of things that were happening in England. We're very much in this together and I regard them as close colleagues and their advice and help has been invaluable. Mr Courtiour and Mr Penrose, as you know, are journalists

and know more than Harold Wilson. They have documented
the stuff in a way that I admire.

But Challes scored a minor victory when Bessell enquired whether
he might be offered immunity from civil actions by his creditors in
Britain; Challes sniffed and said that he did not have the authority
to discuss this.

The meeting broke up shortly after 4 p.m. but it achieved
nothing, apart from leaving Bessell with a hefty bill which he
could not pay. Indeed, Pencourt suspected that he had hired
high-powered lawyers simply to impress his visitors and the pack
of reporters camped outside the office.

Next day, Challes and Greenough, who had booked into a
Holiday Inn nearby in San Diego, arrived at Oceanside. Bessell
now owned four holiday bungalows, which he had bought with
Diane's father's money, and named Cornwall, Devon, Somerset
and Dorset. Once again, to Challes' displeasure, Pencourt were
present. The rest of the media were marooned outside while
the quintet talked for the next three days. They spent most
of the time in the living room of Dorset, the curtains drawn
to prevent photographers capturing the dramatic scene inside:
Bessell pontificating, sipping tea and puffing on cigarettes, Challes
and Greenough scribbling notes, Courtiour leafing through his files
and Penrose staring into the distance, telling himself that he must
not fall asleep because he was witnessing a seminal moment in
British political history.

Bessell insisted on reading from his 60,000-word *aide memoire*
because he said that this was the only way that Challes and
Greenough would understand 'the background and context'
of what had happened. They would have preferred a simple
statement, which they could have used as evidence, but had no
choice and had to listen as he droned on, hour after hour. But,
by the end of the week, they could see what he meant about the
complications of the case and were frantically copying sections of
the *aide memoire*, which they then Sellotaped into one seamless
whole, helped by the master-filer, Courtiour. They told Bessell
that he had given them valuable leads, which they would have
to follow up in Britain; Challes said that he would be back in
Oceanside in the near future to take a formal statement.

This was Pencourt's opportunity to prove to the rest of Fleet
Street that they were still ahead of the pack. On Sunday, 18

December, almost a year after it had bought the serial rights to their book, the *Observer* finally carried a story by them. It was headlined: 'I'll give evidence, Bessell tells police', and described how Pencourt had, exclusively, witnessed Bessell's meetings with the police. They summarised his allegations and slipped in the names of Dave Miller, George Deakin and John Le Mesurier. But it was not an unmitigated triumph. The newspaper censored Pencourt's material; in October, in response to the *Evening News*'s story on Newton, Pencourt had reported that David Holmes was implicated in the plot to kill Scott but now, in December, the newspaper decided not to name Holmes; for no obvious reason, the *Observer* described him as 'a Liberal Party member'. Thorpe was referred to as 'Mr X'. The *Observer* said that Pencourt were writing a book which was due to be published in the New Year, but omitted to mention that it was contracted to serialise it, which showed that senior executives there, who thought that Thorpe was a fine man, still hoped to persuade Trelford to drop Pencourt.

Challes was furious when he read their front-page account of his expedition to California and complained that he was as shocked as anyone that two reporters had infiltrated a confidential discussion between police officers and a witness. He forgot to mention that Pencourt had arranged the meeting and, instead, insisted, 'On no occasion did I spend the evening with Bessell or the journalists while I was in California,' though this was irrelevant. He concluded, 'There has been so much publication of articles that I have gone beyond shock.'

Private Eye also read the *Observer* and pointed out that Trelford seemed half-hearted about Pencourt. The magazine said, 'There were a series of omissions in the story which any *Eye* reader could spot. For instance, by use of the "Mr X" and "a Liberal", Pencourt avoid mention not only of the Rt. Hon. Jeremy Thorpe but also David Holmes, "merchant banker" and former deputy treasurer of the Liberal Party.'[8]

Challes' public protests about Pencourt did not, however, affect his private relationship with them. Early in January he asked Norman Scott if he would meet him. Scott was delighted that the police were finally taking him seriously but had no intention of making it easy for them. He told Challes that he would be prepared to be interviewed, but only if Pencourt were present. Challes needed Scott so he agreed. Scott telephoned Pencourt. He said that he had just spoken to Challes: 'I told him that if Bessell

had Pencourt then I wanted them, too. What is good enough for
Peter Bessell is good enough for me.'

On 9 January, Challes and Greenough set off from Bristol for
Scott's home at Teigncombe, on the edge of Dartmoor. The journey
took longer than anticipated because they got lost and they arrived
at tea time, to find Penrose and Courtiour chatting with Scott
and Hilary Arthur, while Briony gurgled in the background. To
compound the nightmare, news of the interview had leaked to the
rest of the media and reporters and photographers were staking
out the cottage.

Challes began by saying that he was anxious that the conversation did not become public. He looked at Pencourt hopefully, but
they smiled and said nothing. Scott wanted parity with Bessell; he
knew that Pencourt had taped the meetings in California and asked
them to turn on their machine, which further irritated Challes. But
Challes had a job to do. So he gave his opening address: 'You
will appreciate that back in 1975 certain inquiries were done
and were never brought to any satisfactory conclusion. That's
been the problem and we're going right over it again. We want
to start at the beginning and end at the end if we can.' He said that
it would obviously take a long time to run through Scott's story
and moved to the problem of 'outsiders'. He said, 'It is common
practice in this country to talk to witnesses separately. I would
be a bit reluctant for others to be here because there could be
all sorts of allegations and repercussions. It might be said that
you [Pencourt] were here to make sure your book was alright.
My brief is to find out what the true facts are. We're not after
conclusions or opinions but hard facts which will stand up.'

There was silence. Scott smiled, Briony whimpered and Pencourt
did not do the decent thing and leave. Challes decided to press
on and hope that his interview with Scott was not plastered
over the next morning's newspapers, which would not please
his superiors:

I don't want to embarrass anybody at all but we're going
right back over it starting at the beginning. What I want
to be able to say and ensure at the end of the day is that
there is not going to be another inquiry. We are charged with
looking at everything right from start to finish and therefore
it does, of necessity, mean we have to go right back to the
very beginning, Norman. There are a lot of things I want to

clear up. You know, Norman, we've been chopping about all over the place. What I would like to do, Norman, is go back to the very beginning. When's your birthday?

As Scott ran through the story that Penrose had heard many times before he felt his eyes closing. He decided that he had to get some air before he fell asleep and sneaked outside. Courtiour remained on duty in the cottage, alert as ever, as Scott grappled with the perennial problems of his sexuality: 'At the time I hadn't had deeply homosexual relationships but I think I had homosexual feelings. But I also had heterosexual relationships with ladies . . .' This went on for several hours until Challes and Greenough decided that they heard enough, thanked Scott and said that it had been very instructive. Pencourt, meanwhile, did not even bother to transcribe their tapes.

The Pencourt File had now been sent to the printers, for publication in the New Year. Tom Rosenthal, was convinced that there was more than enough new material, notably on Harold Wilson and on the genesis of the plot to murder Scott, to satisfy the *Observer* that it had made a wise investment. In mid-January the newspaper decided to begin serialisation. Then Trelford changed his mind. Pencourt could not understand why he still had reservations about the book, though they suspected that Lord Goodman was behind the decision.

Tom Rosenthal was furious. Trelford wrote to him, justifying the decision not to serialise: he said that it was not the book that he had expected and that he was worried about 'authenticity'. Rosenthal fired off a fierce reply:

In the course of our very pleasant lunch at the Savoy Grill on February 17 1977 I described, I hope succinctly, the overall ramifications of the book . . . and you and your colleagues were given, and took ample opportunity to satisfy yourselves as to the *nature* of the contents and the *authenticity* of the contents before committing yourselves to serialisation. Since that time there has been no radical change of direction in the book, nor has there to date been a single instance of any statement by the authors being proved wrong. Thus we cannot accept any reservations at all either about the nature of the book or its accuracy.[9]

It was kind of Trelford, Rosenthal continued, not to ask for the return of the £50,000 fee but this was not just about money; Pencourt's pride and reputation had been damaged by the *Observer's* decision:

> The fact is that you have been in possession of some very extraordinary journalistic material which for some months you could have used but did not, only for us and the authors to see ourselves 'scooped', literally time after time, in other newspapers. This has resulted in, to put it mildy, adverse comments on the credibility of the book, our publishing house and the authors, and the authors have been particularly disturbed by the fact that on at least two occasions they have produced good extra stories which the *Observer* has then not printed, one of which, to their intense chagrin, appearing subsequently, piecemeal, in three other newspapers . . . Barrie and Roger also feel somewhat under-appreciated because of the relative lack of prominence given to them personally by the *Observer* at a time when they were producing extraordinarily good material and because of the mildly persuasive aura of doubt as to the authenticity of the material they presented.

News of Trelford's decision swept Fleet Street. Several newspapers decided that, now that the *Observer* had bottled out, they would take advantage. Editors dispatched limousines and executives with blank cheque books to Penrose's home in Sanderstead, with the brief to buy the book, no matter how much it cost. First on the scene was the *Daily Mirror*, represented by Terence Lancaster, the respected political editor, and Joe Haines, Wilson's former press spokesman, who had joined the newspaper the year before. The *Mirror* had been chasing the Thorpe–Scott story with almost as much energy as Pencourt and was determined to acquire the book, which it believed contained the missing pieces of the Thorpe jigsaw, though, like the *Observer*, it was really more interested in the sensational material on Wilson and MI5.

A few hours later the *Mirror* agreed a fee of £50,000 (*about £150,000 in 1995*) for serialisation with Gordon Fielden, Pencourt's literary agent, who specialised in German literature and who had never struck big-money deals with national newspapers. The *Mirror* immediately began to organise a week of extracts from *The Pencourt File*. It also arranged a publicity campaign, the centrepiece of which were television advertisements of Pencourt, Britain's answer to Woodward and Bernstein, stalking Downing Street. It had taken many months of isolation and ridicule but that week in late January they were spectacularly rehabilitated.

Pencourt, meanwhile, had one difficult task to perform: they had to let Wilson know that they had written a book that proved that he had been conned by Thorpe. On Tuesday, 24 January they arrived at his new office in Parliament Street, for their first meeting with him since the summer. They exchanged pleasantries with Falkender and him about the pregnancy of Courtiour's wife and Penrose's passion for horses and settled down to discuss their book. It was a gloomy occasion, matched by the surroundings; the office had not yet been decorated and looked as if it belonged to a minor Whitehall functionary. Former American presidents enjoy large pensions, fat book contracts and lucrative lecture tours, the fawning attentions of major corporations and Secret-Service guards but British ex-prime ministers are discarded. If they are independently wealthy, like Alec Douglas-Home, or commercially astute, like Margaret Thatcher, they survive the trauma of life after Downing Street, but Wilson was neither and seemed to have shrunk since Pencourt had listened, mesmerised, when he had explained that he was 'the big fat spider in the corner of the room'.

Pencourt had agreed beforehand that it would be prudent not to mention the *Mirror*'s forthcoming serialisation; they feared that Wilson might ask someone, such as the ubiquitous Lord Goodman, for advice, which might threaten the deal with the *Mirror*. But, apart from this pragmatic omission, they were frank with him. They told Wilson and Falkender that they had believed at first that Thorpe was the victim of a South African plot. But slowly they had pieced together the truth: Thorpe had ordered Scott's murder. Penrose tried to soften the blow and said that the book was not only about Thorpe. He added that South Africa was still an important element in the story; it was just that Thorpe had not been framed. He said:

The book will surprise because it is not just the wretched Thorpe–Scott affair. We've put flesh on, for example, South Africa in the sense that, for example, those men in Washington . . . you remember the Trans-World news agency telling stories about you, Thorpe and Edward Heath. These were stories with documents that came from Whitehall which could not possibly have been with agencies in Washington unless they came from official sources . . .

Wilson rallied briefly: 'Maybe Holmes is tied up with South Africa . . . Why did Newton go to Rhodesia of all places? He could easily have gone to Brussels, Copenhagen, Singapore, Hong Kong.' But then he gave up: 'I think that people will see me as naive in not realising what was going on. But you don't suggest anywhere I knew about the murder?' Pencourt assured him that they were sure that he was innocent. Wilson began rambling again, appalled that he had fallen for Thorpe's story: 'I was involved with Jeremy very much on what I believed to be, and still have reason to think, was the South Africans pushing around the place and that was that. At no point was there was any suspicion in my mind that they were involved in murder. If I had thought that I would have gone to the Metropolitan Commissioner of Police or the Attorney-General.'[10]

Penrose tried to console him: 'We started off on the wrong premise, that the Liberals were innocent. But as we checked Scott it became disturbing because the facts were turning a lot of Thorpe's statements on the head. We know we must have become a terrible embarrassment to you because we seem to have found the wrong hare.' Wilson mumbled, 'Yes, we all chased the wrong hare.'

On Monday, 30 January, the *Daily Mirror* opened its serialisation of *The Pencourt File* with four pages of huge headlines and dramatic allegations. It said:

Today the *Mirror* begins the astonishing story of the inquiry that took two young reporters through Britain's corridors of power. The reporters, Barrie Penrose and Roger Courtiour, became known as Pencourt. They document their stories in a book called *The Pencourt File*. It is a story of espionage and intrigue. A human story. Above all, it is the real-life British drama of Whitehall behind closed doors.[11]

That week the *Mirror* demonstrated that tabloid journalism could tackle serious issues as well as the quality broadsheets. It extracted the main revelations from the morass of mind-scrambling detail and treated its readers to a week of high-class investigative journalism. Other newspapers held their breath and waited, hoping that the

Mirror would make a mistake but, by Wednesday, they were forced, with gritted teeth, to follow up *The Pencourt File*.

There was a brief crisis when Falkender protested after the first extract that Pencourt had exaggerated or misunderstood Wilson and her; but then the *Mirror* revealed that they had heard the tape recordings that Pencourt had made of the meetings and she retreated. Three days of the serialisation were devoted to Wilson, his fears about MI5 and assorted reader-friendly spy stories.

The *Mirror* spent two days on the more complicated Thorpe story and gave the fullest account yet of the conspiracy; Pencourt did not directly accuse him of masterminding the plot to kill Scott although that was the only conclusion that could be drawn from the story. Unlike the *Observer*, the *Mirror* did not mince around when it tackled the Scott affair. Its front-page headline was: 'Enter the Godfather.' It named David Holmes as the man who had had 'shadowy dealings with the gunman, Andrew Newton'. The newspaper also identified John Le Mesurier, George Deakin and Dave Miller as key figures.

Other newspapers waited for Holmes or Thorpe to issue a writ for libel. But nothing happened. And, from that moment, in the village of Fleet Street, opinion began to shift; editors, who had always assumed that Scott was mad and that Pencourt were silly conspiracy-mongers, suggested to their executives that it might be worth 'looking at' the whole story afresh, just in case Pencourt were right. The broadsheet press, whose support had been crucial to Thorpe, now began to back off, for example, the *Sunday Times* ran a two-page story, headlined: 'The Scott affair: the dog, the gun and the money. The basic facts in the mystery that won't go away. The South Wales Connection: was there a plot to kill?'[12]

Pencourt were determined that Thorpe should not wriggle to safety and privately continued to help Challes in an effort to make sure that the police inquiry did not founder. Late in January they persuaded Tony and Donald Johnson, the brothers from Essex who discovered the cache of letters when they were decorating Bessell's flat in November 1974, to meet Challes.

On Tuesday, 31 January Challes telephoned to thank Penrose for fixing the meeting, which had been 'well worthwhile', and to assure him that the police would not arrest anyone before *The Pencourt File* was in the bookshops. Penrose asked him whether he would hit 'the jackpot' and charge Thorpe. He replied, 'That's almost an impossible question to answer truthfully. So much will depend on how things progress from now on in. I mean, some days we think there are good signs and the next day we fall flat on our face and the next day we pick ourselves up. You know, it is so much in the melting pot but you know our views well enough. You know the ends to which we are working.' Finally, Challes emphasised that he would not jeopardise the book: 'You can rest assured nothing is going to happen this week or the early part of next week. I am prepared to sit on other people until the books are in the bookshops. This is the way I would anticipate playing things, if it suits you.'

Like Pencourt, Challes imagined that the book would rock the Establishment but, like wolves, reviewers ripped it to shreds. Most critics simply judged it as a book, not as the culmination of a brave crusade by two freelance journalists. Some, like David Holloway, writing in the *Daily Telegraph*, were also offended by the idea that public figures like Jeremy Thorpe, MP, PC, could behave in the manner alleged by Pencourt: 'Pencourt's wholescale scattering of half-formulated assertions of interference and covering-up, not to say murder plots, merely confuses the issue. If indeed there is an issue.' But a few were more charitable, such as the novelist Julian Symonds, who concluded his long and funny review in the *Sunday Times* with this observation: 'A serious investigation lies beneath the candyfloss. Badly written and sensational as much of the story is, Pencourt did uncover some things – about the possible murder plot and the astonishing behaviour of some Liberals – that it was in the public interest to make known.'[13]

The book did, however, briefly excite politicians in Britain. Tories accused Wilson of damaging national security by talking about – and criticising in a wholly unjustified manner – Britain's intelligence services. Labour MPs, meanwhile, were outraged that a Labour prime minister had been smeared by right-wing extremists in MI5 and called for an investigation. Liberal MPs said nothing.[14]

But Michael Challes and Davey Greenough took no notice of the smart literary critics or the politicians. They plodded on, determined to find out why poor Rinka had been shot.

CHAPTER EIGHTEEN

The sensational stories about dirty tricks by MI5, murder plots and Jeremy Thorpe were soon forgotten by the public, though Pencourt continued to probe the mystery of Rinka. It was now a battle of wits between the police and Thorpe. As Challes plodded on, collecting and filing evidence, Thorpe darted around, begging and threatening people, including Jack Hayward and David Holmes, either to lie or to say nothing. This was a sustained bid to pervert the course of justice, which was a serious crime in itself, and revealed the real Thorpe: a man for whom the law was something that could be fixed if it went wrong, like a flat tyre.

On 5 March Challes and Greenough returned to Oceanside, this time without Pencourt, to take a statement from Bessell and to beg him to return to Britain if there was a trial. Challes told him: 'We don't have a case without you. We couldn't obtain a conviction on your evidence alone but, as we see things, at present you're our principal witness.' But the idea of appearing in court as the main witness against Thorpe did not appeal to him. He said, 'They'll pelt me with rotten eggs.' Greenough tactlessly agreed: 'Quite likely. You should see some of the letters we get.' This was the fatal flaw in the investigation. Bessell was the police's main source but Challes should have realised that he would be ripped apart in the witness box. He was a self-confessed cheat and serial liar and had bought Scott's silence with his 'retainers'. He claimed that Thorpe had talked to him and Holmes in the Commons about killing Scott but it was his word against Thorpe's and there was no doubt who would have more credibility with a jury. Next, he said that Holmes had told him that he had recruited Newton to kill Scott, at Thorpe's behest. But without Holmes's corroboration this was worthless hearsay.

It should have been obvious to Challes that the only man who could send Thorpe to prison was Holmes. He could corroborate Bessell's allegations about Thorpe's various schemes to dispose of

Scott and could explain how Newton was hired. Unlike Bessell, he
was 'respectable' and had no reason to lie. If he could be persuaded
to tell the truth in court then Thorpe would struggle to convince
a jury that it had all been a joke. But Challes' expedition to
the West Coast did produce one vital new lead when Bessell
mentioned that he had always wondered whether Thorpe had,
somehow, paid Newton by diverting donations to the Liberals from
a multi-millionaire called Jack Hayward, who lived in the Bahamas.
Challes nodded, noted Hayward's name and returned to the main
question: would Mr Bessell return to Britain for a trial?

Thorpe was faster to spot the danger posed by Hayward and
by the two letters that he had sent to the Bahamas in March
1974 and in April the following year, asking Hayward to send
two payments of £10,000 to Nadir Dinshaw, whom he described
as his son's godfather and who was 'conveniently resident in
Jersey'. Naturally, he had lied to Hayward about the reasons for
this financial manoeuvre. He had said that he might, perhaps,
have broken the rules governing a candidate's general election
expenses, which was so easy when you were also the leader of
a national party, and that Dinshaw would safely be able to pay
the 'ambiguous' bills which he had run up. He did not inform
Hayward that the money was going to his friend, David Holmes,
to buy letters from Scott and then to hire someone to kill him. He
felt queasy when he thought about these two letters, handwritten
on House of Commons notepaper and undeniable. Thorpe was not
worried about Hayward, who was so rich that he had probably
forgotten about the £20,000, but he was terrified that Bessell
would pop up in London and start talking, which might lead the
police to the Caribbean. So he telephoned Hayward in Freeport
and asked if he could fly to the Bahamas to see him; Hayward
said that there was no need, because he would be in London
soon. They arranged to meet at his solicitor's office in Pall Mall
on 4 April. Hayward recalled, 'Thorpe asked me to put pressure
on Mr Bessell for the money he owed me [£35,000] and threaten
that if he came back to this country I would serve a writ on him for
bankruptcy, which would ostensibly prevent him from returning
to the United States as an undesirable, where he had, of course,
a girlfriend. I didn't take any action against Mr Bessell at all.'[1]
He could not understand why Thorpe wanted to prevent Bessell
returning to England; as far as he knew, he had no intention of

leaving California and no money to do so anyway. He shrugged and concluded that they had fallen out for some unknown reason and returned to the Caribbean.

Thorpe was like a man trying to stem the leaks from a dyke; as soon as he repaired one hole another one appeared. Holmes now threatened to break ranks and tell the truth, which was not surprising since he feared that, if anyone was going to face criminal charges, it would be he and not Thorpe.

In mid-March Challes was telephoned by Sam Hall, a journalist who had been reporting the Thorpe case for Independent Television News. Hall said that he had been told by a colleague at ITN, who lived in Folkestone, close to Holmes's parents, that Holmes had just turned up on his doorstep. Hall told Challes:

> My colleague said that Holmes appeared and was shaking with rage. Holmes said, 'If you want to know where the money came from, it was from Jack Hayward in the Bahamas. He passed it to a man called Nadir Dinshaw in Jersey, who lives at St Brelades Bay. Dinshaw brought it to London in several lots of cash, £400 and £500 at a time.' Holmes said that he wanted the information passed to the police but did not want them to know where it had come from. Then he disappeared into the night.[2]

Holmes later explained: 'Jeremy had thanked me for keeping his name out of it all. He consoled me, saying, "I've made enquiries and if things go wrong you shouldn't get more than seven years. With good conduct you'd be out in four and a half – and you must agree there doesn't seem much point in both of us going down."'[3]

Challes should have rushed off to interview Holmes, who was apparently tired of being used by Thorpe. But he did not because he was investigating an MP and a Privy Counsellor and had to proceed more cautiously than if he had been probing, say, an armed robbery. So, he made more time-consuming inquiries in an effort to find the evidence that would convince his twitchy superiors that the former deputy treasurer of the Liberal Party should be pulled in for questioning.

Finally, on 1 April, Challes decided to swoop. Unfortunately, he could not find Holmes and had to turn to Pencourt for assistance. He telephoned Penrose and said that Holmes had disappeared from his home in Manchester, which he shared with Gerald Hagan.

He said, 'It did seem he left in haste. I don't think he's pulling out, Barrie, but something happened and he left the North. It's extremely odd and came as something of a shock to us. If I could find him I'd go and see him. What I don't want, Barrie, under any circumstances, is a solicitor involved initially. I want to drop in on him, as it were.' The law then allowed Challes to question suspects without a solicitor being present and Penrose promised to try and locate Holmes. This was a classic journalistic deception since Penrose knew very well that Holmes had a flat in Eaton Place, Belgravia, where he always stayed when he was in London. Next day Greenough and Penrose struck a deal: Holmes's address in return for Pencourt being allowed to monitor the arrest. Greenough thought that this was fair and also sensible since Pencourt would be able to confirm that they had picked up the right man.

Challes later explained why he had asked for help from them:

When I arrived at Mr Holmes's home on April 3rd, 1978, this was without appointment and I was accompanied by Superintendent Greenough. Mr Penrose and Mr Courtiour were also in the area because they had shown us where Mr Holmes lived – I was not aware of his address . . . It did spring to mind that D.J. Freeman & Co. were potential solicitors for Mr Holmes. I didn't want to interview D.J. Freeman & Co., I wanted to interview Mr Holmes. Mr Holmes had not made any communication to me that I was to contact him through solicitors. It was not the best course for me to contact a firm of solicitors D. J. Freeman & Co. – who could possibly be the solicitors acting for Mr Holmes. I needed anybody's [sic] help as to Mr Holmes's address. I telephoned a variety of people in an endeavour to contact Mr Holmes and this included one or other of Mr Penrose and Mr Courtiour and many other journalists. Neither of those two people gave me the address. I don't know why not – they would not give it to me – I suggest you ask them. They offered to take us and point out the house where Mr Holmes was, at that time, residing, in order that I could see Mr Holmes and, as far as I was concerned at that time, it was the best way. I went to the area with Mr Penrose and Mr Courtiour – or rather, to be more particular, they drove their car and I followed but it was never my intention that they should be present when I interviewed or arrested Mr Holmes.[4]

Pencourt had summoned a photographer from the *Daily Mirror*, who snapped Holmes being led away by two detectives, which was a welcome development in the static Thorpe story. Challes said that he could not be blamed for this: 'They hadn't photographers with them when I left them. When we came out of the house a few minutes later, there was a photographer there. I remember Mr Holmes expressing distress to me that Mr Courtiour and Mr Penrose should be there. I think he was expressing more distress because a photographer was present.' Holmes was driven to Bristol. He was questioned for two days but did not break. Despite Challes' efforts, Holmes's solicitor soon arrived to advise his client, which ensured that the police obtained nothing of value. Holmes answered a few questions but mostly replied 'No comment,' 'No comment on that' or, 'No comment on that at all.'

Challes was too late; Thorpe had convinced Holmes that they would all be safe, providing that they admitted nothing. But Holmes was not rock-solid; he was a fastidious man and would probably have cracked if he had been treated like an ordinary suspect. After a few hours in custody in Bristol he complained: 'I was appalled by the conditions which people in custody are expected to endure. After a night in the cell at Bristol police station I had to have medical treatment for bed bugs.'

Two days later Challes tried Le Mesurier, the carpet salesman. But he was even less talkative. On his solicitor's advice he refused to say anything, apart from, 'nothing to say.' On 10 May Challes had another tilt at Holmes. But he added nothing to what he had already said and, to Challes' dismay, replied, 'No comment,' to questions that he had answered the previous month.

Some officers in Bristol felt that Challes was out of his depth. They argued that, if they treated ordinary criminals with the consideration which he was showing people like Holmes, then the courts would be empty. Don Taylor, who had been promoted and taken off the Thorpe inquiry, said, 'Everyone was pussyfooting. Challes and Greenough wouldn't stick their necks out. If Thorpe had been anyone else we'd have said let's nick him, let's get him and stick him in the cells. But that never happened. They came in by appointment. Well, you never get anything like that, do you? You've got to get them counting tiles in the cell.'

Even Kenneth Steele, Chief Constable of Avon and Somerset, conceded that it was a sensitive investigation:

We were in a delicate situation and were not going to charge around like a bull in a china shop. It was tricky because of the personalities involved, including a well-known public figure. We were not going to rush things and risk adverse publicity. It is not unusual when you are dealing with people of standing to make appointments. They may be difficult to get hold of and the only way to be certain that they will be available when you want to see them is to agree a date.[5]

Thorpe, however, was fighting in a very ungentlemanly fashion. He turned to his friend Nadir Dinshaw (the shy, God-fearing, Karachi-born businessman who lived in Jersey). Earlier that year he had told Dinshaw that, if he was asked about the £20,000, he should say that it had been part of a business deal with Hayward. Dinshaw said that he would not lie. In mid-April Thorpe returned to the attack. He told Dinshaw that he would be ruined unless he helped. Dinshaw repeated that he would have to tell the truth, which drew this response from Thorpe: 'It will be curtains for me and you will be asked to move on.' Dinshaw was stunned by the suggestion that he might be thrown out of Jersey for telling the truth. But, as a Christian, he refused to condemn Thorpe: 'When people are in desperate straits they do desperate things. Our Lord tells us very clearly not to judge people. I am sure that being gay forced him to act like this. It was a very painful thing to happen. He let me down but I cannot feel anger.'[6] But he would not lie and a few days later he told the police about Hayward's £20,000, sent to him on Thorpe's instructions and paid to Holmes.

Thorpe even enlisted the help of his old Oxford friend Michael Ogle, to try and re-arrange the truth. He asked Ogle, who did not, of course, have any idea what was happening, to 'remind' Holmes about the £20,000. He told Ogle a complex and fictitious story, which involved various loans that Holmes had made to him and problems with 'election expenses'. Ogle met Holmes several times and repeated Thorpe's story about the money. But Holmes was not satisfied and said that he feared that he would be charged by the police. Finally, he told Ogle that he wanted to meet Thorpe to discuss this but Thorpe's lawyers refused to allow this.

Thorpe was running out of options. The police now contacted Hayward in the Bahamas and asked him about the £20,000. Hayward wrote to Thorpe: 'I said that Challes had called me and asked me about two payments of £10,000. I said that I was very worried and asked him what was going on. He wrote back and said that he had no idea.'[7] Like many people, Thorpe underestimated Hayward. He was a tough businessman who could look after himself and did not believe Thorpe; he spoke to his trusted partner, Edward St George, who was in London. St George advised him to meet Challes as soon as possible.

As he flew across the Atlantic, Hayward realised that the letters from Thorpe, in which he had given precise instructions about the transfer of the £20,000 to Nadir Dinshaw in Jersey, proved that he, Hayward, was not involved in whatever crime the police thought that Thorpe might have committed. Hayward recalled:

> I had always kept the letters in a drawer by my bed at my farm in Sussex. My wife had said to me that she needed the space for my socks and underpants and handkerchiefs and said I should get rid of them because they were so old. But thank God I didn't. I put them in an old suitcase in the box room. They saved my bacon. If I hadn't kept them the police might have thought that I knew where my money was going.[8]

He arranged to meet Challes and Greenough at the Tate Gallery in London, where Leonard 'Nipper' Reid, a legendary Scotland Yard detective, worked as a security adviser. Hayward said that Challes and Greenough were ecstatic when they read the letters from Thorpe: 'You could tell what they were thinking: We've got him now! They were very pleased and were almost having orgasms. I took out the letters, one by one. Challes said, "This is what we wanted. They are the last piece in the jigsaw. They prove where the money went."' Now that he had the letters Challes was in chatty, off-the-record mood. He could not understand how Hayward could be so vague about £20,000, which was more than his annual salary. Edward St George laughed and said that Jack had no idea how much he gave away each year; he had even lent Bessell £35,000 because he felt sorry for him.

Then Hayward asked about Scott:

> I said to Challes that this chap Scott must be a revolting character. Challes said that the first thing that Scott did when you met him was to get out the photographs of himself as a young man. Challes said, 'I am not that way inclined but, boy, I can see the attraction of Scott if you are of that persuasion.'

I said that Newton must have been trying to frighten Scott. But Challes said that that was balderdash. He said that they had tested the gun again and again and it jammed regularly. He said that he was sure that if the gun hadn't jammed then Scott would have got the second bullet.

Challes closed in on Thorpe. On 3 June he questioned him at Bath police station in the presence of his new solicitor, Sir David Napley, a former president of the Law Society. Thorpe handed Challes a five page statement. As usual he thought that the truth could be buried beneath a mountain of tautologies and maladroit legal jargon. He denied everything: the affair with Scott, knowledge of the 'retainer' that Bessell had paid, the recruitment of Newton and the siphoning of Hayward's money to Newton. This was a typical passage:

> I wish with no less emphasis entirely to refute any suggestion that I have at any time been a party to any conspiracy to kill or injure Norman Scott or to put him in fear, or that at any time I had any knowledge of or believed in the existence of any such conspiracy. Quite apart from the fact that any desire or willingness to kill or cause harm to any person is wholly alien to my nature, as many would be prepared to confirm, the circumstances which existed at the time when it was subsequently suggested that such a conspiracy may have existed are wholly inconsistent with the alleged pursuit of such a conspiracy.[9]

He added that he would not make any further comment, though he did put it as simply as this:

> Having regard to the unusual way in which these current allegations have emerged there is a real danger that, if specific details relating to matters which can be proved are made known at the present time, they may in the course of the investigation become known or deduced by those minded to further the allegations, with consequent re-adjustment of their version. In these circumstances, I have been advised that whilst it is right and proper that I should re-express the denials which are contained in this statement, it is neither incumbent upon me nor desirable to add anything further.

Nonetheless, Challes pressed on with his prepared questions. Thorpe suggested that, rather than trying to think of different ways to refuse to answer, he should merely say, 'Ditto.' Challes agreed and continued with his questions, echoed by Thorpe repeating, 'Ditto.' It was not a satisfactory interview; even less satisfactory, from Challes' point of view, was the fact that *Private Eye* appeared to have been given a transcript. The *Eye* dubbed Thorpe 'The Ditto Man', which was funny but unhelpful to the police because it suggested that they were leaking to the media, which defence lawyers would certainly exploit if the case ever came to trial. Challes was furious again:

> I agree that whoever wrote the story [in *Private Eye*] must have had access in some way to the answers to the questions which Mr Thorpe gave to me. I knew a complaint had been made to the Director of Public Prosecutions. I have no idea who leaked this but I'm sure it did not come from anyone in my office. My Deputy Chief Constable was concerned about security generally and Mr Greenough and I, together with my secretary, have always been concerned about security in this case and, therefore, when this article appeared, we made sure that there had been no breach of this security.

There was another lull. But journalists tracking the case knew that the police were closing in on Thorpe; the only question was whether they had enough evidence to convince Tony Hetherington, the DPP, to authorise an arrest. On 4 July Challes sent his report to Hetherington; a few days later he was told that there were still gaps in the evidence. The DPP did not relish the idea of charging the former leader of the Liberal Party, who was still an MP and Privy Counsellor, with conspiracy to murder; even less appealing was the prospect of a trial, which would be set against a background of alleged cover-ups by Cabinet ministers, civil servants and Scotland Yard. There was also Harold Wilson, whose indiscretions to Pencourt about dirty tricks by MI5 and BOSS would be dragged in. This would not help anyone, least of all the Labour Prime Minister, James Callaghan, who had contemptuously brushed aside Wilson's demands for a royal commission into the intelligence services.

By late July the press knew that charges were imminent, which would prohibit any further speculative reporting of the case. The

Observer, which had refused to serialise *The Pencourt File* because
it believed that Thorpe was innocent, decided to sneak through one
final investigative article before the guillotine of the contempt law
came down. On 23 July it carried a front-page story by Pencourt
that revealed that Wilson, David Steel, the Liberal leader, Cyril
Smith, Liberal MP for Rochdale, and Emlyn Hooson, Thorpe's
implacable foe, would shortly be interviewed by Challes' team.

There was little else that was new. Pencourt were still obsessed
with 'the South African dimension' and reported: 'There is a
lingering suspicion that South African agents knew of the Scott
affair and tried to turn it to their advantage.' They added grudgingly
that Wilson 'no longer fully believes in the South African conspiracy
story', which suggested, of course, that he partly believed in it.[10] In
inimitable Pencourt style they enlisted Andrew Newton to breathe
new life into 'the South African dimension'. They said that it
was suspicious that he was sent 'job-hunting' in South Africa
and Rhodesia by the people who had hired him to kill Scott.
Newton said, 'There was no job and I ended up in this filthy cell
being questioned by six people. It was a set-up. They took me to
South Africa. You know, Rhodesia's one place – South Africa,
BOSS and people like that, that's another thing.'

On 2 August Challes asked for arrest warrants from a Justice
of the Peace to be issued against Thorpe, Holmes, Deakin and Le
Mesurier. If they had been ordinary criminals they would have
been hauled out of bed and dragged off in handcuffs to the cells
but they were invited to report to Minehead police station on
Friday, 4 August. Challes' team were not happy at the way that
four alleged murderers were being treated. Peter Hinde, who had
not been allowed to mention Lord Snowdon's name at Newton's
trial, said:

> The four of them were going to be arrested in the normal
> way. I was sent up to London and spent a week there. I sat
> in the House of Commons and listened to Thorpe prattling
> on about something. I had to make sure he was at home.
> They were all going to be arrested on Thursday night, the
> 3rd of August. I also made sure Holmes was at home in
> Eaton Place. We clocked him at his place of work and his
> flat. Then the DPP got cold feet and they were allowed to
> report to Minehead police station and were given a table
> and chairs and tea. It was bloody disgraceful. We are talking

about a most serious offence. They should have been arrested by us.[11]

Hinde, who was Greenough's oppo in London, did not enjoy his time in the capital. He said:

> I remember getting off the train at Paddington with Davey and I saw this bloke clocking us. Davey said that I'd been watching too much television. We got on the Underground and the bloke was at the end of the carriage. Then we're walking up to New Scotland Yard and I say, 'He's in the doorway, watching us.' I said, 'I'm going to grab him.' Davey said, 'Don't do that. We'll end up on the front pages.'

Apart from monitoring the movements of Thorpe and Holmes they also interviewed politicians who knew Thorpe well. These meetings could not possibly have proved that he had plotted to kill Scott, but the police hoped that they might yield useful background, illustrating, for example, how he had misled parliamentary colleagues about his relationship with Scott. They saw David Steel, who was polite and helpful. Cyril Smith was 'outspoken and said that Thorpe was a raving homosexual'.[12] They approached Lady Falkender, who was less co-operative. She refused to meet them because, she said, she did not know anything that was relevant to a criminal investigation.

Harold Wilson, however, agreed to meet them at his office in Parliament Street on Thursday, 3 August. This was a remarkable event – a former prime minister being questioned by two provincial detectives about a conspiracy to murder – but it went unreported by the press, apart from a paragraph in the Bristol-based *Western Daily Press*.[13] This was not a conspiracy by the media but a manpower problem: newspapers had deployed their staff around the country at key locations, such as Thorpe's homes in London and Devon, to make sure that they recorded every grimace of what would obviously be a momentous day. This meant that no one noticed that Wilson was being interviewed by the police. Greenough recalled, 'I think Sir Harold was a bit worried what I was going to ask him. I put his mind at rest and said, "I'm not remotely interested in anything concerned with politics. I am only interested in any rumours you heard about Thorpe." He said that he had not heard any. He was very good and and gave me a cup of tea. He gave us a statement saying that he had not heard anything about Thorpe.'[14]

For Peter Hinde, however, the meeting with Wilson was one of the highlights of his career:

> He was very nervous. Perhaps even ex-prime ministers get like that when they are interviewed by policemen. Davey was the tightest bugger on this earth and used to roll his own cigarettes. He used to roll them as thin as matchsticks. We sat there interviewing an ex-prime minister and you'd think this would be the one occasion he wouldn't light up. But Davey rolled a sleek one and leant over and said, 'Sir Harold, have you got a light?' Sir Harold lit it for him and said, 'By God, that won't do your lungs any good.'[15]

The next day, Friday, 4 August, Thorpe, Holmes, Le Mesurier and Deakin arrived at Minehead police station, as the press knew that they would, and were charged with conspiracy to murder. Thorpe was also charged with incitement to murder, a reference to his alleged discussions in 1968 and 1969 with Bessell and Holmes. Thorpe was the only one to say anything when he was cautioned and charged. He said, 'I am totally innocent of this charge and will vigorously challenge it.' After being charged the four men appeared briefly at West Somerset Magistrates' Court and were remanded on bail.

It was 9 a.m. in New York when Peter Bessell heard the news from Tom Mangold, whose exclusive interview with him in spring 1976 had been chucked in the cellar by BBC executives. Bessell wrote:

> 'Well, mate,' said Mangold, 'they're all in the nick!' It was a slight exaggeration. Jeremy, David, Le Mesurier and Deakin had not been arrested in the conventional way. Instead, for Jeremy's benefit, they had been told to present themselves at Minehead police station at noon. After being charged with conspiracy to murder Norman Scott, they were given coffee and sandwiches. In addition to being charged with conspiracy, Jeremy was charged with having incited David to murder Scott in 1968–69. I realised the second charge depended on my uncorroborated evidence, and was far from happy with it.

As Mangold and I talked there was a sudden flash of

lightning followed by an ear-splitting clap of thunder. My room on the 25th floor of the Wellington Hotel had windows on two sides. It seemed to be in the very centre of the storm. It occurred to me that this was an absurdly theatrical climax to a tragic story which had begun for me thirteen years earlier in the dining room of another hotel, the Ritz, in London's Piccadilly.

Norman Scott was now 38 years old and was living on Dartmoor in yet another isolated cottage, called Kestor Way, surrounded by ducks, chickens, a nanny goat and eleven cats. He also had four dogs: Lassie, a Border collie; Emma, a whippet; Cino, a lurcher, and the eponymously named Beagle. He was training three horses and earned a little money from giving riding lessons, but mostly lived a cash-free, self-sufficient life. Meanwhile, Hilary Arthur had disappeared again with their daughter.

He remained neurotic, prone to bouts of self-pity and adamant that Thorpe had ruined his life. But he was nudging middle age and, inevitably, there was a growing maturity. He had been married and had had a long, if tempestuous, relationship with Hilary; he had a son, Ben, whom he never saw, and a daughter, Briony, whom he worshipped. He still talked about the agonies of his sexuality, but to people who had known him as a young man these monologues had a stagey quality about them; he sweated profusely, wrung his hands and spoke in a barely audible voice, just as he had done when he was in his early 20s, but this was an older, wiser and calmer Norman. He enjoyed his life on Dartmoor. 'What I said I had to say. I've done what I had to do and that's over now. They are real people here and I have a great deal of respect in the village. It's not a question of anyone being on my side. It has all been a very private thing. Here I do not talk about what has gone on. I'm just interested in my horses. The Thorpe thing is incidental.'[16]

He was dismissive of most journalists. They had ridiculed or ignored him when he needed their support but they pretended now that they cared because they wanted 'exclusive' stories from him, which was despicable. Pencourt, however, were different. They had always listened carefully and had never patronised him; he did not agree with everything that they had written but they had never lied to him. Above all, they had tackled the Establishment, which had protected Thorpe, and he respected them for that.

As the police had closed in on Thorpe the media became increasingly demanding. Pencourt told Scott that he needed professional advice; the media was making money out of him and it was only right that he was paid for this time. Scott told Pencourt that he was reluctant to ask for money; if he did then people would think that he was fabricating stories for profit. But he agreed to talk to Pencourt's contact, Peter Thomas, who ran a news agency in Wales and who also represented Dave Miller. Thomas suggested that Scott should charge £50 for an interview and £80 for a photograph. Then the American television company, CBS, asked Pencourt if they would help them make a documentary for *Sixty Minutes*, the most influential current-affairs programme in the country, which had a regular audience of 40 million. Pencourt called Scott, who agreed to talk to CBS for nothing.

Early in August the Americans arrived and set up camp at Chagford, in a hotel which was renowned for its superb food. The Americans were led by Mike Wallace, a gnarled anchorman who was almost as famous as the legendary Walter Cronkite. They were briefed in Chagford by Pencourt and began to plan their film, which they thought that the folk back home would enjoy because it was Watergate with an English twist.

On Thursday, 3 August a reporter and photographer from the *Daily Mail* turned up at Kestor Way with the news that Thorpe would be charged the following day. The newspaper cajoled a few innocuous sentences from Scott and photographed him riding in the mist, with the CBS camera crew in the background. Next day, Friday, the *Mail* ran a double-page feature, headlined: 'Down on Dartmoor the best-known recluse in Britain shows off his horses and goes back to the spot where his Great Dane was shot: Norman Scott's busy day starring for American TV'. Mischievously, the newspaper, which knew that Thorpe would be spending the day with the police in Minehead, tacked this paragraph to the end of the story: 'Jeremy Thorpe is expected to visit his Devon constituency today. This morning he will conduct a 'walkabout' in Barnstaple market, talking to stall-holders and passers-by. This evening he will be a guest at a coffee evening run by his supporters.'

The *Sixty Minutes* team were followed immediately by other overseas journalists, who poured into the West Country to report this unbelievable story about the attempt by an important politician, who was a secret homosexual, to murder his former lover. This pre-judged Thorpe but foreign publications did not have to worry about libel or contempt and their approach to the story did, at least, have the merit of simplicity.

Thorpe did not like being stalked by camera-toting reporters who had no respect for English law, which said that a man was innocent until proven guilty. On Saturday, 12 August his patience snapped. Mike Wallace confronted him in the High Street in Bideford, while he was on one of his famous 'walkabouts'. After a brief exchange, Thorpe stormed off, pursued by the CBS crew and a gaggle of other journalists. He went into the local Liberal Club, followed by Wallace. There they had another acrimonious chat. According to Wallace, Thorpe said, 'I will have you charged with contempt at the local magistrates' by sundown if you ask any more questions about the allegations made against me. I am a lawyer and I know the law.'[17] Wallace, an experienced journalist who was well aware of the difference between American and English law, said:

I wasn't surprised by Mr Thorpe's reaction. He was obviously under a great deal of strain and I must confess I have sympathy for the man. I suggested we discuss everything but the actual charge. For example, an interesting subject would have been Mr Thorpe's reactions to the way his constituency has taken the situation. But he immediately told me that if I was aware of English law I would not ask questions like that.

But Wallace did not allow this 'sympathy' to influence his reporting. He opened his report on *Sixty Minutes* with this unequivocal statement:

A tale of homosexuality, attempted murder and cover-up which may sound these days like ordinary stuff. The man in trouble, Jeremy Thorpe, is one of Britain's most prominent poiticians. The Kennedy of Britain, he's been called. A man whose burning ambition was to be his country's Prime Minister. But now Jeremy Thorpe has been charged with incitement to murder. The man he is alleged to have wanted dead is Norman Scott. A male model, a horseman. A man who claims that he was Jeremy Thorpe's lover for five years.[18]

Then Wallace introduced Norman Scott to the American public. He asked him if he had had a homosexual affair with Thorpe. Scott replied, 'Most definitely. Yes, yes.'

The programme, which could never have been broadcast in Britain, continued:

Wallace: The man who says that he was paid to eliminate Scott is Andrew Newton, a professional pilot who accepted the contract to kill for $20,000.

Newton: Yes, I did accept the contract to kill Norman Scott.

Wallace: And the chief witness against Thorpe will be the man who was at one time his best friend and parliamentary colleague, Peter Bessell. Did you ever hear Jeremy Thorpe say that he had to get rid of Norman Scott?

Bessell: Oh yes. He first discussed this with me as long ago as 1968.

Wallace: But all of this was covered up, says Scott, by Thorpe's parliamentary colleagues, by the police and by the British press. Until a couple of young journalists, Roger Courtiour and Barrie Penrose, focused on it in a book they called *The Pencourt File*.

Penrose: We have here a social Establishment that finds it inconceivable, absolutely inconceivable, that someone enjoying power as Jeremy Thorpe did and with a very honourable record in Parliament, could possibly be mixed up in a very murky, in fact, murderous, attempt on the life of a former male model.

Viewers in New York, Washington, Atlanta, Memphis and Los Angeles were then offered an insight into the other Scott, petulant and irrational, who had driven Thorpe to despair:

Wallace: Why would Jeremy Thorpe want you killed, if indeed he did? What would be his motive?

Scott: He just couldn't cope with the situation.

Wallace: What situation?

Scott: Our relationship.

Wallace: But you hadn't had a relationship for over ten years.

Scott: No, that's true.

Wallace:	You told anybody who would listen.
Scott:	This is really bad. I wasn't going around deliberately saying Jeremy Thorpe and I had a relationship. One doesn't do that.
Wallace:	There has to be a motive for murder. No?
Scott:	Yes.
Wallace:	What could the motive be? You must know what you believe that motive was.
Scott	[Long pause]: I suppose. I just don't know.
Wallace:	The fact is from reading newspapers, books, I get the feeling that you did indeed badger Jeremy Thorpe.
Scott:	That's it. You know bloody well I didn't. I'm so sick of this. You know damn well, so why ask a question like that? It's all part of this whole bloody Thorpe thing . . .

Then Scott stomped out. Next day, however, he had calmed down:

Scott:	Well, I've been thinking deeply about it since I spoke to you before and I think that I posed a threat because of my honesty, and don't forget, of course, he knew it was the truth. People were beginning to believe me and not him.
Wallace:	And you were beginning to tell the story in his own constituency?
Scott:	In his own constituency. To people he knew and I knew.
Wallace:	And so he was afraid that finally people were beginning to believe Norman Scott?
Scott:	Yes. So I posed a very real threat.
Wallace:	So he would have said to somebody like Holmes . . .
Scott:	Arrange the deal. Yes. Rub out time. Yes.
Wallace:	Do you want to see Jeremy Thorpe behind bars for ten years?
Scott:	No. I know that sounds absolutely ridiculous. I nearly had my head blown off. But I honestly don't.

Wallace blithely described Holmes as Thorpe's 'closest friend and a homosexual' before returning to Newton:

Newton: I just happened to be around and, wanted a bit,
          for want of a better word, a bit of excitement.
Wallace: Had you ever before been involved in a contract
          to murder?
Newton: No, it was the first time. And it was the first time
          and it was the first time [sic] perhaps to put a
          dream into reality. When it actually happens to
          you, that someone approaches you, it's a chance
          that should never be missed.

Wallace said that the British press sided with Thorpe against Scott,
who was 'depicted as a pathetic creature, a liar, a blackmailer'. He
continued:

But embarrassed members of his Liberal Party knowing, or
suspecting, more than they were prepared to admit publicly,
forced Thorpe to resign his leadership, though he did continue
as a Member of Parliament. And that seemed to be the end of
the affair. But the problem remained Andrew Newton serving
a two years' sentence for shooting Scott's dog.

Sixty Minutes now zeroed in on Thorpe as he toured North
Devon.

Wallace: Mr Thorpe.
Thorpe: Sir.
Wallace: I'm an American.
Thorpe: Well, you could have fooled me. I'm CBS.
Wallace: I'm CBS, too.
Thorpe: Well, that makes two of us.
Wallace: Your former parliamentary colleague, Mr Peter
          Bessell, has told me on film that you did indeed . . .
Thorpe: Yeah. I'm not interested in giving any interviews.
          I'm sorry. It's very nice to see you.

Peter Bessell appeared now, playing the part of the world-weary
philospher:

It comes down to a very simple issue. What Thorpe did was
to arrange for a friend of his, David Holmes, to hire a gunman
to do that which he could not do himself. Kill Norman Scott.

Against that background the issue of personal loyalty does not arise. Whether it is the assassination of Thomas à Becket, Julius Caesar, John F. Kennedy, even Norman Scott, it still comes down to the same thing. It is one person depriving another of their life. And that is a crime which in civilized society is intolerable.

Scott had once been offered big money to tell all. In the spring of 1976, when newspapers were chasing him for the inside story of the 'Bunnies can (and will) go to France' letter, which was about to be released by Scotland Yard, he had been invited to London by the *Daily Mirror*. It told him that it would take thirteen days to debrief him, for which he would be paid £1,000 a day. But he fled home after three days to Dartmoor and his beloved horses, saying that he 'couldn't stand' being in 'an awful hotel' in London. Thorpe's arrest had turned Scott into what Fleet Street called a 'hot property'. But he did not want to jeopardise his hard-won credibility by asking for money. Hence, he managed to earn only £1,200 between Thorpe's arrest in early August and the committal at Minehead in late November, which was a fortune to him but was roughly what a top Fleet Street reporter might claim in expenses in a good month.

Peter Thomas, his 'agent', despaired of him: 'I set up a lot of deals for Norman. But then he used to throw wobblers. But it was nice to dine out on Scott stories. The one thing people wanted to know was, did he have an affair with Thorpe? I was amazed that no one was concerned that a Privy Counsellor and the former leader of a political party might have conspired to kill someone. That didn't matter. They only wanted to know if Thorpe was gay.'[19]

By the late summer of 1978, however, the Thorpe story had become an *event*, which would happen, with or without Scott's help. There would be a committal in the late autumn when, or so everyone assumed, magistrates would swiftly survey the evidence, decide that there was a case to answer and dispatch the defendants to the Old Bailey in London for trial, which would take place in the spring. This meant that journalists had more than enough time to prepare books, films and 'background' features for newspapers.

London Weekend Television signed up Pencourt to work on a documentary, which it planned to broadcast on the day that Thorpe was convicted. The BBC revived the 'Special Unit' which had been closed after Pencourt's departure and rummaged through its archives to retrieve the footage which had been dumped there. Tom Mangold was instructed to produce a definitive film, which was a difficult assignment in view of the way that the Corporation had treated Pencourt. The *Sunday Times* assigned three gifted journalists, Lewis Chester, David May and Magnus Linklater, to produce a book.

Senior journalists who had backed Thorpe and ridiculed Pencourt were forced to defend themselves from accusations that they had backed Thorpe because he was a member of the Establishment. Harold Evans, editor of the *Sunday Times*, was defiant. He said, 'It's not the first time in history we've believed someone who's told an untruth. The *Sunday Times* gave the man in public life some credibility but then I reached the conclusion that he was not to be believed. We had a bad beginning but then we made a swift recovery.'[20]

Sir Charles Curran, the BBC's former Director–General, who had become managing director of Visnews, television's equivalent of a news agency, also did not see any reason to apologise. He was questioned aggressively by Mangold: 'It was quite evident, indeed from an interview I did before Penrose and Courtiour even came on to the story, when I saw Peter Bessell in California in May 1976, he made substantially the same allegations to me, to the BBC exclusively, that were later to become part of the court process. The BBC decided not to go ahead with the story.'

But Curran said that he knew nothing about Mangold's scoop and repeated that he had been right about Pencourt:

The kind of subject that would be acceptable to Penrose and Courtiour would not always be acceptable to me. I wanted an investigation of 'the South African connection' but it was turning into a story on Jeremy Thorpe. I had no wish for Thorpe to be harrassed personally. I was not interested in pushing Thorpe further down the hole. He was dead politically and I was not interested in him.[21]

Mangold said that surely it reflected badly on the entire British press, not just the BBC, that Pencourt's investigation had been financed by a publisher rather than by a newspaper or television channel. Curran disagreed: 'It depends on how you judge other people's decisions. If you say that we took the wrong decision, too bad. You are saying that every failure to follow up a story is a monstrous sin. I don't take that severe view.'

While the media were gearing up for the bonanza of the Old Bailey trial Detective Chief Superintendent Challes was briefing the lawyer who would prosecute Thorpe and the others. In early August he approached a young barrister called John Bull, who was prosecuting a major drugs case in Bristol, and told him that he was offering him the chance to work 'on the most important case of your career'.[22] Bull agreed but pointed out that, since he was not a Queen's Counsel, he could not lead the prosecution. The obvious candidate was the QC who led the Western Circuit, which covered the West Country, but unfortunately this was Sir Peter Rawlinson, who was also a Tory MP. It was impossible for Rawlinson to prosecute the former leader of the Liberal Party so he was ruled out. The next obvious candidate was the top Welsh barrister but again there was a difficulty; he was Emlyn Hooson, Liberal MP and critic of Thorpe. Finally, Peter Taylor, the Leader of the North Eastern Circuit, was chosen.

The people facing the biggest problem were the hierarchy of the Liberal Party. They agreed that, of course, Thorpe was innocent until proven guilty but enough was known about the case to raise the vote-losing question: How could a man like Thorpe have led the Liberals for almost a decade? He might or might not have been involved in a conspiracy to murder Scott but much was undeniable: for example, it was plain that he had been intimate with Scott, had known about the 'retainers' and had persuaded Bessell to write a letter claiming that he was being blackmailed by Scott. It was agreed that he had to be jettisoned before further damage was inflicted on the Party.

Thorpe, who was still the spokesman on foreign affairs, had assured Steel, who had succeeded him as leader, that he would resign as an MP and stay away from the Party conference at Southport in September if he was charged. Steel recalled:

He changed his mind on both counts, the first partly under pressure from his constituency, and both, I suspect, on legal advice. He was pleading not guilty and so he had to portray a normal life to the outside world, regardless of the embarrassment to the Party. The MPs and party managers were furious. The annual Assembly is our guaranteed shop window and here was Jeremy going to walk straight through it, against all entreaties. Sure enough, he didn't just appear, but, with his usual showmanship, the doors at the back of the hall were flung open and he marched down the crowded aisle with Marion to a half-standing ovation. When he got to the platform, I greeted him and showed him to his seat. One journalist shrewdly observed, 'Mr Steel shook him warmly by the hand while looking as if though he would rather have gripped him by the throat. No one was in the least interested in our worthy debates and resolutions. He virtually wrecked the conference and the rest of us had to put up with it.'[23]

One newspaper reported:

Soon after Mr Thorpe appeared he found himself sitting alone on the platform. He arrived in time for the debate on Rhodesian sanctions in which it was thought he would speak but the debate only lasted a few minutes and he did not contribute to it. Most of the Party's MPs were on the platform when the former Liberal leader arrived. But they left just after the end of the debate and Mr Thorpe was the only MP left on the platform.[24]

Thorpe's friends – and he still had some – were appalled. He had saved the Party and now, when he most needed support, it was turning its back on him. Whatever he had done the fact remained that, without him, the Liberals would not exist. Steve Atack had known Thorpe since 1971. He was a former firebrand chairman of the Young Liberals, and a militant gay rights activist, neither of which helped his ambition to become an MP. He said, 'The Party behaved in the most illiberal, vindictive and thoroughly ungrateful manner I have ever witnessed in a political movement. The way that the Party erased his contribution was breathtaking.'[25]

But senior Liberals did not care what Thorpe's friends said; there was another, potentially explosive problem: money. Jack Hayward was unhappy that he had been dragged into a squalid court case and wanted to know what had happened to almost a quarter of a million pounds that he had given to Thorpe, under the impression that he was financing the well-meaning underdog of politics, rather than paying for the murder of a mad recluse who lived on the moors in the West Country. He had been assured that his first donation of £150,000 had been used to clear the Party's overdraft of £100,000 but that does not seem to have happened. £50,000 went into funds which Thorpe controlled; Thorpe claimed that this money was used to bolster the Liberals in seats that they had a chance of winning. Another £40,000 went into a 'reserve' fund (this seems to have been raided later to pay off debts incurred during the election in June 1970). That left about £60,000, which was spread thinly around the Party's various overdrawn accounts. Hayward was not certain how much he sent to Thorpe after the first cheque but thought that it was around £70,000. However, he had 'no doubt' that £20,000 went to Andrew Newton, the airline-pilot-cum-hitman who was hired by David Holmes to frighten and/or kill Norman Scott. He was also baffled about a cheque for £40,000 that he sent to Thorpe in May 1974. He thought that it had been paid into a bank account bearing the name the Liberal Party General Election Fund but, when he checked with the bank, was told that no such account existed. He said, 'There were false accounts all over the place. But only Jeremy knew where the money went. I just don't know where it went.'

David Steel promised a thorough inquiry and appointed Michael Steed, the Manchester academic who had just become Party President, to lead it. Steel was an honourable and honest man but he was also the new leader of a party that had almost been destroyed; the Liberals could not afford a financial scandal after the nightmare of the Old Bailey trial, which meant that the investigation into Thorpe's use of Hayward's money was swiftly concluded and forgotten.

Steed said that his brief was to discover whether Hayward's money had been properly used and that he was not required to look into the way that Thorpe had handled other donations during his time as treasurer and leader, which was just as well. Steed said:

There were a lot of rumours about other money but we were only asked to investigate what happened to Hayward's donations. Anyway, we didn't have a clue about other sources of money. Thorpe explained how he spent the money, apart from the £20,000 which never went near the Party. We were very critical. He spent money as he saw fit. He thought that since he had raised it he should decide how to spend it. But he didn't pocket money himself.[26]

That was small consolation. The inquiry revealed a party that had been so grateful that it had a charismatic, headline-grabbing leader that he had been allowed to use its funds as if they were his personal savings. Steel said:

> However unorthodox Jeremy's handling of funds, especially Hayward's substantial donations, all was accounted for except the £20,000 [used to pay Newton] which never came near the Party . . . But the report was severely critical and it was universally felt in the Party hierarchy that he had no further role in that body. Party members – not knowing all these ramifications – continued to assert that there was surely a place for him; but no one felt inclined to offer him one.[27]

This was measured and regretful but, in private, Steel was incandescent. In mid-November he telephoned Jack Hayward in the Bahamas, who was due to fly to England to give evidence at the committal in Minehead. Hayward recalled:

> David said, 'Jack, we must meet before you go to Minehead.' He said that I should ring him as soon as I got to London, which I did. We had lunch in a small restaurant near the Commons. He said straight away, 'Jack, I never realised how generous you had been to the Party.' He knew about the first payment I'd made but he didn't know about all the rest. He didn't know about all the accounts that Thorpe had asked me to send the money to.
>   Then he said, 'Jack, I have known this man a long time and it's only just become apparent that there are two characters.' He said, 'Jack, you must defend yourself. Forget loyalty. You are two men swimming to a raft from a shipwreck. He will tread on your shoulders and push you under to get on it. He deceived us all. Save yourself now.'[28]

CHAPTER NINETEEN

On Monday, 3 November 1978, three years after Rinka, the Great Dane, was murdered by Andrew Newton on Exmoor, the small, unremarkable Somerset coastal resort of Minehead had its first, and last, taste of international fame. In the winter the town's population hovered at around 10,000 souls, who spent the damp, dark days waiting for the holidaymakers. But, like every resort, Minehead had been devastated by the all-inclusive foreign package; Britons, who had once been grateful for the candy floss, slot machines and chilly waters of their own seaside, now spent their precious two weeks roasting on Mediterranean beaches, dancing the nights away in discos and getting marvellously drunk for less than the cost of a couple of lukewarm pints back home.

The arrival of the Thorpe circus did more than put Minehead on the front pages; hundreds of expense-account journalists, television crews, authors and lawyers poured in, packing the hotels, eating expensive meals, clogging the telephone lines with surcharged, long-distance calls and renting anything with four wheels and an engine. The locals did not care whether or not Thorpe had masterminded Rinka's execution but they were grateful that the dog had died six miles away on Porlock Hill, just inside the borders of Somerset, so that the committal had to be held there. That Monday morning the media swarmed around the nondescript 1930s redbrick building which housed the court and the police station. Photographers and camera crews were not allowed inside the precincts so they picketed the entrance, filming the defendants and witnesses as they swept into the car-park. The street was lined with television outside-broadcast units, the companies' logos emblazoned across the sides of the trucks, and, high above, cameramen perched on gantries, to capture a different perspective of the drama.

All the stars of the Thorpe saga were there, led by Thorpe, Scott and Bessell. Barrie Penrose and Roger Courtiour arrived in

Penrose's trusty Volkswagen Beetle, transformed from penniless purveyors of silly, sub-Watergate conspiracy theories to prosperous authors. They had abandoned their clunking briefcase, which had served them so well, and invested in two Swiss-made miniaturised tape recorders. Every day they smuggled their expensive new toys into court; there was no need for them to record the proceedings, but they felt that they wanted a permanent record of the event that vindicated their crusade. Peter Bessell jetted in from California, deeply tanned, with hair that appeared to have been dunked in luminous orange paint and wearing lightweight suits which included the latest shiny, non-crease synthetic fibre. When Bessell took the stand in court the overall effect was striking; he glowed, literally, like a warning beacon.

There were distinguished barristers, such as Peter Taylor and Gareth Williams, who were to become household names. There was Thorpe's solicitor, Sir David Napley, a former Conservative candidate and past President of the Law Society, who wore beautiful suits and rode around in a brownish Rolls Royce, which the media unilaterally decided was gold, in keeping with the owner's image. He was an entertaining, warm man, who looked younger than his 63 years, but he was not self-effacing. He kept a supply of champagne in the boot, despite suffering from gout, and told the press that he was the best and most expensive solicitor in the country. He said that he intended to represent Thorpe at the committal and demonstrate the theories outlined in his book, *The Techniques of Persuasion*, that a fine solicitor like him could present a case as competently as any barrister.

Jack Hayward also turned up, as rumpled and amiable as ever, escorted by a legal adviser, and checked into a modest converted rectory. To the relief of the press, who were scrabbling for quotes and photographs, he was happy to pose for pictures and utter a few non-contentious sentences, though the law meant that he could not comment on the forthcoming proceedings.

Norman Scott stayed at his cottage on the moors, tending his animals and insisting that he had better things to do than sit astride his horse or play with his dogs for the benefit of the cameras; but secretly he revelled in the attention. David Holmes rented a farmhouse on Exmoor where he contemplated the cost of loyalty to his friend Jeremy.

Despite the press frenzy, the committal was only supposed to be a private rehearsal for the main event, which was the trial. Under

British law magistrates have to decide whether there is sufficient evidence in criminal cases on which 'a reasonably minded jury, properly directed, might convict'.[1] But, in 1967, Parliament passed the Criminal Justice Act in an effort to avoid lengthy committals. This said that a defendant could agree to be committed for trial if the magistrates were satisfied that the written evidence submitted by the prosecution justified it. The accused could, if he or she wished, ask for what was called a Section Seven hearing, where the prosecution would have to lay out its evidence in detail. But a Section Seven hearing could not be reported by the media unless the defence requested it.

For the accused there were obvious advantages in a Section Seven. The prosecution had to reveal its case, which the defence could probe for weaknesses; the defence could also cross-examine the prosecution's witnesses but did not have to call their own. At 10.27 a.m. the three magistrates charged with deciding whether Thorpe, Holmes, Le Mesurier and Deakin should be dispatched to trial by jury sat down in the court, packed with thirty-seven journalists and authors (over a hundred more had failed to obtain seats) and sixteen members of the public. There were barristers, solicitors and assorted legal aides, who did not have to bother with wigs and gowns since this was a committal. Their desks seem to have been splattered with red paint; these were the hardback copies of *The Pencourt File*, which was the key source for the prosecution.

Napley was also enthusiastic about the book. He had dreamt up an unusual defence for Thorpe: that Bessell and Pencourt had 'orchestrated' the entire story. Napley knew that this was absurd but he hoped that, by linking Bessell and Pencourt, he would plant the idea that they were making pots of money out of his client, which might offend the magistrates and would definitely outrage a jury of humble wage-earners if the case went to trial.[2] In an effort to obtain proof of this 'orchestration' he asked a detective agency in Plymouth to 'tail' Pencourt around Minehead and monitor their improper clandestine meetings with Bessell and other witnesses. But the agency did not have any detectives available so he deputed a member of the North Devon Liberal Association called Kenneth Ayre to track them. But Ayre reported that Pencourt spent their days innocently and did not go near Bessell, which rather undermined Napley's thesis.[3] Napley also blundered spectacularly in his strategy for the hearing by assuming that other defence lawyers would meekly accept that reporting restrictions should remain in force.

Barrie Stephens, Deakin's solicitor, and Gareth Williams, QC, a tough 48-year-old Welshman who led the Wales and Chester Circuit, decided to ask for them to be lifted to demonstrate that their client had nothing to hide, in contrast to Holmes and Thorpe. Williams had taken an immediate dislike to Thorpe, who, he told friends, reminded him of Richard Nixon.[4] He thought that Deakin was innocent of serious wrongdoing but believed that Thorpe had manipulated Holmes to hire Newton. He never wavered from this view and, indeed, was more hostile to Thorpe than the prosecution team. So, that Monday morning, at around 10.30 a.m., Williams rose to his feet and, to the consternation of the chairman of the magistrates, Edward Donati, a retired architect, and the delight of the press, asked for reporting restrictions to be lifted because his client 'welcomed the fullest scrutiny'.[5] Donati, who usually dealt with drunks and errant motorists, frowned at this unexpected development. Then the clerk of the court, Frederick Winder, rescued him; he said that Donati had no discretion in the matter and had to grant Williams' request.

There was uproar amongst the journalists. They were known in the trade as 'wordsmiths' and had been sent to Minehead because they could write colourful sketches, not because they possessed reliable shorthand. In London newspapers told their court specialists, who could take accurate, verbatim notes all day without pausing for a stiff drink, to get to Minehead as fast as possible, no matter what it cost. Le Mesurier did not mind about this development since he had paid Newton almost £20,000 and, in return, had been assured by Newton that he would be portrayed as a peripheral figure in the affair. Holmes was emotionally exhausted and was beyond caring. But Thorpe was furious; Deakin's 'betrayal' meant Scott's allegations would be splashed across the front pages of every newspaper in the country. He had hoped that the case would be dismissed and that he would emerge victorious, with a chance of rebuilding his career. But Deakin had ruined everything; Thorpe knew that, whatever the magistrates decided, Scott would have the revenge of publicity he had always craved.

The committal lasted until mid-December. Every day brought new and unbelievable allegations, of a passionate homosexual affair between a young male model and a charismatic politician, bribery, cover-up, fraud and, finally, a murder plot. And, thanks to Deakin, the Welsh entrepreneur who dealt in fruit machines and who wore dazzlingly bright suits, Minehead became a gripping soap opera, which was enjoyed by tens of millions of people in Britain and around the world. The story was simple in outline. Jeremy Scott had seduced Norman Scott in 1961. They had an affair but Scott was unstable and became obsessed with Thorpe and with his Insurance card, which he believed Thorpe should have stamped. Thorpe bought Scott's silence with weekly 'retainers', which were paid by Peter Bessell. In the early 1970s, as Thorpe edged towards real power, he became increasingly worried about Scott. So he told Bessell and Holmes that Scott had to be killed by, for example, poisoning him and throwing him down a disused tin mine in Cornwall. But they stalled him. Then Scott married and Thorpe relaxed. The marriage failed and Scott resumed his campaign to destroy Thorpe. Bessell was now living in California so Holmes took charge and, with the help of Deakin and Le Mesurier, hired Andrew Newton to kill Scott.

In essence, this was the Crown's case, though it was often explained in grittier language (Scott's description of his seduction by Thorpe read like an excerpt from a gay hard-porn magazine) and had many complex sub-plots. For example, there was the mystery of The Postcard. From their own investigations the press knew that many years earlier Thorpe had sent a postcard to a friend, whom they thought was called Brecht Van de Vater. There was the delicious, but unsubstantiated, rumour that the Establishment had protected Thorpe because The Postcard proved that Tony, otherwise Lord Snowdon, Princess Margaret's ex-husband, was, somehow, involved in the Thorpe–Scott affair. (He was not.) But neither the prosecution nor the defence had any intention of dragging the Royal Family into the case and refused to mention The Postcard at the committal, which disappointed reporters, who had been looking forward to exposing 'the Royal connection'.

To add a final, surreal touch to what was, by common consent, the most extraordinary story that journalists had ever covered, the voice of the clerk of the court, Frederick Winder, echoed constantly around court. For reasons that were never satisfactorily explained, he had been given a microphone which seemed to date from the early twentieth century. This was strapped to his face, so that he looked as if he was wearing an oxygen mask. Winder had to repeat everything witnesses said, which was picked up by an equally ancient tape recorder. Secretaries then transcribed his tapes, which became witness depositions. Unfortunately, the mask was neither sound-proof nor comfortable, so that Winder seemed to be shouting that he was suffocating.

Journalists occupied the dock at Minehead, where the accused usually sat, while Thorpe sat, alone, in the front of the court, formally dressed in the unfashionable three-piece suits which had been his vote-winning trademark, watched by his faithful wife, Marion, and his mother, Ursula, who sat further back. The other defendants were scattered around the court. Holmes was stony-faced and immaculate in a dark business suit, Deakin was neither serious nor elegant and Le Mesurier was large and hot.

At first the press thought that they were wasting their time. Guy Rais, a ramrod-backed, mustachioed gentleman who looked more like an RAF squadron leader than a reporter for the *Daily Telegraph*, was one of the leaders of the press pack. As the committal opened he assured his colleagues that they would soon be back in Fleet Street but then he changed his mind and announced that Thorpe and the others were 'obviously guilty'.

Pencourt became key sources for the press, who found it difficult to follow the twists and turns of a story which began in 1961. At first Pencourt responded politely to every question – they lost count of the number of times they had to spell out Le Mesurier's name – but then they realised that there were book sales here and suggested to their publisher Tom Rosenthal that he should ship some copies of *The Pencourt File* to Minehead. Reporters there were baffled by the labyrinth of stories about Harold Wilson, MI5, BOSS and Norman's missing Insurance card but were grateful for the index, where the names of the protagonists were neatly laid out. Guy Rais was particularly impressed by Pencourt's knowledge and connections with people who mattered. So he asked them if they could arrange for Thorpe's trial to be held in Winchester, because that would be 'good for exs' (aka expenses). But he said that he would be just as happy with the Old Bailey since he would be able to check the court reports in the London *Evening Standard* before he filed his own stories.

The prosecution case depended on three witness: Bessell and Newton, who had both been offered immunity, and Scott. To a British audience, who did not follow West Coast hairdressing and sartorial fashions, Bessell looked like a man who should not be trusted. This impression was reinforced by his testimony. Under cross-examination from the defence lawyers he adopted a self-flagellatory posture; he said that he was a liar, cheat and womaniser, though he insisted that he had only told big lies to protect his friend. Unburdening himself in this way, as if he was participating in one of the evangelical television programmes that were so popular in California, did little to enhance his credibility. Bessell himself later admitted that he had felt an irresistible urge to confess and thought that it had been inspired by the courtroom, which reminded him of the chapels where he had once preached.

He was also damaged by his contract with the *Sunday Telegraph*, which had bought the serial rights to his book on the Thorpe–Scott affair. Napley argued that this meant that he had a financial interest in the outcome of the case, though, luckily for Bessell, he did not discover that the contract included a bonus if Thorpe was convicted; the newspaper had agreed to pay £25,000 for six extracts if Thorpe was acquitted but promised Bessell that it would double the payment if he was found guilty.

Napley savaged him, too, over the immunity from prosecution that he had been offered by the Director of Public Prosecutions, which Napley said was a licence to lie with impunity. This was an exaggeration because Bessell could still have been prosecuted for perjury but Napley had made his point: Bessell's word was worthless. Bessell was not surprised by any of this. Many weeks earlier, when he had been in negotiations with the *Telegraph* and the DPP, he had told himself that he should not agree to either deal because it would look as if he was lying for profit, knowing that he could not be prosecuted. But that had not stopped him.

Newton was even less convincing. He adopted the persona of a publicity-shy gangster and roared into the car-park in a metallic-blue Opel. The windows had been darkened to frustrate the press and, as an added insurance, he had donned a balaclava to hide his face since he did not want photographers to immortalise him for nothing. He dressed casually, like a golf professional, for the witness box. It was impossible to believe anything he said. When he had been tried at Exeter in spring 1976 he protested that he had only been trying to frighten Scott, who had been blackmailing him. But he told a different story now: he said that Holmes had hired him to kill Scott but insisted that he had decided not to carry out his assignment and had pretended that his gun had jammed.

The defence lawyers tore him apart in a series of black-comic exchanges. Gareth Williams was especially effective. He asked if Newton had told 'a fair number of lies' to save his own skin. Newton seemed to think that this was funny and agreed. Williams asked if he hoped to make money from the case. Oh yes, said Newton. He added cheerfully that it was his 'only source of income' and was determined to 'milk it' for all it was worth. Then Williams wondered whether he had ever sought psychiatric treatment. By now Newton realised that he was being made to look a chump and replied grumpily, 'No, but I am sure you will recommend me for some.'

The defence had a harder time with Norman Scott, who dressed for the occasion in a smart dark suit. His testimony centred almost entirely on Thorpe, so his chief interrogator was Napley. Like many people Napley underestimated Scott. He began in a quiet, sympathetic manner, as if Scott was on the brink of a nervous breakdown, which was a mistake since Scott always became fierce and cogent if he thought people were not showing him the proper respect. Napley opened with what he imagined was a devastating question. He asked Scott to identify the red-covered book which he had brought to court the previous day; wasn't it, and here he paused, like a comic about to deliver the pay-off line, *The Pencourt File*? No, said Scott, it was a book of Anglo-Saxon poetry. Reporters roared with approval. Sexual politics had not yet made an impact on hardened Fleet Street professionals like them; hence, they had dismissed Scott as a limp-wristed homosexual who would be reduced to a tearful pulp by clever defence lawyers. But, judging from the way he handled Napley, reporters agreed that he was obviously a much tougher customer than this and they settled back to enjoy what promised to be an entertaining contest.

The jousting between solicitor and witness lasted for a day and a half, as Napley endeavoured to prove that Scott could not tell the difference between fact and fiction. But Scott fought back. He was in fine form, confusing Napley by switching personalities effortlessly, from sensitive to steely to wry, and blurring fact, opinion and invention to create a narrative that was simultaneously convincing and suspicious. He had infuriated many people over the years – lovers, police, reporters and lawyers – and now he made Napley wish that he had, after all, employed a barrister to deal with him. Whenever Napley thought he had him he wriggled free. Scott admitted that he had often lied in the past but insisted that he was now telling the truth; for example, to further guffaws from the press, he said that he could prove intimacy with Thorpe because he could describe what he called 'warts or nodules' on his body. There were many memorable exchanges like this. Napley suggested that Scott had spent his life searching for 'love and affection' and, having been rejected by people, had turned to animals. Not so, said Scott, he loved his son and daughter more than he loved animals. The more that Napley patronised him, the angrier Scott became. Napley quoted William Congreve's immortal passage: '"Heaven hath no rage, like love to hatred turned / Nor Hell a fury, like a woman scorn'd."' Scott flashed back, 'I am not a woman.'

The press agreed that Scott had won on points, as did barristers throughout the country, who had been irritated by Napley's suggestion that he could do their job. The magistrates were also not impressed by Napley. On 13 December they ruled that there was enough evidence to justify a trial by jury, which the defence said should be staged at the Old Bailey since the nearest Crown Court, at Exeter, was not suitable for such a high-profile case. Although they gave the impression that they were successful businessmen, Deakin and Le Mesurier were each granted Legal Aid for the trial.

Thorpe had remained silent until now. Then he declared, 'I will plead not guilty and will vigorously defend this matter.'

On 27 March 1979 James Callaghan, the Labour Prime Minister, lost a vote of confidence in the House of Commons by one vote after his erstwhile Liberal allies deserted him. In theory he could have soldiered on but tradition demanded that he had to call a general election. Polling day was set for Thursday, 3 May. Thorpe had been busy raising money for his defence, helped by friends at the Reform in Pall Mall, who had set up 'a Jeremy Thorpe Defence Fund'. They had raised £30,000, including a donation of £5,000 from Sir James Goldsmith, the businessman who had made his fortune in food and publishing.[6]

After Callaghan's announcement the Liberal leadership assumed that Thorpe would accept that he could not contest North Devon while he was awaiting trial on charges that carried a possible life sentence. But Thorpe did not agree. On 4 April he applied to the Lord Chief Justice for the trial, due to begin on 30 April, to be postponed by fourteen days; he was given eight days, which meant that he would have to appear in court on Tuesday, 8 May, four days after polling. Senior Liberals were incandescent. They said that the Party had enough problems without a candidate who was about to stand trial accused of conspiring to murder his homosexual lover. But Thorpe did not care; in his own mind, he was the greatest Liberal since Gladstone and would be vindicated by the acclaim of his faithful supporters in the West Country. He declared, 'This will be my eighth election and I am delighted to be back in the fray. The adrenalin really starts pumping.'

Liberals were under pressure everywhere because the Conservative leader Margaret Thatcher had made it clear that she had no time for the old One Nation Toryism, which was no better than socialism. Voters were faced with the starkest choice since the war: between her aggression and Callaghan's caution. The Liberals always did well when the ideological lines between the two giants were blurred; when there was a clear division voters tended to chose between the Conservatives and Labour and dismiss the Liberals as also-rans. Thorpe had a majority of almost 6,000 from the election of October 1974. In normal circumstances that would have been cut in 1979, but he would probably have survived. However, these were not normal times.

Auberon Waugh stood as a candidate for the Dog Lovers' Party. His manifesto stated that anyone who loved dogs should reject Thorpe because he had been unmoved by the death of Rinka, the Great Dane. Thorpe should have ignored Waugh but instead tried to have him jailed for contempt of court, which did not do much for his public image.

Boredom also played a part. Although Thorpe was only 50 years old, a baby by the standards of politics, he had been the local MP for twenty years. He was also wounded by the hostility of the Party leadership. Apart from John Pardoe, who was fighting, unsuccessfully, to hang on to North Cornwall, no prominent Liberal offered support; David Steel, the leader, sent a curt tape-recorded message, which did as much harm as good. Thorpe did his best. He jumped over fences, shook hands and did the usual impersonations, but the magic had gone. People turned away from him, embarrassed by the shell of their old hero.

On 3 May eleven Liberals were elected to the Commons, compared to the fourteen in the previous Parliament. But Thorpe was not one of them; his Conservative opponent romped home in North Devon with a majority of almost 8,500.

CHAPTER TWENTY

A few minutes before 10 a.m. on Tuesday, 8 May, Jeremy Thorpe strode into the Old Bailey, accompanied by Marion and his uncle, Sir Peter Norton-Griffiths, a distinguished 74-year-old ex-military intelligence officer and barrister. They were welcomed by Jack Kemble, Keeper of the Central Criminal Court, and escorted to a room alongside Number One Court which was normally reserved for discussions between barristers and their clients. It was an unusual reception for a man charged with conspiracy to murder and showed that nothing had changed since Minehead: Thorpe was still being treated by the courts as if he was a visiting dignitary.[1]

Photographers and camera crews waited in the street for the other defendants and star witnesses, watched by 100 not-very-enthusiastic members of the public. Peter Bessell, who had jetted in from California, was unmistakable; he had acquired a new, non-shiny wardrobe but his hair was still resolutely orange, despite desperate efforts in his bathroom at Oceanside to dye it a less strident colour. This distressed Bessell, who was pleased with his new suits but thought that his hair made him look like an 'out-of-work actor'.

In an attempt to rekindle the excitement of Minehead, newspapers melodramatically dubbed this 'The Trial of the Century', which was fittingly being heard in Number One Court, the most impressive court at the Old Bailey. They also compared it to a show that was transferring by popular demand from the provinces to the West End and which would be bigger and better than before. But this amusing analogy turned out to be wholly inaccurate because the trial rarely matched the breathtaking drama of Minehead.

The script and cast were essentially the same. The charge sheet giving the dates of the alleged conspiracy had been amended since December and Napley had given way to a barrister called George Carman, since solicitors could not take the floor at the Old Bailey, which must have been a relief to him after the drubbing he had received from Scott. But otherwise this was Minehead with a judge in a scarlet robe instead of magistrates in lounge suits.

Despite the hype journalists knew privately that the opening would be an anti-climax because the main prosecution witnesses, Bessell, Scott and Newton, would merely be repeating their testimonies from Minehead. But the final stages promised fresh delights because Thorpe, Holmes, Deakin and Le Mesurier would have to give evidence; reporters were particularly excited by the thought of the front page stories that would be spawned by Thorpe wriggling under cross-examination. For example, he would have to explain the famous 'Bunnies' letter, Hayward's £20,000 that had gone via the gullible Nadir Dinshaw in Jersey to Holmes and then to Newton, and his various, undisputed efforts to nobble witnesses.

Pencourt, meanwhile, had better things to do than sit around speculating with fellow hacks in Fleet Street pubs. They had been signed up by London Weekend Television to work on a two-hour, £250,000 documentary, which would be broadcast as soon as Thorpe was convicted, and were hunting for scoops. They were delighted, therefore, when they found William Shannon, the hairdresser-turned-shoe-salesman, who had twice been picked up by Thorpe in the King's Road, Chelsea in the mid-1960s. Then, since they were anxious that justice should be done, they tipped off Detective Chief Superintendent Michael Challes, who persuaded Shannon to appear as a witness at the Old Bailey. Pencourt and Challes were triumphant; Shannon disapproved of Scott because sex was a private matter but he was honest, outrageously camp and would tell the truth under oath. They told each other that his appearance at the Old Bailey would say more about Thorpe's sexual preferences than a hundred 'Bunny' letters.

By the opening of the trial the LWT film was finished. It was an updated version of *The Pencourt File*, minus the jumble of stories that had nothing to do with Thorpe. LWT executives declared it crisp and convincing and said that, as far as they were concerned, it proved that Thorpe was guilty as charged. They congratulated Pencourt and waited for the verdict.

In the weeks leading up to the trial Taylor and Bull, the prosecuting counsel, wrestled privately with complex legal and ethical problems. They knew that the defence had an obligation to win, using whatever means were necessary, but, as prosecutors, they believed that they had a duty to present the evidence against Thorpe and his co-defendants fairly and objectively, even if that undermined their own case. First, they had to decide whether to downgrade the charges. John Mathew, Holmes's barrister, had suggested at Minehead that his client would be prepared to plead guilty to a lesser charge, of conspiracy to frighten. But Taylor and Bull believed that they had to prosecute a conspiracy to murder and refused to become involved in private trade-offs with the defence. They also knew that the charge of conspiracy to frighten was so petty that it would be laughed out of court; in layman's terms it would mean that Holmes had planned either to strike, or pretend to strike, Scott, which was hardly an offence warranting a jail sentence. They might have been tempted by a plea from Holmes of conspiracy to cause grievous bodily harm, in return for him telling the truth about Thorpe, but Holmes's legal advisers would not consider any charge that carried the possibility of a jail sentence. They also toyed with the idea of charging Thorpe with fraud, based on his handling of Hayward's money, but decided against this because it would confuse the jury.[2]

Then there was Bessell. After Minehead he told Challes that his testimony had been fatally undermined by the immunity from prosecution that the DPP had granted him; surely, he asked Challes, it would help if he waived this? Challes agreed but Taylor did not; he said that it would be best to stick with the immunity deal. This was surprising since Taylor knew that defence lawyers would argue that Bessell had a licence to lie.

Even more surprising was the prosecution's attitude towards his contract with the *Sunday Telegraph*. Before the committal his solicitor had asked the DPP for an opinion on the clause that said that the newspaper would double its payment if Thorpe was convicted. But an official there said that since Bessell would be attacked 'on all sorts of grounds anyway one more may not make that much difference'.[3] Napley had not known about this clause when he questioned Bessell at Minehead. But, when Taylor and Bull obtained a copy of the *Telegraph* contract, they were 'horrified' by the double-your-money provision in it because they knew that it would utterly discredit him in the eyes of a jury. But they did not think that it was their place to persuade him to amend or cancel it; however, they did brief the defence on it, though they knew that they were destroying one of their star witnesses.

They also decided that they would not use the information that they had gathered from the police and intelligence services on Thorpe's relations with young men whom he picked up in the street and in pubs. They thought that this was irrelevant and inadmissible. If they were prosecuting a known member of the IRA, who was charged with blowing up the Stock Exchange, they agreed that it would not be right to introduce material – and the judge would probably not permit it anyway – which showed that the man was a member of the IRA who had a history of convictions for similar offences. So they decided that they would not need William Shannon, which astonished the police.

Thorpe's lawyers were relieved by this decision. They knew that his homosexuality did not prove the conspiracy charge but, on the other hand, it would gravely damage his credibility if the prosecution had shown that he had lied about his sexual preferences. The other defence lawyers, especially Gareth Williams, representing Deakin, thought that Taylor was being over-cautious. They also had files that indicated that Thorpe was a promiscuous homosexual and told friends that, in Taylor's position, they would have tried to introduce this in open court.

These were important decisions but Thorpe received the decisive boost when Mr Justice Cantley was appointed trial judge. He was 68 years old and, unlike many of his colleagues, was not the product of a wealthy home and Oxbridge. His father was a general practitioner in Manchester, where Cantley went to school and university. He became a moderately successful barrister, specialising in personal injury and contract law, and took Silk in 1954. In 1965 he became a High Court judge, though he spent most of his time in the North of England. From 1970 until 1974 he was presiding judge of the Northern Circuit. Even his friends were surprised that he had been given the plum of the Thorpe trial, in preference to better-known and cleverer judges. They said that he had probably been selected because he had spent most of his judicial career outside London and was, therefore, untainted by metropolitan prejudice.

But there were fears that he might, perhaps, not be a wise choice. Critics said that he was limited intellectually, which would be a problem because both prosecuting and defence teams contained some of the sharpest legal minds in the country. Next, they said that he was a snob, which meant that he would instinctively favour Thorpe. He could be arrogant and impatient, which might be acceptable at a court in, say, Salford, where the press corps consisted of an old soak from the local rag, but would be disastrous at the Old Bailey where the cream of the world's press was watching. Finally, he was unworldy, which was likely to prove a handicap in a case where homosexual love and revenge were the dominant themes.

It was rumoured in the legal profession that he had not slept with a woman until he married in 1966, when he was in his mid-50s. He believed that sex did not exist outside marriage, which was, of course, his prerogative but made it difficult for him to understand characters like Bessell, Scott and Thorpe, who were, in different ways, driven by sexual urges. In 1970 Cantley was trying a case involving a young man whose sex life had been ruined in a bulldozer accident. He asked the man's barrister if his client was married. The barrister said that he was not and Cantley replied, 'Well, I can't see how it affects his sex life.'

After four days of legal submissions and opening addresses Peter Bessell stepped into the witness box. Peter Taylor guided him sympathetically through his complex story and then, just before lunch on Tuesday, 15 May, John Mathew, Deakin's tough and wily barrister, rose to begin the cross-examination. Thanks to the prosecution, Mathew knew about his unwise, double-your-money contract with the *Sunday Telegraph*. So, he launched his attack by asking if it was true that he would make more money from his literary endeavours if Thorpe was sent to prison.

Bessell looked for help to Taylor and Bull but they were staring into space. So, just as he had done at Minehead, he threw himself on the mercy of the court, confessing his many previous sins, such as womanising, cheating and lying. But Mathew was merciless. He said, 'I started cross-examining Bessell at twelve-twenty and by one o'clock he was absolutely dead. It was the best forty minutes I have ever had in court. It went like a dream. We all went to lunch and said, "That's Bessell gone."'4 But Taylor and Bull did not enjoy their lunch. They agreed that there had been 'a chill' in court when Bessell admitted that he would double his money if Thorpe was found guilty. To add to their gloom a bailiff told them that the jury were disgusted by the *Telegraph* deal. Mr Justice Cantley, however, was delighted with the demolition of Bessell. He had already made it clear that he did not like him and now dropped any pretence of neutrality.

Pencourt were not in court to monitor these developments. Cantley had ejected them after Carman, representing Thorpe, had protested that their presence might, in some mysterious way, undermine justice. He said that it was possible that they would be called as witnesses, though neither the defence nor prosecution had any intention of doing so. Pencourt thus found themselves treated like criminals, which was odd since they had done nothing wrong except investigate an alleged conspiracy to murder Scott. They hired barristers to try to persuade Cantley to re-admit them but he shared Carman's fantastic theory that they might have 'orchestrated' the whole story with Bessell to make money. He said, 'This is a serious matter for the defendants, if not for your clients. It is a bit of a goldmine they have found. I rule that Mr Penrose and Mr Courtiour should remain out of court during the evidence of Bessell, Newton and Scott.'

So they were not present as Bessell spent four humiliating days in the witness box. Mathew and then Carman ignored his claims about the conspiracy, which was sensible since much of what he said could be corroborated from other sources; instead, they concentrated on discrediting him. They wore him down, slowly building a picture in the jury's mind of an amoral character who would do anything for money, which was true but did not mean that he was lying about Thorpe. They talked about the immunity from prosecution which he had been offered by the DPP as if it was a permit to commit perjury, which it was not, and suggested that he had concocted his entire story with Pencourt so that they could both write bestselling books. This was absurd but, after four days, they had convinced the jury that Thorpe was the victim of a plot by unscrupulous reporters and an ex-MP with orange hair. This was a gut instinct, rather than a rational assessment based on the facts, but was an important victory for the defence. Cantley threw himself into the bash-Bessell spirit of the proceedings, chortling, grinning and lobbing in his own jibes about Bessell's 'whoppers'.

On Friday, 18 May it was Norman Scott's turn to give evidence. He told the usual story to Peter Taylor but it was familiar stuff and lacked the dramatic impact of Minehead. Scott also seemed jaded, like an actor who has played a role brilliantly for weeks and then finds one night that inspiration has vanished. His cross-examination began the following Tuesday. After being briefly questioned by Williams and Denis Cowley, for

Le Mesurier, neither of whom had much interest in his stories about Vaseline, biting pillows and the missing National Insurance card, George Carman rose to his feet to prove that Thorpe had never slept with Scott.

Cantley, meanwhile, did his best to steal the limelight from Carman. He sniped constantly at Scott, whom he found even more repulsive than Bessell. Observers in the court watched the jury carefully as Cantley made his wounding little jibes; from the jurors' faces it seemed that they were taking the lead from him and that they had already decided that Scott was a horrible man who could not be believed. Though it was obviously not an enjoyable experience for Scott to be treated like this, it has to be said that it was difficult not to laugh as Cantley chastised him, like a father dealing with a difficult child. When Scott started to talk about The Postcard Cantley, who had vowed that the Royal Family would not be dragged into this sordid affair, snapped, 'You are not giving a proper answer. That was just a bit of dirt thrown in. Listen to the question and answer and behave yourself.' Then Scott started shouting about the damage Thorpe had caused him, emotionally and physically. Cantley was pleased that, after sobbing inaudibly for so long, he had found his voice: 'If only you spoke like that when you began your evidence, we could have heard everything you said. It shows you can speak up.' But he had to be firm again when Scott said that he would not answer any more offensive questions from Carman. After asking him whether he wanted to go home, which was an unusual suggestion for a judge to make to a witness, Cantley persuaded him to continue, by pointing out that, upsetting though it might be for him, questioning like this was part of a court case. Carman plodded on, despite Cantley's interruptions. He adopted the same tactics that he had used so effectively on Bessell; he wanted Scott to damn himself so that the jury would ignore the undisputed facts of the case. So he nudged him into admitting that he was a serial liar who was obsessed with his National Insurance cards, which Scott described memorably as 'my lifeblood'.[5] He fought valiantly but Carman was slicker and cleverer than Napley; he also had the backing of a judge who appeared to be a founder member of the Jeremy Thorpe fan club.

But Carman decided to make his own damaging admission. He asked Scott, 'You knew Thorpe to be a man of homosexual tendencies in 1961?' Scott replied that he did. This was untrue or was, at least, a gross over-simplification, but it demonstrated Carman's skill in teasing the right answers from witnesses. Scott should have told Carman that he had been desperate, lonely and confused when he had taken the late Mrs Tish, his Jack Russell, to the Commons to meet Thorpe and had certainly not been thinking about sex. Carman pressed on: 'He was the most famous and distinguished person you had met at the time?' Scott agreed. Carman continued, 'You were flattered that for a short time he introduced you into a different social world. I suggest you were upset and annoyed because he did not want to have a sexual relationship with you.' Then Scott lost patience. He said, 'Of course that is ridiculous because he did.' This was a sensational exchange. Carman's admission that Thorpe once had 'homosexual tendencies' raised more questions than it answered – for example, he did not say whether these had remained latent or whether Thorpe had actually slept with a man – but, nonetheless, it was the first time that Thorpe had admitted publicly that he had been, or would have liked to have been, a homosexual. He had always protested that he had never been a homosexual and, therefore, could not have had an affair with Scott.

Unlike the press, which splashed the story across the front pages, Taylor and Bull were unmoved. Thorpe's lawyers had asked them earlier if they would agree a formula to deal with his homosexuality but they had refused because they believed that his sexual preferences were not relevant to the conspiracy charge. Carman's grudging statement did not change anything; they ignored it though they thought that they might now be able legitimately to question Thorpe on his sex life when he gave evidence.

Ironically, the other defence lawyers were more hostile by now to Thorpe than the prosecution. Holmes's solicitor, David Freeman, told friends that Thorpe was an 'unpleasant windbag with superficial charm' who had conned poor, gullible Holmes into the plot to kill Scott. John Mathew, Holmes's barrister, told colleagues that, if his client gave evidence, he would confirm that Thorpe had wanted Scott killed, while Gareth Williams had always thought that Thorpe was devious and manipulative.

Deakin had already given evidence at Minehead and would obviously do so again at the Old Bailey. But Carman and Sir David Napley knew that it would be disastrous if Holmes and Le Mesurier took the stand because Thorpe would have to follow them. They were certain that he would not survive a grilling under oath; he might be able to convince the jury that he had not instructed Holmes to hire Newton but he would certainly be exposed as a liar on other counts. Any lingering doubts that Carman and Napley might have had were removed when the prosecution showed them a sexually explicit letter from Thorpe to a friend called Bruno, who lived in the United States, which they had obtained from intelligence sources there (the prosecution refused to say how they had acquired the letter, though there were unconfirmed rumours after the trial that the FBI was involved). Carman and Napley agreed that it would be a catastrophe for Thorpe if the letter became public, which would definitely happen if he gave evidence; so they agreed that, whatever the consequences, he would remain silent.

Luckily for Thorpe, Holmes and Le Mesurier remained loyal. Holmes later explained that this had not been easy: 'If I had given evidence on oath it would have been necessary to have told the truth about the occasions when Jeremy wanted Scott killed. But in saving myself I would have convicted Jeremy on the incitement charge and that I could not do. I was not going to let him down at the last moment. I am not trying to sound noble. It was just unthinkable after ten years of trying to help him.'[6]

Le Mesurier also wrestled with his conscience:

Although he looked very grave in the dock, Thorpe was cheerful downstairs. He was convinced that, provided we did not flap or panic, we would get off. He claimed we could totally discredit the prosecution case. The whole thing, he said, had come through the sewer and no British jury would convict on that sort of evidence.

But this mum's-the-word policy caused difficulties with my QC, Denis Cowley. I had to keep emphasising to him that the idea was for all of us to walk away. I told him the idea was not to save myself by dropping everyone else in it. But Mr Cowley thought that his job was to get me off and said I should make a statement from the dock disassociating myself from Thorpe and Holmes. But Thorpe was dead against anything that threatened to destroy the illusion of a united front. He wrote me such a persuasive note in the dock that I told Mr Cowley that I could not do as he wanted.[7]

The press and public, however, did not know about these

manoeuvres; they believed that, once the Crown had presented its case, all the defendants would have to give evidence. Journalists thought that it was inconceivable that Thorpe would refuse to do so; if he did, they said, it would be tantamount to an admission of guilt. While they waited for his appearance, which would, they were sure, be the highlight of the entire trial, they sat back to enjoy the testimony of Newton, the buffoon-cum-villain, who had put on such a marvellous performance at Minehead. The prosecution did their best but he was a wretched witness. He claimed now that he had been hired by Holmes to kill Scott, not to frighten him, but unfortunately he had insisted at his own trial in 1976 that he had not wanted to hurt Scott and had only wanted to stop him blackmailing him. He was further weakened by the immunity from prosecution that he had been granted and by his self-confessed ambition to make as much money as possible from the case. The defence lawyers tore him to pieces, helped by the judge, who obviously wished that he had the power to send him back to prison or, possibly, to the gallows. Newton fought hard in a series of spirited exchanges with Cantley and the defence lawyers:

Newton: I have admitted trying to kill Norman Scott at the Royal Garden Hotel [in London].
Cantley: You are not on trial here, you know.
Newton: I am sorry, my Lord, I am.
Cantley: Well, you're not. Take that from me and don't talk nonsense. You can tell us if there is anything which happened on the moor but you are not going to make a speech to the jury.
Newton: That's all right. What I wanted to say would probably not interest you.

His tussles with John Mathew, defending Holmes, were also a delight:

Mathew: You find it difficult to remember what is fact and what is fiction?
Newton: I think you are falling into the realms of sorcery with words.
Mathew: I was quoting what you said on a previous occasion.

Newton: I am being taken out of context.

Mathew: I will put it into context. Did you answer, in reply to the very first question which was put to you in cross-examination at Minehead: 'I do sometimes find it difficult to distinguish between fact and fiction regarding this case'?

Newton: Oh yes, I do remember saying that.

Then it was Jack Hayward's turn, to the relief of the judge, who called him 'a nice respectable witness', in contrast to the odious Bessell, Scott and Newton. Hayward told the story of the hundreds of thousands of pounds that he had given to the Liberals and then stepped down from the box. But he was puzzled that the judge did not want him to describe in detail, for the benefit of the jury, how Thorpe had used his money. Hayward said, 'Thorpe's lawyers told my lawyers, "Thank God he is only on a murder charge and not fraud because there is no doubt money disappeared all over the place."'[8]

Other defence lawyers agreed. They thought that Thorpe's financial activities were 'smelly' and were never properly investigated; one told a friend that Thorpe had certainly used Hayward's money to pay Newton, though he added that he could not, of course, say so publicly.

The trial was now moving towards the climax: Thorpe's appearance in the witness box. Then, on Thursday, 7 June came the bombshell: Holmes would not be giving evidence. Reporters knew that this also meant that Thorpe and Le Mesurier would remain silent. The day passed quietly, as George Deakin repeated his dull little story, and then, as feared, Denis Cowley, for Le Mesurier, and Carman, for Thorpe, announced that their clients would not be saying anything in their own defence.

The following Monday, 11 June, Peter Taylor began his closing address. He should have made a few punchy and simple points, which the jury could have grasped, but instead, spoke for two days, which was too long. As he spoke, reporters studied the faces of the jurors and decided that they were lost and bored as he made his erudite points about the nature of evidence in a conspiracy. But observers thought that the jurors were moved by Taylor's aside that Thorpe's life was 'a tragedy of truly Greek or Shakespearian proportions'. This was a curious remark for a prosecutor to make about a man who had lied and cheated so often to save his career but it appeared to reinforce the view of Cantley, who had behaved throughout the trial as if Thorpe deserved support not condemnation.

Taylor was followed by John Mathew for Holmes, who said that his client had plotted to frighten, but not kill, Scott. Then he bashed Scott, Bessell, Newton and Pencourt. Gareth Williams adopted a different approach; he said that his client was an ordinary working man, who had been deceived by men of power, such as Thorpe. Denis Cowley spoke briefly about Le Mesurier, but no one paid much attention.

Then Carman rose. He repeated his earlier admission that his client had once been cursed with what he called 'homosexual tendencies' but, apart from that, he had done nothing wrong. And he had certainly not had an affair with Scott or plotted to kill him. This was predictable stuff but Carman was not finished. To the horror of Holmes and Le Mesurier he invited the jury to consider whether they might have organised a conspiracy without telling Thorpe, which was a spectacular betrayal even by Thorpe's standards. Le Mesurier said:

> That was the worst moment of the entire trial. I couldn't believe my ears when Carman came out with that. It was diabolical. David and I were furious. For Thorpe's counsel to suggest that, after all we'd done for his client, was unforgivable. My solicitor told me later that he'd been frightened that something like that might happen. 'On the strength of that speech,' he said, 'you could have gone down for five years.'[9]

Holmes was also appalled: 'I couldn't believe it. Then I realised that the whole nightmare had not been worthwhile.'[10]

Finally, on Monday, 18 June, Mr Justice Cantley began his summing-up, which was supposed to be a clear, balanced analysis of the facts, allegations and issues for the benefit of a jury of laymen who might, understandably, have become muddled after so much high-powered legal debate. But Cantley did not see his role in these terms; his two-day speech was so biased in favour of Thorpe and his co-defendants that reporters thought that he had either gone mad or was making an elaborate private joke. Sometimes, as he burrowed into the body of the evidence, he seemed to be suggesting that Thorpe and the others might be guilty, but whenever that happened he changed direction quickly, like a driver who discovers that he has gone down a one-way street the wrong way. But these subtleties appeared to escape the jurors, who only seemed to perk up when he made his big points.

He told them that Bessell, Scott and Newton were liars and should not be believed. He said of Bessell, 'He is plainly a very intelligent, very articulate man. He must have impressed the voters of Cornwall very much. He told us that he was a lay preacher at the same time as being, as he put it, sexually promiscuous. And therefore a humbug.' He described Scott thus: 'He is a crook. He is a fraud, a sponger . . . He is a whiner. He is a parasite. But of course he could still be telling the truth . . . I am not expressing any opinion.' He was also unimpressed by Newton: 'He is a chump, a conceited bungler. I doubt whether he has paid any income tax. One has to look at his evidence with great care.'

But Cantley was much kinder to the defendants, who were, he said, men of 'hitherto unblemished reputation'. He was particularly keen on Thorpe: 'He is a Privy Counsellor, a former leader of the Liberal Party and a national figure with a very distinguished public record.'

On the morning of Wednesday, 20 June he brought the proceedings to a close. He told the jury that, first, they had to consider the charge that the four defendants had conspired to murder Scott:

> Put it that way because that is the correct way to apply the burden of proof. If the answer to that is, 'No, we are not sure,' that is an end to it, because if there was no conspiracy, none of the accused can be guilty of it. If your answer is, 'Yes, we are sure,' then you should proceed conscientiously to examine the evidence against each of the defendants in turn. If you find a doubt about any of the accused, he is entitled to be acquitted.

On the other charge, that Thorpe incited others to murder Scott, he said, 'Again you must ask yourself if you are sure that early in 1969 Thorpe seriously and genuinely tried to persuade Holmes to murder Mr Scott. If you are completely sure, you will convict, but if there is any reasonable doubt you will acquit.' He smiled and said that he would only accept a unanimous verdict. 'You may go now. Take as long as you like. There is no hurry. We shall wait for you.'

The jury trooped out to consider whether Jeremy Thorpe and the other three, whose names they kept forgetting, had plotted to kill Norman Scott. Mrs Celia Kettle-Williams, a middle-aged woman who taught English and home economics at a comprehensive in south-east London, had arrived at the Old Bailey on Tuesday, 8 May for jury service expecting to be assigned to a humdrum case and was thrilled when she was told to report for the Big One in Court Number One. The lawyers, who could veto prospective jurors, thought that it was more important to find out whether they had read *The Pencourt File* than how they voted. Thus, four were rejected, which gave Kettle-Williams her chance to participate in history. She said, 'I was delighted. I had not followed the committal in the press but I liked Jeremy Thorpe.' She was also a member of the Liberal Party, which she did not mention because no one asked her. But, to be fair, she was not the sort of person to let her political beliefs influence her; it was an honour to be asked to serve on the jury of the biggest court case in living memory and she was determined to do her best.[11]

Then came another unexpected honour. She said, 'I went to the loo and came back and found out that I had been elected forewoman. The other jurors said that I was the only one who had sounded confident when I took the oath. I suppose that was because I was a schoolteacher and was used to speaking in public.'

Journalists had worked hard since Thorpe had been charged the previous summer and had thick files of interviews and background material, which proved, or so they thought, that he had had an affair with Scott, that he had deployed Bessell to buy Scott's silence and, when that failed, had commissioned his friend, Holmes, to make sure that Scott never bothered him again. But the media and the police had not known, of course, that the case would be tried by a judge who thought that it was disgraceful that a statesman like Thorpe should be embarrassed by having to stand trial. However, they should have realised the intrinsic weakness of any prosecution which depended on the testimonies of Scott, a vengeful hysteric, Bessell, a self-confessed fraud, and Newton, a braggart who would say anything for money. They also overlooked the fact that this was Britain. Some of the jurors might, in theory, have been Liberals, anarchists or revolutionaries but they had been brought up in a society where the idea of class, that a privileged minority were inherently superior, was implanted deep in the subconscious of the majority – and to the jurors Cantley and Thorpe would unquestionably have belonged to the elite who, rightly or wrongly, had always run the country.

The only person who could have threatened Thorpe was David Holmes but the police had not been allowed to question him with the vigour with which they handled ordinary suspects in Bristol. In the absence of a confession from him there was only circumstantial evidence, which proved nothing. For example, the police and the media thought that it had been established beyond doubt that Jack Hayward's £20,000 had gone, via the hapless Nadir Dinshaw, to Holmes and then to Newton; as they studied the faces of the jurors reporters had whispered to each other that they were obviously finding it hard to grasp the technicalities of cash transfers between the Caribbean and Jersey.

By late afternoon that Wednesday the jury were exhausted and needed a break. They were ferried to the Westmoreland Hotel, near Lord's, the home of cricket in St John's Wood, where they were warned by the court ushers who accompanied them not to discuss the case. Kettle-Williams said, 'We had a lovely dinner. Then the ushers said that they would take us all for a walk in the park because it was so hot. But they put us on our honour not to listen to the news in our bedrooms.'

Jeremy Thorpe was also relaxing that steamy night. The defendants had been on bail but this was withdrawn, as was customary, when the jury retired, and they were shipped off in a police van to Brixton prison. Thorpe, who was handcuffed to George Deakin, lay on the floor of the vehicle to avoid being photographed. While Deakin, Holmes and Le Mesurier were packed off to share cells with other prisoners Thorpe discovered that he was suffering from a stomach upset which required treatment in the prison hospital. When the journeymen reporters who were covering the trial heard about this they realised that Thorpe was still being treated as if he was the victim of a ghastly misunderstanding. But it was not their job to express these kind of forthright opinions in print. Next day Thorpe, Holmes, Deakin and Le Mesurier returned to the Old Bailey. Despite what Le Mesurier called the 'unforgivable' closing statement by Carman, they spent that Thursday in a private room there, chatting and playing cards, under Le Mesurier's tutelage.

Thorpe spent Thursday night in the hospital in Brixton prison, still suffering from a stomach upset, while his three co-defendants endured the discomfort of the cells. The jury, meanwhile, wound down in the Westmoreland Hotel.

Next morning, Friday, 22 June, they assembled again at the Old Bailey and at 2.34 p.m. Kettle-Williams led her colleagues back into Number One Court. They had been out for fifty-one hours and forty-nine minutes. The jury had worked hard. But it was a complex case, involving issues such as homosexuality, and characters, including an hysterical male model and a distinguished public figure, from a different world. Reporters agreed that, confronted by this bewildering array of issues and people, the jury had probably just accepted the judge's opinion, that Thorpe was innocent, even if it had taken him two days to say so. This was the phenomenon described by Ludovic Kennedy. Many years before this trial he had written:

> The mean intelligence of any jury is apt to be low; this apart, few have any experience in assessing the value of evidence, in separating the relevant from the trivial, and most, after the first day or two, find their concentration waning. Never mind, they say to themselves, the judge will tell us what to do in his summing-up. They cling to this thought as a swimmer to a spar . . . The judge remains the great leveller, the last safety net, the junction where prejudice and calumny end and fair play begins.[12]

Thorpe, Holmes, Deakin and Le Mesurier had been enjoying a lunch of smoked salmon, beef and French wine, courtesy of Clement Freud, the Liberal MP and bon vivant who was Thorpe's friend, when they were told that the jury were back. The court was packed for the verdict. Thorpe stood, motionless, staring at infinity, as Kettle-Williams announced that all four were not guilty. Deakin grinned. Le Mesurier gripped Thorpe's arm. Holmes swayed. Then Thorpe turned, smiled at Marion and said, 'Darling, we won!' and tossed three cushions, which he had needed to support his weak back, over the dock, as if he was back on the hustings as Jeremy Thorpe, MP, PC.

Reporters stampeded out to telephone the sensational news to their offices, oblivious of Cantley's injunction to remain seated in his court. The defence lawyers now petitioned limply for costs, the award of which, to the legal *cognoscenti*, was significant. Deakin was granted costs, because he had co-operated with the police, but the applications by lawyers for Holmes and Le Mesurier were rejected, because they had been so unhelpful. Thorpe's lawyer George Carman did not trouble the judge; in financial terms this did not matter to his client, who had a substantial defence fund.

Thorpe now assumed the inappropriate demeanour of a conquering hero. Instead of leaving court quietly, to ponder his future, he strode out of the Old Bailey into the sunshine, greeting the gawping crowds with his arms aloft. This was the old Thorpe, who had such faith in himself; it did not cross his mind that his refusal to testify had damned him. This was classic Thorpian self-delusion; the jury might have decided that he had not plotted to kill Scott but it was obvious to anyone who had listened to the evidence, apart from Mr Justice Cantley, that he was not fit to be entrusted with the management of a sweet shop, let alone a political party.

David Holmes slunk away, shattered by Thorpe's betrayal. His barrister, John Mathew, said:

It was the most incredible scene I have ever seen. When the verdict came in Holmes was swaying like a drunken boxer. He was totally gone, out on his feet, supported by the wardens. But Thorpe had a look of total equanimity, a sort of told-you-so expression. In five seconds he was unfazed and was thanking the coppers in the dock and kissing the lady usher. He was saying to the press, 'I will see you outside.' Poor old Holmes. I went down to the cells and took him to my car. I ran him down the road and put him in a taxi.[13]

That evening, while Thorpe celebrated, Holmes had a quiet dinner with close friends. His long-standing companion, Gerald Hagan, said, 'He was exhausted. He couldn't believe that it was over. He saved Jeremy but I don't think that they ever met again.'[14]

Journalists who had followed the case were devastated. Barrie Penrose and Roger Courtiour joined the LWT team who had prepared the documentary on Thorpe for a tearful, end-of-project dinner, hosted by Michael Grade, LWT's Director of Programmes. The Thorpe programme was never broadcast. The BBC also dropped its film, which had been masterminded by Gordon Carr and Tom Mangold, for whom the story had been a succession of unhappy near misses. The *Sunday Times* journalists, Lewis Chester, Magnus Linklater and David May, who had written a book describing how Thorpe had plotted to kill Scott, watched their manuscript being ripped to libel-free pieces by lawyers.

Norman Scott was at home in Devon, surrounded by his animals and journalists. He shrugged when he was told that Thorpe had been acquitted, as if the verdict was irrelevant, which, in a sense, it was; Thorpe might have been free but he had lost everything that mattered to him. From the moment that they became infatuated with each other in 1961 it had been inevitable that one of them would be ruined; that Friday in June 1979 Scott knew that he had won.

Andrew Newton, the failed hitman, rose to the occasion with this typically ungrammatical, one-line grumble: 'I am not too wrapped up in that judge.'

Thorpe returned with Marion to their handsome house in Orme Square. Bottles of champagne were opened, which he reportedly enjoyed, having recovered miraculously from the painful stomach upset that had necessitated two nights in the hospital at Brixton prison. Later he emerged with Marion and his mother, Ursula, on the balcony, waving to passers-by, who did not understand why this pasty-faced man in a suit that looked as if it had been bought in a jumble sale, an old lady with white hair and glasses and a matronly figure who was smiling inanely were pretending to be royalty.

Next day, newspapers which had once idolised Thorpe delivered their verdicts: The *Daily Telegraph* declaimed, 'Mr Thorpe exercised the undoubted right of every citizen, but his public image might have been better served had he explained the course of his behaviour publicly and on oath.' The *Daily Express* said that Thorpe would be remembered 'not for his political achievements but for this case'. The *Daily Mirror* wrote: 'He has been cleared of the criminal charges against him but the uncontested evidence puts an end to his public life.'

Peter Bessell, who had returned to his holiday 'bungalows' in Oceanside, was numbed. The *Sunday Telegraph*, which had been condemned for its contract with him, refused to publish his extracts. For once, money was not all that counted; he was paid for his work but that was no comfort to him. He knew that he was despised for betraying an old friend and had craved a respectable platform to explain himself. He had planned to say that Thorpe was not a bad man; he had many admirable qualities but, like everyone, had his faults, which, alas, had proved fatal. Since no newspaper would publish his story, he had to issue statements, in the hope that someone would print them: 'Jeremy has suffered enough. I just hope he can find peace. I did what I did because I felt it was my duty but there were times when my courage nearly failed me.'

That was as much sympathy as Thorpe received. Harold Wilson, whose decision to summon Pencourt in the spring of 1976 had led to Thorpe's downfall, refused to comment. David Steel obviously hoped that Thorpe would vanish, possibly to a desert island without telephones. 'I hope that after a suitable period of rest and recuperation he may find many avenues where his great talents may be used.' But Steel made it clear that these 'great avenues' did not include the Liberal Party, which was still embarassed that it had been led by a man who had used Party funds to try and silence a former lover.

Auberon Waugh was completing his book on the trial but managed to find time to help *Private Eye* publish a 'Special Acquittal Souvenir' issue, with a photograph of Thorpe on the cover under the bubble: 'Buggers can't be losers'. Peter Cook, the other giant of British satire, was also inspired by the verdict. He produced an hilarious parody of Cantley's summing-up, which most people thought must have sprung from his fertile mind but which was actually not that different from the original.

Understandably, the press, which had invested large sums compiling dossiers on Thorpe, wanted to know how the jurors had reached their verdict. The law covering newspaper revelations on debates inside the jury room had been unclear for many years and there were some circumstances when reporters could describe a jury's discussions, though, it must be added, there was so much confusion about the law that no one was sure what was legal and what was not. A few weeks after Thorpe's acquittal the *New Statesman* decided to test the law and published a long exclusive interview with one of the Thorpe jurors.[15] The *New Statesman* did not name the juror but that was its only concession to the tradition of jury secrecy. The story appeared to confirm the suspicions of reporters who had covered the trial: notably, that the charges had been ill-conceived, that Cantley's interventions and summing-up had been crucial and that Bessell's 'double-your-money' contract with the *Sunday Telegraph* had discredited him totally as a witness.

Other journalists followed up the *New Statesman* scoop. They expanded the magazine's theory that the prosecution had failed to convince the jury that Thorpe was a homosexual who had had an affair with Scott. They concluded that the jury must have decided that Thorpe's sexuality was not relevant. This puzzled reporters because they had always thought that the entire case rested on his honesty and his possible motive for wanting to eliminate Scott; if he had never slept with Scott then, clearly, he had no reason to want to see Scott killed, or even frightened.

The press also wondered how the jurors had tackled the problem of Newton's jammed gun. From the verdict it seemed that they had decided that Newton could have unjammed it if he had really tried and that, therefore, he had never intended to kill Scott, which was, of course, what he had said when he was tried at Exeter in 1976.

According to other journalists and lawyers the jury had simply not understood the world that Thorpe, Holmes and Scott inhabited. One observer said, 'I can only guess but I think that the jury was swayed by the judge, who liked Thorpe. I imagine that they decided that Scott was lying about his affair with Thorpe. I also do not think that the jury knew that Holmes was a homosexual.' Other observers said that the jury must have accepted the defence's curious theory: that Holmes had hired Newton without telling Thorpe because Scott was distracting him from his duties as Liberal leader and that Newton had then allied himself with Scott to blackmail Thorpe. All this was interesting but it did not matter: Thorpe had been tried and acquitted and that was that.

On Sunday, 1 July, two weeks after Thorpe walked out of the Old Bailey, the Reverend John Hornby unwisely held what he called a 'Thanksgiving Service for Marion and Jeremy Thorpe' in his eleventh-century church in the village of Bratton Fleming, Exmoor, in the heart of what had once been Thorpe's constituency. Hornby, who also administered to the village's temporal needs by chairing the local Liberal Association, anticipated the kind of crowds that had once greeted Thorpe on his barnstorming tours of North Devon, and had arranged for the service to be broadcast on loudspeakers in the village hall, for those who arrived too late to find a place in the church.

That morning Thorpe, Marion and young Rupert took their places in the front pew. Behind them were dozens of journalists and a handful of curious locals. The village hall was empty. Hornby, who had not sought permission from his superiors for this unusual service, pressed on and said that he had chosen the lesson for the day from Ecclesiastes: 'Let us now praise famous men.' He told the Thorpes and the media:

> We have the opportunity to give thanks to God for the ministry of his servant Jeremy in North Devon. In the long dark days of Minehead and the Old Bailey, God granted Marion and Jeremy that fantastic resilience which has aroused the admiration of the whole world. The darkness is now passed and the true light shines. This is the day the Lord hath made! Now is the day of our salvation! Thanks be to God, for with God nothing is impossible!

The media tittered and scribbled but the Archdeacon of Barnstaple, the Venerable Ronald Herniman, was not pleased that Hornby had compared Thorpe's acquittal with the Resurrection. Herniman told the *Daily Telegraph*:

> Both clergy and laity feel the service was unfitting, unseemly and unsavoury and has soiled the Church, and I agree with them. There is a great deal of unhappiness about the result at the Old Bailey. As far as most people are concerned, the trial ended with a big question mark over the case. People have said, 'Just because a man is acquitted does not mean he is innocent.' The resentment among people of all ages is remarkable. They feel nauseated.

But Hornby said he had no regrets: 'I pray that God will drive out from human hearts the evils of suspicion and hatred. Jeremy has been the best MP North Devon has ever had or could have. The service was a very English occasion and a suitable ending to the Jeremy Thorpe story.'

EPILOGUE

Jeremy Thorpe

The Reverend John Hornby's 'Thanksgiving Service for Marion and Jeremy Thorpe' in his little church on the edge of Exmoor, which had been such an excruciating embarrassment, was the beginning of a living death for Thorpe. He had been acquitted and was, therefore, in law at least, innocent. But that did not save him. His peers and the public were less impressed than Mr Justice Cantley by Eton and Oxford, his collection of Chinese ceramics and by the letters 'PC' for Privy Counsellor after his name; he might not have plotted to kill Scott but he had behaved abominably.

As the years rolled by Thorpe always recorded his achievements in *Who's Who*, as if he was still a player in the Great Game of Politics: 'Chairman, Jeremy Thorpe Associates (Development Consultants in the Third World) since 1984. Pres. North Devon Liberal Democrats (formerly North Devon Liberal Assoc.) 1987 – United Nations Association, Chairman, Executive 1976–1980; Chairman, Political Committee, 1977–1985.[1] But this was an illusion. His life effectively ended when he waved triumphantly from the dock in Number One Court; he was only 50 years old but the Establishment, which had ensured that he was not sent to prison, dispatched him into exile. Imprisonment might, perhaps, have been kinder because it would have conferred on him a marketable celebrity. The British are a generous nation and would have pardoned his past sins; after a few years in a comfortable open prison, writing his memoirs, he would have emerged, like Richard Nixon after Watergate, as the elder statesman who had paid for his mistakes and was wiser for having done so.

John Profumo, the Minister for War who had been forced to resign in 1963, had been rehabilitated because he had done the decent thing and admitted his errors. (He was awarded the CBE in 1975 for his services to charity.) But Thorpe could not do that because he was too arrogant to admit that he had been a fool and because, like many secret homosexuals of his generation, he could not face the truth about himself. In December 1979, six months after the trial, he emerged to confront the world. He arrived with Marion and his son Rupert, aged nine, at the parish church of Buckingham Palace, St Peter's, Belgravia, to take part in a fund-raising concert for the United Nations' Human Rights Day and the International Year of the Child.[2] Journalists are predators; like lions stalking a herd of wildebeest, they circle the rich and powerful, waiting to pounce on one who is fatally weakened. The same writers who had once scoffed at Pencourt's allegations now turned on Thorpe. One wrote:

> Thorpe's spirit, once his personal trademark, seemed to flicker to life only infrequently, and his bitterness appeared to weigh like a coat of lead . . . His features were immobile, his eyes wide open and unblinking like two round marbles set in Plasticine. He looks permanently sad or briefly amused; contentment seems banished. 'I think he's so dignified,' said one woman as he passed. 'He's not dignified,' contradicted her friend. 'He's crushed, totally crushed.'[3]

He wanted to fight North Devon again for the Liberals but was told that his services were not required. He tried to find another constituency but he was a non-person, whom the Party wanted to forget. He still thought that he could joke his way back to public favour but there was a growing fear now that the best lay behind him and that the future would be nothing but memories of the past. He was rejected by everyone. He tried to persuade television companies to hire him as an interviewer but they did not want a middle-aged has-been who had inspired tasteless jokes about dead dogs. He was shortlisted for a job as race-relations adviser with the Greater London Council, but did not get it.[4]

The most wounding episode came in March 1982 when, at the age of 52, he was chosen from forty-two candidates to be director of Amnesty International's British section, on a modest salary of £14,000 a year. But many Amnesty staff and members were furious and demanded that the appointment be rescinded. The protests were led by David Astor, co-founder of Amnesty in 1961 and, ironically, a former editor of the *Observer*, which had once been a stalwart supporter of the Liberal Party. Astor said,

'Amnesty is a big, world-wide organisation with very important responsibilities to people in prison. It depends on its own reputation for integrity and good judgement. Jeremy has not shown himself to be a man of good judgement. It was a great mistake to offer him the job. He has some very old friends. I hope his appointment will not be confirmed.'[5]

Thorpe tried to rally support but it was hopeless and a few days later he announced that he was withdrawing. He was obviously bitter, as he made clear in his resignation letter: 'What astounds me is that people who claim to believe in human rights should display so much prejudice and pettiness.' Astor advised Thorpe to learn from John Profumo, who had accepted that his public life was over and had toiled anonymously for charity. But he said that Thorpe insisted on 'playing a role as if nothing has happened'.

A few people remained loyal. Malcolm Harper, director of the United Nations Association, said that he was proud that Thorpe was the chairman of their political committee. He said, 'Many people have cold-shouldered him but we felt that he had been acquitted and he has been very valuable to us.'[6] He also retained the affection of many people in North Devon, who thought that he had been victimised by horrible newspapers in London and who remembered him as a hard-working and caring MP. In 1987 they invited him to become President of the North Devon Liberal Democrats.

But by now there was another, serious problem: he was suffering from Parkinson's disease. His friends thought that it had been triggered by the strain of the Scott controversy but that seems unlikely. Parkinson's, named after James Parkinson, the surgeon who discovered it in 1817, afflicts about one person in 1,000 and, according to orthodox medical opinion, is 'not caused by stress, anxiety, emotional or family upsets'.[7]

Like other progressive neurological illnesses, such as multiple sclerosis and motor-neurone disease, it is incurable and cruel. A cocktail of drugs can slow but not halt the development of the many distressing symptoms caused by the brain's inability to manufacture a substance called dopamine, which helps transmit messages to the spinal cord, nerves and muscles. These symptoms include shaking of the hands, rigidity and akinesia, otherwise a pronounced slowness of movement, and handwriting which shrinks to a tiny scrawl. As the condition worsens the victim is twisted sideways, arms held close to the side; walking becomes an uncontrolled trot, the face freezes and the voice is reduced to a faint slur. Often the mind is unaffected but most sufferers are prone to depression, either caused by drugs or by the anguish of being imprisoned in a body that is rotting.

Friends said that Thorpe tried to keep going, supported by Marion, who remained devoted to him. One recalled: 'They were having a party and Jeremy was trying to help Marion. He was rushing around with plates and you wondered if you could catch them if he dropped them. I know he made at least three very good jokes but I couldn't hear them. It was awful.'[8] By the early 1990s he was ready to try anything to try to reverse the disease. He had a foetal cell implanted in his brain in an effort to stimulate the production of dopamine, but it had no effect.

His young gay friends were faithful, even though some disapproved of his old hypocritical lifestyle. Steve Atack said, 'You will not find anyone who is more pro-JT than me.' He said that they had never discussed Thorpe's homosexuality but he conceded that Thorpe had not been honest: 'I criticised people for not coming out and saying that they were gay. But I can see that it was hard for them. Politicians of that generation who said that they were gay would have been finished.' He said that the trial had done more than ruin Thorpe; it had also set back the cause of gay rights because 'it reinforced the idea that gays were untrustworthy people who resorted to blackmail'.[9]

Some gays were less understanding. Bernard Greaves, who had warned the Party in the mid-1970s that Thorpe was courting disaster by cruising gay pubs and bars, told me: 'The key is the fact that he had to conceal the fact that he was gay. He was an Establishment figure who wanted to be respected and loved. He turned against people who could have helped him. He was just too old to adapt to gay liberation.'[10]

Most of Thorpe's heterosexual friends vanished after the trial. For example, Dominic Le Foe, who had once been Thorpe's public-relations guru, commented, 'He is a sad and pathetic figure. I never wished him any harm but he let me down. The Fates couldn't have taken a more potent revenge. The Furies must be laughing their heads off. He can't perform now.'[11]

Some, however, argued that he had been unfairly pilloried. Michael Ogle, who shared rooms with Thorpe at Oxford, said, 'Jeremy was acquitted. I think that the jury would have liked to convict Holmes but acquit Jeremy. But the judge said they couldn't do that. I believe there was a conspiracy but without Jeremy's knowledge.'[12] John Pardoe, the rugged former Liberal MP for North Cornwall, said, 'I was not surprised by the verdict. If you really wanted to murder someone would you conspire with that extraordinary crowd? It was ludicrous. A pilot who had never flown a plane successfully and that crowd from Wales. It was all fantasy stuff.'

Ann Dummett, who, as Ann Chesney had been President of the Liberal Club at Oxford, said, 'I was shocked and upset by the case. Men with pinball machines. I suspect without any evidence that the British intelligence services wanted to get rid of Wilson and Thorpe.'[13]

But others distanced themselves from him. Stanley Brodie, who had once been a member of Thorpe's entourage at Oxford, said, 'He was acquitted but, on the other hand, he put himself in a compromising position. He suffered cruelly but that is life. Unfairness is meted out every day.'[14]

But the key to it all was Thorpe himself. Christopher Bourke, another Oxford contemporary, told me: 'You should write to Jeremy. He is a very approachable man. Or speak to Marion. The wrong kind of people have been asking to speak to them for years so we all have to be careful.'[15]

The voice on the answerphone in my study in London was an inaudible whisper. It was summer 1995 and British Telecom, which once took a month to repair a fault, was now a digitalised money-making machine. So, I punched in the numbers 1471, and a robotic, semi-female voice gave the long and unfamiliar number of the last caller. I scribbled it down and then dialled.

'Hello.'

'Sorry, who I am speaking to?'

'Marion Thorpe.'

'Ah, yes, this is Simon Freeman. I think Mr Thorpe has just called me.'

I explained that I had written to Mr Thorpe asking if he would be prepared to discuss 'a documentary project' I was researching, which was neither a lie nor the whole truth; these were early days and it did not seem sensible to reveal that a book was the ultimate objective. Marion Thorpe had a firm, assertive voice, in contrast to her husband's sad murmur. She said that, perhaps, he might be prepared to meet but he was not well and distrusted reporters, who always wanted to ask him about matters that were best forgotten. I said that I might be in North Devon soon and wondered whether I might drop in and pay my respects to Mr Thorpe. Well, said Marion, that would be, um, very nice.

I packed my overnight bag and headed off to Thorpe's home in Higher Chuggaton. Five hours later I located the hamlet, which consisted of a few scruffy houses dozing in the summer heat. I asked an old man, who was tending his parched garden, whether he could direct me to Mr Thorpe's house; he pointed to a lane off the main road. The large wooden gates at Thorpe's cottage were open so I drove in and parked. The main cottage was a postcard idyll and was flanked by a converted barn and double garage. I knocked on the door and a few seconds later Marion Thorpe, sturdy, tanned and wearing an old dress and sandals, appeared. I said that I just happened to be in the area, which was not very convincing in view of the fact that Higher Chuggaton was on the way to nowhere, and wondered if Mr Thorpe was available. She smiled and said that he was not; I asked if he might be free tomorrow, at, say, 11 a.m. She said that might be possible.

Next morning, at 10.59 a.m., I was back. It would be nice, I thought, if Thorpe finally told the truth; he was dying and had nothing to gain now by further lies. Then Marion opened the door. She had paid me the compliment of dressing formally, as if she was going to one of those prestigious functions, such as a garden party at Buckingham Palace, which her husband had once so enjoyed. She ushered me into the living room, where french windows opened on to a glorious garden, and offered coffee. Then she said that she would fetch Jeremy. A few minutes later he came in, bent forward and half-running, wearing a colourful outfit of bright blue shirt, cravat and red trousers. Parkinson's had stripped him of flesh; his arms had been reduced to sticks and his face was a skull and staring eyes. Marion said that he was having problems with his new false teeth, which brought a heart-rending little protest from him that, until now, his teeth had always been fine.

But I soon realised that he did not want pity. It was difficult to understand him but Marion was able to interpret much of what he said, which turned out to be the familiar Thorpian mix of bluster and threats. He stared at my bag and asked if it contained 'a recording device'. Then he launched into a long monologue. He did not grant interviews although he had talked to another writer, who was preparing a biography, on condition that he would be allowed to check the manuscript for 'inaccuracies'. He would not help me with 'a sex trawl' and then, despite the face which had been frozen by illness, managed to glower. This was the old Thorpe, who thought that he could be protected by the law. It was hard to catch the details but the thrust was clear: he had teams of lawyers who would hammer any journalist who suggested that he was less than one hundred per cent honest and heterosexual. This was ridiculous; even before the trial he had never sued for libel.

I interrupted his rambling discourse on the terrible consequences awaiting disrespectful writers. What did he think of Harold Wilson? 'A great friend and a democrat,' said Thorpe, with rare clarity. What did he remember about Heath's offer of a coalition in 1974? But his reply defeated even his wife. Then he lost patience. He was not going to give an interview. He had no intention of helping me; he was thinking of writing his autobiography and said that he did not want to 'scoop' himself. He mumbled something else, which Marion translated: 'Why should I write your book for you?' He did, however, agree to 'clarify points of fact'. This was encouraging and I said that I would send him an interesting article, which the *Sunday Times* had published in 1974, to check it for factual errors. Thorpe said that he would be happy to help.

He was tiring visibly and I rose to leave. Then Marion asked if I would like to see the barn, which they had converted many years ago. Thorpe led the way, in that tragic shambling run, and began the guided tour. I nodded politely, although I could not understand a word, as Thorpe pointed out a magnificent piano, which, Marion volunteered, she rarely played these days. It was a beautiful room and yet it felt like a mausoleum.

He led me up some stairs and pointed unsteadily at the photographs of himself as the young star of the Liberal Party and at the commemorative mugs, given to him by the local Liberal Association to mark his election victories. For an instant it seemed that he was smiling at the memory of the good days, before Norman Scott and Parkinson's destroyed him.

I drove off and parked a few miles away. It had been an unsatisfactory and troubling encounter. Thorpe was obviously neither nice nor honest – though to be fair, that is true of many ambitious, competitive people, journalists as well as politicians – but he was not an evil man and did not deserve to be suffering like this. Yet even now, as his body rotted painfully, with no reputation to defend, he could not admit that Scott had been telling the truth all those years ago. Then I turned on my tape recorder, which had been switched on throughout the meeting. There was only the hiss of the machine; I had been recording a ghost.

As agreed, I posted the article from the *Sunday Times* to Thorpe. Many weeks later he replied. Though he was grievously ill he had not lost the ability to duck and weave behind a fog of verbiage. He wrote:

> As you will be aware I have never ruled out the possibility that I might write an autobiography or use my material in some other way, and have now come to the decision to keep such material for my future use. I believe you appreciated I did not want to scoop myself.
>
> I am, however, prepared from time to time to consider any particular aspects upon which you seek assistance with a view to clarifying matters which you propose to include in your project . . . I would be prepared to do this for the sake of factual accuracy but only with the clear understanding that it would in no way be suggested that I have either authorised or approved such a project and nothing will be written or said to suggest that the project or any part of it has been the subject of any assistance or approval by me.[16]

He said, however, that he would not make any comment on the *Sunday Times* article because 'this would be a back-door way of obtaining partial authorisation, which I am anxious to avoid'. Nor would he make any comments about his life: 'If I was to do then I might just as well use this for an autobiography.'

To add the final mad touch, he made his usual threats: 'Let me make it clear the form of assistance which I have suggested is on the basis that your project will be fair and balanced. Let me say frankly, from the information received from various quarters, some doubt can be thrown on this objective . . . May I take it that you would be willing to show me your final draft?'

Penrose agreed with me that there was no point in pursuing him. But Thorpe would not let go. He was still writing threatening letters to me in January 1996:

> I refer to paragraph three of my letter of 11 October which sets out the guidelines on the basis of which I would be

prepared to help. To summarise, this would mean that I would not be willing to provide material which I would need for my own biography – otherwise I would be scooping myself. Secondly, your request was fair and reasonable and thirdly, that your approach was fair and reasonable. May I raise again the question of seeing your final draft in the cause of accuracy.[17]

Meanwhile his friends had decided that it was time that the truth should be told, whether he liked it or not. John Fryer had met Thorpe in 1970 when he was a pimply 19-year-old activist in Oxford's Liberal Club. Twenty-five years later he was a respected and openly gay writer and broadcaster, whose front door at his terraced house in London's East End announced that he was 'Honorary Consul of Mauritania in the United Kingdom'. Fryer, who had been a Liberal candidate in general and European elections, told me, 'Jeremy was one of the most charming people I have ever met. He was charismatic and extremely funny.' But he added that there was no point in denying what many gay Liberals had always known: that, before his illness, Thorpe had been a promiscuous homosexual. He conceded that Thorpe would not thank him for this: 'I am quite sure that he would rather everyone left the whole thing alone. But it's gone past that now. He is a subject of interest and it's better to be accurate. It is all too easy, especially for someone who is not involved in this world, to make it sound sordid.'

He said that by the early 1970s Thorpe's sexual predilections were widely rumoured in gay Liberal circles: 'It was not that people said, oh, Jeremy is gay, just that he had a flirtatiousness that went beyond charm. But it would have been impossible for him to come out then, even if he had wanted to. He liked to know that there were certain people who he could have a naughty conversation with over a drink.' He cultivated young Liberals, said Fryer, with whom he could 'discuss politics and have sex'. Fryer said, 'He had a network of people. They introduced him to men. It wasn't necessarily rough trade. But they weren't proper relationships. It was just sex.' But by the mid-1970s gay Liberals were becoming irritated by his double life:

When it all went wrong we felt that he had brought it on himself, by not accepting that things had changed. It wasn't

really a problem that he was a gay but he saw it as one.
He started fabricating things and lost a lot of support in
the Party because he would not come clean. He brought a
lot of his problems on himself. He wanted the best of both
worlds – his fun and a family. Today, he just doesn't figure
in the consciousness of the gay movement. He chose not to
be involved with gays so they are not interested in him.[18]

Others were less sympathetic. For example, Lady Falkender could
not forgive him for tricking Harold Wilson into declaring that he
was the victim of a plot by the South Africans. She told Penrose:
'He must have known what would happen to Harold but he
didn't care. I don't have any illusions about him any more.'[19]
Falkender realised that Thorpe had learnt nothing from the past
when he arrived, unannounced, with Marion, at her mews house
in London. They asked her if she could arrange a peerage for him,
which struck her as an extraordinary cheek in view of the way
he had behaved. Then, mischievously, she passed on his request
to Lord Jenkins, the former Labour Home Secretary and founder
of the Social Democrats, which had merged with the Liberals to
form the Liberal Democrats.[20]

Norman Scott

He came striding out of the magnificent eleventh-century Devon
long house, picking his way through the cats who were sleeping
in the summer heat and the hordes of clucking ducks and geese,
and beamed at Barrie Penrose. He was wearing a denim shirt,
jeans and wellington boots and, despite a stoop, radiated health
and looked closer to 45 than 55. He had defied Mr Justice
Cantley, who had described him as 'an hysterical, warped
personality, a crook, a fraud, a sponger, a whiner and a
parasite'. Cantley was dead and Thorpe was dying but he was
fit and thriving.

He ushered us into his living room. He said that he avoided
journalists now after an unpleasant experience with the *News of
the World* six years earlier, on the tenth anniversary of the trial.
The newspaper had 'borrowed' photographs of his teenage son
Ben, by his marriage to Susan Myers, and had published them.
'Ben was furious with me,' Scott said. 'We had not seen each
other for many years and were just getting to know each other.

Then the *News of the World* happened. Ben thought that I had sold the photographs.'

But Penrose was different because Pencourt had treated him as a human being, not a piece of refuse. It would be an exaggeration to describe them as friends but they sounded like veterans of a military campaign as they argued and laughed about the awful Van de Vater, who made Norman scrub his back in the bath, the missing Insurance card and Thorpe's flings with young men whom he picked up in the street. As always, Scott had chosen to live far from the rest of humanity. The long house – of such historic importance that it was pictured on the cover of the standard work on Devon architecture by the late Sir Nikolaus Pevsner – was perched on the edge of Dartmoor, high above the village of Trowleigh.

He moved here in 1985 after friends, whom he said preferred to remain anonymous, offered him the house, rent-free for life. He had some savings, bequeathed to him by another friend, and earned a small but steady income by schooling horses. As always, too, he was self-sufficient. He also owned, roughly, seventeen cats, who ensured that mice did not go anywhere near the house, a sheep dog, a whippet and two champagne pugs, called Polly and Dora, who sat by his side, staring at him, their black masks set in the distinctive querulous scowl which made pugs the fashion accessory of 1995.

This was not the effeminate, hysterical creature of Cantley's summing-up. He was rational and cracked jokes about Thorpe's selfishness in bed; but there was a disturbing side to him. I said that it was hard not to feel sorry for Thorpe, but he would have none of this; he laughed and slapped himself, delighted that the man who had infected him with 'the disease' of homosexuality was suffering.

The living room was crammed with paintings and photographs of Norman hunting and show-jumping. On the mantelpiece was a photograph of Conway Wilson-Young, the rich young man whom Scott had once lived with and who had died of a drug overdose in New York in 1985. In the hall were rows of black riding boots, testimony to Scott's career as a horseman.

Parked by the gate was a Land Rover, which, he said, was essential for this terrain. Twenty years earlier, when he was living in Devon and demanding action be taken against the dreadful Thorpe, he had never insured or taxed his cars but the local police, wary of getting involved with such a troublesome character, had always left him alone. When Penrose asked him whether he bothered with insurance and tax now he said that, of course, he did, otherwise he would be breaking the law. The *News of the World* had suggested that he lived in constant fear; it said that he was 'haunted by Thorpe's creepy face' and 'only felt safe when morning comes'. The newspaper said that he kept 'a well-locked chest, containing all my papers on the case, safe and near, in case it all blows up again'. But this was not the Scott of summer 1995.

His personal life, however, had not been easy. Susan Myers had divorced him and had ignored his requests to be allowed to see his son Ben. Then, in the late 1980s, Myers committed suicide. As he was sorting through her personal papers Ben found Norman's Christmas cards and realised that he was his father. There was a reconciliation, which was wrecked by the *News of the World* article. Scott's brothers and sisters had disowned him long ago but he said that he was still close to Briony, his daughter by Hilary Arthur.

He walked outside to groom his horses, trailed by Polly and Dora; life was not perfect but he was probably as close to happiness as he had ever been.

David Holmes

Holmes died in the middle of 1990 from a re-occurrence of the cancer which he had fought as a young man, though Thorpe's friends whispered unkindly that he had, in fact, perished of AIDS. Michael Ogle, who acted as a go-between in the summer of 1978, when Thorpe was trying to agree a cover story with Holmes, said, 'He died of AIDS. If you get up to those tricks consistently it tends to happen.'[21] But Holmes had perished in spirit long before. The disgrace of the trial was painful enough for a man who abhorred publicity and who was terrified that his homosexuality, and promiscuity, would be exposed. But he could have endured it if Thorpe, the friend whom he loved, had remained loyal.

Holmes's friends were disgusted by Thorpe's behaviour. Dinah Plunkett said that he 'had laid down his life for Thorpe'[22] and was rewarded with ostracism. Gerald Hagan told me: 'David was a gentleman. He stuck his neck out for Thorpe and he was betrayed.

He was hoodwinked. Scott was a woman wronged and wanted revenge but David didn't realise that. If I had known what David was doing I would have told him to tell Thorpe to sort out his own affairs.'[23]

After the trial Holmes's life had disintegrated; he had prospered as 'a business consultant' because he was suave and respectable but no company wanted to be advised by a man who had hired an 'airline pilot' to frighten or kill a homosexual male model.

In January 1981, he was arrested early one morning in the Old Brompton Road for importuning. A few days later West London magistrates heard that Holmes, aged 50, who described himself as the manager of a roller disco in North London, had approached several men, before walking off with a man in tight jeans. When he was arrested he pleaded with the police: 'Look, I promise to go straight home, only not this. I'll never come back here again, please.'

His solicitor, John Underwood, said:

Because of the Thorpe case it caused a bit of a stir. But it was a typical case of importuning. He was walking down the Old Brompton Road mildly cruising but unfortunately he was cruising a cop. It was standard stuff. You are in a funny gay world here. We did our best to get him off but it was an open and shut case. He said he was going to see a girlfriend but the magistrates didn't believe him.[24]

The fine was only £25 but the real punishment was the headlines in the tabloid press: 'The sex shame of Thorpe's friend' and 'Thorpe friend in court on sex charge'.[25]

He tried to fight back in June with a series of articles in the *News of the World*, the fee for which he donated to charity. He explained that he had lied to protect Thorpe, who had demanded that Scott had to be killed, just as the prosecution had always alleged. In the first instalment, headlined: 'World exclusive: Truth behind the biggest political scandal of the decade: Kill Scott! pleaded Thorpe', Holmes said, 'From now to eternity I deny the charge of conspiracy to murder. But the incitement charge which Jeremy faced was true and if I'd gone into the witness box I'd have had to tell the truth.' But it was too late; Holmes was ruined.

His solicitor from the Old Bailey, David Freeman, said:

He was a very nice chap. One of the nicest I have ever defended. I remained in touch with after the trial because I liked him. My wife liked him immensely. Thorpe was the *Deus ex machina*. No doubt about that. My man was no leader but he was far better read than Thorpe. He was taken in by Thorpe's tremendous superficial charm. Who will rid me of this pestilent Scott? So, Holmes rode forth and buggered it all up.[26]

His barrister, John Mathew, said, 'He was a very charming, quiet chap. His problem was loyalty to Thorpe. But for that, he would never have got involved in anything like this. He was under Thorpe's control, no question about that. Thorpe was an overpowering person. If Holmes had gone into the witness box at the trial he would have had to admit that there was a conspiracy.'[27]

Sir Jack Hayward said, 'He was delightful and charming. A gentleman. I am sure that Thorpe controlled the whole thing.'

Peter Bessell

Bessell died in California in 1985, after struggling for years against the lung ailments caused by heavy smoking, and the strain of having to lie his way out of a succession of financial crises. Yet his Diane had only fond memories. She married Bessell in 1978 and typed his manuscript, which became *Cover-Up* in 1980. Bessell cruised effortlessly in the book between self-justification, where he blamed everyone but himself for his failed business career; self-abasement, when he shared his sins with the reader, as if he was in the confessional box; long indignant passages, where he railed against Thorpe and the system that had protected him; and boasts about his countless sexual conquests.

Diane talked after his death about depositing his papers in the British Library in London, as if he had been an international statesman rather than a backbench MP, failed businessman and incorrigible womaniser. She wrote to me:

Peter was full of life – passionate and charismatic yet kind and sensitive. He adored attractive, intelligent women, along

with music, theater, great books, ideas and nature. He had
a first-rate mind, was curious about everything, and as a
result could build things and solve mechanical or electrical
problems as well as analyse the state of the world. His book
dwells on the more flawed examples of his judgement and
actions. It is not a self-serving tale.[28]

Sir Jack Hayward should certainly have disliked Bessell but could
not: 'Peter was a real ladies' man. He loved animals, which appealed
to me. He tried to con me but I had a soft spot for him. I just felt
sorry for him. I couldn't find any major mistakes in his book. I
think when he wrote it he knew he wouldn't be around that long
and wanted to get it down as it was. He was trying to clear his
conscience.'[29]

John Pardoe, MP for North Cornwall from 1966 until he was
swept away in 1979 in the aftermath of the Thorpe scandal, said,
'I liked Peter but I can't say that I ever trusted him. But he was
incredibly loyal to Jeremy.' Lord Hooson, who, as Emlyn Hooson
had represented a Welsh constituency for seventeen years, said,
'Bessell was a strange and complicated character who turned out
to be completely under the dominance of Thorpe.'[30]

But there were many who had nothing kind to say. Dominic Le
Foe, Thorpe's former public-relations adviser, said, 'Bessell was
a congenital liar and a confidence trickster. He was a peculiarly
perverted man. I think he was a necrophiliac although I don't
know if he ever got the chance to indulge that. He was one of
the weirdest men I have ever met. And he was close to Thorpe,
which says everything about Thorpe.'[31]

Even the obituary writers could not find it in their hearts to be
kind to poor Bessell: 'He will be remembered for the notoriety and
ignominy he drew upon himself as the chief prosecution witness
in the trial of Mr Jeremy Thorpe in 1979. He was discredited
and dismissed as a liar and fantasist. Bessell admitted that he
was a compulsive liar and agreed that he had "a credibility
problem".'[32]

Andrew Newton

Newton's reputation as an amoral buffoon was reinforced by his
performance in the witness box at the Old Bailey. But some people,
such as John Le Mesurier, thought that the persona he presented

– 'flippant, cynical, self-righteous, stupid and television-fed into a sort of mindless conceit'[33] – disguised a devious criminal mind. He did not allow the condemnation of the judge, defence and prosecution lawyers and the press to distract him from his main object in life: to make money. He hawked a synopsis of what he liked to call his 'autobiography' around Fleet Street. This offered a fascinating glimpse into the mind of a man for whom right and wrong were meaningless single syllable words. He wrote:

The book begins with Andrew Newton's own graphic account of the shooting on Exmoor in the winter of 1975. It moves to the dramatic events that followed the shooting and then switches back to Andrew's life as a well-paid airline pilot with a glamorous bachelor existence.

The proposal – to be a hired killer. Fascinating description of clandestine meetings, amazing characters and plots all lead to the first meeting with Scott.

His own feelings and reactions begin to play an important part as the moment for putting the gun to Scott's head draws near.

After the shooting: the weeks in which he was the hunted quarry – by the police and his fellow conspirators who tried to murder him.

The arrest, his trial and the beginning of the cover-up. Instructions to protect the names of leading politicians and assurances of compensation after prison.

On release, the remarkable story of Andrew's single-handed – and entirely successful – efforts to prove the identities of those in the murder conspiracy. The Newton Tapes – as they have come to be called – revealed together with intriguing story of how they came to be made.

Drama as the instigators of the plot make new attempts to remove Andrew from the scene: highly placed people and another attempt on his life.

For the first time answers to questions raised by the inumerable newspaper reports and: Were the Liberals involved?

The South African connection – what part did it play? And was there only 5,000 pounds to be gained?

The book answers these questions and satisfies the perplexing query: Why did he do it? An important question is the tortuous psychological journey of Andrew Newton and his own feelings, emotions and thoughts – articulately expressed – and on every aspect of the affair.

Harold Wilson, Jeremy Thorpe, David Holmes and many others have been named in the context of this affair. Andrew Newton – with his meticulously gathered tapes and documents so far never revealed – demonstrates how each one slots into the story.

And for the first time – evidence of a police conspiracy.

Only Andrew Newton can tell the whole story – and prove it.

But no one was interested. Apart from the fact that it read like a comic strip, he had lied so often that it was impossible to believe a word.

In 1990 he had another crack at making money from the story. He claimed that MI5 had arranged a £50,000 win on the Premium Bonds in 1981, as payment for his help in a plot to discredit Harold Wilson and Thorpe. Newton obviously hoped that a newspaper would 'bite' and pay him for the 'inside story' but again there were no takers.[34]

In August 1993, now aged 46 and with a new name, Hann Redwin, he was in the news again. Earlier that year he had befriended a 39-year-old divorcee called Caroline Mayorcas at the expensive Hogarth Health Club in Chiswick, where she taught aerobics. In August he persuaded her to climb the Eiger in Switzerland. He was hardly the ideal companion; he had last tackled the mountain ten years earlier and had no qualifications as a guide. The death of Mrs Mayorcas in a fall, which he survived with only cuts, enraged her parents, Basil and Pamela Rogers. They claimed that their daughter had just withdrawn a large amount of money from her bank account, which was far more than was needed for a short holiday in Switzerland. Basil Rogers said, 'If I had a gun, I'd shoot that man between the eyes. My beloved daughter trusted him with her life – I wouldn't have trusted him with tuppence.' Pamela added, 'He is a convicted criminal and a liar.'[35]

At the inquest in London the following January, Redwin-Newton was cleared of any blame for her death, though newspaper headlines described him 'the villain of the Eiger'. He protested that he was just unlucky: 'Maybe I live in the fast lane, but I seem to have to have an alibi for every day of my bloody life. All I am trying to do is get on with my life.'[36]

Then he embarked on a career as 'an advocate', which, he explained, meant that he represented friends in civil court actions. He popped up in March 1993 in the Chancery Division in London, acting for a woman called Rosalieve Lowsley and her ex-husband Michael, who were demanding the settlement of a debt from a former business partner. As usual, there was a romantic angle; the court heard that Newton was engaged to Mrs Lowsley. Adrian Jack, the barrister who opposed Newton, described him in court as 'a notorious criminal, thoroughly unsuitable to represent the plantiffs'.[37] Jack later said, 'He was very suave but you couldn't trust him as far as you could throw him. But he was intelligent and sophisticated and knew his way around the law.'[38]

John Le Mesurier

Le Mesurier was the invisible man of the Thorpe affair, whose only comment to the police was, 'I have nothing to say.' By the end of the trial at the Old Bailey he had become such a marginal figure that people referred to him as 'the other one'.

He persuaded the court – and the media – that he was a jolly fat chap who had only become involved in the conspiracy after Newton had shot Rinka. He insisted, via his barrister, that he had just been trying to help his mates, George Deakin and David Holmes, sort out a problem. But after he was acquitted he changed his story. Like Newton, he thought that he could make a great deal of money by writing the true story of the conspiracy. But he discovered that lying had a price.

In July 1979 he touted the outline of his 'true story' around Fleet Street, which was a mistake. The *News of the World* did not buy it but, having read the synopsis, revealed that Le Mesurier was now claiming that he had masterminded the conspiracy. Under the headline: 'Thorpe Trial: Exclusive: I'm the one who set it all up', the *News of the World* reported that Le Mesurier, whom it described as a 49-year-old businessman, said that he had organised the plan to silence Scott 'permanently' and that he had briefed Newton and organised the payments to him after he was released from prison. But he maintained that Thorpe did not know about the plot. This destroyed the 'exclusivity' of his proposed memoirs and he skulked off.[39] Two years later he was back in Fleet Street, trying to sell another version of the 'real story'. But once again no one was interested.

That was the last time he tried to sell his story. He returned to Wales, where he moved into the video-rental business. The company collapsed amid allegations that he had been peddling pornography.

George Deakin

Like Le Mesurier, he made no impact on the audience at the Old Bailey, despite Mr Justice Cantley's quip that he was 'probably the sort of man whose taste ran to a cocktail bar in his living room'.

After the trial he vanished; unlike Le Mesurier, Holmes and Newton he did not try to sell his story to the press; indeed, he was very annoyed when they admitted later that he had been as unimportant as he had always insisted.

He figured only twice in the press: a few weeks after the trial, when his wife suffered a miscarriage, and in spring 1980, when he faced minor charges connected with the licensing of gaming machines. By 1995, however, he was enjoying a prosperous, crime-free retirement in Wales.

Dave Miller

He was haunted by the Thorpe affair. According to Peter Thomas, the journalist who was briefly his agent, Miller tried to move into the playgroup business in the 1990s. But his application for a licence was 'put on ice' by the local social services.[40]

Harold Wilson
(created Lord Wilson of Rievaulx, life peer in 1983)

After a long, unhappy retirement Wilson died, aged 79, at 12.30 a.m. on Wednesday, 24 May 1995 at St Thomas's Hospital, London, with the two most important women in his life, his wife, Mary, and his former secretary, Marcia Falkender, by his side. Falkender told reporters:

He was very peaceful. No words were exchanged as he drifted in and out of consciousness. The hospital staff looked after him beautifully. He felt no pain. There were no real words between us, just a squeeze of the hand. It was the end of an era for myself and many, many people whose lives he touched. His passing is a great loss. It will leave a hole in my life. He was one of the great prime ministers, who devoted his entire life to the Labour Party and through it the creation of a more modern, equal and open Britain. He was a man of unique intelligence and stature and a rare capacity for kindness who lived to the end as simply as when he started. A gentleman and a statesman in the finest sense.[41]

Other friends said that they were glad that he had finally found rest; he had been philosophical about the inevitable decline in his physical powers but had hated the deterioration in his once-formidable mental abilities.

Although he had been largely ignored by the media since his retirement as an MP in 1983, his death showed that he was already established as one of the most fascinating and influential British politicians this century; he was the only post-war Prime Minister to win four general elections and will certainly be ranked alongside those Conservative colossi, Winston Churchill and Margaret Thatcher, in terms of his influence on British society.

Newspapers dissected his career in minute detail but were particularly interested in what they called the 'unsolved mysteries' of his reign: why did he resign when he was only 60 years old and did he have an affair with Falkender? Some commentators claimed that they had solved the first mystery. They said that Wilson had resigned because his doctor, Joe Stone, had warned him early in 1974 that he was suffering from Alzheimer's disease, which leads to confusion and, eventually, complete memory loss, turning the sufferer into a virtual vegetable.[42] So, this theory suggested, Wilson decided that he would quit before his mind began to fail him. Other writers argued that his mental decline dated from an interruption in the oxygen supply during an operation in 1980 for bowel cancer.[43] Two acclaimed biographers offered more complex interpretations for the resignation, in which political calculation played as great a part as his health.[44]

Falkender argued that his departure from Downing Street was also linked to the fact that Wilson knew that the Establishment was still searching for evidence that would damn him as a fool, a traitor or a crook. In September 1995 she told Barrie Penrose:

'He was upset by the pressure. There was no doubt about that. He said to me, "You don't understand the pressures . . . they are so great I am going to go." I think it was the cumulative effect. They made him go.'

She was more precise, though, about the second, great mystery. 'He loved pretty women but he was no womaniser. Did I fancy Harold? No. He had a wonderful brain and I thought that he was God. I absolutely adored him but he used to tell smutty jokes and put milk bottles on the table. How could I have an affair with a man like that?[45]

On 13 July 1995 Falkender organised a memorial service at Westminster Abbey. The guest list was a tribute to Wilson's stature – Prince Charles, John Major, the Prime Minister, and every living ex-prime minister, apart from Lord Home, who was too frail to attend – but there was one unexpected and unwelcome guest: Jeremy Thorpe. Falkender was furious when she saw Thorpe, guided by Marion, totter to the front of the abbey, where he sat down, alongside the most honoured guests. Then, when the service was over, an usher told her and Wilson's family that they had to wait for the VIPS, including Thorpe, to leave. As she watched him limp away, towards the massed ranks of press and television, she said that she knew that here was a man who would never understand the difference between right and wrong.

Sir Jack Hayward

Hayward spent the rest of his life giving huge sums of money to charity, which was acknowledged in 1985 when he was knighted. In May 1991 he had the chance to indulge every football fan's fantasy: to buy a club. Wolverhampton Wanderers, which he had supported as a boy and which had been one of the mightiest clubs in the country in the 1950s, was close to bankruptcy in spring 1990; then Hayward stepped in with a cheque for £2.1 million. By late 1995 he had spent over £20 million but did not regret one penny, even though Wolves were still just another once-great team in the decaying industrial heartlands.

He remained the same unspoilt, rumpled character whom Thorpe took for a fool. Over a lunch of sandwiches in a London hotel, which he chose because they were jolly good value, he told me: 'I'm too trusting. I like everyone. And Jeremy was very charming and amusing. But everyone was taken in by him, weren't they?'[46]

The Police

By 1995 all the detectives who had worked on the Thorpe case had long retired. Michael Challes died that year, still brooding about the most important case in his career.

Men of the Law

Sir Joseph Cantley, who died, aged 82, in January 1993, was haunted by the Thorpe trial. Peter Cook immortalised him as 'Sir Joseph Cocklecarrot' in a savage satire on his summing-up. He had many admirers in the judiciary but no one thought much of the way he had handled the case. One obituarist wrote: 'Cantley's friends detected in him a deep revulsion to the thought that, if Mr Thorpe were convicted, any judge would have been duty-bound to have imposed a very substantial term of imprisonment, even on someone of such a high reputation and impeccable public record.'

Lord Goodman deftly rewrote history and said that he had barely known Wilson or Thorpe and had certainly not been involved in the events leading to the trial at the Old Bailey. The obituaries after his death in May 1995 did not mention Thorpe, which was a posthumous triumph for Goodman. He had fought hard to protect him but had dropped him when Pencourt closed in for the kill and spent the rest of his life insisting that he had not been involved with Thorpe.

For both prosecution and defence lawyers the trial was just another case, albeit a more interesting one than the usual murders and armed robberies. But some defence lawyers privately said that Thorpe was a devious, cold-hearted snob who was probably guilty of fraud if not conspiracy to murder. But they were professionals, who put aside personal feelings when they donned wigs and robes; their job was to secure their clients' freedom.

Peter Taylor, who led the prosecution, was appointed Lord Chief Justice in 1992. In May 1996 he resigned because of ill health. His junior, John Bull, became Resident Judge of the Crown Court at Guildford, Surrey. The trial established George Carman as one of the top advocates in the country. Gareth Williams was awarded a life peerage in 1992 and became Lord Williams of Mostyn and a senior front-bench spokesman for Labour in the House of Lords. John Mathew continued to work out of his chambers in Lincoln's Inn.

The Journalists

Barrie Penrose and Roger Courtiour never worked together again. Courtiour spent two years in the Middle East and then returned to the BBC, the organisation that he had always loved and which had treated him so shabbily. He became a respected senior producer, with a string of prestigious documentaries to his name. In 1979 Harold Evans apologised to Penrose for the *Sunday Times*' coverage of Thorpe and invited him to join the newspaper. He stayed there for over a decade, serving Evans, his successor, Frank Giles, and, finally, Andrew Neil, before moving to the *Sunday Express* as Investigations Editor. He left the *Express* in spring 1995 to pursue a freelance career.

The Thorpe affair was the major blot on Evans' distinguished editorship. After Rupert Murdoch's purchase of the *Times* and *Sunday Times* in 1981 Evans moved to edit *The Times* but less than a year later resigned. After a series of low-profile jobs he moved to the States with his second wife Tina Brown and became president of Random House.

Donald Trelford's reign at the *Observer* ended in 1993 when the newspaper, which had haemorrhaged readers and money for many years, was bought by the *Guardian*. Trelford became a freelance sports columnist and pundit on the media.

Sir Charles Curran, the BBC Director-General who found the Thorpe affair so distasteful, died in 1980, aged 58, three years after leaving the Corporation. Tom Mangold, the reporter whose interview in 1976 with Peter Bessell was, sadly, never broadcast, enjoyed a long and successful career as an investigative reporter with the BBC's *Panorama*.

The Juror

Celia Kettle-Williams, the schoolteacher and Liberal supporter, returned to her comprehensive school in south-east London. Then she retired quietly to Sussex, where she brooded on the fact that no one had ever acknowledged her role in 'The Trial of the Century'. She blamed Auberon Waugh for this because his *The Last Word*:

An Eye-Witness Account of the Thorpe Trial incorrectly named Linda Binns as the jury forewoman. She said, 'I was very upset when I read the book. I had told my family and friends that I was the forewoman and then this book came out. It looked as if I had been lying.'[47]

She wrote to Waugh, who apologised for his mistake. She said, 'Linda Binns was the same age as me and also had grey hair. She sat at the front during the trial and I was behind her. But I was the forewoman and should have sat in the front. We changed places when I gave the verdict. But Mr Waugh said that he had poor eyesight and didn't notice.'

The law insists that jurors must accept that they are performing an anonymous duty but, since they are human, they are just as susceptible to flattery and attention as anyone else. So, Kettle-Williams was delighted when Sir David Napley, Thorpe's solicitor, said that he wanted to meet. 'He was worried what I would do after the Waugh book came out. I had lunch with him and his wife at a Chinese restaurant. He told me that he had always thought that I was anti-Thorpe. I told him that had been Linda Binns, not me. After lunch he took me to Charing Cross Station in his Rolls Royce.'

But she was more concerned about whether the jury had been right than personal glory. She said:

> The homosexuality thing was very much played down in court, wasn't it? I think it was wrong not to tell us. I wonder why the prosecution didn't make more of it?
>
> When we agreed on the verdict I put my head in my hands and thought: Have we done the right thing? God, are we right? It was a heavy responsibility but no one was killed or hurt, were they? We were very ordinary people and we did our best. You can't do more, can you?
>
> [She paused] And Jeremy Thorpe was ruined, wasn't he?

Simon Freeman
London, July 1996

SOURCE NOTES

I must acknowledge three books, which helped me enormously in the writing of *Rinkagate: The Rise and Fall of Jeremy Thorpe*:

Lewis Chester, Magnus Linklater and David May, authors of *Jeremy Thorpe: A Secret Life* (André Deutsch, 1979), gave me a clear chronology and much valuable material on Thorpe's background and career, although his acquittal at the Old Bailey meant that they had to delete a great deal of information from their manuscript for legal reasons.

Next, I have drawn heavily on Peter Bessell's massive book, *Cover-Up*. He published this privately in the United States in 1980, using a company called Simons Books Inc., and could only afford to print 2,000 copies. This was a pity since it was a fascinating account of his relationship with Thorpe and Thorpe's extraordinary obsession with Norman Scott. Unless stated otherwise quotations from Bessell in *Rinkagate* come from *Cover-Up*.

Finally, I have taken some unchallenged quotations from *The Pencourt File*, written by Barrie Penrose and Roger Courtiour and published by Secker and Warburg in 1978.

Simon Freeman

Chapter One

1 The *Sun*, 21 March 1979. She was 48 years old and the mother of two teenage children when she killed herself. She had been depressed since her husband's death five years earlier.
2 The *Sunday Times magazine*, March 1974. This article included the most revealing interviews ever given by Ursula or her son. But Thorpe and his wife Marion refused to discuss it when I (S.F.) visited their cottage in Devon in August 1995. He said that he was thinking of writing his autobiography and did not want to 'scoop' himself by helping an author. Quotations from Thorpe and his mother in this chapter are taken from the *Sunday Times magazine*.
3 S.F. interview with Christopher Bourke, August 1995.

4 The *Evening Standard*, 6 September 1995.
5 S.F. interview with Quentin Crewe, September 1995.
6 S.F. interview with Stanley Brodie, July 1995.
7 S.F. interview with confidential source, September 1995. He spoke on condition that he was not identified.
8 Like many Liberals she tired of the Party's incessant internal bickering; in 1957 she became Labour MP for Carmarthen.
9 *British Biographies: The 20th Century* (Chambers, 1993).
10 Walter Ellis, *The Oxbridge Conspiracy* (Michael Joseph, 1994).
11 S.F. interview with Lord Rees-Mogg, August 1995.
12 According to Trinity College's records Thorpe matriculated in October 1949 and left after taking his Finals in the summer of 1952. This meant that he took four years, instead of three, to complete his law degree. Friends said he took off the academic year, 1950–1951, to run for the Presidency of the Oxford Union.
13 Sir Robin Day, *Sir Robin Day, Grand Inquisitor* (Weidenfeld & Nicolson, 1989).
14 S.F. interview with Stanley Brodie, August 1995. Subsequent quotations in this chapter come from interviews by S.F. in August–September, 1995.
15 He switched to Labour in 1957 and was Labour MP for Ipswich from 1957 until 1970. His brother, Michael, led the Labour Party from 1980 until 1983.
16 S.F. interview in 1995 with source who asked to remain anonymous.

Chapter Two

1 Chris Cook, *A Short History of the Liberal Party 1900–1992* (Macmillan, 1993).
2 S.F. interview with Lillian Prowse, September 1995.
3 The *Sunday Times magazine*, op. cit.
4 S.F. interview with Lillian Prowse.
5 S.F. interview with Michael Barnes, October 1995.
6 S.F. interview with Lillian Prowse.
7 S.F. interview with Dominic Le Foe, September 1995. Mr Le Foe was Director of the Players' Theatre, underneath the arches at Charing Cross Station, London.
8 ibid.
9 S.F. interview with confidential source, September 1995.
10 The *Sunday Time magazine*, op. cit.
11 He showed that he meant business a few years later when he was still a humble back-bencher. He acquired the status symbol of his own office in Bridge Street, an annexe of the Commons which overlooked Big Ben. Most of the building was used by MPs' secretaries or for storage but there were half a dozen rooms which were available for ordinary members. When an office became vacant Thorpe's name was one of hundreds in the ballot box; he won. He told colleagues that he had been lucky but there were mumblings that he had fixed the draw. No one ever proved this but there were echoes here of Oxford, when his victories in elections were overshadowed by doubts about his methods.
12 S.F. interview with Sir Russell Johnston, October 1995.
13 The *Sunday Times magazine*, op. cit.
14 S.F. interview with Vater, August 1995.
15 From Peter Bessell's *aide-memoire*, Bessell began work on this 100-page

document in the summer of 1976, after Thorpe's suggestion in the *Sunday Times* that Scott had been blackmailing him, to 'remind himself of events'. Bessell denied that he was thinking then of writing a book, although the *aide-memoire* formed the basis for *Cover-Up*.

16 Barrie Penrose (B.P.) spoke to Scott many times between 1976 and 1996. Scott had a good but unstructured memory, which meant that B.P. often pieced together one incident, such as Scott's first encounter with Thorpe, from interviews spanning twenty years.

17 S.F. writes: Since Thorpe married twice and fathered a son he was technically bisexual. Josiffe, who later changed his name to Scott, also had affairs with women. He was married once and had a son; he also had a daughter by another woman.

18 B.P. interview with Norman Scott, October 1995.

19 B.P. 'archive', 17 January 1979.

20 S.F. interview with Scott, August 1995.

21 B.P. interviews with Scott 1976 and 1985. Scott explained what happened that night many times – in statements to police, at the commital in Minehead, the Old Bailey and to Penrose. His accounts became more graphic over the years. In his first statement to the police in December 1962 he denied that Thorpe had penetrated him but he claimed in 1979 that he had been too embarrassed to describe what had happened: 'I was trying make myself out to be a cleaner person than I was.'

22 James Baldwin, *Giovanni's Room* (Penguin, 1990).

23 B.P. 'archive'. Statement to the police by Thorpe, June 1978.

24 B.P. interview with Scott, August 1995.

Chapter Three

1 Quotations by Josiffe come from interviews with B.P., between 1976 and 1995, some of which appeared in *The Pencourt File*. Occasionally I have also drawn on Josiffe's statements to the police over the years, as well as his evidence at the committal in 1978 and the trial at the Old Bailey in 1979.

2 S.F., interview with Le Foe.

3 B.P. interview with Mary Collier, August 1995.

4 B.P. interviews with Huntley, 1976 and 1979.

5 ibid.

6 S.F. interview with Sir Russell Johnston, October 1995.

7 *A Short History of the Liberal Party*, op. cit.

8 'Opinion: Homosexual Rights – time that a victimised minority gained acceptance', by Ian Harvey, the *Sunday Times*, 25 April 1976.

9 Bryan Magee, *One in Twenty: a Study of Homosexuality in Men and Women* (Secker and Warburg, 1966).

10 Francis King, *Yesterday Came Suddenly* (Constable, 1993).

11 ibid.

12 ibid.

13 S.F. interview with Francis King, October 1995.

14 Barbara Castle, *The Castle Diaries, 1964–1976* (Macmillan, 1990).

Chapter Four

1 B.P. 'archive'.

2 B.P. interview with Scott, August 1995.

3 B.P. 'archive'; statement to the police by Lady Dunleath, 1979.

4 B.P. interview with Lady Dunleath, August 1995.

5 John Vassall, *The Autobiography of a Spy* (Sidgwick & Jackson, 1975).

6 In the mid-1970s, after he had been released from prison, Vassall became friendly with Humphrey Berkeley, Conservative MP for Lancaster from 1959 until 1966, who was a member of a penal-reform group, and told him about intimate relationships that he had enjoyed with MPs before he had been jailed. Berkeley saw that one of these MPs had been knighted and quietly informed the Conservative leader, Margaret Thatcher.

  B.P. interviewed this MP in October 1995 but agreed not to identify him. He told BP: 'I knew Vassall socially. I felt sorry for him because he was a lonely man. I had no relationship with him and I knew nothing about his treachery.'

7 Richard Lamb revealed that Denning had written this secret report in his acclaimed study, *The Macmillan Years, 1957–1963* (John Murray, 1995). Lamb named Marples in his book here but not Freeth, because he was still alive.

8 B.P. interview with Lord Denning, 1995.

9 B.P. interview with Denzil Freeth, December 1995.

10 B.P. interview with confidential source, October 1995.

11 Nigel West, *A Matter of Trust, MI5 1945–1972* (Weidenfeld & Nicolson, 1982).

12 Francis King, *Yesterday Came Suddenly*, op. cit.

13 ibid.

14 S.F. interview with King, October 1995.

15 B.P. 'archive'. Sheila Weight statement to the police, 9 January 1979, supplemented by B.P. interview with her, August 1995.

16 B.P. 'archive'. Charles Weight statement to the police, 9 January 1979.

17 The following quotations from Scott in this chapter come from interviews with B.P. 1976–1995.

Chapter Five

1 B.P. 'archive'. Thorpe wrote this in March 1965.

2 *Jeremy Thorpe: A Secret Life*, op. cit.

3 S.F. interview with Sir Russell Johnston, October 1995.

4 'Twilight of the Establishment' by Walter Ellis, the *Sunday Times*, 17 September 1995. Henry Fairlie first used the term, 'the Establishment,' in the *Spectator* in September 1955, to describe what he called 'the whole matrix of official and social relations within which power is exercised' in Britain. But, forty years later, newspaper commentators and academics thought that this Establishment – based on public schools, Oxbridge and gentlemen's clubs and composed of public-spirited men who married into each other's families – had disappeared.

5 S.F. interview with Tom Dale, August 1995.

6 Curiously, Bessell became very angry when journalists suggested that he had also owned a shop called Jaycell Same Day Dry Cleaners. He did not mind being called a conman and an adulterer but he insisted in his mammoth book, *Cover-Up*, that 'no member of my family had any connection with such a business', as if dry cleaning was a crime against humanity.

7 S.F. interview with Chris Drake, July 1995.

8 B.P. 'archive'. Bessell's letter is dated 8 April 1965.

9 B.P. 'archive'. The letter is dated 14 April 1965.
10 B.P. 'archive'. Stainton's letter is dated 7 May 1965.
11 B.P. interviews with Scott, 1976–1995.

Chapter Six

1 B.P. interview with Mary Collier, August 1995.
2 Lord Beaumont letter to S.F., August 1995. He said that Bessell only repaid 'a miniscule amount'.
3 *A Short History of the Liberal Party 1900–1992*, op.cit.
4 S.F. interview with Sir Trevor Jones, September 1995.
5 S.F. interviews with Gerald Hagan, July and August 1995.
6 *A Short History of the Liberal Party, 1900–1992*, op.cit.
7 S.F. interview with Pincham, November 1995.
8 ibid.
9 In April 1968 Bessell announced that he would not contest Bodmin again.
10 B.P. interview with Richard Wainwright, 1978.
11 S.F. interview with Michael Meadowcroft, August 1995.
12 B.P. interview with Richard Wainwright, 1979.
13 S.F. interview with Sir Russell Johnston, October 1995.
14 S.F. interview with Michael Steed, August 1995.
15 Bessell's *aide-memoire*, September 1976 and repeated in *Cover-Up*, op.cit.

Chapter Seven

1 S.F. interview with Lord Rees-Mogg, August 1995.
2 S.F. interviews with Bernard Greaves, August – September 1995.
3 S.F. interview with Mike Steele, November 1995. Steele resigned as Liberal press officer in 1972 and returned to the Commons as a lobby correspondent.
4 S.F. interview with Tom Dale, August 1995.
5 The quotations from Steel, Grimond and Thorpe here are taken from the *Sunday Times magazine*, March 1974.
6 Peter Hennessy, *Whitehall* (Secker and Warburg, 1989).
7 B.P. interview with Baroness Falkender, October 1995.
8 B.P. interview with Falkender, May 1977.
9 S.F. interview with Jeremy Thorpe, Cobbaton, North Devon, August 1995.
10 S.F. interview with Tom Dale, August 1995.
11 B.P. interview with Lady Falkender, November 1995.
12 Philip Ziegler, *Wilson: The Authorised Life* (HarperCollins, 1995).
13 Ben Pimlott, *Harold Wilson* (HarperCollins, 1992).
14 B.P. 'archive'. Reproduced in *Cover-Up*.
15 B.P. interview with William Shannon, February 1979.
16 In 1995 Shannon was living in retirement in Spain with a former Automobile Association patrolman.
17 B.P. interview with Scott, August 1995.
18 S.F. interview with Mike Steele, November 1995.
19 Obituary, Caroline Thorpe, July 1970.
20 The *Sunday Times magazine*, March 1974.
21 Bessell's *aide-memoire*, 1976. Bessell did not include this story in his book, *Cover-Up*, perhaps because it was too tacky even for him. Holmes's companion, Gerald Hagan, thought that Bessell had made up the story. It is true that there

was no corroboration but Bessell had no reason to lie in his *aide-memoire*, which he never intended should be published.

22 S.F. interview with John Fryer, August 1995.
23 The *Daily Mail*, 4 April 1968.
24 S.F. interview with Mike Steele, November 1995.
25 S.F. interview with John Fryer, August 1995.
26 S.F. interview with Bernard Greaves, August 1995.
27 SF writes: I am grateful to Bernard Greaves for supplying me with copies of Liberal Party documents and speeches from 1968.

Chapter Eight

1 Information based on interviews by B.P. with Scott, October – November 1995.
2 Bessell described this conversation – and subsequent crisis talks about Scott – in *Cover-Up* and at the Old Bailey in 1979; apart from a few minor details Holmes confirmed Bessell's accounts in the *News of the World* in June 1981.
3 B.P. interview with Captain Myers, September 1995.
4 B.P. interview with Scott, September 1995.
5 *Jeremy Thorpe: A Secret Life*, op. cit.
6 ibid. This book provides a clear analysis of Liberal Party finances in the early 1970s, although senior Liberals disputed its accuracy.
7 John Campbell, *Edward Heath: A Biography* (Pimlico, 1994). Some pundits argued that the vote was a protest against England's shock 3–2 defeat by West Germany in the World Cup in Mexico.
8 The *Sunday Times magazine*, March 1974.

Chapter Nine

1 David Steel, *Against Goliath: David Steel's Story* (Weidenfeld & Nicolson, 1989).
2 B.P. 'archive': Scott statement to the police, dated 10 June 1971.
3 ibid.
4 B.P. interview with Scott, 1995. Except where noted further quotations from Scott in this chapter come from conversations with B.P., 1976–1995.
5 B.P. 'archive': Scott, police statement, dated 10 June 1971.
6 *Jeremy Thorpe: A Secret Life*, op. cit.
7 When Penrose and Courtiour interviewed Holmes late in 1976 B.P. said that he 'did not deny' that he had discussed killing Scott when he had met Bessell in the States. However, Holmes denied to the *News of the World* in 1981 that he had talked to Bessell in this way.
8 B.P. 'archive': Scott police statement, dated 10 June 1971.
9 *Against Goliath: David Steel's Story*, op. cit.
10 *Jeremy Thorpe: A Secret Life* and *Cover-Up*, op. cit.

Chapter Ten

1 B.P. interviews with Scott, 1976–1995. Unless noted further quotations from Scott in this chapter come from conversations with B.P.

2 Gordon Winter, *Inside BOSS* (Penguin, 1981). This was Winter's account of his life as an agent for BOSS. He wrote it after he fled from South Africa to Ireland. But he had such a cavalier approach to facts that the book attracted numerous writs for libel.

3 On 31 January 1976 Harold Wilson leaked a story to the *Daily Mirror* that Winter was a South African spy who was masterminding a smear campaign against Thorpe.

4 *Jeremy Thorpe: A Secret Life*, op. cit. Supplemented by B.P. interviews with Lee Tracey, 1979 and 1995.

5 In autumn 1995 B.P. traced a retired Special Branch officer. He told B.P. that MI5 had deliberately 'frightened' Winter out of Britain.

6 The *Sunday Telegraph*, 25 February 1973; the *Daily Telegraph*, 26 February 1973.

7 Newspaper reports on Marion Stein, including the *Sun*, 21 March 1979.

8 The *Daily Mail*, 20 July 1949.

9 The *Daily Telegraph*, 15 March 1973.

10 *Cover-Up*, op.cit. There is no corroboration for this anecdote but there is no doubt that Thorpe was a practising homosexual after he married Marion.

11 Edward St George told S.F. in 1995 that the sale of Freeport for 100 million dollars would have earned Thorpe and Bessell between 5 to 7 million dollars in commission.

12 The *Sunday Times magazine*, March 1974.

13 ibid.

14 S.F. interview with Dick Taverne, 1995.

15 There is an excellent account of the collapse of London and County Securities in *Jeremy Thorpe: A Secret Life*, op. cit.

16 S.F. interviews with Hayward and St George, London 1995. They said that if Thorpe had asked for a modest loan of, say, 50,000 dollars to help Bessell they would have agreed; but they did not like being taken for fools.

17 S.F. interviews with Jack Hayward and Edward St George, 1995.

18 *Jeremy Thorpe: A Secret Life*, op.cit. Edward St George confirmed this quote to S.F. in 1995.

19 That was not Hayward's view in 1995. He told S.F. that he was now sure that Bessell and Thorpe had been accomplices.

Chapter Eleven

1 John Campbell, *Edward Heath: A Biography*, op. cit.

2 This was known as the Yom Kippur War because Egypt and Syria attacked Israel on the afternoon of Saturday, 6 October 1973 which was the Day of Atonement, the holiest date in the Jewish calendar. Israel counter-attacked and drove deep into Egypt and Syria. A ceasefire was declared on 24 October.

3 Cyril Smith, *Big Cyril: The autobiography of Cyril Smith* (W.H. Allen, 1977).

4 John Campbell, *Edward Heath: A Biography*, op. cit.

5 S.F. interview with Sir Trevor Jones, September 1995.

6 Chris Cook, *A Short History of the Liberal Party, 1900–1992*, op. cit.

7 David Steel, *Against Goliath: David Steel's Story*, op. cit.

8 In his acclaimed biography of Edward Heath, John Campbell wrote: 'For himself, he [Thorpe] would have loved to be able to accept' a job in Cabinet.

9 Raymond Carr, former Warden of St Anthony's College, Oxford, reviewing Roy Jenkins' biography of Gladstone in the *Evening Standard*, 7 October, 1995.

10 In 1996 Susan Barnes is better known as Susan Crosland, bestselling novelist.
11 S.F. interview with Magnus Linklater, August 1995.
12 S.F. interviewed Barnes' source in September 1995. He confirmed the conversation with Barnes in 1973 but asked not to be identified.
13 S.F. interview with Susan Barnes, August 1995.
14 The *Daily Telegraph*, 12 July 1993.
15 S.F. interview in 1995 with Barnes' friend. He asked to remain anonymous.
16 S.F. interview with ex-MP who asked not to be named, July 1995.
17 B.P. interview with Scott, 1976.
18 Scott was always precise when he described his accommodation over the years; he insisted to B.P. in May 1996 that it was 'a bungalow', not a cottage.
19 *Who's Who*, (Adam and Charles Black, 1983).
20 *The Pencourt File*, op. cit.
21 ibid.
22 ibid.
23 Pencourt deployed all their investigative skills to try and discover whether Scott was telling the truth. They covered the episode in detail in *The Pencourt File*; they established that a helicopter had, indeed, landed near Scott's 'bungalow' but failed to identify the occupants.
24 In the mid-1970s, when he was still pretending to be a bona fide journalist, Winter said that he had approached the *Sunday People* and the *Sunday Mirror* in 1971, not 1974. However, in his autobiography, *Inside BOSS*, op.cit., published in 1981, he insisted that he had not tried to sell the story in 1971 because BOSS forbade him; he claimed that he was 'activated' because of the election in 1974. In spring 1996 B.P. told S.F. that he believed that Winter was telling the truth.
25 The *News of the World*, June 1981.
26 Gleadle statement to the police; published in *The Pencourt File*, op.cit.
27 The *News of the World*, June 1981.

Chapter Twelve

1 Chris Cook, *A Short History of the Liberal Party, 1900–1992*, op. cit.
2 S.F. interview with John Pardoe, 1995. Pardoe said that Thorpe had lost 'his whole feel for leadership'.
3 Jack Hayward gave this letter, and later appeals for money from Thorpe, to Det. Chief Supt. Michael Challes in April 1978. The letter was central to the prosecution case at the trial at the Old Bailey in 1979. It was reproduced in full in *Jeremy Thorpe: A Secret Life*, op. cit.
4 Auberon Waugh, *The Last Word: An Eye-witness Account of the Thorpe Trial* (Michael Joseph, 1980).
5 The *News of the World*, 1981.
6 ibid.
7 S.F. interviews with Gerald Hagan, 1995.
8 *The Pencourt File* and *Jeremy Thorpe: A Secret Life*, op.cit. Pencourt broke new ground with their description of Scott's experiences in this period but the *Sunday Times* writers were able to draw on evidence from the committal and trial and, not surprisingly, their account is more coherent.
9 B.P. 'archive': Le Mesurier: unpublished interview. He made similar claims in the *News of the World* in 1979 a few months after the trial at the Old Bailey.

10 B.P. interview with Scott, 1995.

11 ibid.

12 S.F. interviews with Bernard Greaves, 1995. He knew the exact time of his meeting with Smith because he had kept his diary for the year.

13 Smith did not refer to the meeting with Greaves in his autobiography, *Big Cyril*, op. cit.

14 The *News of the World*, June 1981.

Chapter Thirteen

1 B.P. interview with Scott, 1996.

2 The *News of the World*, June 1981.

3 B.P. interview with Detective Inspector Ivan Pollard, 1995.

4 The *News of the World*, June 1981.

5 *Private Eye*, 12 December 1975; quoted in *The Last Word: An Eye-witness Account of the Thorpe Trial*, op. cit.

6 S.F. interviews with Gerald Hagan, 1995.

7 Cyril Smith, *Big Cyril: The Autobiography of Cyril Smith*, op. cit.

8 ibid.

9 *The Pencourt File* and *Jeremy Thorpe: A Secret Life*, op. cit.

10 Various newspapers, including the *Guardian* and the *Sun*, 30 January 1976.

11 S.F. interviews with John Fryer, Michael Steed and Bernard Greaves, 1995.

12 Cyril Smith, *Big Cyril: The Autobiography of Cyril Smith*, op.cit.

13 Barbara Castle, *The Castle Diaries, 1964–1976*, op.cit.

14 Cyril Smith, *Big Cyril: The Autobiography of Cyril Smith*, op. cit.

15 The *News of the World*, June 1981.

16 David Steel, *Against Goliath: David Steel's Story*, op.cit.

17 The timing of these statements inspired various elaborate conspiracy theories. Falkender told Pencourt that the Palace had asked Wilson to resign that day to distract attention from news of the marital problems of Princess Margaret. As a result, Pencourt speculated in their book *The Pencourt File* that the Establishment had arranged everything to ensure that Newton's trial was overlooked by the media. There is no evidence to support this theory.

Chapter Fourteen

1 The two acclaimed biographies of Wilson, by Philip Ziegler and Ben Pimlott, op. cit., quoted extensively from Pencourt's account of this meeting. Both authors accepted the veracity of Pencourt's report. In 1978, when Penrose and Courtiour published their book, *The Pencourt File*, Wilson suggested that they had either misquoted or misunderstood him. But then Pencourt indicated that they had an unchallengeable record of their interviews with him, in the form of tape recordings, courtesy of their magic briefcase; after this, Wilson sensibly refused to discuss Pencourt.

2 Ben Pimlott, *Harold Wilson*, op. cit.

3 B.P. 'archive': *The Red File*.

4 Auberon Waugh, *The Last Word: An Eye-witness Account of the Thorpe Trial*, op. cit.

5 B.P. 'archive': *The Red File*.

6 *Private Eye*, 17 September 1976.

7 S.F. interview with Alan Protheroe, August 1995.

Chapter Fifteen

1 B.P. 'archive'.
2 *Private Eye*, 29 October 1976.
3 B.P. interview with Scott, December 1995.
4 B.P. interview with Brian Cook, December 1995.

Chapter Sixteen

1 Arnold Goodman, *Tell Them I'm On My Way* (Chapmans, 1993). Goodman did not mention his tireless defence of Thorpe in his autobiography. He made one short reference to Thorpe in the book, when he said that he 'turned the case over' to another solicitor, Sir David Napley, when 'it seemed that Thorpe's problems would take him into a criminal court'. Yet Tom Dale, Thorpe's personal assistant, told S.F. in 1995 that he had instructions to contact Goodman if journalists asked about Scott. Goodman also protested to Sir Charles Curran, the Director-General of the BBC, after Pencourt interviewed Scott in spring 1976. Goodman did admit, however, that he always counted Thorpe as a friend.
2 There are excellent accounts of Falkender's relationship with Wilson in the biographies of him by Philip Ziegler and Ben Pimlott, op.cit.
3 Joe Haines, *The Politics of Power* (Jonathan Cape, 1977).
4 The quotations are taken verbatim from *The Pencourt File*, op.cit.
5 The quotations from Wilson and Falkender come from B.P.'s 'archive'.
6 B.P. 'archive': John Le Mesurier interview, unpublished, 1981.
7 The *Evening News*, 20 October 1977.
8 The *Daily Express*, 26 October 1977.
9 B.P. 'archive': opinion of James Comyn QC, 28 November 1977.
10 B.P. 'archive': police statement by Chief Superintendent Michael Challes of the Avon and Somerset Constabulary, 5 September 1978.

Chapter Seventeen

1 B.P. 'archive': witness statement by Daniel Farson, dated 31 October 1977. Repeated in *Cover-Up*, op. cit.
2 B.P. interview with Don Taylor, August 1995.
3 *Jeremy Thorpe: A Secret Life*, op. cit.
4 The *Daily Mirror*, 15 December 1977. In a story on Challes' meeting with Bessell in California the *Mirror* reported that Challes had not known that Penrose and Courtiour were journalists.
5 B.P. 'archive': witness statement by Det. Chief Supt. Michael Challes, 5 September, 1978. Unless noted otherwise quotations from Challes in this chapter come from this statement.
6 B.P. interview with Don Taylor, August 1995.
7 *Cover-Up*, op. cit.
8 *Private Eye*, 23 December 1977.
9 B.P. 'archive': letter from Tom Rosenthal to Donald Trelford, 26 January 1978.
10 B.P. 'archive': Quotations from Pencourt's meeting with Wilson come from

the verbatim transcript of the conversation, which was tape-recorded by Pencourt.

11 The *Daily Mirror*, 30 January 1978.

12 The *Sunday Times*, 26 February 1978.

13 The *Sunday Times*, 12 February 1978.

14 American critics were marginally more generous when *The Pencourt File* was published in the States in December 1978. For example, the *Christian Science Monitor* headlined its review: 'Britain's Woodstein: Journalistic duo stays on Thorpe's trail'. The *Monitor* said that 'the hero of the book is undoubtedly Pencourt himself [sic] – two intrepid investigative journalists who, like Carl Bernstein and Bob Woodward before them, came as one to root out evil in high places'. A newspaper in Hartford, Connecticut, also compared Pencourt to Woodstein; its review was headlined: 'Britain's Watergate'.

Chapter Eighteen

1 B.P. 'archive': Jack Hayward, witness statement (undated).

2 *Cover-Up*, op. cit.

3 David Holmes, the *News of the World*, 28 June 1981. Unless noted otherwise quotations from Holmes in this chapter come from this series of articles.

4 B.P. 'archive': witness statement by Det. Chief Supt. Michael Challes, 5 September 1978. Unless noted otherwise quotations from Challes in this chapter come from this statement.

5 B.P. interview with Kenneth Steele, 1995.

6 S.F. interview with Nadir Dinshaw, October 1995.

7 S.F. interviews with Sir Jack Hayward, 1995.

8 ibid.

9 B.P. 'archive': Jeremy Thorpe statement to Det. Chief Supt. Michael Challes, 3 June 1978.

10 The *Observer*, 23 July 1978.

11 B.P. interview with Peter Hinde, October 1995.

12 ibid.

13 On 4 August 1978 the *Western Daily Press* ran a front-page story, headlined: 'Scott: Charges Out Today'. It said that four people were expected to be charged that day over 'the Norman Scott affair'. The tenth paragraph said that Wilson had been interviewed in London the previous day by Det. Supt. Davey Greenough.

14 B.P. interview with Davey Greenough, 1995.

15 B.P. interview with Peter Hinde, 1995.

16 The *Daily Mail*, August 1978.

17 The *News of the World*, 13 August 1978. The story was headlined: 'Thorpe warns TV men'.

18 B.P. 'archive.'

19 B.P. interview with Peter Thomas, December 1995.

20 B.P. 'archive': London Weekend Television interview with Harold Evans.

21 B.P. 'archive': Tom Mangold interview with Sir Charles Curran.

22 S.F. interview with confidential source, 1995.

23 David Steel, *Against Goliath: David Steel's Story*, op. cit.

24 The *Dundee Courier*, 15 September 1978.

25 S.F. interview with Steve Atack, September, 1995.

26 S.F. interview with Michael Steed, December 1995.

27 David Steel, *Against Goliath: David Steel's Story*, op. cit.
28 S.F. interviews with Jack Hayward, 1995.

Chapter Nineteen

1 *Jeremy Thorpe: A Secret Life*, op.cit.
2 After Thorpe was acquitted Napley, who died in 1994 aged 79, told B.P. that he knew that the 'orchestration' theory was nonsense. He said that he had just been doing his job, which was to defend Thorpe.
3 In March 1979 Napley admitted that he had ordered Pencourt to be followed. Charles Vaggars, who was chairman of the North Devon Liberals, told B.P. in 1995 that he had not known about this and, if he had, would have stopped Napley.
4 S.F. interview with confidential source, 1995.
5 Peter Chippendale and David Leigh, *The Thorpe Committal* (Arrow Books, 1979). This book, by two *Guardian* journalists, gave an excellent, verbatim account of the committal.
6 *Jeremy Thorpe: A Secret Life*, op.cit.

Chapter Twenty

1 *Cover-Up*, op. cit. Bessell's perceptive and very funny account of the trial showed that he could have made a good living as a writer.
2 Unless stated otherwise, passages on the tactics and opinions of lawyers in this chapter are based on interviews by S.F. in 1995 with confidential sources.
3 *Cover-Up*, op.cit.
4 S.F. interview with John Mathew, summer 1995.
5 In his *The Last Word: An Eye-witness Account of the Thorpe Trial*, op.cit., Auberon Waugh said that Scott's remark 'deserves a place in the dictionary of quotations'.
6 The *News of the World* May–June 1981.
7 B.P. 'archive': unpublished interview with Le Mesurier.
8 S.F. interviews with Jack Hayward, 1995.
9 B.P. 'archive': unpublished interview with Le Mesurier.
10 The *News of the World*, May – June 1981.
11 S.F. interviews with Kettle-Williams, summer 1995. The law prohibited S.F. from asking her about the jury's discussions.
12 Ludovic Kennedy, *The Trial of Stephen Ward* (Victor Gollanez 1964). Quoted by Peter Bessell in *Cover-Up*, op. cit.
13 S.F. interview with John Mathew, summer 1995.
14 S.F. interviews with Gerald Hagan, 1995.
15 The story in the *New Statesman*, which appeared on 27 July 1979, and a similar account in the *Sunday Times* book, *Jeremy Thorpe: A Secret Life*, op.cit., led to a fundamental change in the law. Section 8 of the Contempt of Court Act of 1981 made it an offence 'punishable by up to two years' imprisonment to obtain, disclose or solicit any particulars of statements made, opinions expressed, arguments advanced or votes cast by members of a jury in the course of their deliberations in any legal proceedings'. By 1996, there was growing pressure from journalists, lawyers and civil liberties' campaigners for this law to be relaxed to allow informed debate about the jury system, while, at the same time, continuing to protect jurors from unwelcome attention.

Epilogue

1 *Who's Who* (A. & C. Black, 1995).
2 The *Evening News*, 11 December 1979.
3 ibid.
4 The *Evening Standard*, 12 August 1983.
5 David Astor, statement to the *Press Association*, 27 February 1982.
6 The *Evening Standard*, 12 August 1993.
7 Dr J.M.S. Pearce, *Understanding Parkinson's Disease* (Family Doctors Publications in association with the British Medical Association, 1995).
8 The *Evening Standard*, 12 August 1993.
9 S.F. interviews with Steve Atack, 1995.
10 S.F. interviews with Bernard Greaves, 1995.
11 S.F. interview with Dominic Le Foe, 1995.
12 S.F. interviews with Michael Ogle, 1995.
13 S.F. interviews with Ann Dummett, 1995.
14 S.F. interviews with Stanley Brodie, 1995.
15 S.F. interviews with Christopher Bourke, 1995.
16 Jeremy Thorpe letter to S.F., 11 October 1995.
17 Jeremy Thorpe letter to S.F., 17 January 1996.
18 S.F. interviews with John Fryer, 1995.
19 B.P. interviews with Lady Falkender, 1995.
20 B.P. interview with confidential source, 1995.
21 S.F. interviews with Michael Ogle, 1995.
22 S.F. interviews with Dinah Plunkett, 1995.
23 S.F. interviews with Gerald Hagan, 1995.
24 S.F. interview with John Underwood, 1995.
25 The *Daily Star* and the *Sun*, 24 January 1981.
26 S.F. interview with D.J. Freeman, 1995.
27 S.F. interview with John Mathew, 1995.
28 S.F. interview with Diane Bessell, 1995.
29 S.F. interviews with Sir Jack Hayward, 1995.
30 Lord Hooson letter to S.F., August 1995.
31 S.F. interview with Dominic Le Foe, 1995.
32 *The Times*, 28 November 1985.
33 Auberon Waugh, *The Last Word: An Eye-witness Account of the Thorpe Trial*, op.cit.
34 *The Times*, 3 March 1990.
35 The *News of the World*, 27 November 1993.
36 The *Daily Telegraph*, 29 January 1994.
37 The *Mail on Sunday*, 14 November 1993.
38 S.F. interview with Adrian Jack, July 1995.
39 The *News of the World*, 15 July 1979.
40 B.P. interview with Peter Thomas, 1995.
41 The *Daily Mail*, 25 May 1995.
42 ibid.
43 The *Independent*, 25 May 1995.
44 Biographies of Wilson by Ben Pimlott and Philip Ziegler, op. cit.
45 B.P. interviews with Lady Falkender, 1995.
46 S.F. interviews with Jack Hayward, 1995.
47 S.F. interviews with Celia Kettle-Williams, 1995.

Index